# 108 Flowers

## Book 2

Ning Yeh

Collect and enjoy the other volumes and videos in this series:

## 108 Flowers

### Book 1

African Violet • Amaryllis • Anemone Poppy • Apple Blossom • Azalea • Bamboo • Banana • Begonia • Bell Flower • Bird of Paradise • Blackberry Lily • Bleeding Heart • Blue Bonnet • Bougainvillea • Calla Lily • Camellia • Canna • Carnation • Cattleya • Cherry Blossom • Chili Pepper • Chinese Magnolia • Christmas Cactus • Chrysanthemum • Clivia • Cockscomb • Coral

### Book 3

Hollyhock • Hyacinth • Hydrangea • Iris • Japanese Iris • Jasmine • Kapok • Lantern Hibiscus • Lichee • Lilac • Lily • Lily of the Nile • Lily of the Valley • Loquat • Lotus • Magnolia • Manihot Hibiscus • Morning Glory • Myrtle • Narcissus • Night Bloom • Orchid • Orchid Tree • Paeonia • Pansy • Passion • Peach Blossom

### Book 4

Peony • Persimmon • Plum Blossom • Poinsettia • Pomegranate • Poppy • Primrose • Protea • Pumpkin • Ranunculus • Rose • Shrimp Plant • Silk Gourd • Snapdragon • Strawberry • Sunflower • Tiger Lily • Torch Ginger • Touch-Me-Not • Trumpet Creeper • Tulip • Water Lily • Watermelon • Whale Flower • Winter Sweet • Wisteria • Bamboo Shoot

First Edition
© 2013 Ning Yeh and Lingchi Yeh
Huntington Beach, California
ISBN: 978-0-9618305-2-6
All Rights Reserved
Printed in Taiwan

# Contents




Learn with Videos

(Optional and sold separately)

www.orientalartsupply.com

# Preface

When my first-born was little, I sang "Danny Boy" to put him to bed. I tried other songs, but my son would always want to hear "Danny Boy" again. I learned my lesson. So when my second child came along, I stayed singing "Edelweiss." My daughter never asked for another song.

Likewise, producing *108 Flowers* was a learning experience. Each flower subject had its unexpected moments. Book 1 was an awakening, "Are you nuts? Who told you to set the goal at 100 plus lessons?" Having spent a lifetime in school, I know the passing grade is 60. Book 2 brings me closer to that goal.

In 1985, my first Chinese Brush Painting TV program won an Emmy for Best Instructional Television Series. Since then, I continued with several successful television, print, and video programs. *108 Flowers* is an attempt to summarize many of the flower lessons I have developed, in a simple and concise way. Like staying with my kids' lullabies, it is designed for enjoying the basics.

Producing *108 Flowers* was a lone journey of *The Old Man and the Sea*. The second phase was particularly challenging in motivating oneself to continue. But the belief that even one good lesson may inspire and spark the interest of someone across time and space kept me focused. I know the Old Man was never alone. Many would share his struggle and appreciate his effort.

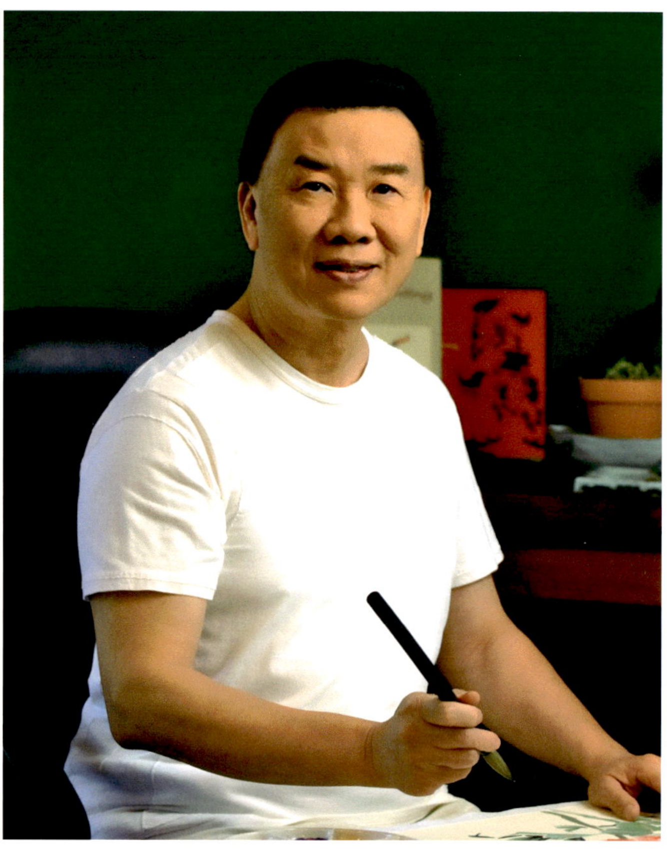

As one of 007's theme songs goes, "You Only Live Twice: one for yourself and one for your dream." Fortunately for me, these two lives merge seamlessly. Painting is a beautiful dream. I have created a dream world and I am living a dream. I dream about doing better and believe I can. Through teaching, I am able to share this dream with others.

With the right instruction and equipment, I know many will enjoy brush painting as much as I do. Still, I am constantly amazed at how well folks have done with my lessons. With this book, brush painting is indeed "a piece of cake."

# Flower Painting Basics

## Set Up

**Felt**
Use a piece of white felt under the paper.

**Water Bowl** (porcelain with 3 divisions)
Leave 1" between water and the rim.

**Stackable Porcelain Dish Set**
A set comes with 5 dishes. Use them to store Chinese chips and frequently used colors (like green).

**Flower Plate**
Keep most colors in pasty condition. Arrange colors from light to dark according to brush loading sequence.

**Mixing Plate**
Choose one white saucer for blending purposes.

**Paper Towel**
Fold a couple of sheets under the mixing plate.

**Spray Bottle**
Use a small pump spray bottle that produces a fine mist to moisten the colors.

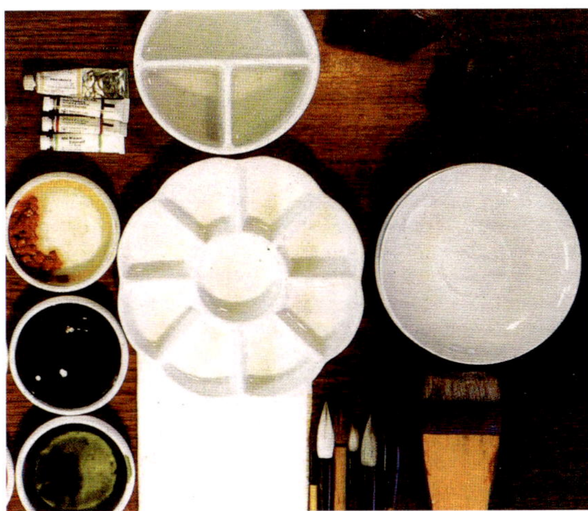

## Materials

**Paper**
OAS (Oriental Art Supply) Premium Double Shuen: best choice
Practice Shuen: for practice
Colored Shuen: for white flowers

**Brushes**
OAS Flow: most petals and dots
OAS Large Flow: larger petals and leaves
Orchid Bamboo: pointed petals, leaves, and branches (use Small, Medium, or Large depending on stroke sizes)
Mountain Horse: sharp lines
OAS Happy Dot: fine dots
Mixing Brush: use a small, tough-bristle brush to prepare colors

**Colors**
*Chinese Chips*
Yellow, Vermillion, Red, Indigo

*Da Vinci Gouache*
White

*OAS*
Best Bottle Ink

*Schmincke Horadam Aquarell Tubes*
Cadmium Red Deep (better than Chinese Red)

*Winsor & Newton Artist's Water Colour Tubes*
Indigo (better than Chinese Indigo), Perylene Violet, Winsor Violet, and other colors as specified in each lesson

## Preparation

Use individual dishes for Ink and White.

Melt Yellow chunks with 2 tablespoons of water in a small jar (for 1 hour or more). Use a mixing brush to smash the softened Yellow into a thick liquid.

Store Chinese chips in stackable dishes. Pour the whole package of chips into the dish. Gather the chips to one side. Spray wet the chips. Allow time for the chips to stick together and onto the dish. When painting, wet the chips with a light spray. Use a mixing brush to work colors into a thick paste.

Use a flower plate for colors. Arrange colors in groups (the greens, the reds, etc.), and in sequence (from light to dark).

Squeeze the watercolors into each section of the flower plate. Use a dry mixing brush to flatten the colors. Keep dark colors pasty. Add a touch of water to the lighter colors. If colors dry up, lightly spray them with water.

Depending on each lesson, the ink, white and/or colors may need to be diluted with water or kept in a pure or thick/pasty condition.

## Working with Brush and Color

### Holding the Brush

Use the first section of the thumb and index finger to hold the middle section of the brush handle. Slide the middle finger down the front and press the nail of the ring finger from the back. Keep the small finger attached to the ring finger.

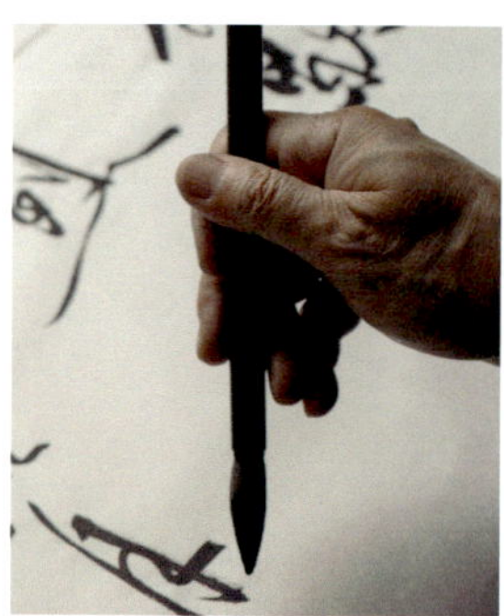

### Preparing the Tip

Wet the brush bristles in water. Stroke the bristles with pressure on the rim of the water bowl. Wipe all sides dry on the paper towel and form a tip.

### Loading Water

After forming the tip, we begin by loading water.

Dip only 1/4" of the tip a couple of times into water. Stroke off the excess along the rim of the water bowl. That is all the water we need on the brush. The secret is wet tip, dry body.

### Loading One Color

Load one color 1/8" into the tip. Blend until the color fades about 1/4" into the tip. Dip the tip 1/8" into the color again. If the color is thick, blend the tip a little.

To test the color, tilt the tip and press the brush with half-length of the bristles making contact with the paper. Lift the brush.

If we see a solid shape with no fading, we have loaded the color too deep. There will be no transparency and no variation. Flat colors produce no joy.

We should see a shape with the point showing more intense color, and then the color fading into nothing.

### Loading Multiple Colors

The exciting moment comes when we see multiple colors blend spontaneously in one brush stroke. We usually load the lightest color first then progressively load stronger and darker colors. Each successive color covers a shorter length of the bristles. For instance, we load Light Green 1/4", add Dark Green 1/6", then add Ink 1/8". Blend.

### Positioning the Brush

After spending the effort to load colors on different parts of the brush, painting with just the tip becomes self-defeating. Color variations will not show. We need to use the brush body with the tip. With the brush tilted, pressure is exerted to allow the body of the brush to make contact with the paper.

By design, only half the length of the brush body is intended for painting. We never paint with the full length of the bristles. For example, the Flow brush is 1" long. So the effective part of the bristles is only 1/2".

We do watercolor. It is obvious that color needs to work with water. We save half of that 1/2" for water. Therefore, the most we load color will be 1/4" deep.

**Where to Begin a Stroke**

From the diagrams in this book, we can study the intensity of colors in a stroke to learn the direction of the movement and the path of the brush tip. The color is more intense at the beginning of the stroke and then it fades. The brush tip may travel in the middle of a stroke or along the edge.

**How to Move the Brush**

BONE STROKE

The bone stroke is used to do branches, twigs, stems, and leaf veins. Hold the brush vertically and land on the paper with a little pressure. Apply pressure while keeping the brush vertical throughout the stroke. The tip travels in the middle of the stroke. End the stroke with pressure and withdraw backward.

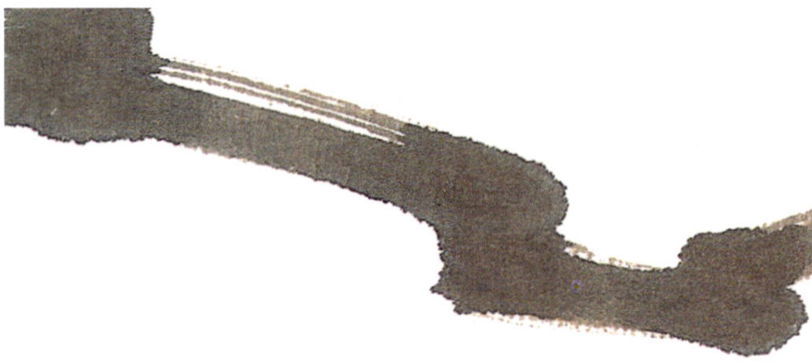

SHARP LINES

Blade-like strokes are used to do sharp leaves like bamboo, grass blades, stamens, and flower veins. Hold the brush vertically and use your arm to move the brush. Do not flex the wrist. In many cases, sharp lines are delivered with a choo-choo train like motion. The brush travels in the air with constant rotations. The tip glides through the paper.

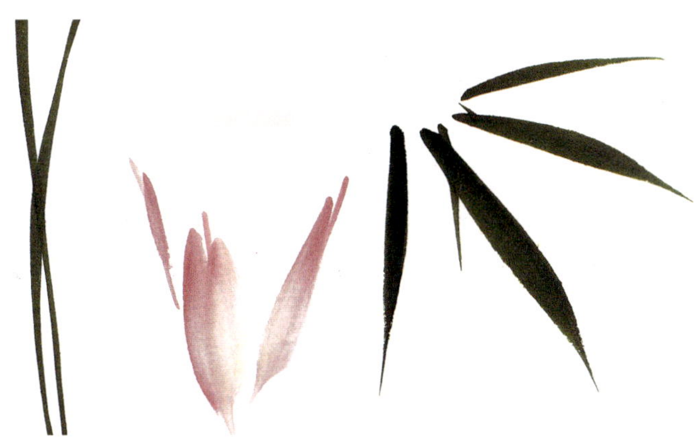

SHAPES

Wider strokes are used to create fuller petal and leaf shapes. Tilt the handle and press the body halfway onto the paper. Using the side of the brush, move the brush like a mop with the body in front and the tip trailing behind or along one edge. Lift the brush off the paper or round-off the tip to finish the stroke. We can vary this brush motion—push, scoop, slide, arch, S-curve, etc.—to make different shapes. Two or more strokes can also be combined to make a single petal or leaf shape.

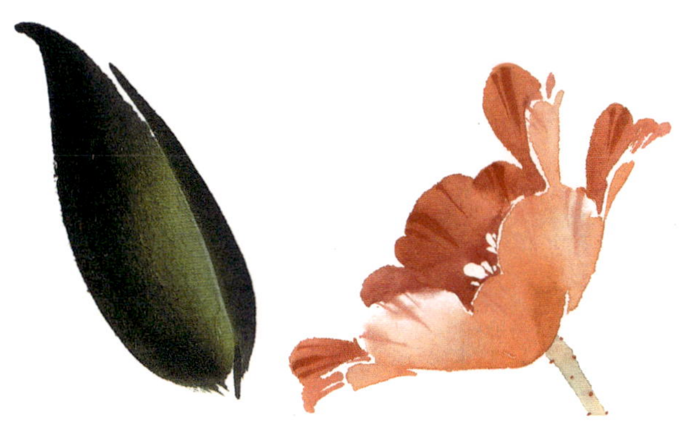

HAPPY DOTS

Happy dots are lively strokes of various shapes and sizes used for pollen, tiny buds, calyxes, petal markings, and knots on the branches. Land the tip with slight pressure, push and lift with a scooping motion.

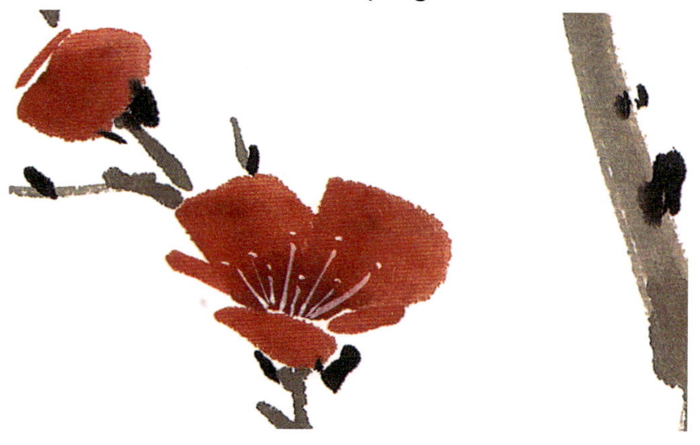

**Other Techniques**

BUILD A WALL

Just like doing a paint job, we line the edge first, and then fill in the rest. "Build a wall" means to draw a block along the edge of a shape and use it as a platform to launch other strokes. Chinese are well-known for building walls.

LEAVE A HAIRLINE SPACE

When painting next to a wet shape, leave a hairline space. This prevents strokes from bleeding into each other. It also adds a sense of light to our shape. Frequently, "build a wall" and "leave a hairline space" go hand-in-hand —like the canal lining the city wall.

LOWER THE BOOM

In many cases, we do the top of a petal from one end with one color. We work the root or base of the petal with another color from the opposite end. I call this "lower the boom." After doing the top stroke, reverse the brush. Tilt and press the brush body halfway onto the paper. Move the brush like a mop, pushing the root stroke into the top stroke. Rather than allowing the brush tip to travel through, we simply press the brush body down. This allows the strokes to blend.

NO CHICKEN FOOT

When painting a group of elements, such as stems, branches, twigs, or stamens, avoid making three or more lines cross or join at the same point, like a chicken foot. Alternate the joints.

FISH LOOKING FOR THE SAME FOOD

Related elements share the same root, like fish looking for the same food. The roots of the strokes should be arranged so that petals tuck into the calyx, or leaves are guided back to the same branch.

ARROWHEAD

In a composition, the root points of the objects determine their relative depth. Center objects are usually the closest, so their base or root points should be the lowest. Let middle strokes join at a lower point, then let side strokes join further up to form a pleasing arrowhead—but NO CHICKEN FOOT.

## Idea of Flowers

Spontaneous-style brush painting expresses the spirit and the essence of a subject rather than its realistic detail. Flowers are personified and represent the spirit of the artist.

Think of a flower as a lady—with a cup-shaped head and a graceful stem; with leaves that reach out like arms, hug the stem like a waist, and fan out like a skirt. Some flowers may be cute and playful; some may be elegant and showy; some may even be Mu Lan, the lady warrior.

**Blossom**

Each cup-shaped blossom is made up of petals, stamens, and pollen dots. Show attitude and movement by tilting and turning the cup in different ways. The rim of the cup forms a circle or oval, with the petal roots converging at the base—like fish looking for the same food. The foreground petals form a "U" shape and the background petals reach out to form a rainbow on the top perimeter. The backside (or underside) of a petal is typically lighter than its front side (or topside). Differentiate lighter and darker tones to give the flower a three dimensional quality.

**Stem, stalk, and branch**
The stem, stalk, and branch are the bones or elements of strength to support the flowers. Be bold, go off the paper to suggest height or to emphasize flow.

**Calyxes and tubes**
Some flowers have calyxes and some have tubes. These form a slender neck or collar connecting the blossom to the stem. Strategically arrange calyx strokes to frame the flower's lovely face. Some calyx leaves can be a mini skirt for the flower.

**Leaves**
Leaves typically grow in layered clusters along the stem. Arrange the top layer of leaves like the lady's arms and shoulders. Young leaves typically head upward and form "check marks." Show graceful, outstretched arms by reaching out with profile leaves. Strive for balance, not perfect symmetry. For example, one arm could be waving in the air, the other bent downward.

The middle leaf cluster forms the waist. Keep leaves tight around the stem. Leaves may be foreshortened.

The lower leaf cluster is the skirt. Vary the hem. Create ruffled, uneven edges. Show layers by adding shadow leaves. Flowers may wear skirts, petticoats, or slips.

**Host, guest, and liaison**
Introduce a family to your composition—fully-opened flowers, profile flowers, teenagers, and baby buds. Arrange them in an interesting formation with a "host" element as the focal point, a supportive "guest" element, and a "liaison" group. They live happily ever-after in our painting.

As you study the lessons that follow, see if you can identify these basic principles and techniques in each composition. Have fun with them.

## Symbols in this Book

I have used a few symbols in these lessons:

♌ indicates which brush to use or that it is time to change brushes.

❖ indicates which color to use or that it is time to load/change colors.

Color A + Color B means load Color A 1/4" into the tip. Add Color B 1/8" into the tip. If we are using similar colors, we do not need to clean the brush when we change or load additional colors.

The Chinese characters at the beginning of each lesson indicate the Chinese name of each flower. Their English transcriptions and meanings are also included.

Arrows on each diagram indicate the direction and orientation of strokes. The numbers and letters on each diagram are referenced in the written steps.

8028

# Corn

Iu
Yù: Jade

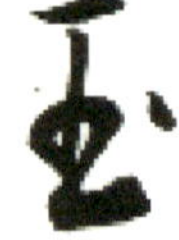

Shu
Shŭ: Sichuan

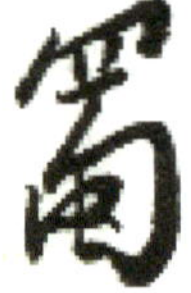

Shu
Shŭ: Crop name

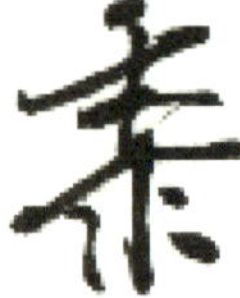

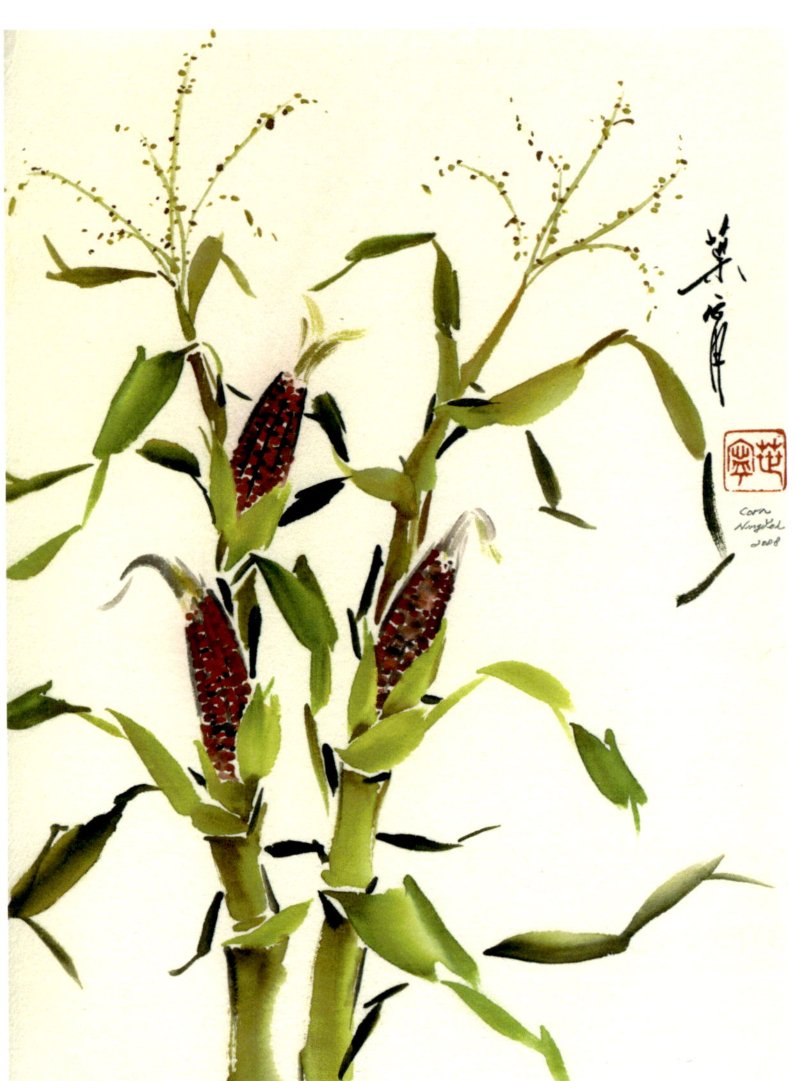

Certain subjects are made for brush painting. Corn offers so many intriguing elements. Forget bamboo! Crooked trunks and torn leaves work great on corn.

**MATERIALS**

Paper: Double Shuen

♌ Brushes
Flow

❖ Colors
*Chinese*
Yellow, Vermillion
*Da Vinci*
White
*Schmincke*
Cadmium Red Deep
*Winsor & Newton*
Indigo, Perylene Violet
*OAS*
Best Bottle Ink

**PREPARATION OF COLORS**

Yellow
White: diluted
Vermillion: thick
Red: Cadmium Red Deep
Dark Red: Perylene Violet + Red
Light Green: Yellow + Indigo
Dark Green: Yellow + Indigo
Ochre: Yellow + Vermillion + Light Green
Brown: Dark Red + Light Green
Ink
Ink Red: Dark Red + Medium Ink

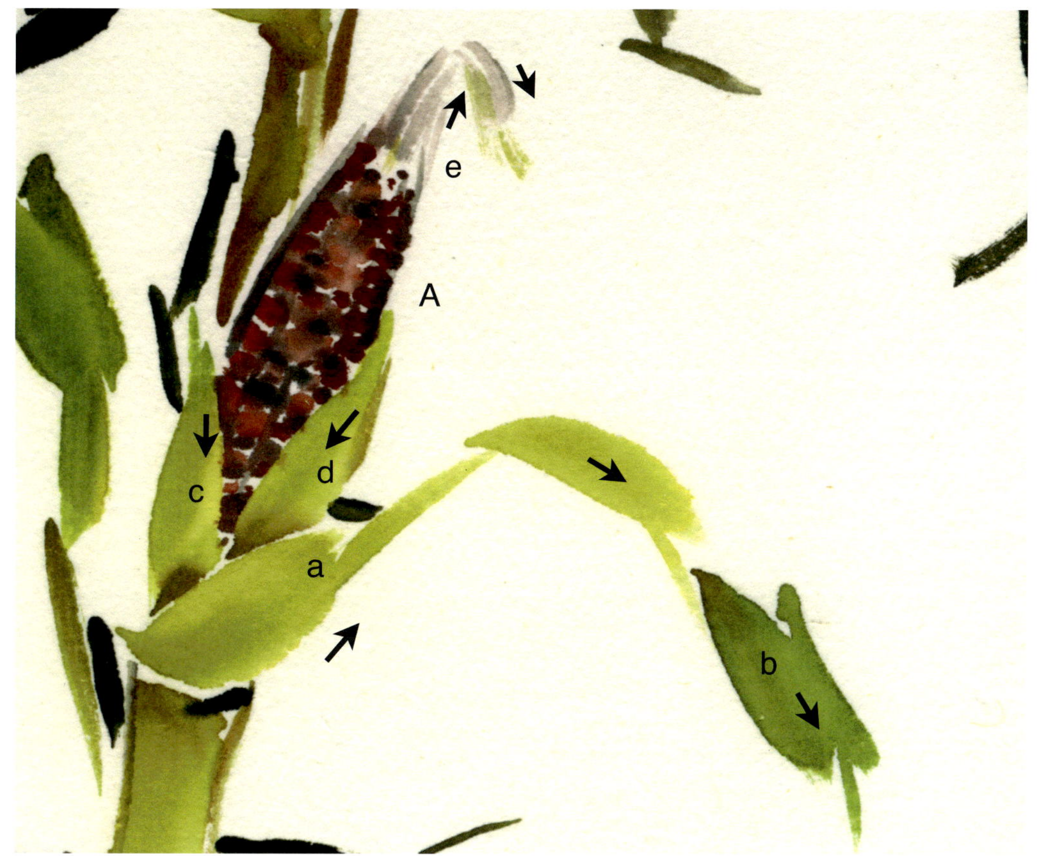


**STEPS**

Corn A
Base Leaves
♌ Flow
❖ Yellow + Ochre + Light Green
Do the base of a sheath leaf, then extend a fold (a).

❖ Light Green + Brown
Add the topside of the leaf with two strokes (b).

❖ Yellow + Ochre + Light Green
Do the topside of a couple of wrappings or husks (c, d).

❖ Brown
Add the roots of the wrappings from the base up.

Line Work
♌ Flow
❖ Ink Red
Work the outlines of a corncob. Do a series of intermittent lines to show a few columns. Add shadow dots horizontally. Leave the top area of the corncob open.

Corn Dots
❖ Red
Work corn dots (kernels) in columns in the middle area of the corncob.

❖ Dark Red
Work darker dots.

❖ Ink Red
Complete the corn dots. Leave the top of the corncob unfinished.

❖ Ink Red
Using a dry brush with the tip split open, work silks on top of the corn (e).

❖ Ochre
Give the silks a touch of color.

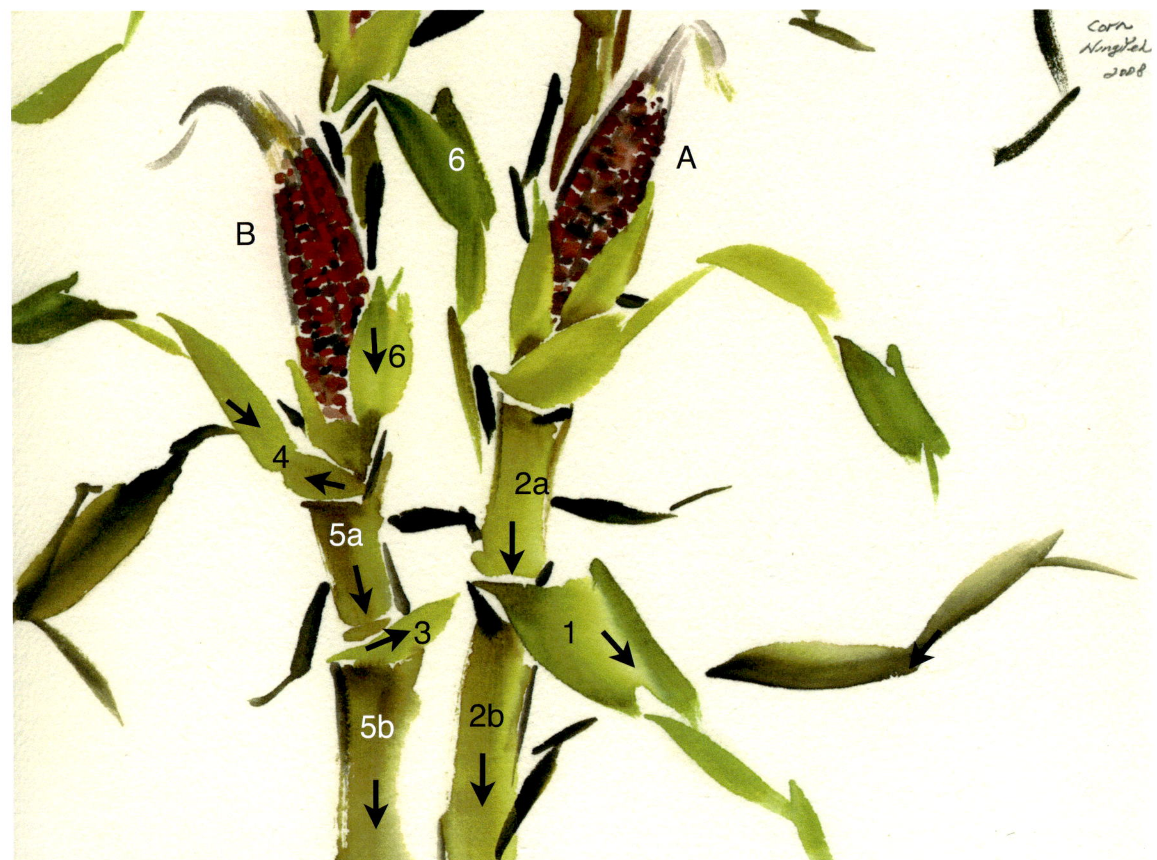


Leaves and Trunks

❖ Ochre + Light Green + Brown

Do a folding leaf (1).

❖ Ochre + Brown

Do sections of the trunk (2a, 2b).

❖ Dark Red + Ink

Add shadows. Lovely.

Corn B

❖ Ochre

Do a foreshortened leaf (3).

❖ Ochre + Brown

Work the base of a leaf. Lead a leaf into the base (4).

❖ Ochre + Brown + Ink Red

Do sections of a second trunk (5a, 5b).

❖ Yellow + Ochre + Light Green

Show the topside of a wrapping or husk (6).

❖ Brown

Add a leaf base and connect the wrappings.

Line Work

❖ Ink Red

Work the outlines of a second corncob.

Corn Dots

❖ Red

Work corn dots (kernels) in columns in the middle area of the corncob.

❖ Dark Red and Ink Red

Complete the corn dots. Leave the top of the corncob unfinished.

Silks

❖ Ink Red

With brush tip split open, work hairs (silks) on top of the corn. Do a ponytail this time.

❖ Ochre

Give the silks a touch of "I dream of Jeannie with the light brown hair" color.

Corn C

❖ Yellow + Ochre + Light Green + Dark Green + Brown

Work a leaf (1).

❖ Dark Green + Ink

Extend an arm crossing behind the other trunk (2).

❖ Ochre + Brown

Work a trunk section under the leaf.

❖ Ochre + Brown + Ink

Tuck a trunk section behind the second corncob (3).

❖ Yellow + Ochre + Light Green

Show a wrapping on the right (4a).

❖ Ochre + Brown

Give it a taller companion on the left (4b).

Line Work

❖ Ink Red

Work the outlines of a third corncob.

Corn Dots

❖ Red

Work corn dots in columns in the middle area of the corncob.

❖ Dark Red

Complete the corn dots. Clean and dry the brush. Add a few touches to smooth the edges of the corncob.

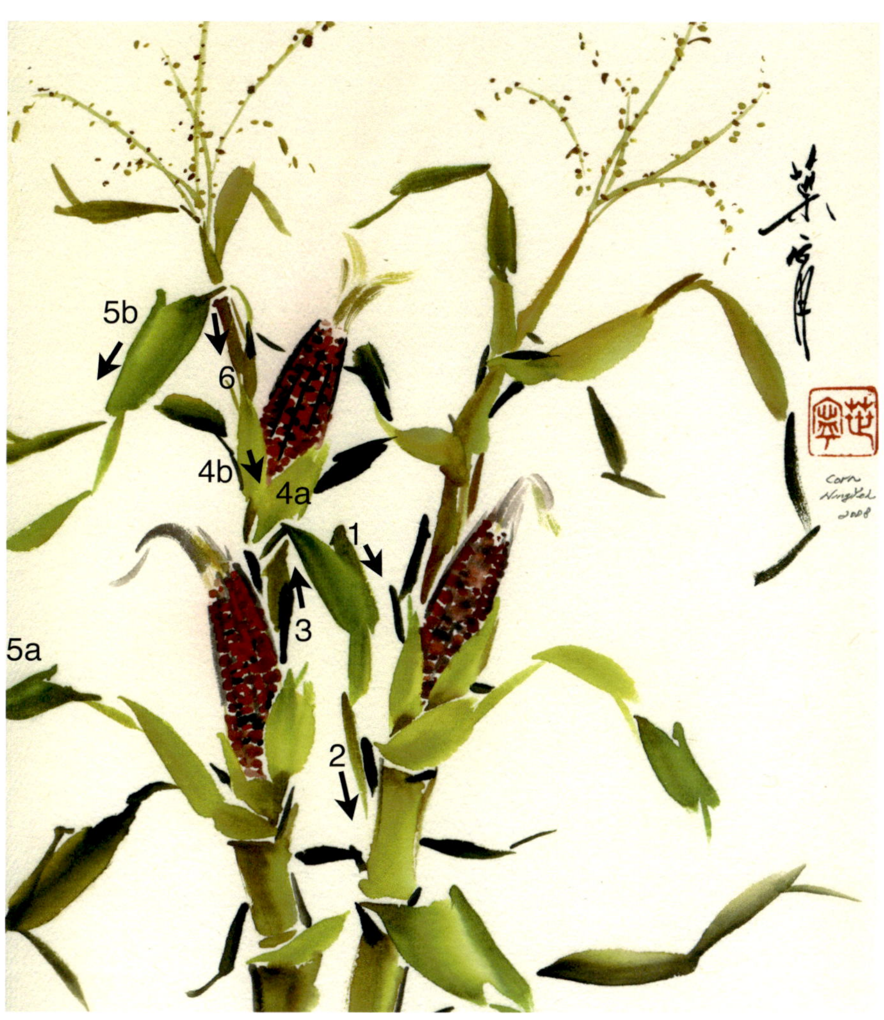


Silks

❖ Brown

Add hairs called silks on top of the corncob.

❖ Ochre

Give the silks a touch of color.

❖ Ochre + Dark Green + Brown

Show the topside of a leaf (5a). Work a leaf on top (5b).

❖ Ochre

Extend the leaf and show folds.

❖ Brown

Extend a narrower section of the trunk (6).

❖ Ochre

Show a turn to tuck the leaf into the trunk.

❖ Brown

Add a trunk section on top.

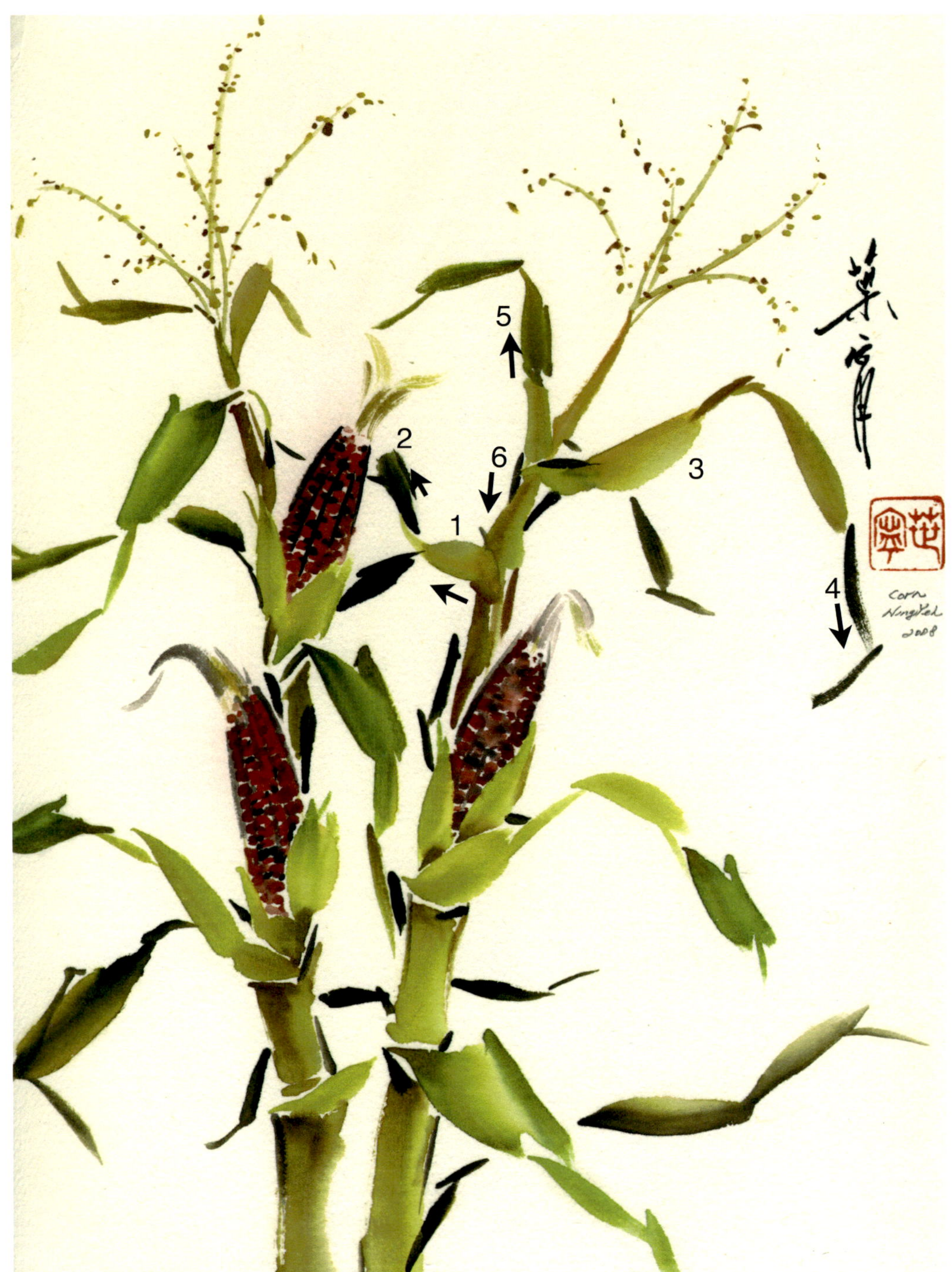


❖ Ochre
Work the base for a leaf (1).

❖ Light Green + Dark Green + Brown + Ink
Show the topside of the leaf (2).

❖ Ochre + Light Green
Extend a leaf to the right (3).

❖ Brown + Ink
Extend the tip of the leaf (4). Isn't this fun? A whole new world!

❖ Ochre + Light Green + Dark Green + Brown
A world is not enough. We add a companion (5).

❖ Ochre + Brown
Do sections of the trunk to tie the leaves together (6).

A Thai dancer.

❖ Ochre + Brown
Let us do a companion dancer with two leaves (1, 2).

❖ Ochre
Extend a shoot from the trunk (3). Work the tassel or the male flower with curving stems (4, 5).

❖ Ochre
Add dots. Dots are always the most fun part of a painting. We hit the jackpot here. We can do hundreds of them, along the stems going left and right. We can extend from the tip of the stems and do more.

❖ Brown
Add darker dots.

❖ Yellow + Ochre + Light Green + Dark Green + Brown + Ink
We really do not need to load these many colors, but why not? Do shadow leaves (6-12).

❖ Ochre + Ink Red
More dots.

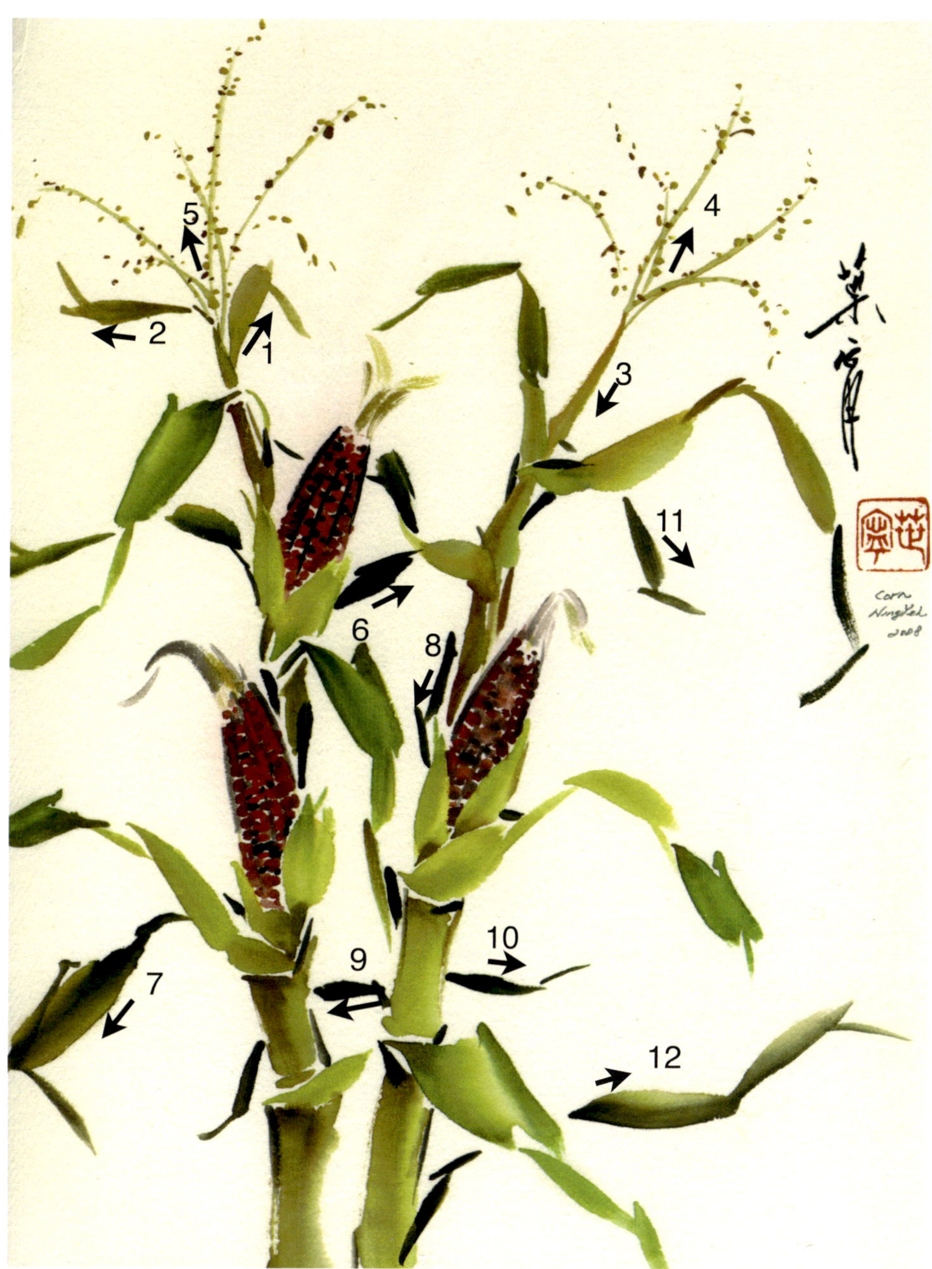

# 8029
# Cotton Rose

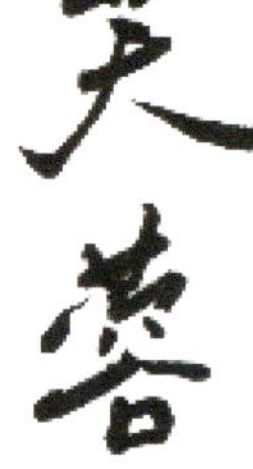


Mu
Mù: Wood

Fu Rung
Fú Róng: Nickname of lotus

Cotton rose blossoms with several colors on the same tree and in the same cluster. Some flowers are white and pink during the day, becoming deep red at night. Enchanting.

**MATERIALS**

Paper: Double Shuen

Brushes
Flow, Large Orchid Bamboo, Happy Dot

❖ Colors
*Chinese*
Yellow
*Da Vinci*
White
*Schmincke*
Cadmium Red Deep
*Winsor & Newton*
Indigo, Permanent Magenta, Alizarin Crimson, Perylene Violet
*OAS*
Best Bottle Ink

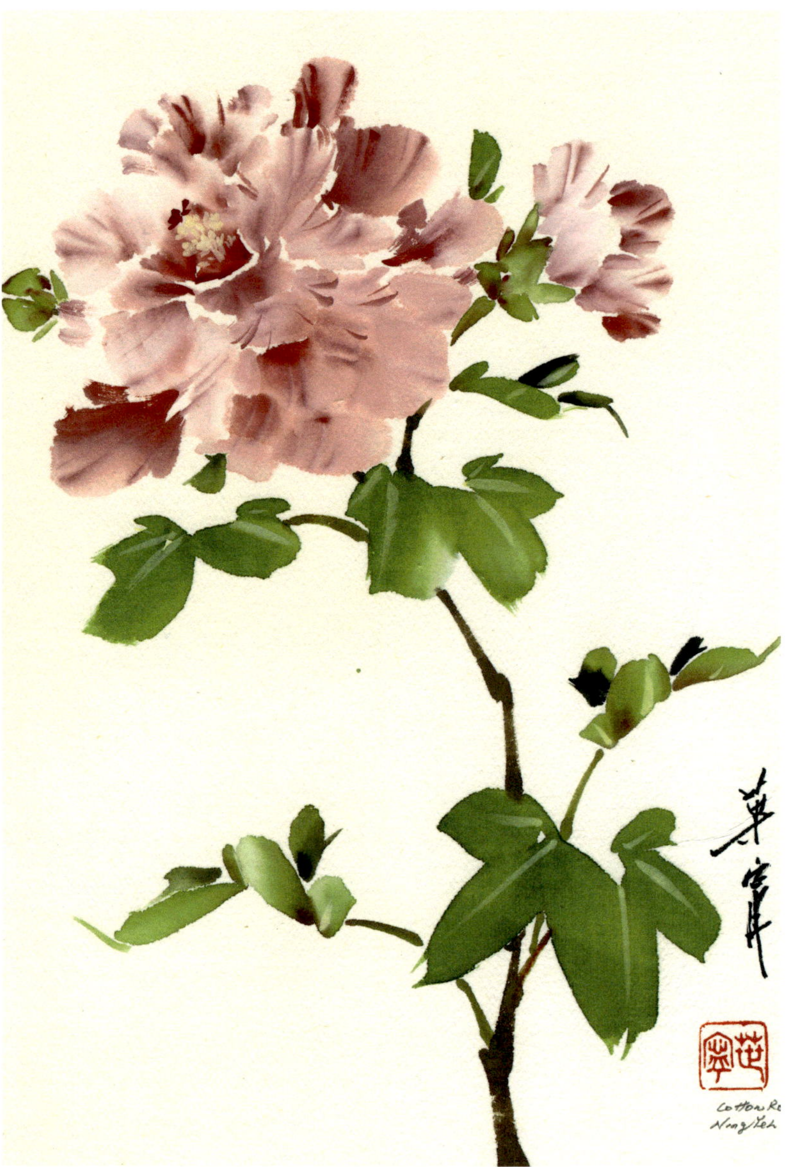

**PREPARATION OF COLORS**

Yellow: thick liquid
White: diluted
Red: Cadmium Red Deep
Magenta: Permanent Magenta + Red
Crimson: Alizarin Crimson + Red
Dark Red: Perylene Violet + Red
Light Green: Yellow + Indigo
Dark Green: Yellow + Indigo
Brown: Dark Red + Light Green
Ink
White: pasty

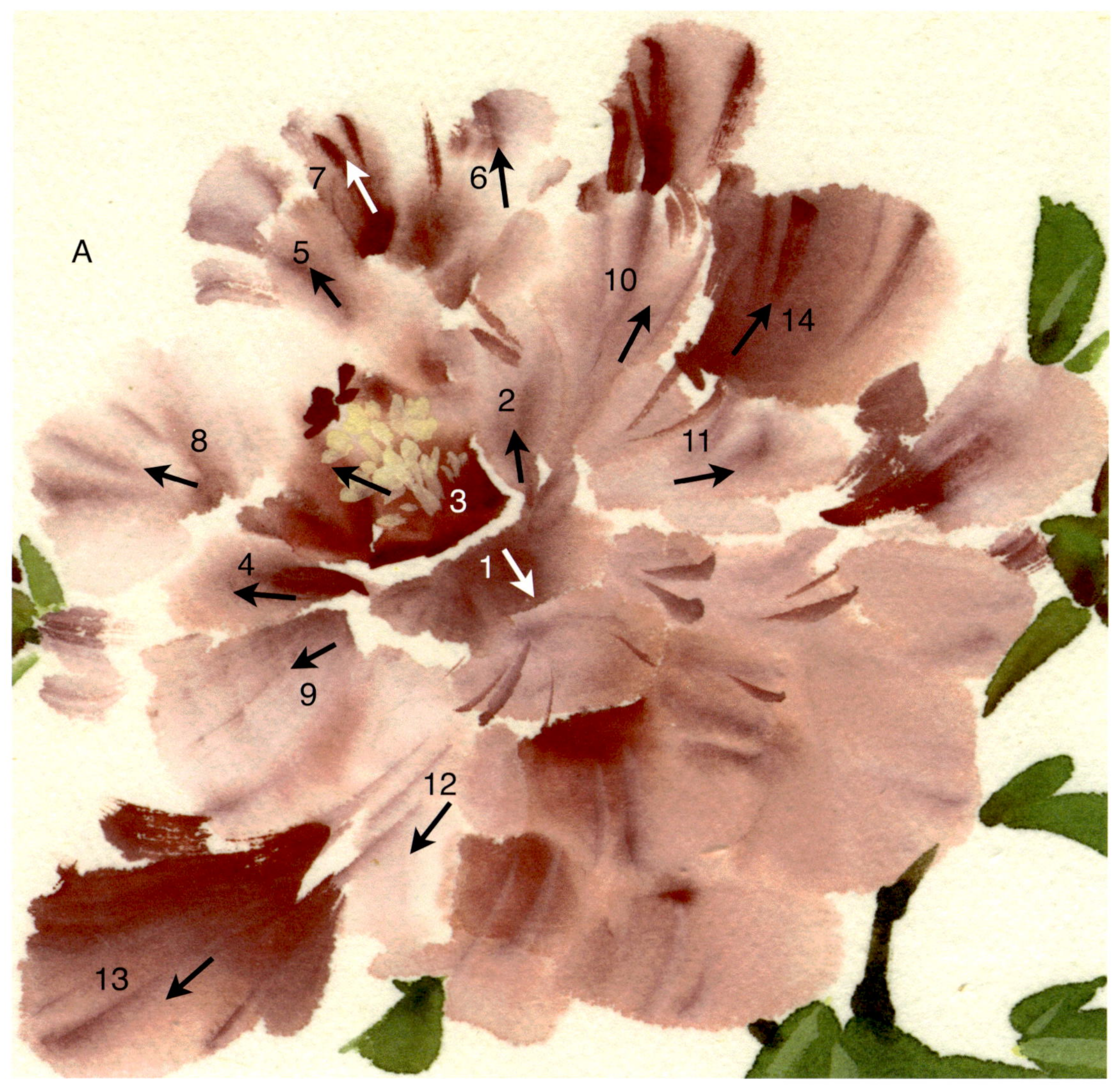


**STEPS**

Flower (A)
Center
ℓ Flow
❖ White + Magenta
The flower center consists of several clusters. Each cluster can be viewed as a small flower. Work a center petal with two strokes in the middle and a shorter stroke on each side (1). Add a petal to the right of the center petal with three strokes (2).

❖ Red + Crimson + Dark Red
Build walls above the petals, leaving a hairline space. Push strokes up (3) and add a petal to the left (4). Together, these petals can be seen as a small flower.

❖ White + Magenta
Work two petals as wings (5, 6).

❖ Magenta + Red
Add petals between the wings (7). This can be viewed as small flower on the upper right.

❖ White + Magenta
Work another small flower on the upper left (8).

❖ White + Magenta
Work strokes to show wings reaching out on both sides (9, 10, 11, 12).

❖ Magenta + Red + Crimson
Add darker petals on each side to complete the cluster (13, 14).

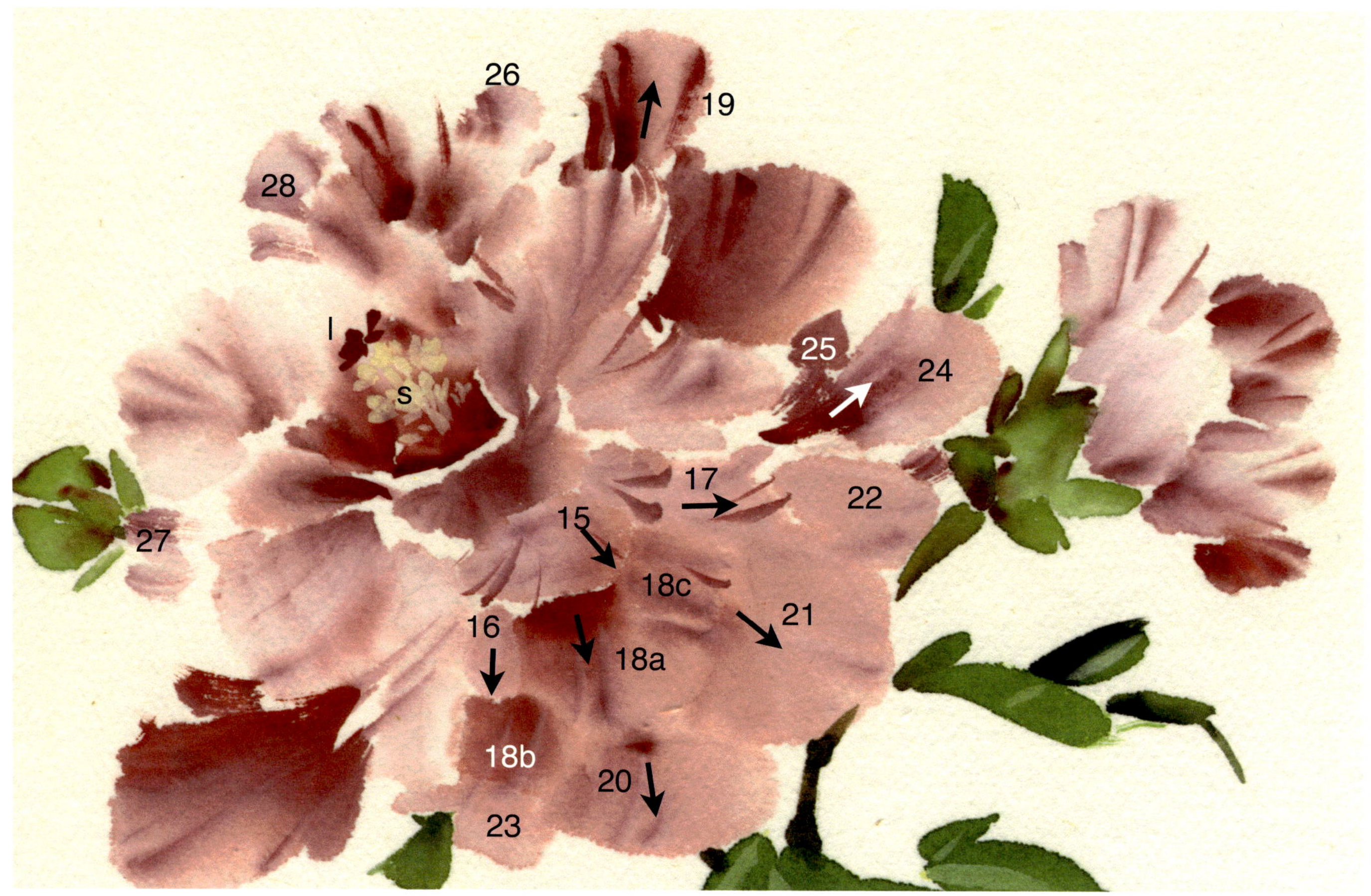


❖ White + Magenta
Show a lighter petal below the center petal (15). Extend wings on both sides (16, 17).

❖ Crimson
Add darker petals to complete the lower cluster (18a, 18b, 18c). Extend a few strokes on the right (19). Expand a skirt below with wider strokes (20, 21, 22, 23).

❖ White + Magenta
Work additional petals below (24, 25). Elongate the side ones (26) and show shorter ones on top (27, 28). We have a full and balanced flower with multiple clusters.

ℓ Happy Dot
❖ White + Magenta
Add veins on the petals. Accentuate the clusters by treating each as a separate small flower with its own center. Lead lines to the separate centers, long and short, host and guest. Press along the edge of the petals and lift inward.

ℓ Flow
❖ Pasty White + Yellow
Work stamen dots into a "tree shape" (s). Show a center group, side groups, and a group on top. Add stems. Work a few small dots on both sides of the stems, fading into the shadow.

❖ Magenta + Dark Red
Show five lady dots (l) above the stamens.

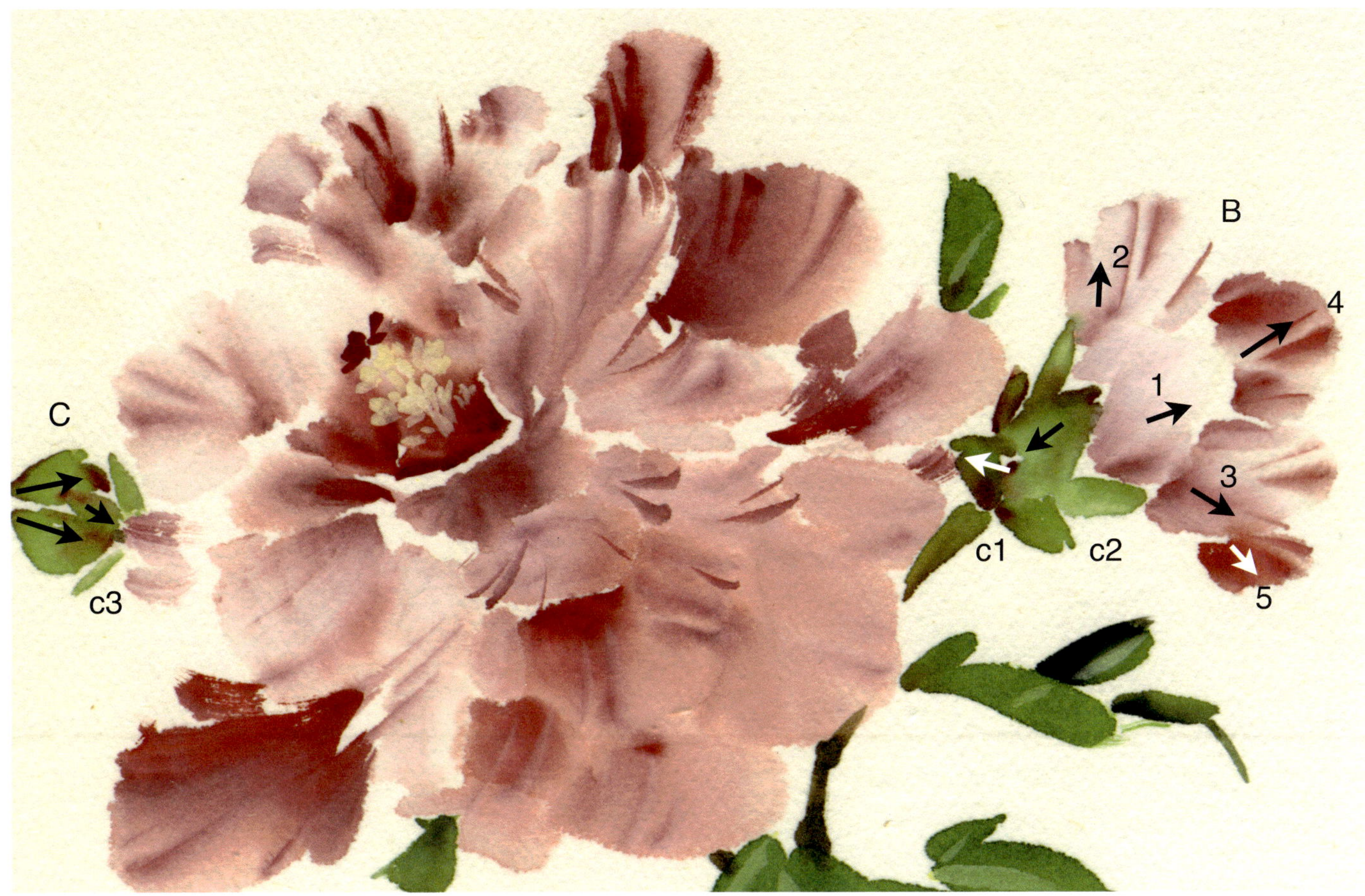


Teenager (B)

❖ Light Green + Dark Red

The calyx of the flower has two layers. Show a lower layer of calyx leaves drooping (c1). Work a top layer of calyx dots from the top down (c2).

❖ Dark Red

Add roots to the top layer of calyx dots.

❖ White + Magenta

Work petals showing their backsides. Do a center petal (1). Add wing petals on each side (2, 3).

❖ Magenta + Red

Work petals showing their front side (4, 5).

ℒ Happy Dot

❖ White + Magenta

Add veins to the teenage flower.

ℒ Flow

❖ Light Green + Dark Red

Work a stem below the teenager.

Bud (C)

❖ Light Green + Dark Red

Do calyx dots (c3). Work a couple of strokes to show the top of the bud.

❖ Light Green + Dark Red

Add the roots of the bud.

Leaves

ჲ Large Orchid Bamboo

❖ Light Green + Dark Green

A mature leaf has five sections. Do a leaf below the flower (1). Show the left and center sections with two strokes each. Work the right side. Finish with smaller wings on both sides. Work a leaf swinging to the left (2).

❖ Light Green + Dark Red

Do a set of profile leaves showing their undersides below the teenager flower (3, 4).

❖ Light Green + Dark Green

Work a large leaf to anchor the lower area of the composition (5).

Branches

ჲ Flow

❖ Brown

Keep the brush body dry. Add stems below the flower, teenager, and bud. Lead a branch down, leaping over the lower leaf. Connect the leaves onto the branch with stems.

ჲ Large Orchid Bamboo

❖ Light Green + Dark Red

Work a set of profile leaves reaching out on both sides (6, 7). Add stems to bring the leaves back to the branch.

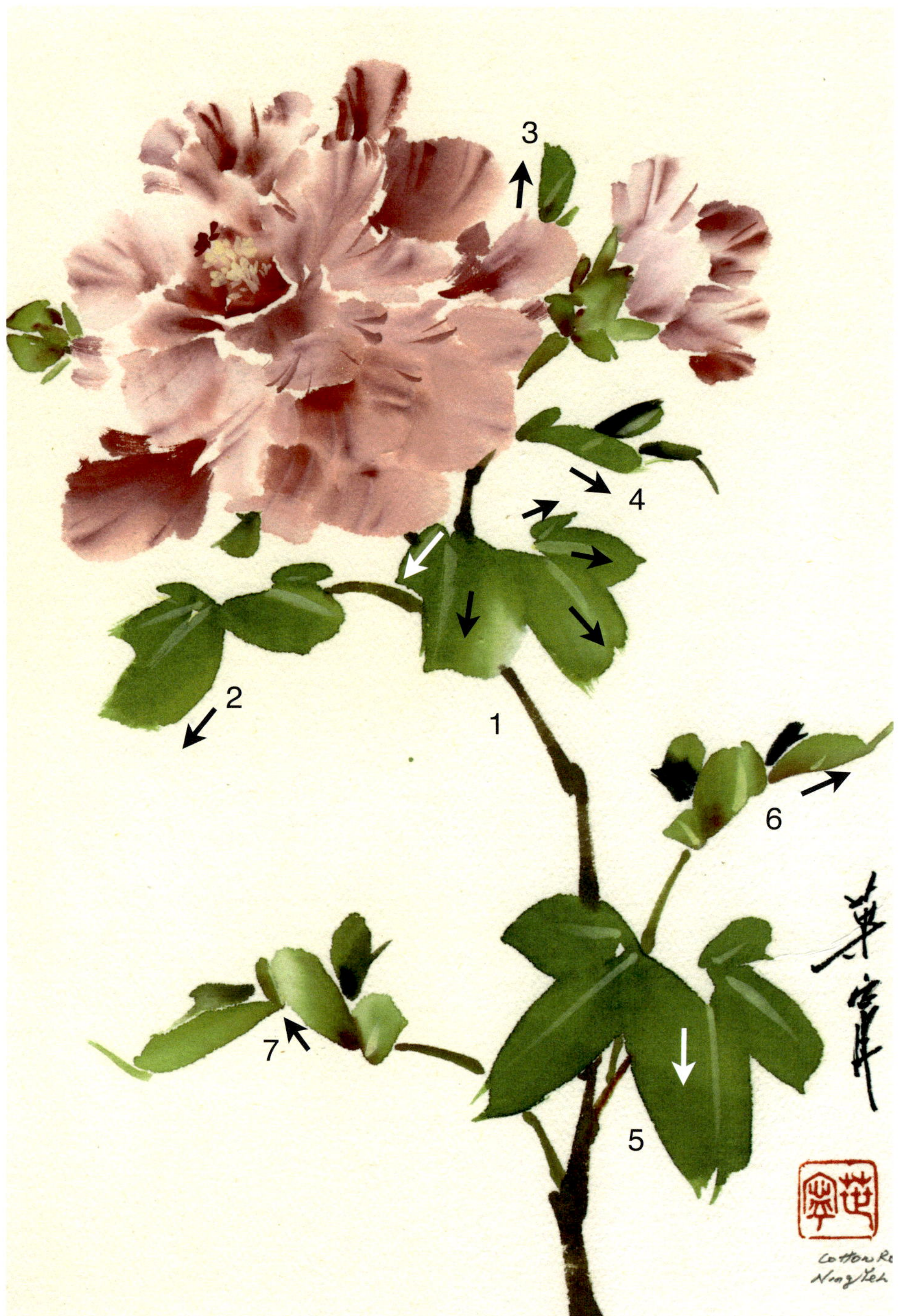


❖ Light Green + Dark Green + Ink

Work the shadow side of the profile leaves.

ჲ Happy Dot

❖ White + Yellow

Add a center vein to each section of the leaves.

8030

# Cyclamen

Shian
Xiān: Fairy

Ke
Kè: Guest

Lai
Lái: Arrive

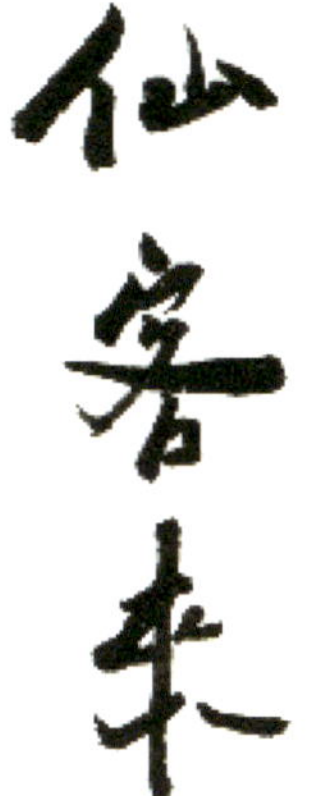

Cyclamen is a symbol of hospitality. Xiānkèlái, the Chinese name, means "honored guest arriving." The bud bows downward. When the flower opens, the five petals flip up into a crown, like an official greeting the emperor.

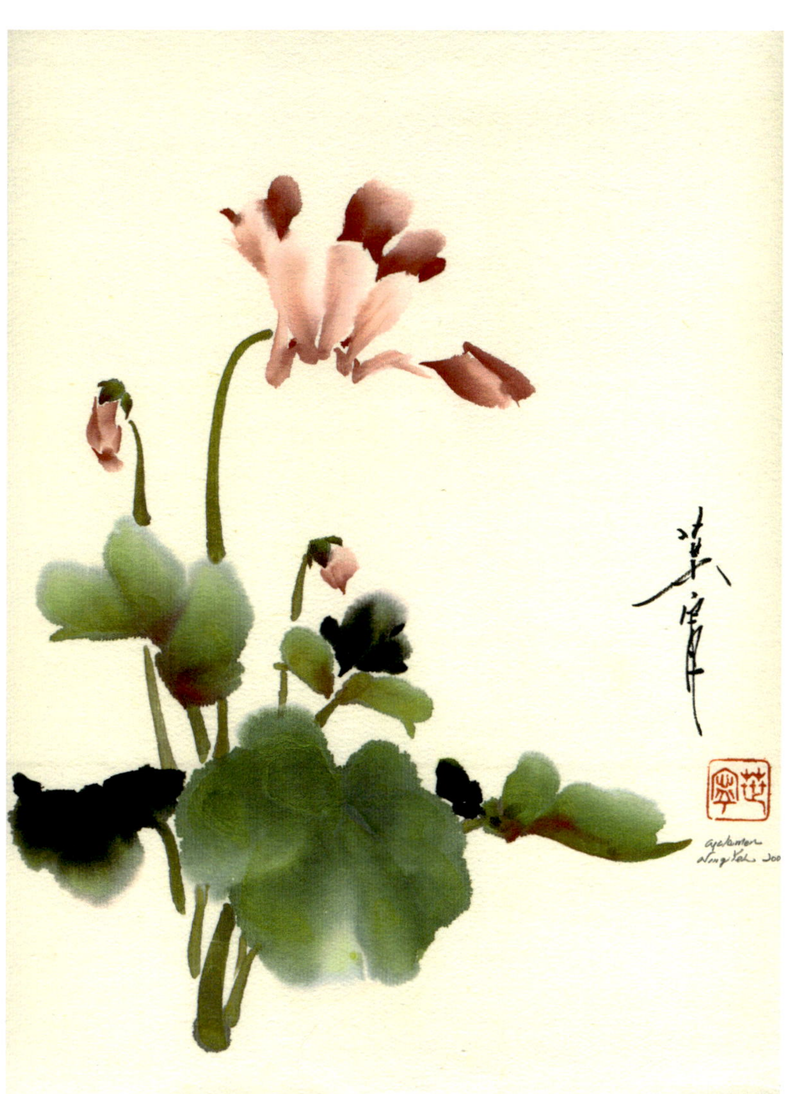

**MATERIALS**

Paper: Double Shuen

ᔕ Brushes
Flow, Large Flow, Happy Dot

❖ Colors
*Chinese*
Yellow
*Da Vinci*
White
*Schmincke*
Cadmium Red Deep
*Winsor & Newton*
Indigo, Permanent Magenta, Alizarin Crimson, Perylene Violet
*OAS*
Best Bottle Ink

**PREPARATION OF COLORS**

Yellow: thick liquid
White: diluted
Red: Cadmium Red Deep
Magenta: Permanent Magenta + Red
Crimson: Alizarin Crimson + Red
Dark Red: Perylene Violet + Red
Light Green: Yellow + Indigo
Dark Green: Yellow + Indigo
Brown: Dark Red + Light Green
Ink

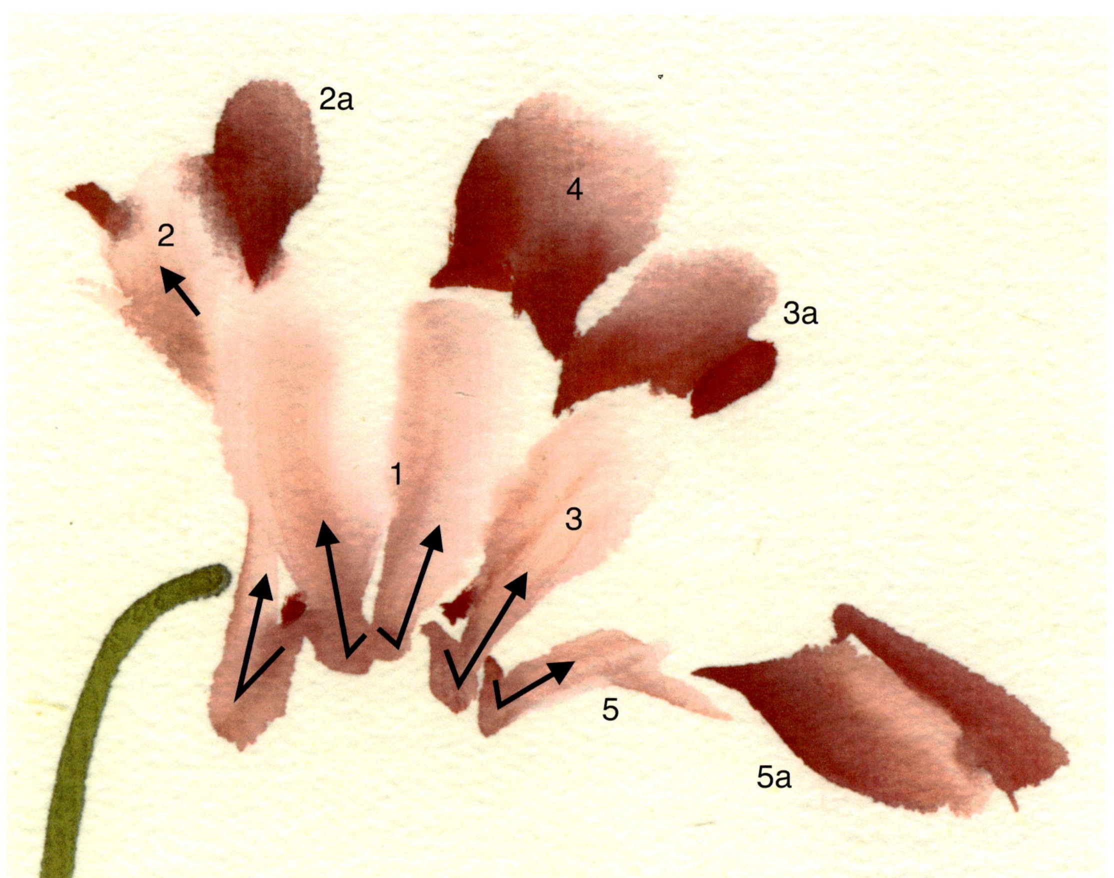


**STEPS**

Flower

Front Petals

ℓ Flow

❖ White + Magenta

The flower has five petals with roots like check marks. The front petals show their backsides and are, therefore, lighter. Work a center petal. Do a check mark then press to the left. Add the right side with pressure at base then press upward favoring the right (1).

Work a profile petal on the left . Do a reverse check mark overlapping into the center petal. Show the top of the petal peeking above the center petal (2).

Add a petal to the right of the center petal with a check mark root. Move up with pressure to the left (3).

Back and Shadow Petals

❖ Magenta + Crimson + Dark Red

Build walls above the front petals, leaving a hairline space. Push strokes upward to show one full petal in the center (4) and the shadow side of the right profile petal (3a). Show their roots between the front petals. Show the shadow side of the left profile petal (2a).

ℓ Happy Dot

❖ White + Magenta

Do the root of a petal with a check mark then settle with pressure heading upward to the right. Lead a tip stroke out following the baseline like a freeway exit (5).

ℓ Flow

❖ White + Magenta + Crimson + Dark Red

Work the topside of the petal with two strokes. (5a)

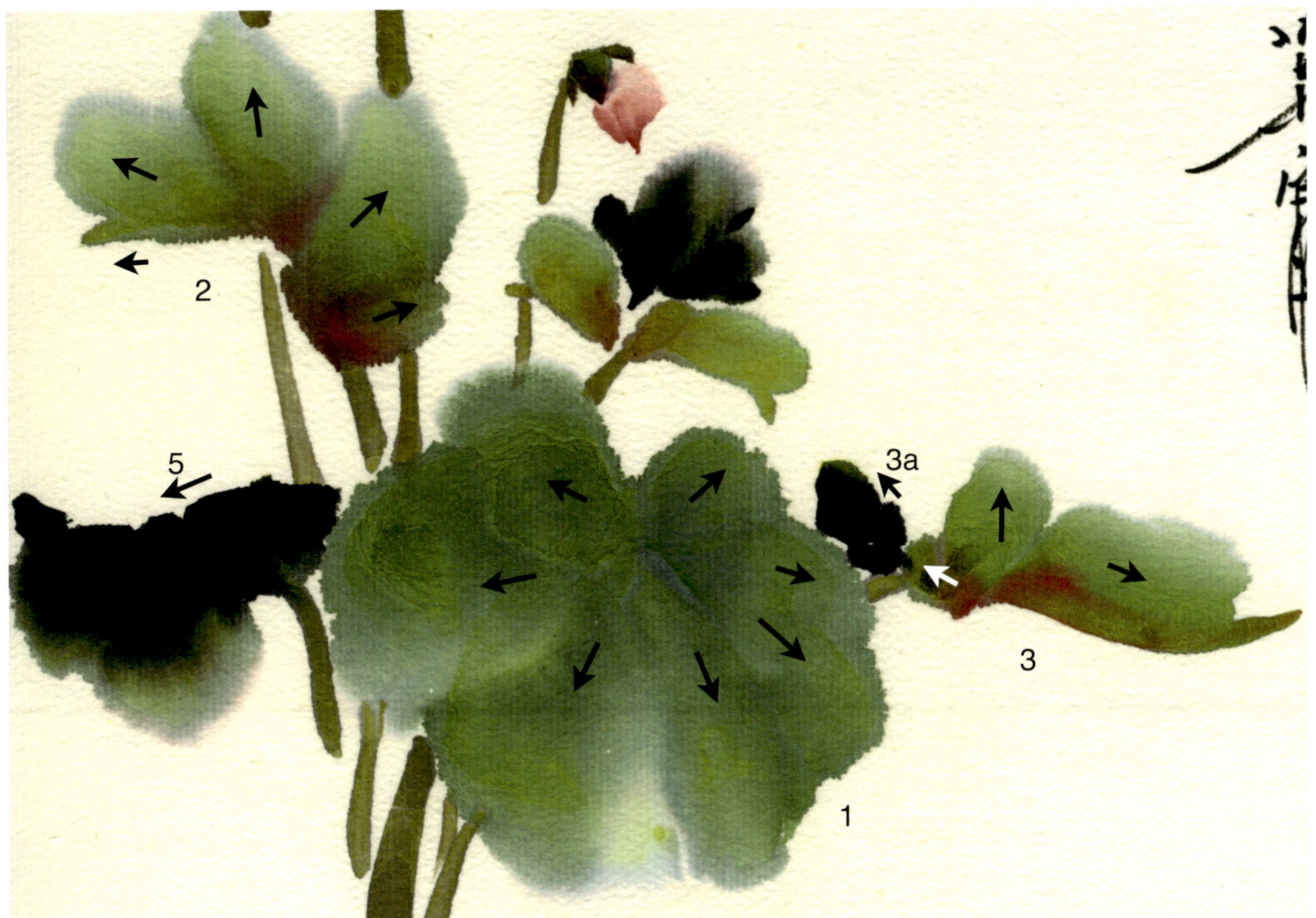


Full Leaf (1)
∂ Large Flow
❖ Light Green + Dark Green
The leaf is heart-shaped with serrated edges. Do the left side of the leaf. Start with a small stroke to show the center of the leaf. Press strokes out to the left. The first stroke arches up, the second pushes out, the third elongates. The fourth stroke shows the center vein to finish the left side. Similarly, work the right side smaller.

Profile Leaves
❖ Light Green + Dark Red
We do folding leaves showing their backside or underside. Set the baseline. Push the first stroke out. Add a small stroke to its right and elongate the strokes to its left. Follow the baseline with a "freeway exit" (2).

Avoid making the baseline too straight. We torture ourselves to show more curves. Do the same to our leaves.

Work another profile leaf on the right (3). Push up first. Add a small stroke on the left, elongate the right side then lead the tip out like a "freeway exit." The exit stroke can swing either upward or downward.

❖ Light Green + Dark Green + Ink
Add the shadow side of the folding leaf (3a).

Stalks

ℒ Flow

❖ Brown (Dark Red + Light Green)

When doing stalks, we do the lower middle ones first. End them lower to show they are in the front. Do the side ones next and end them higher. Group the stalks into an arrowhead, like fish looking for the same food .

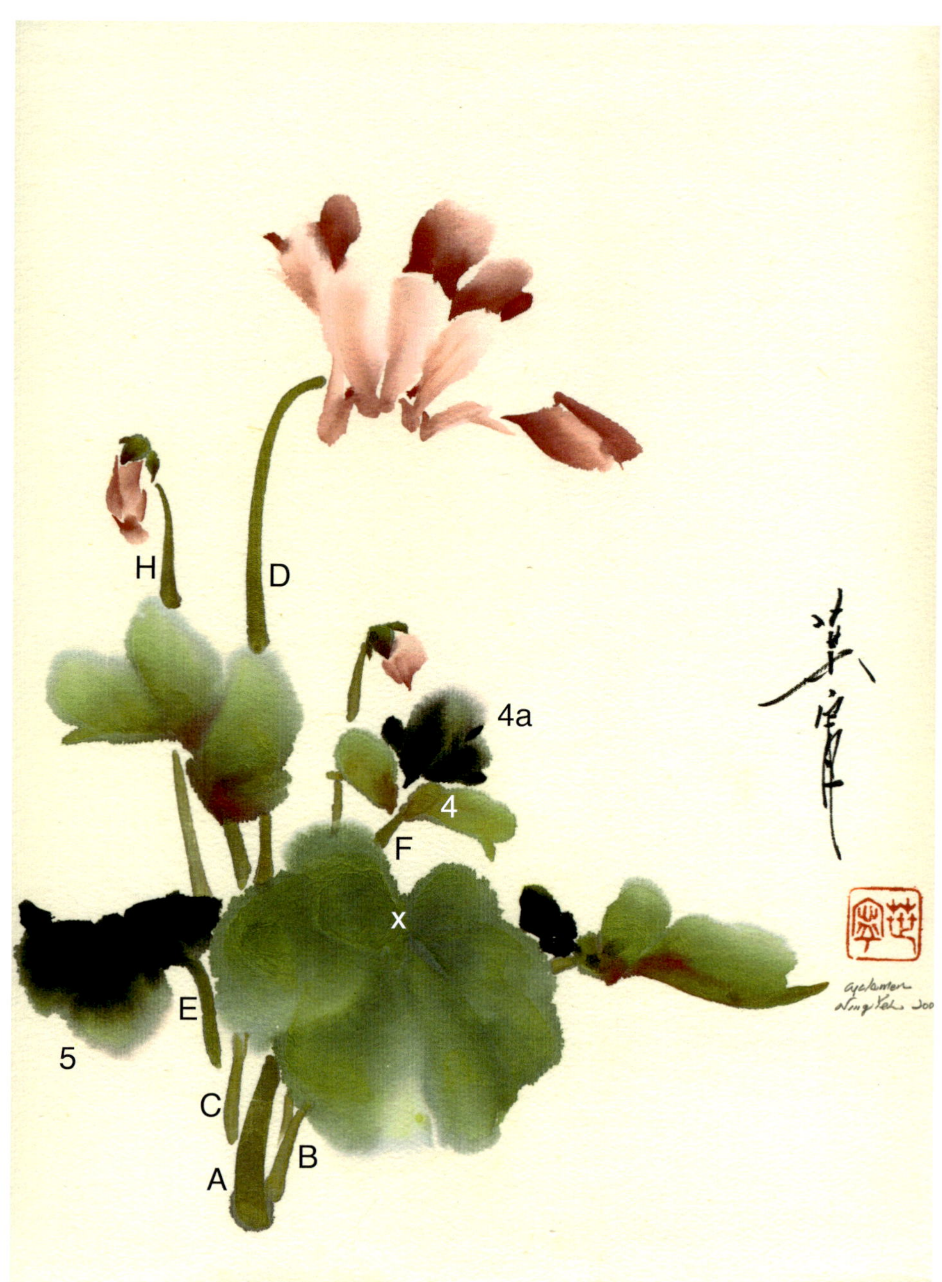


Begin the leaf stalks from the indent of the heart (x) and lead them down (A, B, C).

Starting above the petal roots, curve a stalk reaching into the center of the flower. Lead the stalk down (D).

❖ Light Green + Dark Red

Do a liaison leaf reaching to the back with both sides flipping up (4).

❖ Light Green + Dark Green + Ink

Work the topside with strokes moving from the center out (4a). Add a shadow leaf drooping to the left. Present the dark leaves in a triangle (5).

❖ Brown

Lead leaf stalks down.

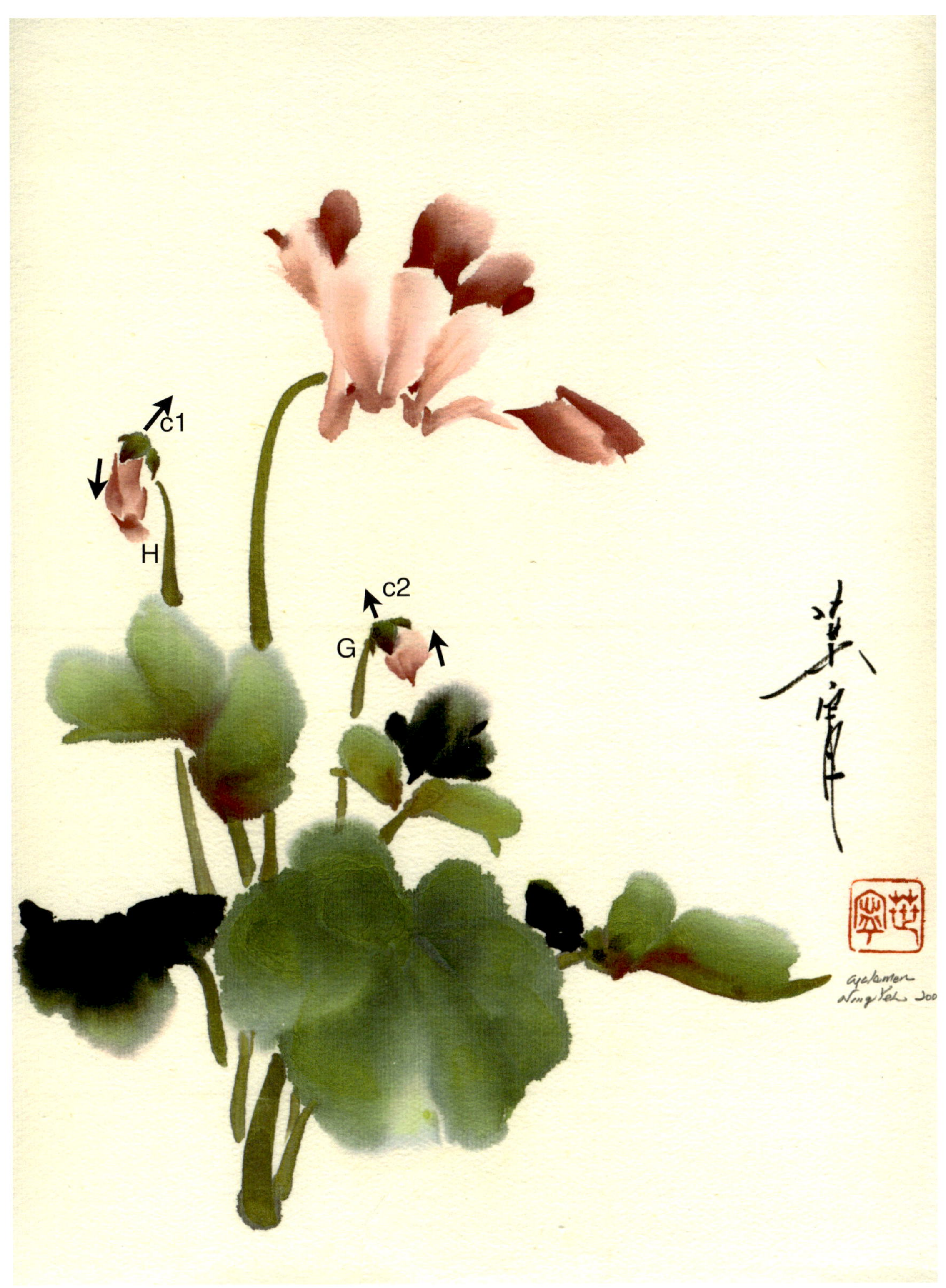


❖ Light Green + Dark Red
Do a couple sets of calyxes. Work three dots upward for each set (c1, c2).

❖ White + Magenta
Do a bigger bud on the left side (H). Work two wrapping strokes from the calyx downward to show one petal. Add more petals below and to the side.

Do a baby bud (G). Work strokes pushing into the calyx.

❖ Brown
Add stalks to the buds.

We have a simple composition with everything.

8031

# Daffodil

Iang
Yáng: Ocean, foreign

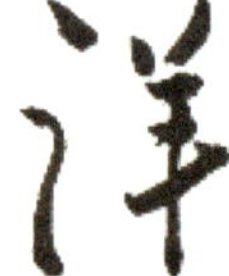

Shuei
Shuǐ: Water

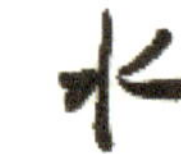

Shian
Xiān: Fairy

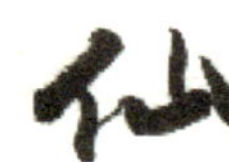

Over the last couple of centuries, foreigners came to China by sea. Chinese call foreign things "yáng" meaning "ocean."

Narcissus is Shuǐ Xiān or Water Fairy in Chinese. Daffodil came from abroad. It is Yáng Shuǐ Xiān.

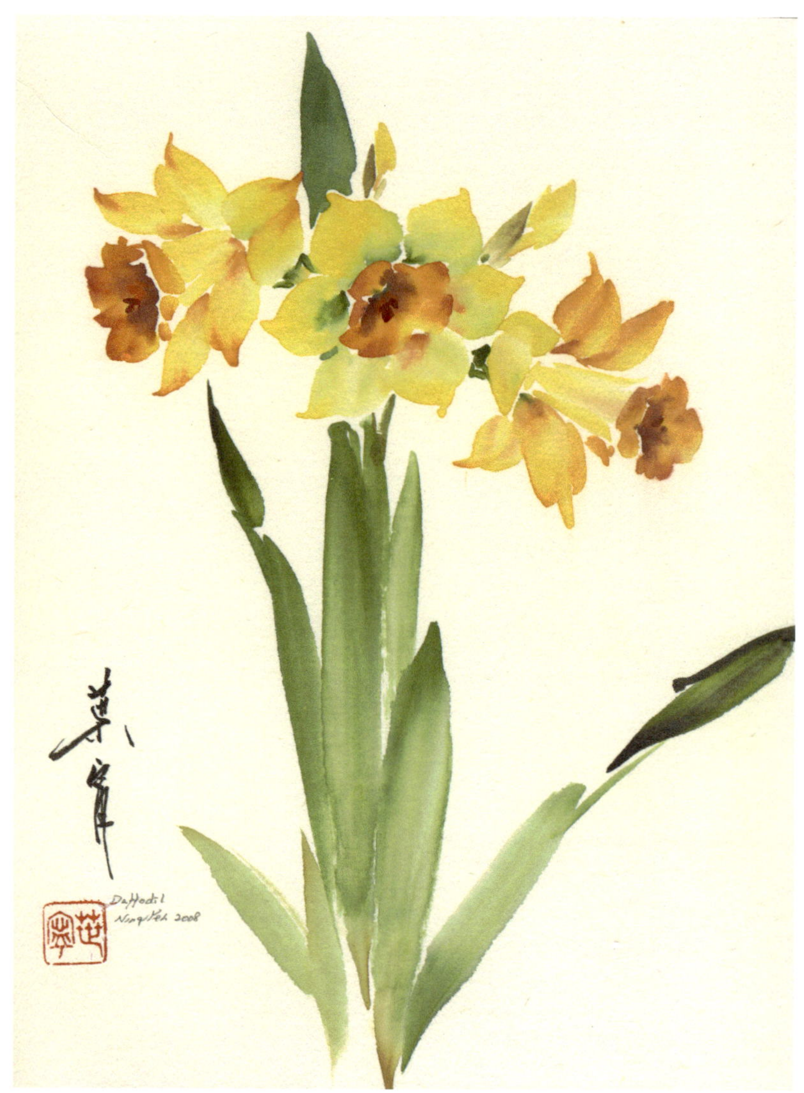

## MATERIALS

Paper: Double Shuen

ℛ Brushes
Flow, Large Orchid Bamboo

❖ Colors
*Chinese*
Yellow, Vermillion
*Da Vinci*
White
*Schmincke*
Cadmium Red Deep
*Winsor & Newton*
Indigo, Perylene Violet
*OAS*
Best Bottle Ink

## PREPARATION OF COLORS

Yellow
White: diluted
White Yellow: White + Yellow
Vermillion: thick
Red: Cadmium Red Deep
Dark Red: Perylene Violet + Red
Light Green: Yellow + Indigo
Dark Green: Yellow + Indigo
Beige: Dark Red + Light Green + Yellow + White
Brown: Dark Red + Dark Green
Ink

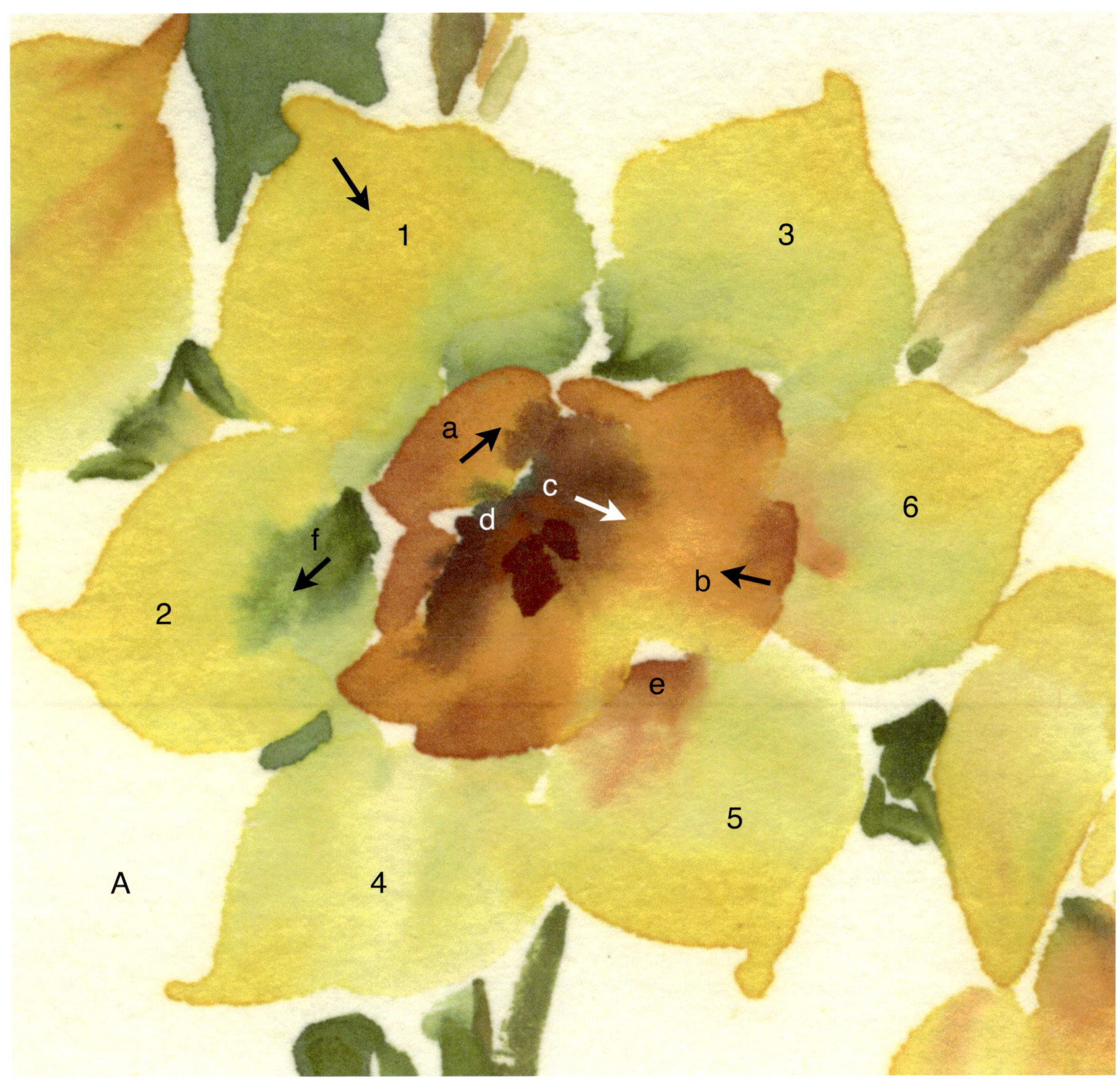


**STEPS**

Middle Flower (A)

Center

ᔑ Flow

❖ Yellow + Vermillion

Do the front of the flower center with three strokes showing a "U" shape (a).

❖ Vermillion

Work strokes from outside in forming a fan (b). Leave the center area open.

❖ Dark Red

Work strokes outward from the center (c).

❖ Light Green + Dark Green

Add the base of the center if needed (d).

Petals

❖ Yellow

Do six petals forming a circle around the flower center. Work each from outside in with two strokes. Leave space open near the petal roots (1-6).

❖ Vermillion

Add shadows at the roots of some petals (e).

❖ Light Green

Work shadows at the roots of the remaining petals (f). The shadows reflect the colors of objects nearby. Use Vermillion or Light Green freely.

Profile Flower Reaching Left (B).

Anchor Petal (1)

❖ Yellow + Vermillion

Show the tip of the petal. Arch upward to the left. Work a stroke to smooth the middle. Add a stroke to show the lower right side. Smooth the base.

Center

❖ Yellow + Vermillion

Do the front of the flower center showing a "U" shape (a). Keep some distance away from the anchor petal.

❖ Vermillion

Work strokes from outside in forming a fan (b). Leave the center area open.

❖ Vermillion + Dark Red

Work strokes outward from the center blending into the fan. Leave a hairline space (c).

Tube (d)

❖ White Yellow + Yellow

Work strokes to show the center tube.

❖ Vermillion

Add the root of the tube.

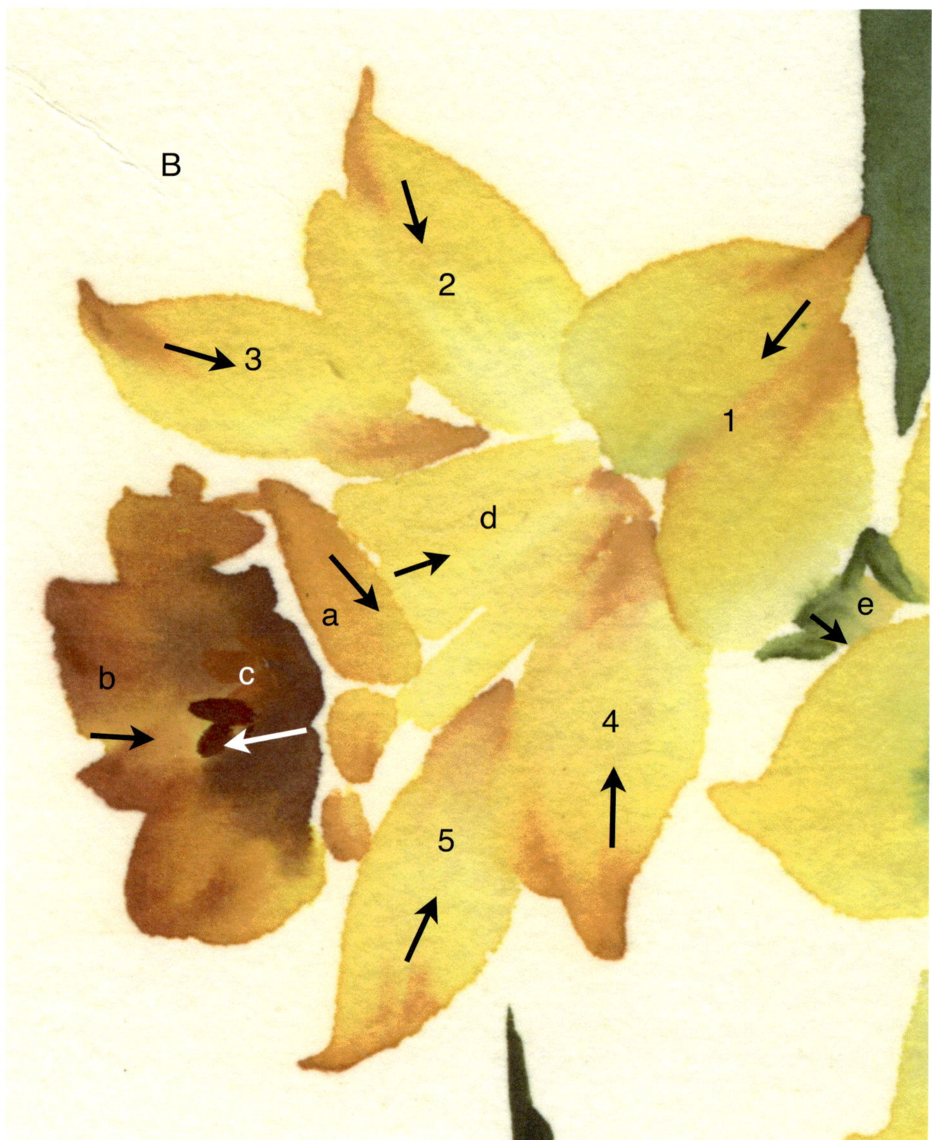


❖ White Yellow + Yellow + Vermillion

Do petals on both sides of the center tube (2, 3, 4, 5). Leave space open near the roots.

❖ Vermillion

Add shadows at the petal roots.

❖ Light Green

Do strokes behind the flower to suggest a trumpet leading to the middle flower (e).

Profile Flower Reaching Right (C).
Anchor Petal (1)
❖ Yellow
Work a petal with two strokes.

Center
❖ Yellow + Vermillion
Do the front of the flower center showing a "U" shape (a). Keep some distance away from the anchor petal.

Work strokes from outside in showing a fan (b). Leave the center area open.

❖ Vermillion + Dark Red
Work strokes outward from the center area, leaving a hairline space (c).

Tube
❖ White Yellow + Yellow
Work strokes to show the center tube (d).

❖ Yellow + Vermillion
Do petals on both sides of the center tube (2-6). Leave space open near the roots.

❖ Vermillion
Add shadows at the petal roots.

❖ Light Green
Add shadows on the lower petal.

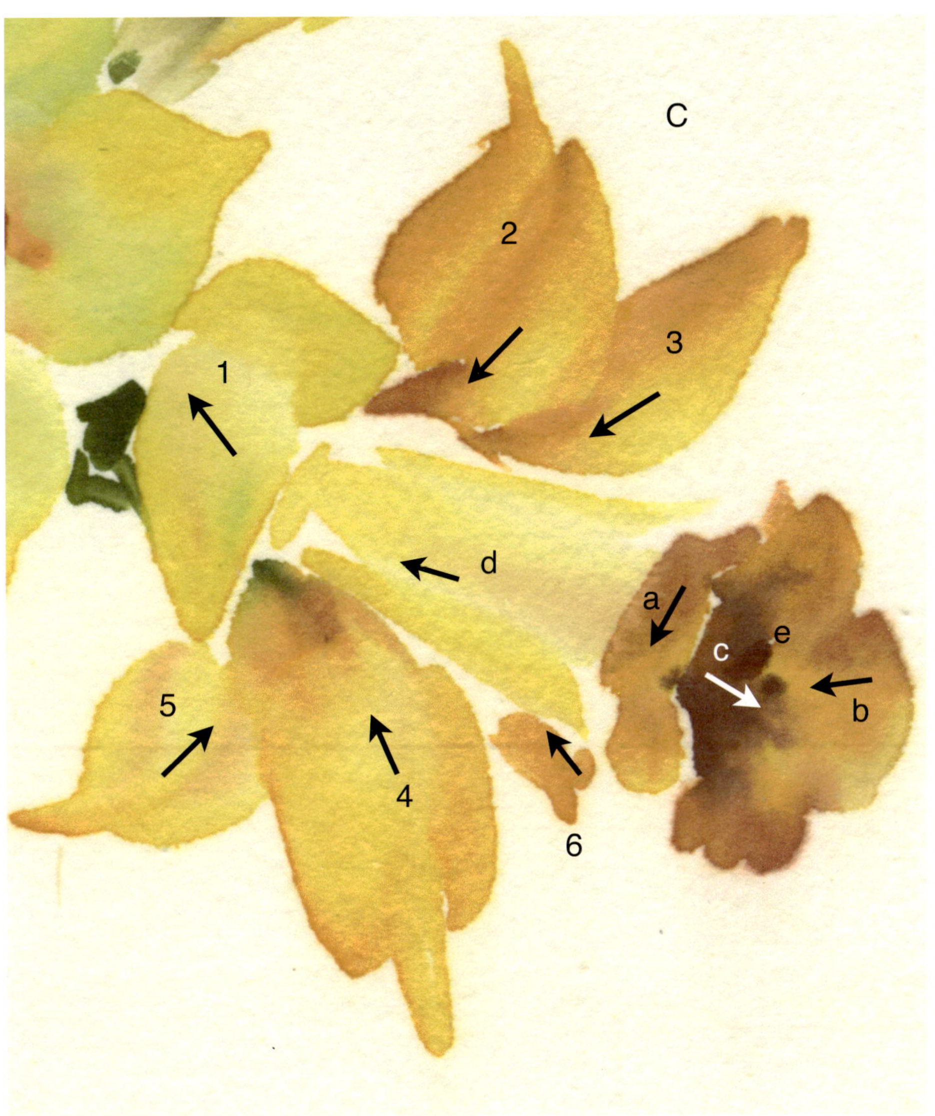


❖ Light Green
Do strokes to suggest a trumpet behind the flower.

❖ Yellow + Vermillion
There are nearly invisible stamens in the center. We do a few dots just to silence the critics.

❖ Dark Red
Add up to three dots to show the lady in the center (e).

Leaves

♌ Large Orchid Bamboo

❖ Light Green + Dark Green

Work a leaf from the top (D). Leap over the center flower and come down (E) .

Do a few leaves on both sides (F, G, H).

Show one profile leaf moving to the right (I).

❖ Beige

Add the roots of the leaves.

Work a couple of smaller leaves on the left (J, K).

❖ Light Green + Dark Green + Ink

Add the topside of the leaf dashing to the right (L). Show a folding top on the tall leaf to the left (M).

Buds

♌ Flow

❖ Beige + Brown

Do two sets of sheaths, each with two strokes (o1, o2).

❖ White Yellow + Yellow

Show the tip part of the buds (P, Q).

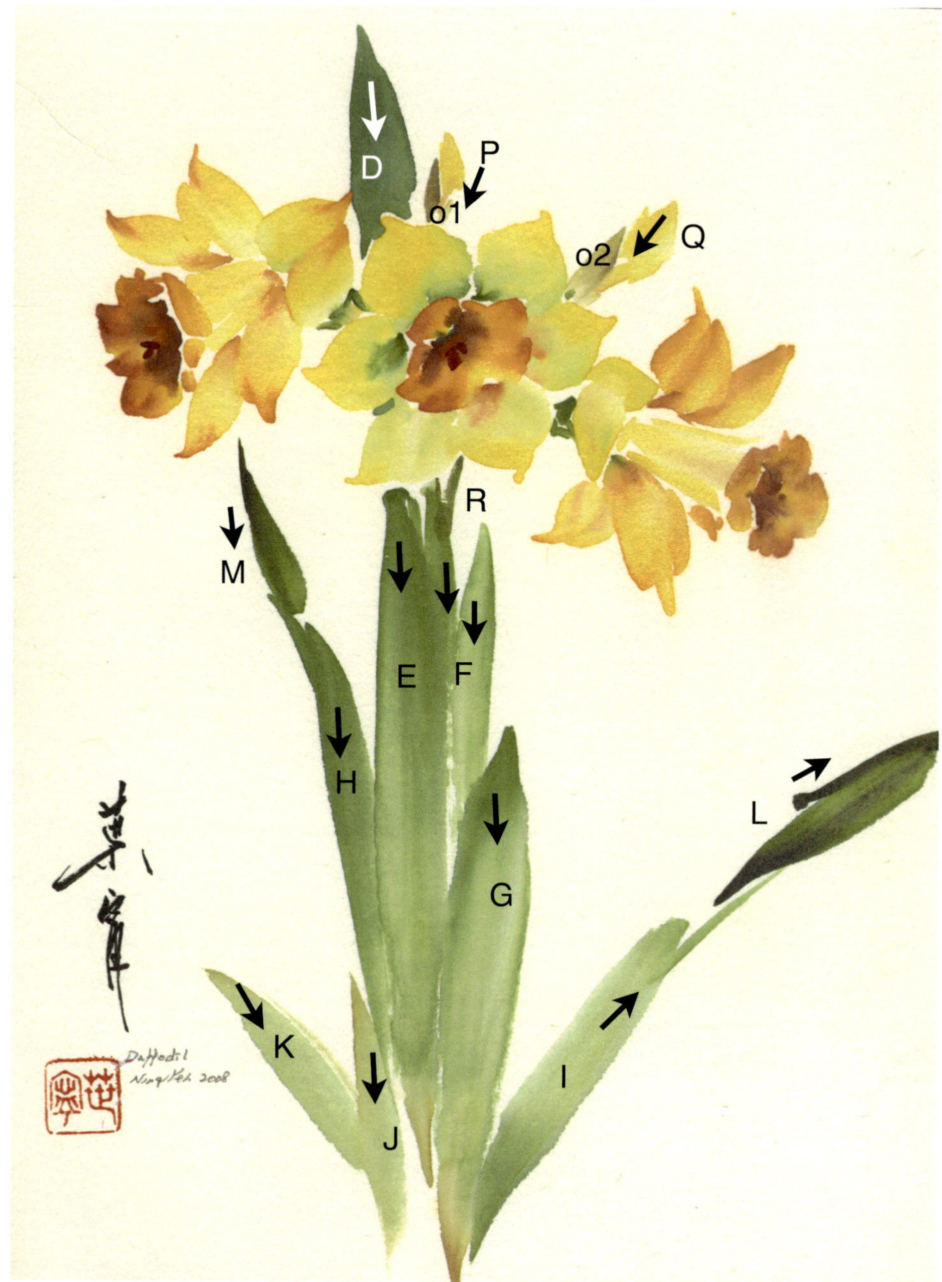


❖ Vermillion

Add the roots of the buds.

❖ Vermillion + Light Green

Do stems to connect the flowers and the buds into the leaf (R).

8032

# Dahlia

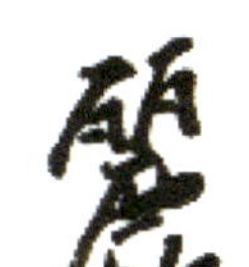

Dai
Dà: Big, grand

Li
Lí: Beauty

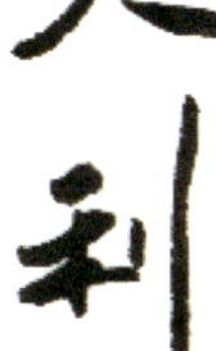

Dai
Dà: Big, grand

Li
Lì: Profit

In Chinese, the word beauty and profit share the same sound: lì. Dahlia is grand beauty or big profit. In the beautiful town of Dàlǐ in Yúnnán, I rode a horse carriage to an old temple and shared a lovely morning studying this flower. My dàlí came from Dàlǐ.

### MATERIALS

Paper: Double Shuen

ᘯ Brushes
Flow, Large Orchid Bamboo, Happy Dot

❖ Colors
*Chinese*
Yellow
*Da Vinci*
White
*Schmincke*
Cadmium Red Deep
*Winsor & Newton*
Indigo, Permanent Magenta,

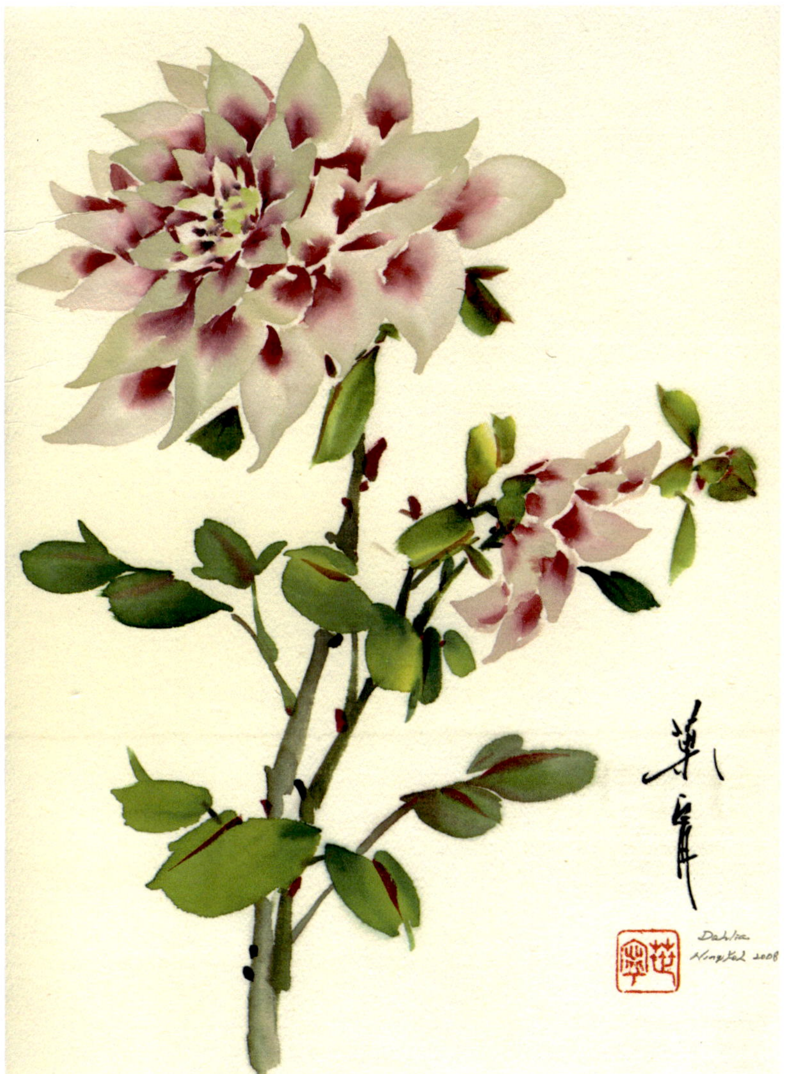

Alizarin Crimson, Perylene Violet
*OAS*
Best Bottle Ink

PREPARATION OF COLORS
Yellow
White: diluted
Red: Cadmium Red Deep
Pink: White + Yellow + Magenta + a touch of Light Green
Magenta: Permanent Magenta + Red
Crimson: Alizarin Crimson + Red
Dark Red: Perylene Violet + Red
Light Green: Yellow + Indigo
Dark Green: Yellow + Indigo
White Green: White + Yellow + Light Green
Ink

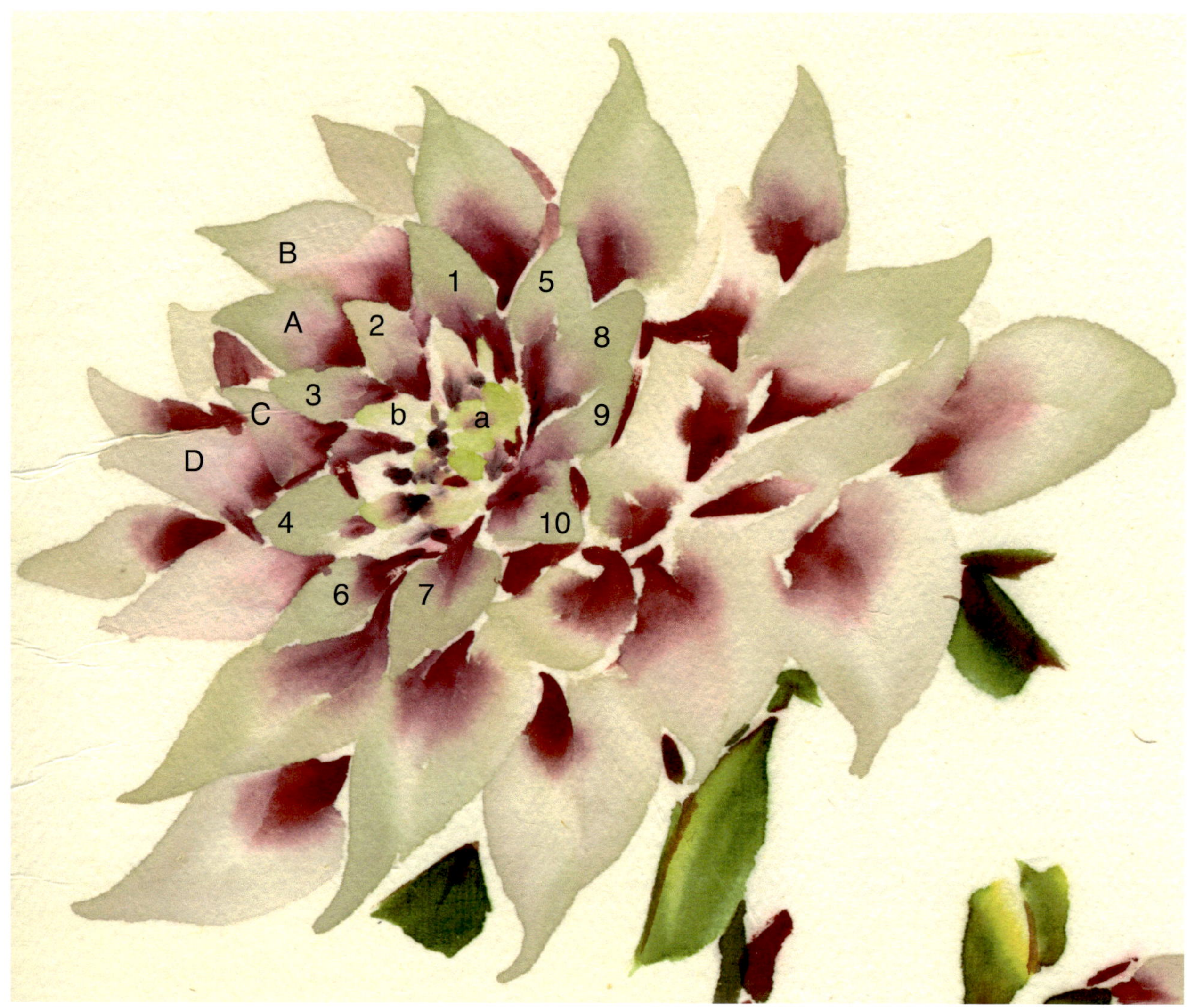


**STEPS**

Full Flower
𝒮 Flow
❖ White Green
Do a pumpkin shaped center (a).

❖ Dark Red + Ink
Seal the middle of the pumpkin with dark dots.

❖ White Green
Add a ring of short petals around the pumpkin. Work strokes from top down (b).

❖ Dark Red + Ink
Work the dark root of each petal from the base up.

❖ White + Pink
Expand the flower with a ring of petals. Work each petal with two strokes. Leave some space in the middle of each petal (1-10).

❖ Dark Red
Work a darker color from center of the flower outward into the middle of each petal. You see how easy this is.

❖ White + Pink
Work larger petals on the top. Do each petal with two strokes. Leave some space in the middle of each petal. The petals bow to the middle slightly (A-D).

❖ Crimson + Dark Red
Work a dark root for each petal from the base up.

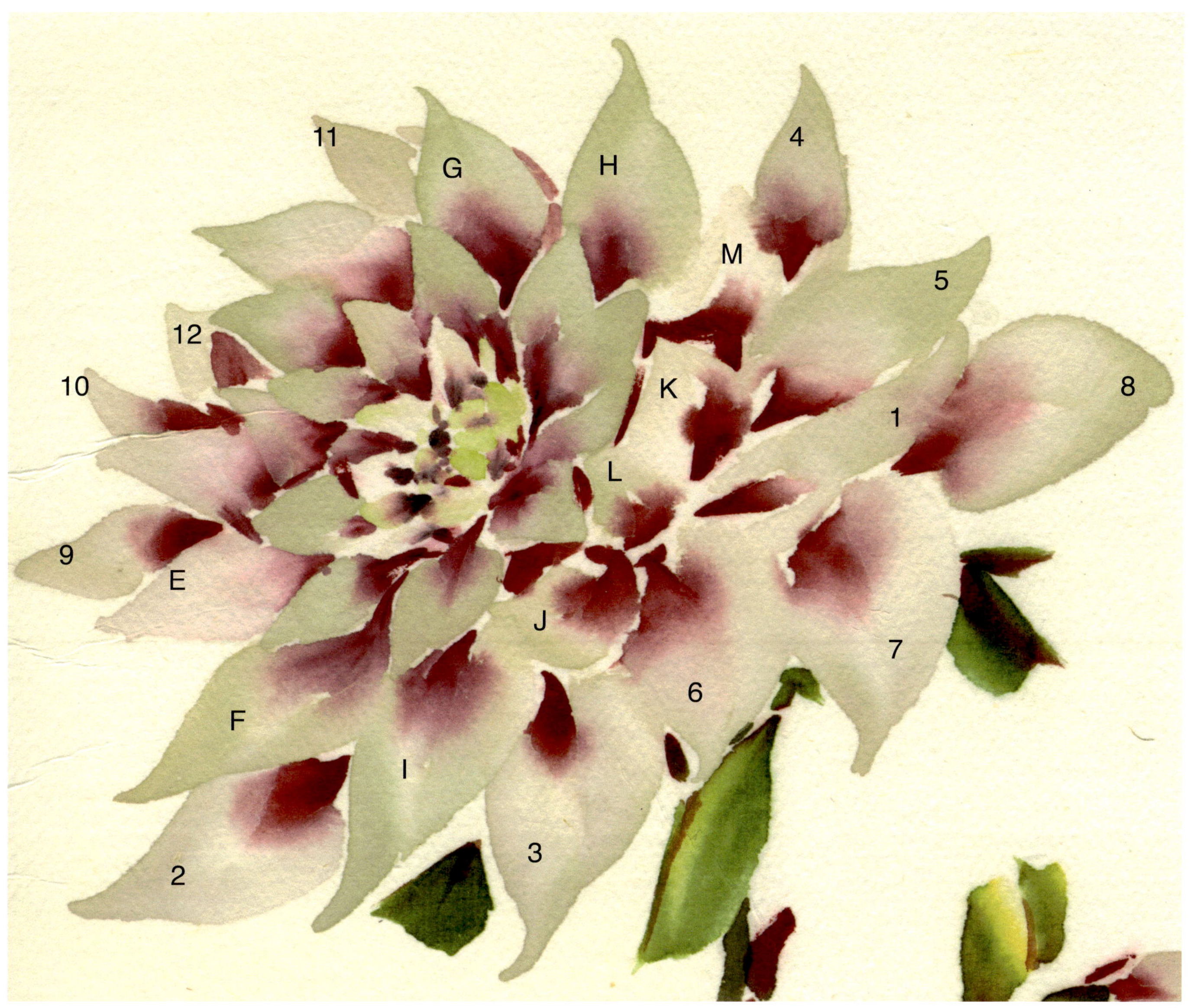


❖ White + Pink
Do long petals on both sides (E, F, G, H, I).

❖ Crimson + Dark Red
Add the roots of the petals from the center out.

❖ White + Pink
Do petals with tips turning upward along the front of the flower center (J, K, L, M).

❖ Crimson + Dark Red
Seal the gaps between the petals. Add root strokes to the base of the front petals.

❖ White + Pink
By now, we are addicted to this. Let us work a few larger petals to form a skirt for the flower (1-8).

❖ Magenta + Crimson + Dark Red
Add the roots of the petals from the center out.

❖ White + Pink
Do a few more petals on top. Develop the perimeter into a balanced oval shape (9-12).

❖ Magenta + Crimson + Dark Red
Add the roots of the new petals.

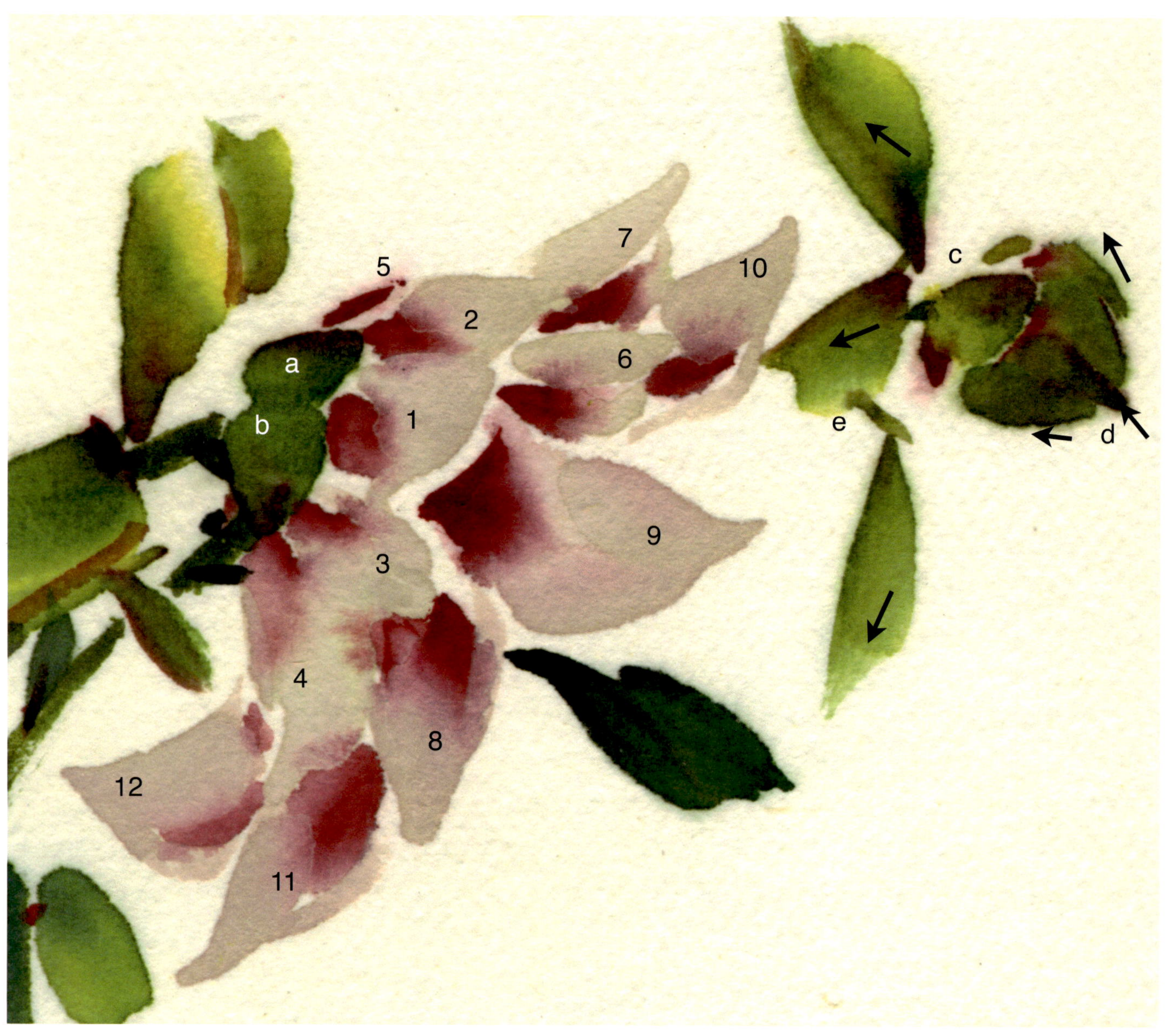


Guest Flower

❖ Light Green + Dark Red
Do calyx dots (a, b).

❖ White + Pink
Work a layer of petals into the calyx (1-5).

❖ Magenta + Crimson + Dark Red
Add a shadow in the middle of each petal.

❖ White + Pink
Work one more layer of petals (7-12).

❖ Magenta + Crimson + Dark Red
Seal the middle of the petals.

Bud

❖ Light Green + Dark Red
Do some calyx dots below (c). Add a bud (d).

Leaves

❖ Light Green + Dark Red
Let us work a few leaves to form a skirt for the bud (e). The leaves of dahlia are serrated. Usually the leaves are three to a group.

♌ Flow

❖ Light Green + Dark Red
Work a few leaves to form a skirt for the full flower (1) and guest flower (1a).

♌ Large Orchid Bamboo

❖ Yellow + Light Green + Dark Green
Do a cluster of leaves as the Grand Central Station for our composition. Show a center leaf. Add wings on both sides (2).

Work a larger group of leaves to anchor the lower area. Do the center leaf with two strokes. Work a leaf on each side of the center leaf (3).

♌ Flow

❖ Light Green + Dark Red
Add stems and branches to the flowers and bud. Lead them past the center leaf cluster. Leap over the lower leaf group. Add stems to connect the leaves into the branches.

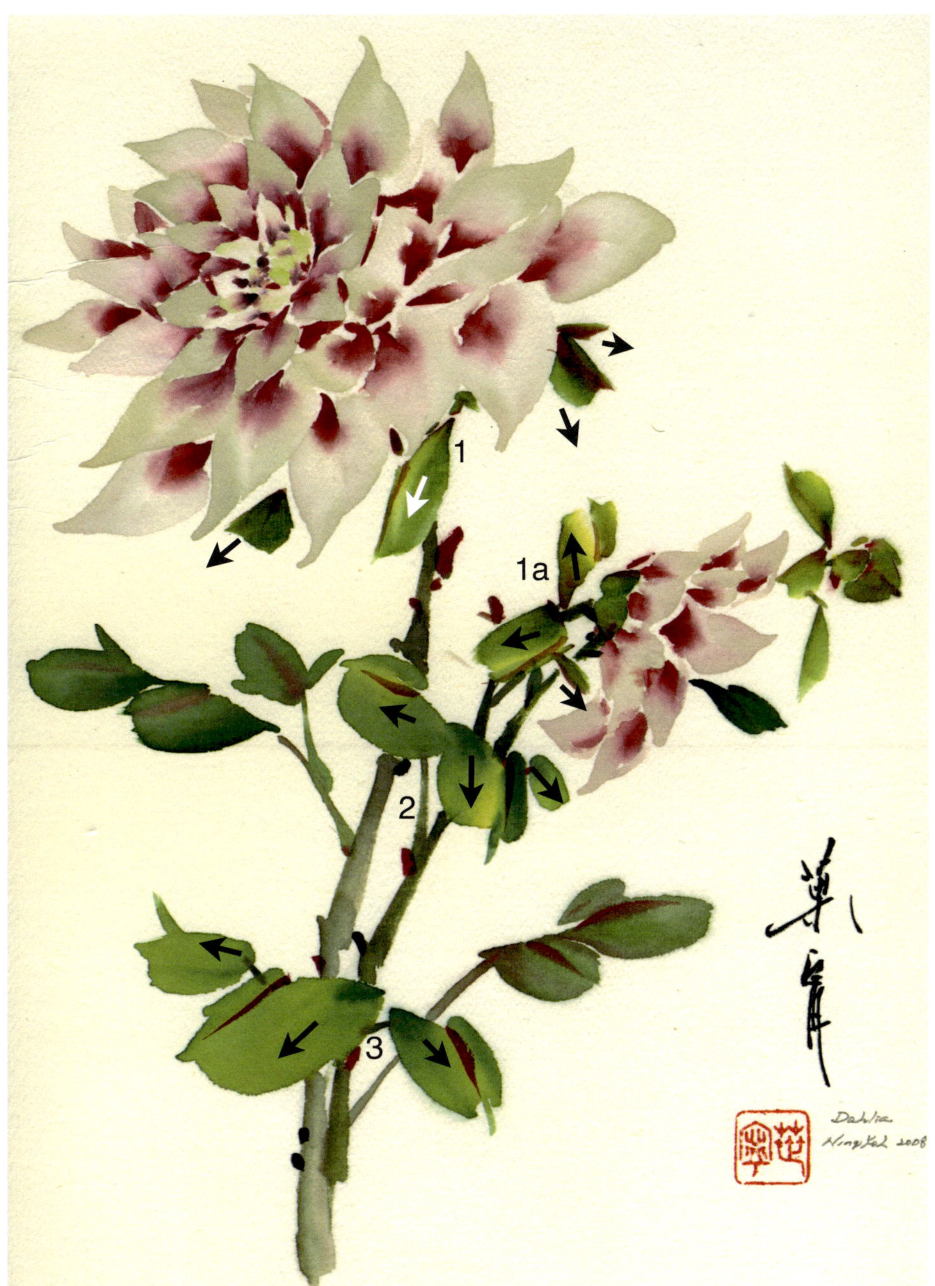

❖ Light Green + Dark Green + Ink
Work a group of leaves reaching to the right (4).

Add a dark leaf to the guest area as a reaching arm (5).

Work a couple of groups of leaves reaching to the left side (6, 7).

❖ Light Green + Dark Red
Add stems to bring the leaves into the branch.

❖ Dark Red
Do some dots to show new growths on the branches.

❖ Ink
Add some ink dots. I just have to do them.

♌ Happy Dot
❖ Light Green + Dark Red
Work a center vein for each full leaf.

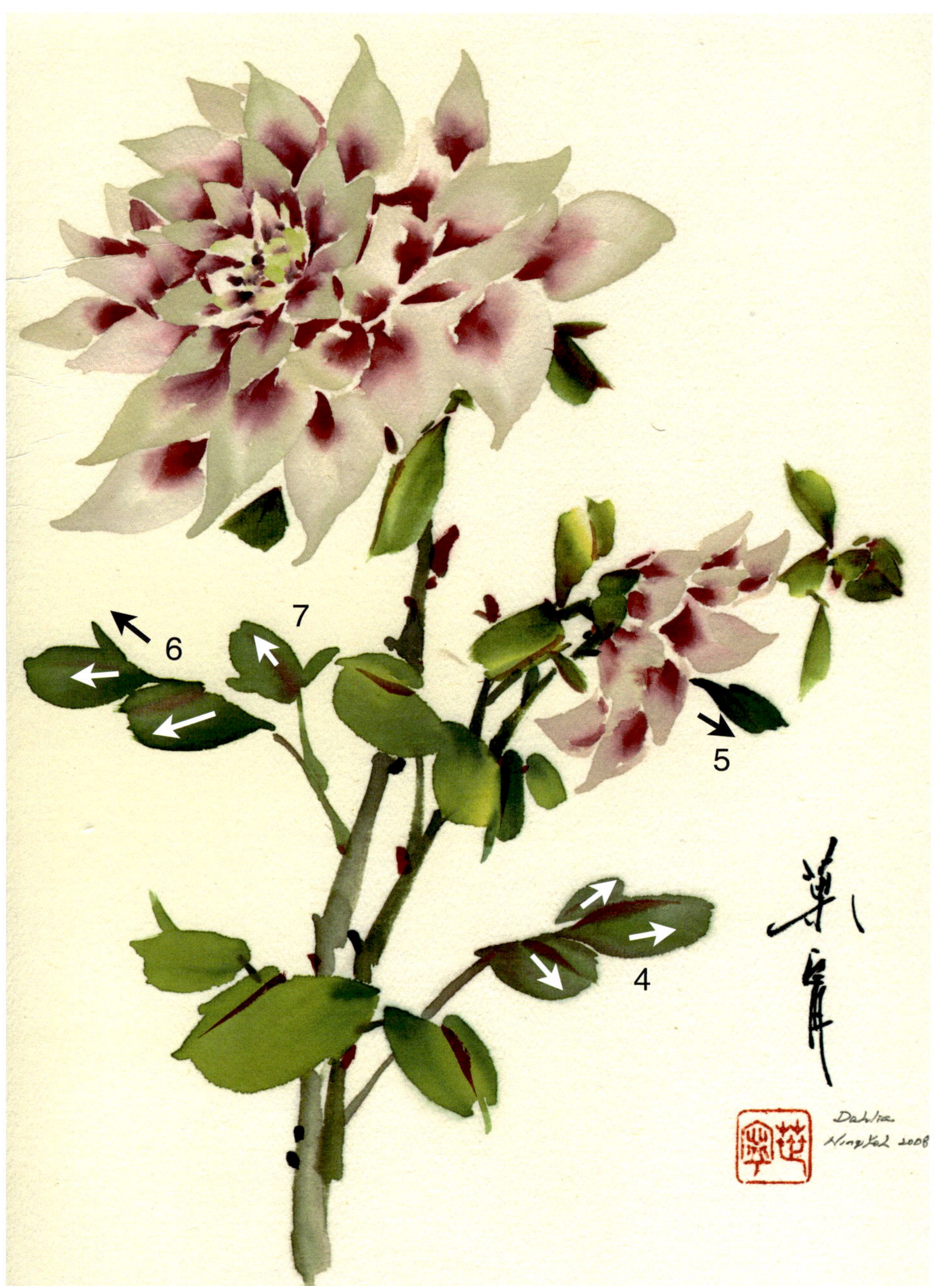

8033

# Datura

Man
Màn: Extend

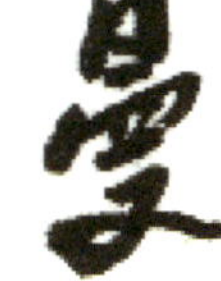


Tuo
Tuó: Uneven

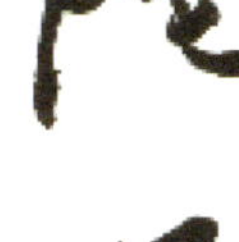


Luo
Luó: Net, silk

羅

Màntuóluó is a beautiful name. It has the romantic notion of an extended silky net. In some cultures, Datura is used as a love potion—but only with care, because datura is a poison that can cause the mind to become delirious and can be fatal. Ignore the warning, Romeo. I know you are desperate.

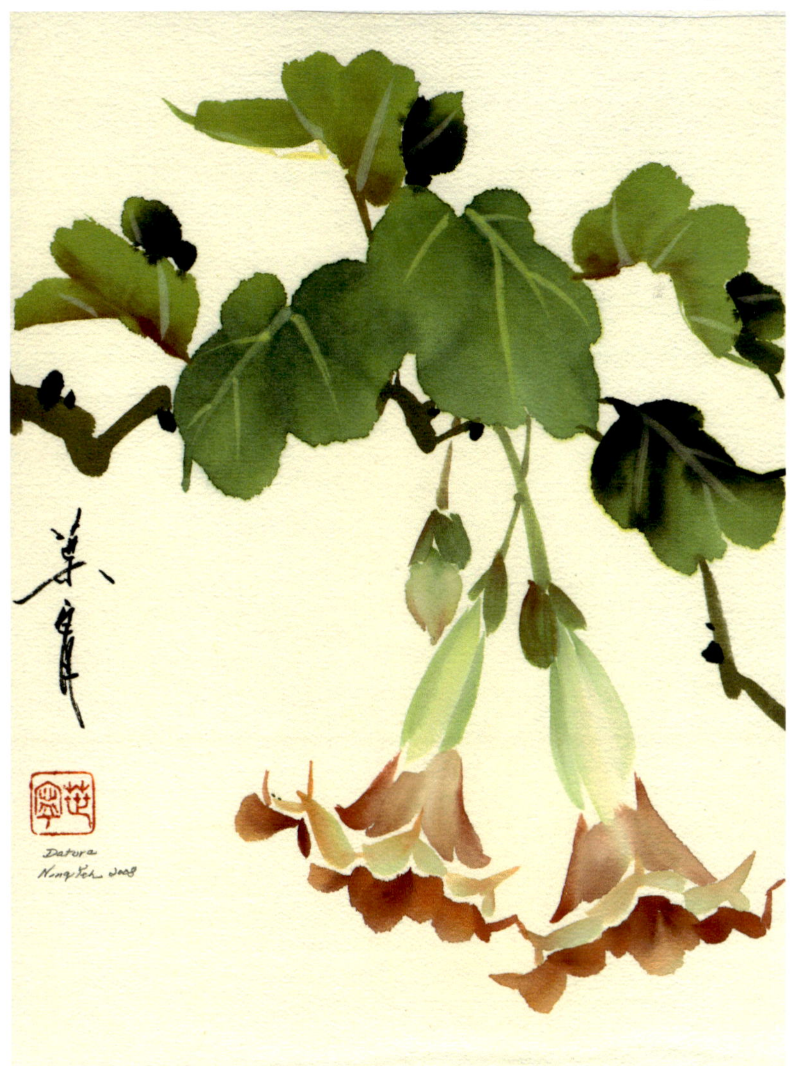

**MATERIALS**

Paper: Double Shuen

Brushes
Flow, Large Flow, Small Mountain Horse

❖ Colors
*Chinese*
Yellow, Vermillion
*Da Vinci*
White
*Schmincke*
Cadmium Red Deep
*Winsor & Newton*
Indigo, Perylene Violet
*OAS*
Best Bottle Ink

**PREPARATION OF COLORS**

Yellow: thick liquid + White
White: diluted
Vermillion: thick
Red: Cadmium Red Deep + Vermillion
Dark Red: Perylene Violet + Red + Vermillion
Light Green: Yellow + Indigo
Dark Green: Yellow + Indigo
Peach: Yellow + Vermillion + White
White Green: White + Light Green
Brown: Vermillion + Ink
Ink

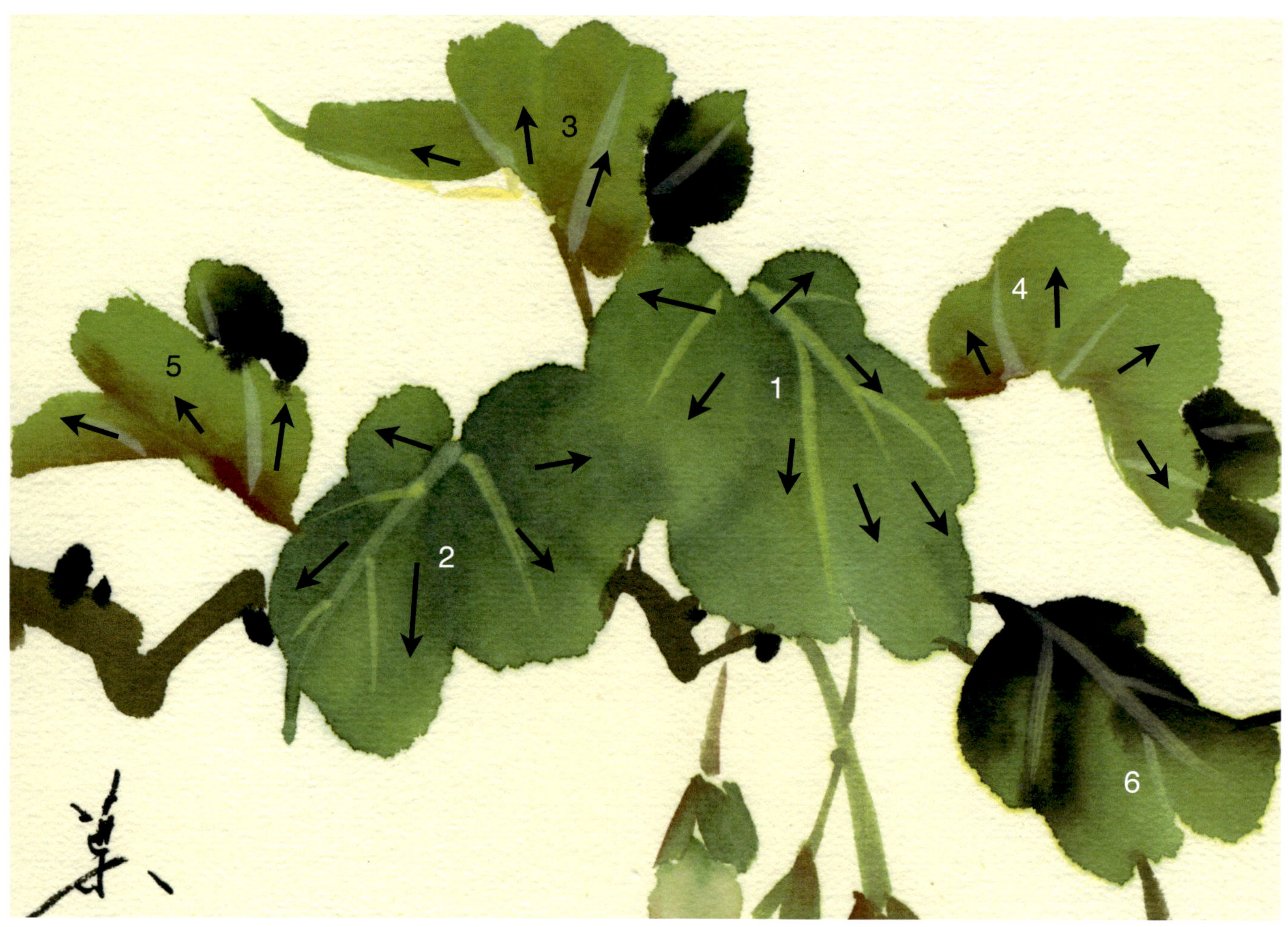


**STEPS**

Leaves

ᔕ Large Flow

❖ Light Green + Dark Green

The datura leaf is elongated with wavy edges. Set the orientation of a leaf heading to the right. Work the left side of the leaf. Starting from the center of the leaf, push a stroke left, arch up, and slide down. Do the right side of the leaf smaller (1).

Work a second leaf moving to the left, a little lower (2).

❖ Light Green + Dark Red

Do profile leaves showing their undersides. Put one folding leaf on the upper left (3). Work a stem. Push strokes upward and radiating to the left. Extend a tip out.

Work one more folding leaf going to the right (4). Start with a short stroke. Do the second stroke taller. Tilt the third stroke. Lengthen the fourth and extend the tip to the right. We see a pair of happy eyes.

Let us do one more profile leaf going to the left (5).

❖ Light Green + Dark Green + Ink

Work the shadow side of the folding leaves. Project all the strokes from the same starting point as the leaf strokes below. Show "valleys and hills" along the top edge. Do not flatten the contour of the leaves.

Add one more drooping leaf on the lower right (6).

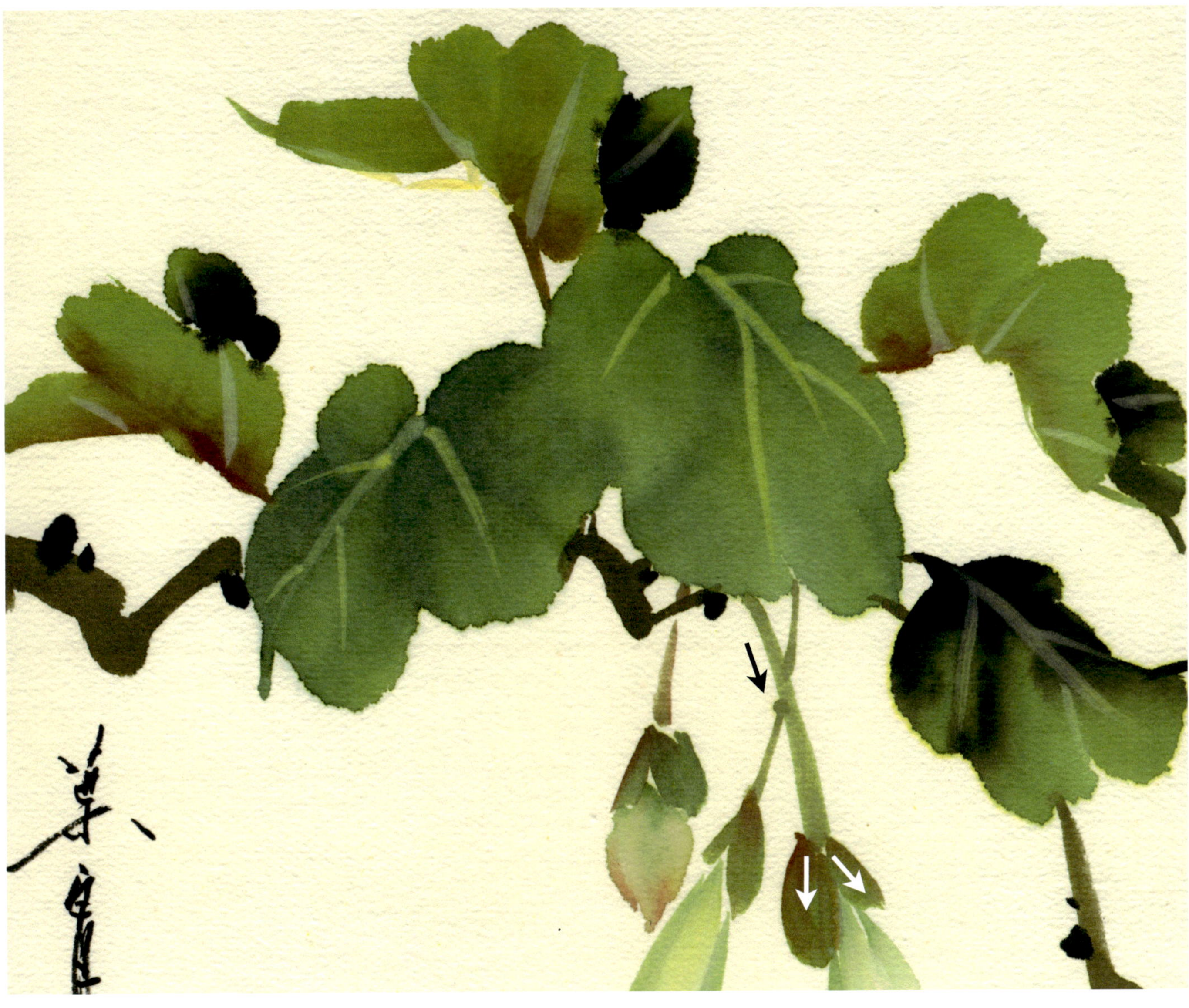

Veins

ℓ Small Mountain Horse

❖ White + Yellow

Add a center vein and pairs of alternating side veins. Avoid "chicken foot" and parallel lines. Profile leaves do not show center veins. Move all the veins upward from the baseline of the profile leaves.

Branches and Stems

ℓ Flow

❖ Brown

Run the main branch from left to right. Leap over leaves. The branch is heavier at the beginning and gradually getting thinner. Tuck the leaves onto the branch with stems.

❖ Ink

Add happy dots.

Flowers

❖ Light Green + Dark Red

The datura has large trumpet shaped flowers drooping from long stems. Run long stems for the flowers. Put sets of calyxes at the end of the stems.

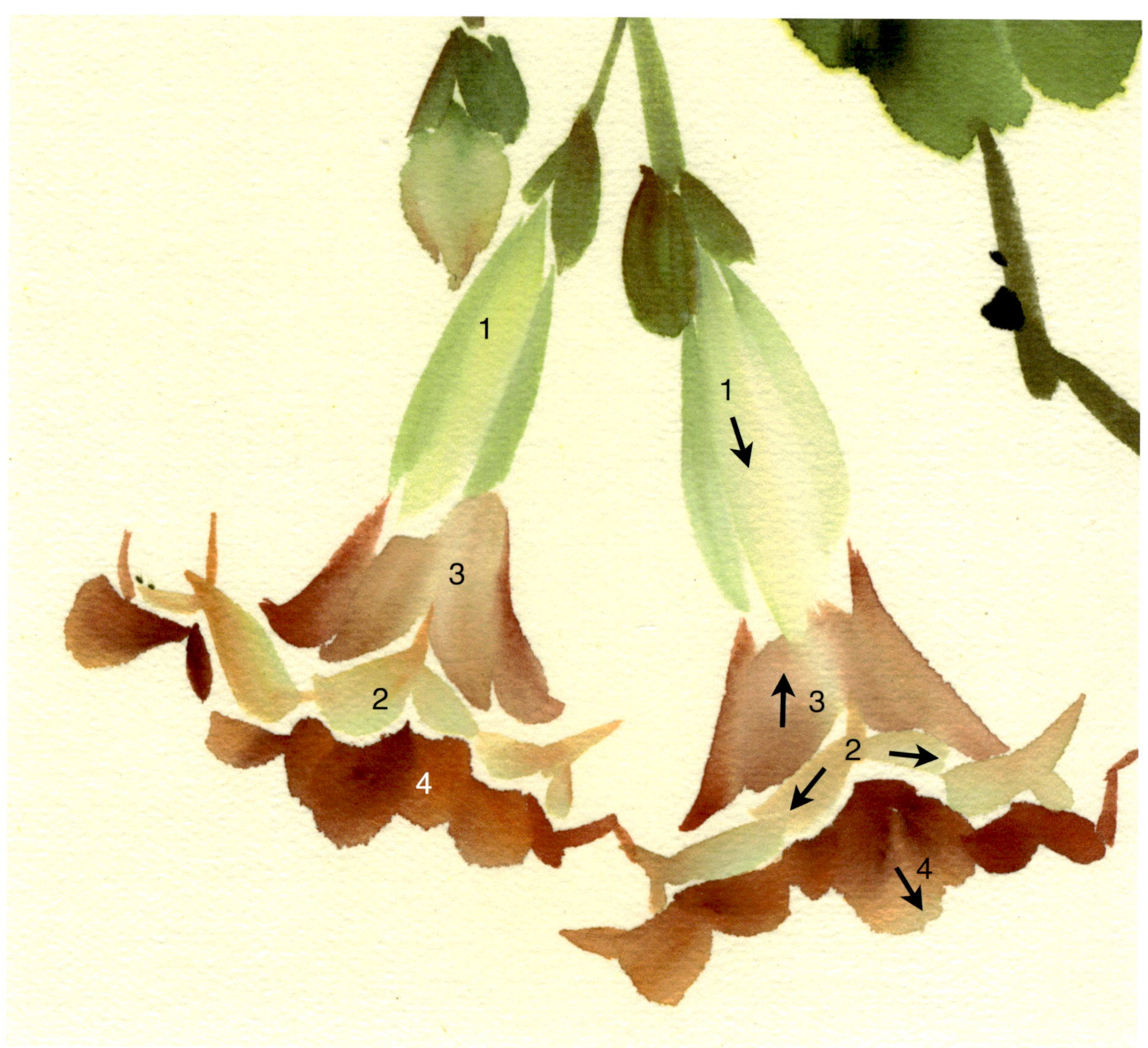


❖ White + Yellow + White Green
Do the flower tubes from the calyx down, lift the brush at the end (1).

❖ White Green
Add strokes to widen the tubes on both sides.

❖ White + Peach
Do the flipped-up tips of the front petals a little distance away from the tubes. Work the center ones. Show the tip, press and lift on both sides (2).

❖ Vermillion
Add petals on both sides of the center ones. The inside shoulders are longer than the outside shoulders.

❖ White + Peach + Vermillion + Red
Connect the petals to the tubes with tapering strokes (3). Do the center part with two strokes moving upward.

❖ Vermillion + Red
Add strokes tapering on each side to complete the trumpet. Let the strokes be. Do not force them to be perfectly connected. Brush painting is about the spontaneous spirit of strokes.

❖ Vermillion + Red + Dark Red
Work the inside of the trumpet (4). Work shadow side petals with downward strokes lining the bottom edge. Show different widths and attitudes. Some of the tips can be extra long and turning. Reach out and touch.

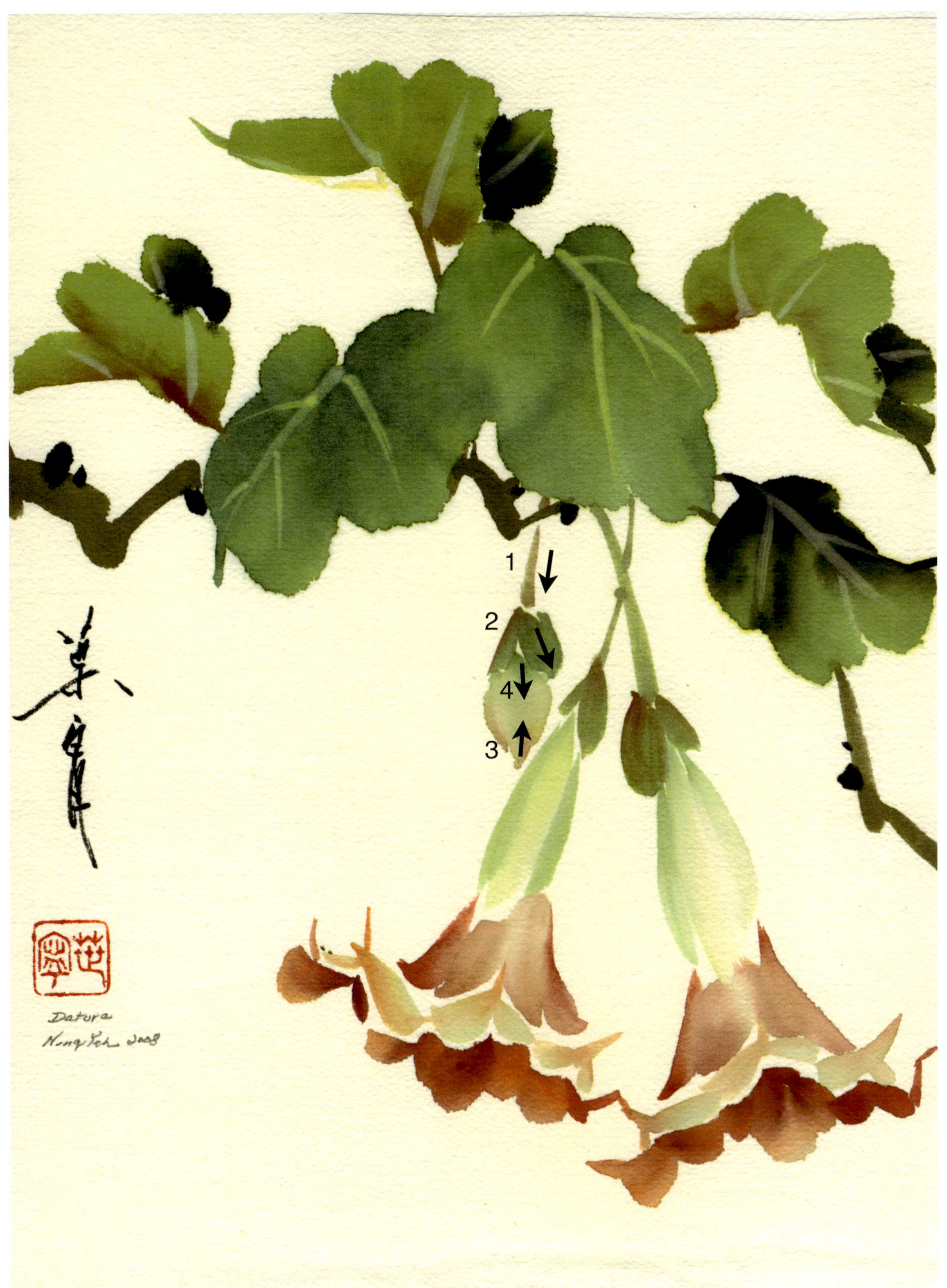


❖ Light Green + Dark Red
How about a baby makes three? Do another shorter stem (1).

❖ Light Green + Dark Red
Add calyx dots at the end of the stem (2).

❖ White + Peach + Vermillion
Do the tip part of the bud (3).

❖ Light Green
Add the root of the bud (4).

# 8034

# Day Lily

Shiuan
Xuān: Day lily

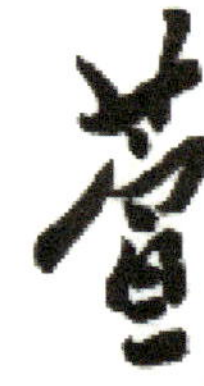


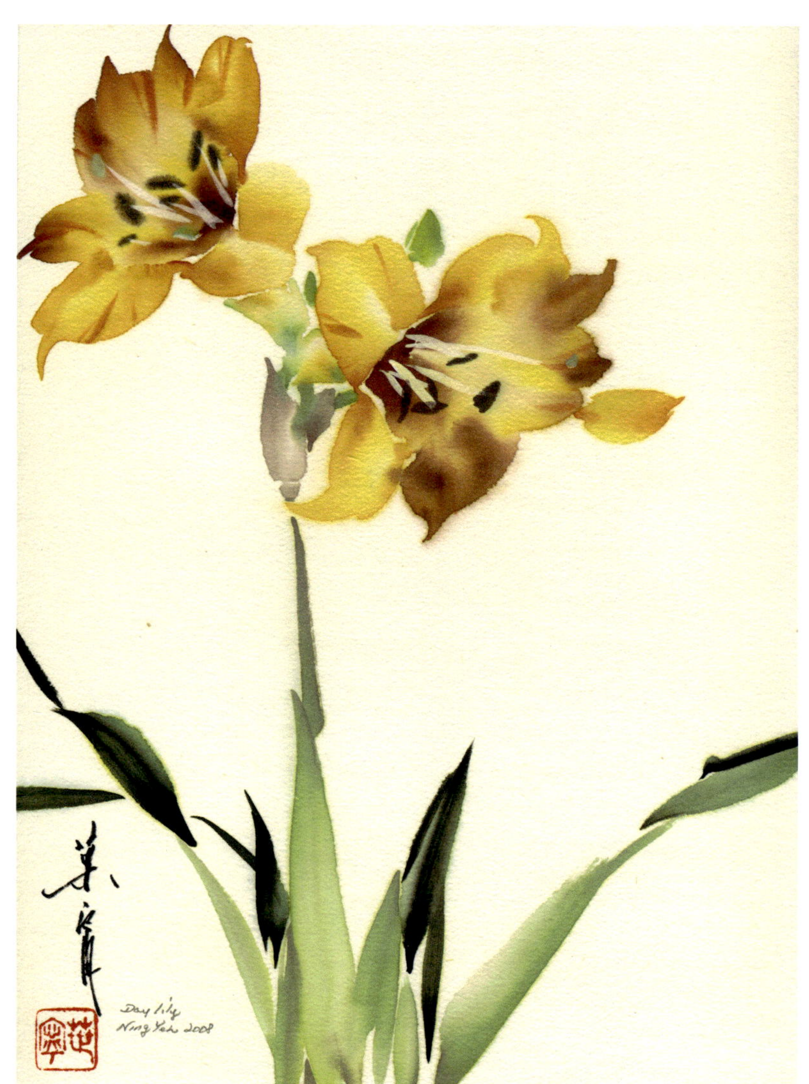


Xuān is the Chinese name for day lily. It means motherly love. One feels the warmth of the sun in this flower.

Day lilies and swallows are everywhere in Chinese villages. Chinese see them as constant reminders of great maternal love.

**MATERIALS**

Paper: Double Shuen

♌ Brushes
Flow, Large Orchid Bamboo, Large Flow

❖ Colors
*Chinese*
Yellow, Vermillion
*Da Vinci*
White
*Schmincke*
Cadmium Red Deep
*Winsor & Newton*
Indigo, Perylene Violet
*OAS*
Best Bottle Ink

**PREPARATION OF COLORS**

Yellow
White: diluted
Vermillion: thick (or Yellow + Red)
Red: Cadmium Red Deep
Dark Red: Perylene Violet + Red (in 2 spots for flowers and leaves)
Light Green: Yellow + Indigo
Beige: Light Green + Dark Red + White + Yellow
Ink
White: pasty

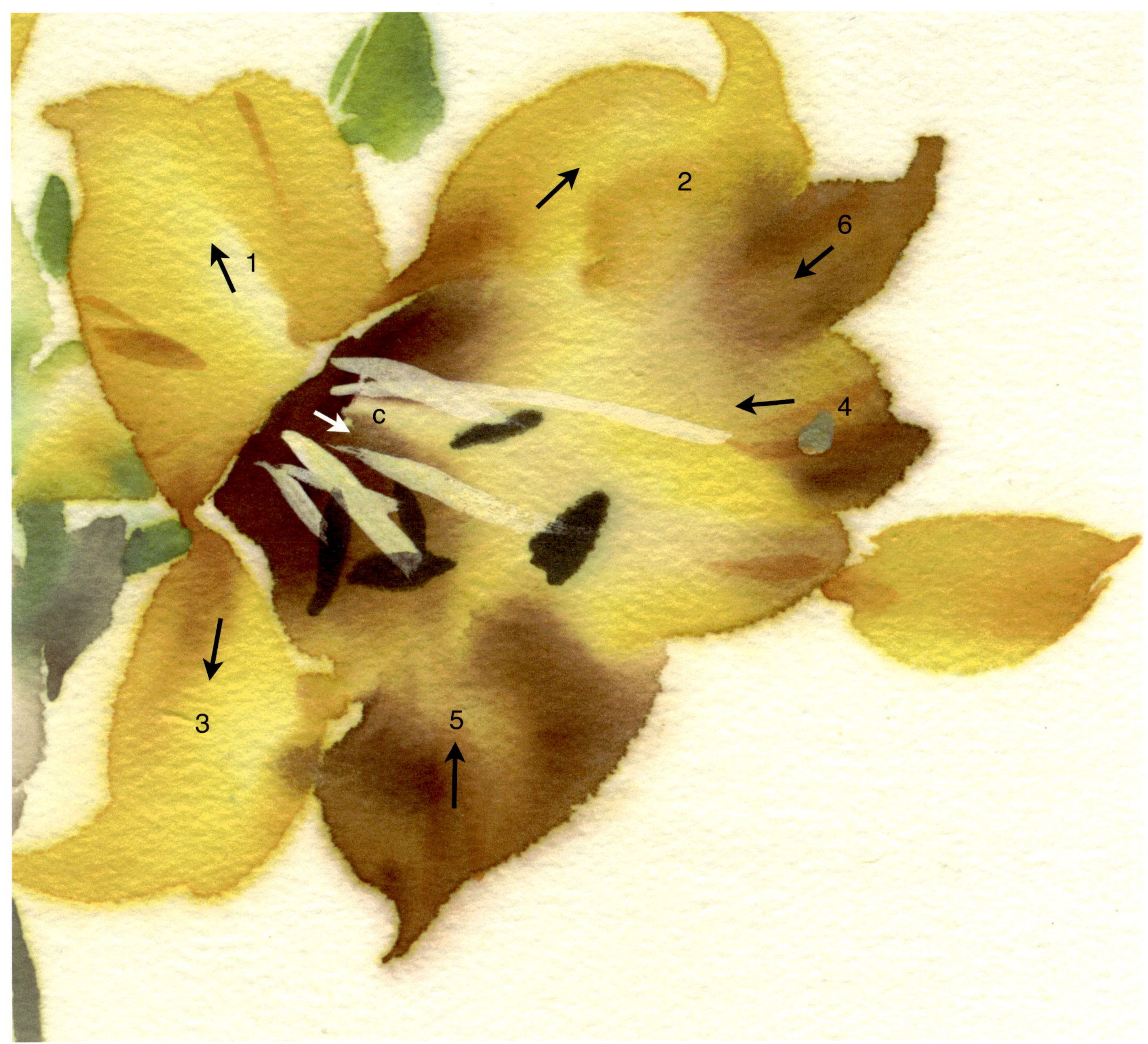


**STEPS**

Flowers
Drooping Flower
ᔓ Flow
❖ Yellow + Vermillion
The day lily has six petals forming a trumpet with a long tube. Do a center petal by working two strokes upward with the side of the brush (1). Add petals on both sides of the center petal (2, 3) to form an upside down "U" curve.

ᔓ Large Flow
❖ Yellow + Vermillion + Dark Red
Work three petals of varying sizes moving strokes from outside into the center (4, 5, 6). Show a circular perimeter. Leave the center area open.

ᔓ Flow
❖ Yellow + Vermillion + Red + Dark Red
Build a wall along the edge of the "U" curve, leaving a hairline space. Push strokes outward and seal the center (c).

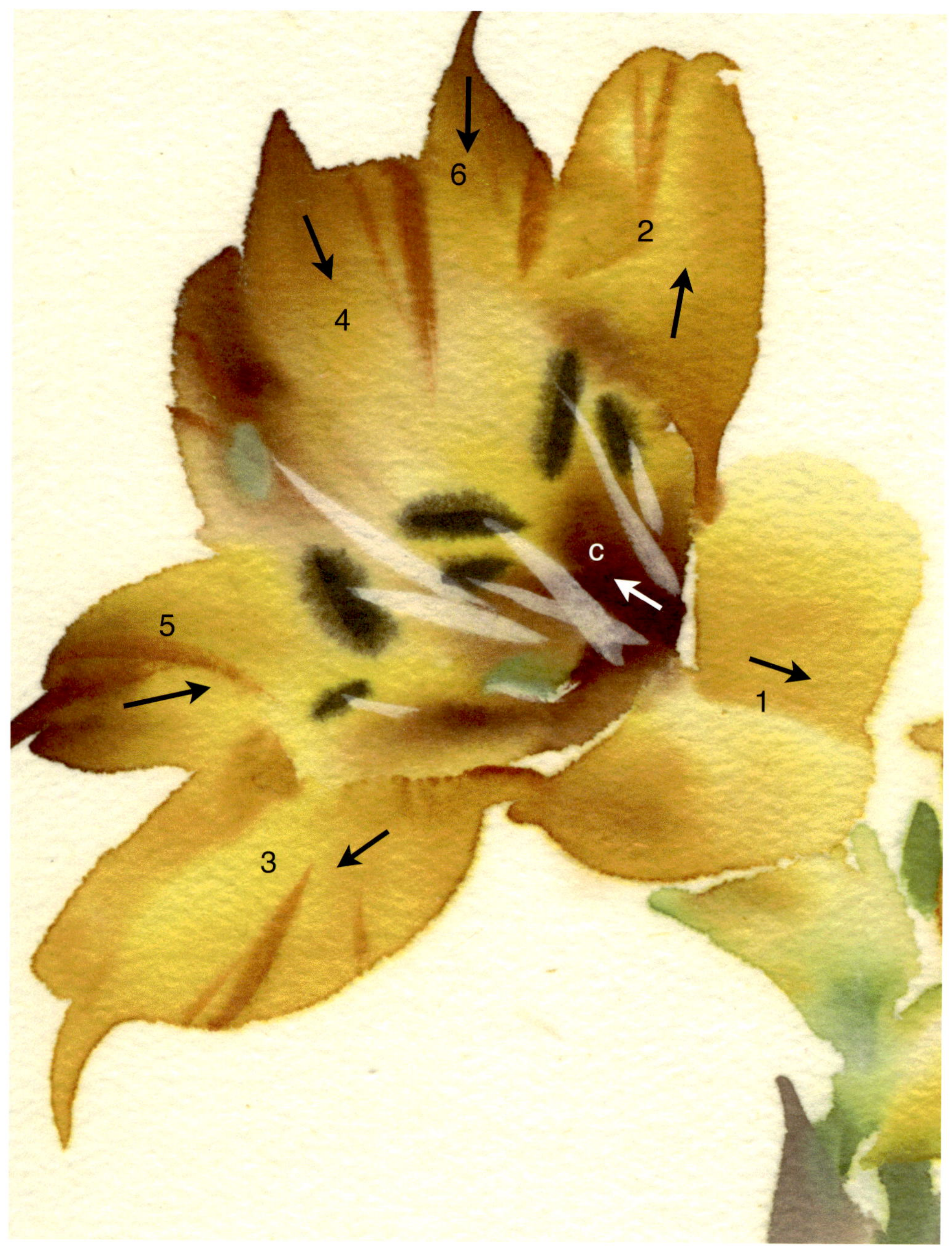


Flower Rising

❖ Yellow + Vermillion

Work the center petal with two strokes (1). Attach to the edge of the center petal. Work petals on both sides to complete a "U" curve (2, 3).

♌ Large Flow

❖ Yellow + Vermillion + Dark Red

Work a large petal off-center to the right from the tip down into the center (4).

♌ Flow

❖ Vermillion + Dark Red

Add smaller petals on both sides (5, 6). Leave the center open.

❖ Red + Dark Red

Build walls along the "U" curve, leaving a hairline space. Move strokes up to seal the center (c).

❖ White + Light Green

Add a touch of green to any open spaces in the center.

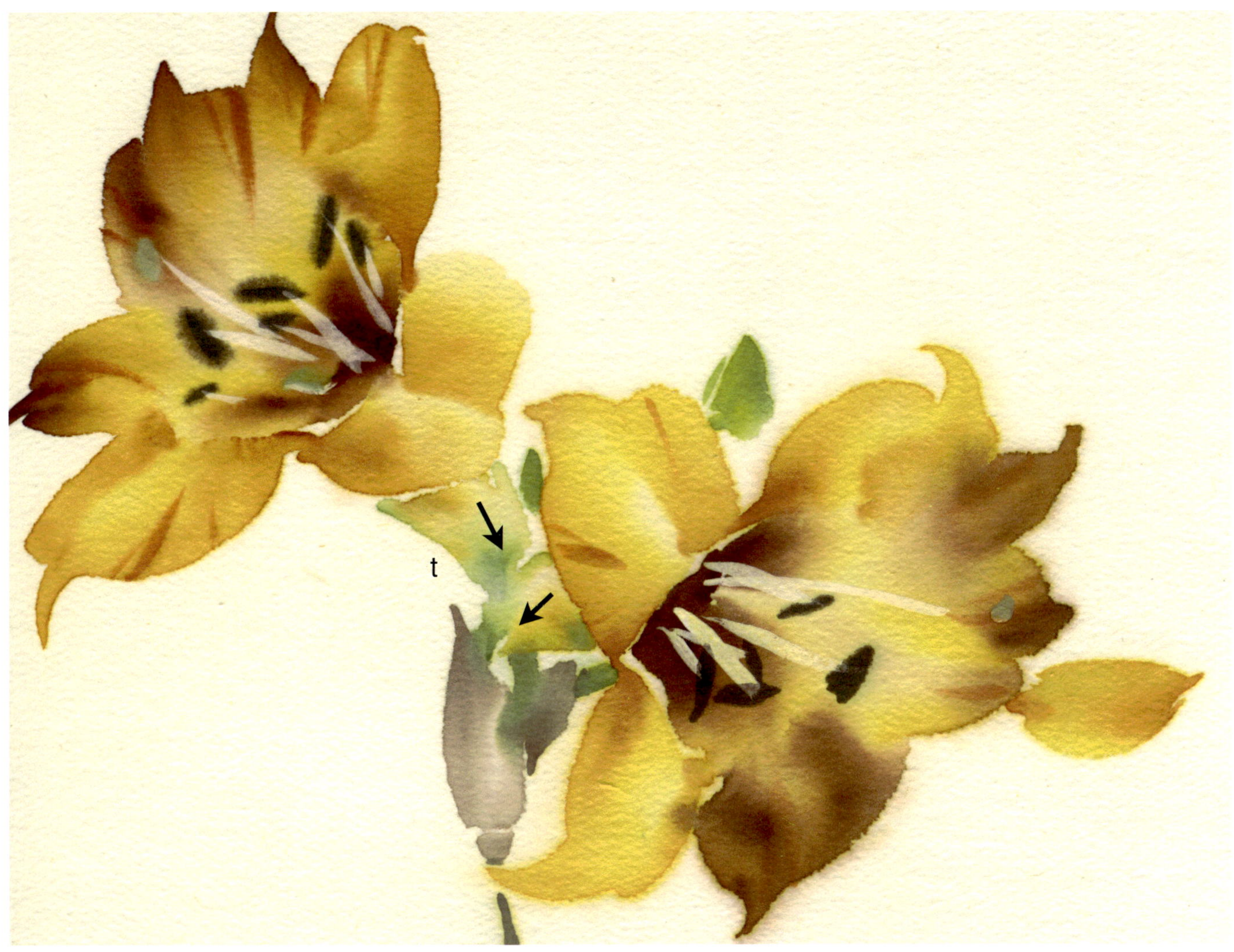


ᔓ Happy Dot

❖ Yellow + Vermillion + Red + Dark Red

Work clusters of veins from outside in. Press and lift. Group them into host and guest. Show long and short. Curve them heading into the center.

❖ Pasty White

Work up to seven lines in the center of each flower for pollen dots and the lady.

ᔓ Flow

❖ Dark Red

Do up to six bossy pollen dots on the tips of the stamen lines of each flower. Vary their angles. Cluster them. Save the longest line.

ᔓ Flow

❖ Pasty White + Vermillion + Light Green

Add a lady dot at the tip of the longest line.

❖ Yellow + Vermillion + Light Green

Work a tube behind the center of each flower (t).

❖ Light Green

Add a base to each tube.

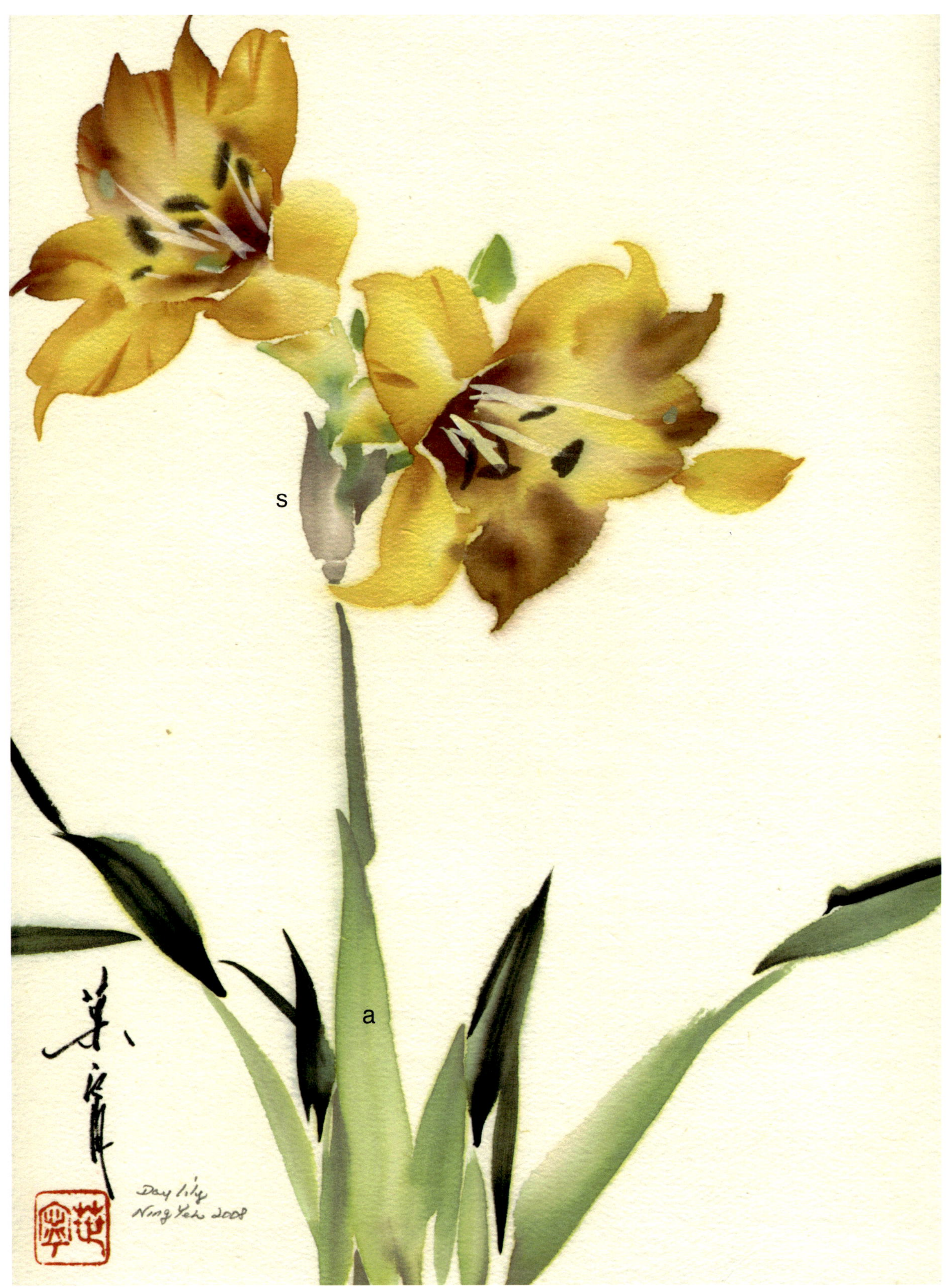


❖ White + Beige
Work a sheath below the flower tubes to house the flowers. Do the left side with two strokes. Add a base. Show the right side of the sheath split open (s).

♌ Large Orchid Bamboo
❖ White + Yellow + Light Green + Beige
Mark an invisible line where the main stalk will run below the sheath. Do an anchor leaf as the receiver for the stalk (a). Work two strokes down, and add the base of the leaf with a stroke moving upward.

Do a cluster of supportive leaves on both sides of the anchor leaf. Lead leaves off the paper to suggest more height. These leaves are in front of the stalk with their backsides showing (b-e). Work a profile leaf on the right (f).

❖ Light Green + Beige
Run a stalk into the anchor leaf (g).

♌ Flow
❖ Yellow + Light Green
Work a couple of small buds (C, D). Add stems into the sheaths for the buds.

❖ Yellow + Vermillion
Do a bigger bud on the right (E).

❖ Vermillion
Add the root of the bud.

♌ Large Orchid Bamboo
❖ Light Green + Dark Green + Ink
Do leaves with their topsides showing (h). Show some crossing leaves (i). Add a top fold to the profile leaf on the right (j).

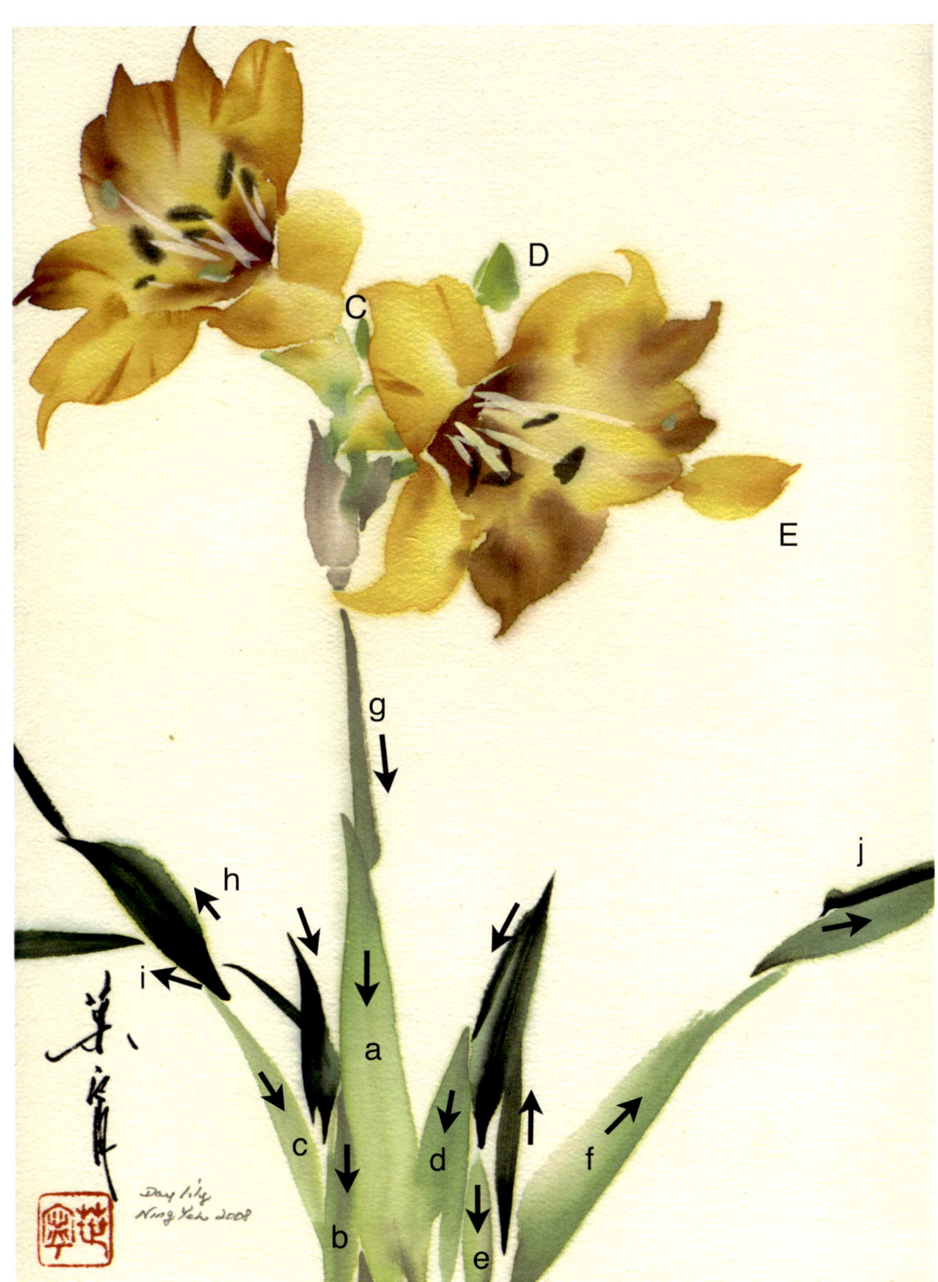

8035

# Dendrobium Orchid

Shr
Shí: Rock

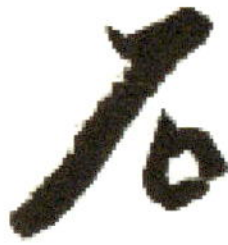

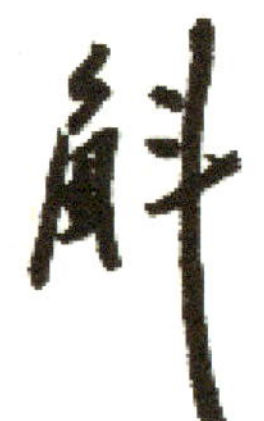

Hú: ?

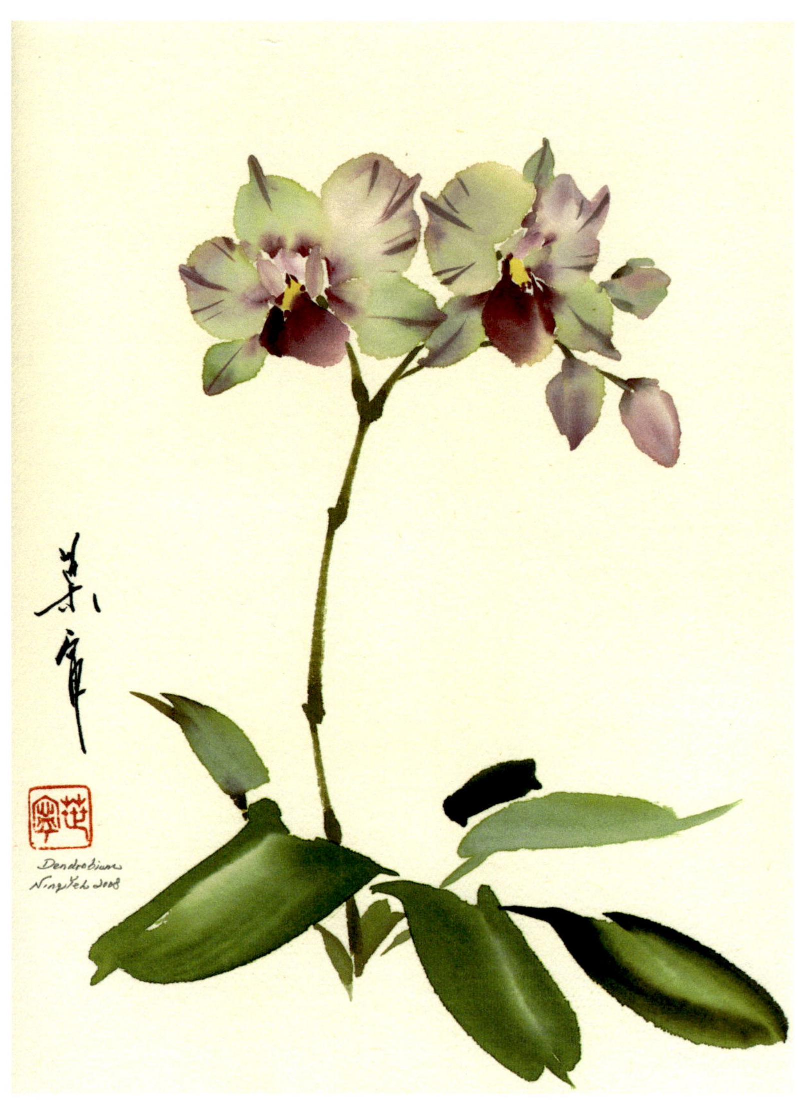


So many orchids, so little time. I know the Chinese name of this orchid. But I do not know the meaning of the character. I do not know how to pronounce the character. After extensive research in vain, I gave up.

## MATERIALS

Paper: Double Shuen

♌ Brushes
Flow, Large Flow, Small Mountain Horse

❖ Colors
*Chinese*
Yellow
Da Vinci
White
*Schmincke*
Cadmium Red Deep
*Winsor & Newton*
Indigo, Permanent Magenta, Perylene Violet
*OAS*
Best Bottle Ink

## PREPARATION OF COLORS

Yellow
White: diluted
White Yellow: White + Yellow
Red: Cadmium Red Deep
Pink: White + Magenta
Magenta: Permanent Magenta + Red
Dark Red: Perylene Violet + Red
Light Green: Yellow + Indigo
Dark Green: Yellow + Indigo
White Green: White + Light Green
Brown: Dark Red + Dark Green
Ink

## STEPS

Host Flower (A)
Center Petal (1)
ௐ Flow
❖ White + Pink
The center petal is shaped like a baby with a hood, bib, arms, and body. Do two strokes to show a baby's hood (a).

❖ Pink
Add two strokes like raised arms on both sides of the hood (b, c).

❖ Yellow
Show a center dot like the baby's bib (d).

❖ White + Pink + Magenta + Dark Red
Push two strokes out to show the main body of the petal (e).

Wing Petals (2, 3)
ௐ Flow
❖ White + White Green + Pink
Do a pair of wings from outside in. Show the tip. Arch the top, smooth the middle and add a stroke to show the lower side.

❖ White Green + Pink
Add the roots of the wing petals from the center outward.

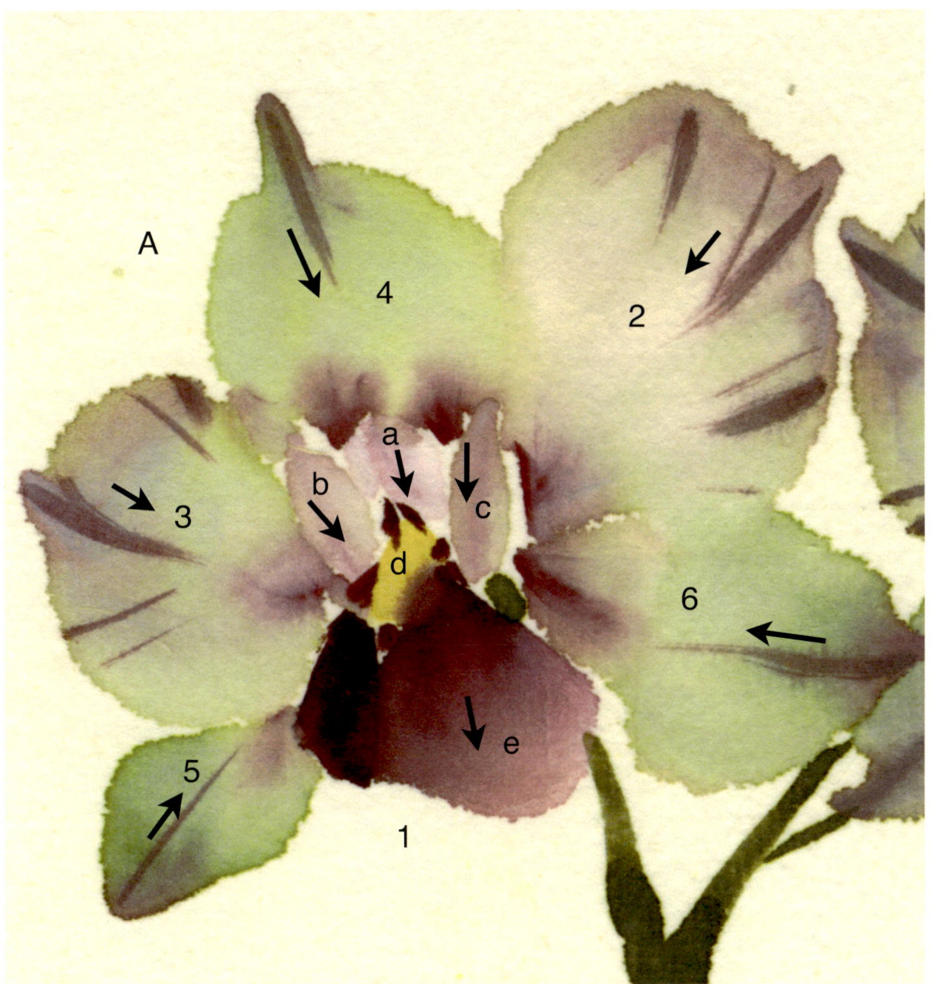


Propeller Petals (4, 5, 6)
❖ White Green + Light Green + Pink
Work three petals from outside in. Show the tip and two embracing strokes for each petal.

❖ Pink + Magenta
Add the roots of the propeller petals.

❖ Dark Red
Add dots to close the small openings in the center.

Veins
ௐ Small Mountain Horse
❖ Brown
Show ruffles on the wing petals by doing some veins. Add a center vein to each of the propeller petals. Do veins from the edge of the petals inward. Press and lift.

Guest Flower (B)

Left Wing (1)

♌ Flow

❖ White + White Green + Pink

Let us do the second flower a little differently. We begin from the wing petal this time. Do the petal from outside in. Show the tip. Arch the top, smooth the middle and add a stroke for the lower side. Show half of the petal without its root.

Center Petal (2)

❖ White + Pink

The center petal is shaped like a baby. Work an arm (a). Add the baby's hood with two strokes to the right of the arm (b).

❖ White Green + Pink

Do the other arm a little lower (c).

❖ Yellow

Show a center dot like the baby's bib (d).

❖ Pink + Magenta + Dark Red

Show the main body of the petal with two strokes (e).

Right Wing (3)

❖ White + White Green + Pink

Do the petal from outside in. Show the tip. Arch the top, smooth the middle and add a stroke to show the lower side.

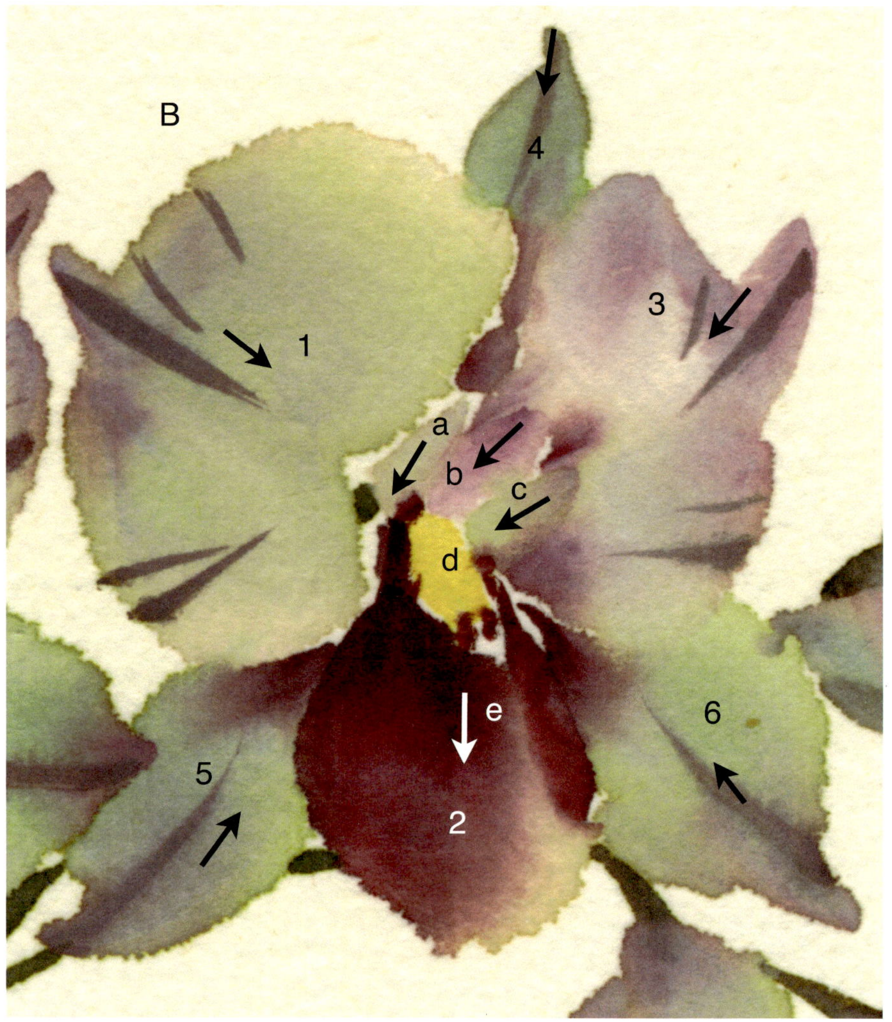


❖ Pink + Magenta

Add the root of the wing petal from the center outward.

❖ Magenta + Dark Red

Add dots to close the small openings in the center.

Propeller Petals (4, 5, 6)

❖ White + White Green + Light Green + Pink

Work three narrower petals from outside in. Show the tip and two embracing strokes for each petal.

❖ Magenta + Dark Red

Add the roots of the propeller petals.

Veins

♌ Small Mountain Horse

❖ Brown + Pink

Show ruffles on the wing petals by doing some veins. Add a center vein to each of the propeller petals. Do veins from the edge of the petals inward. Press and lift.

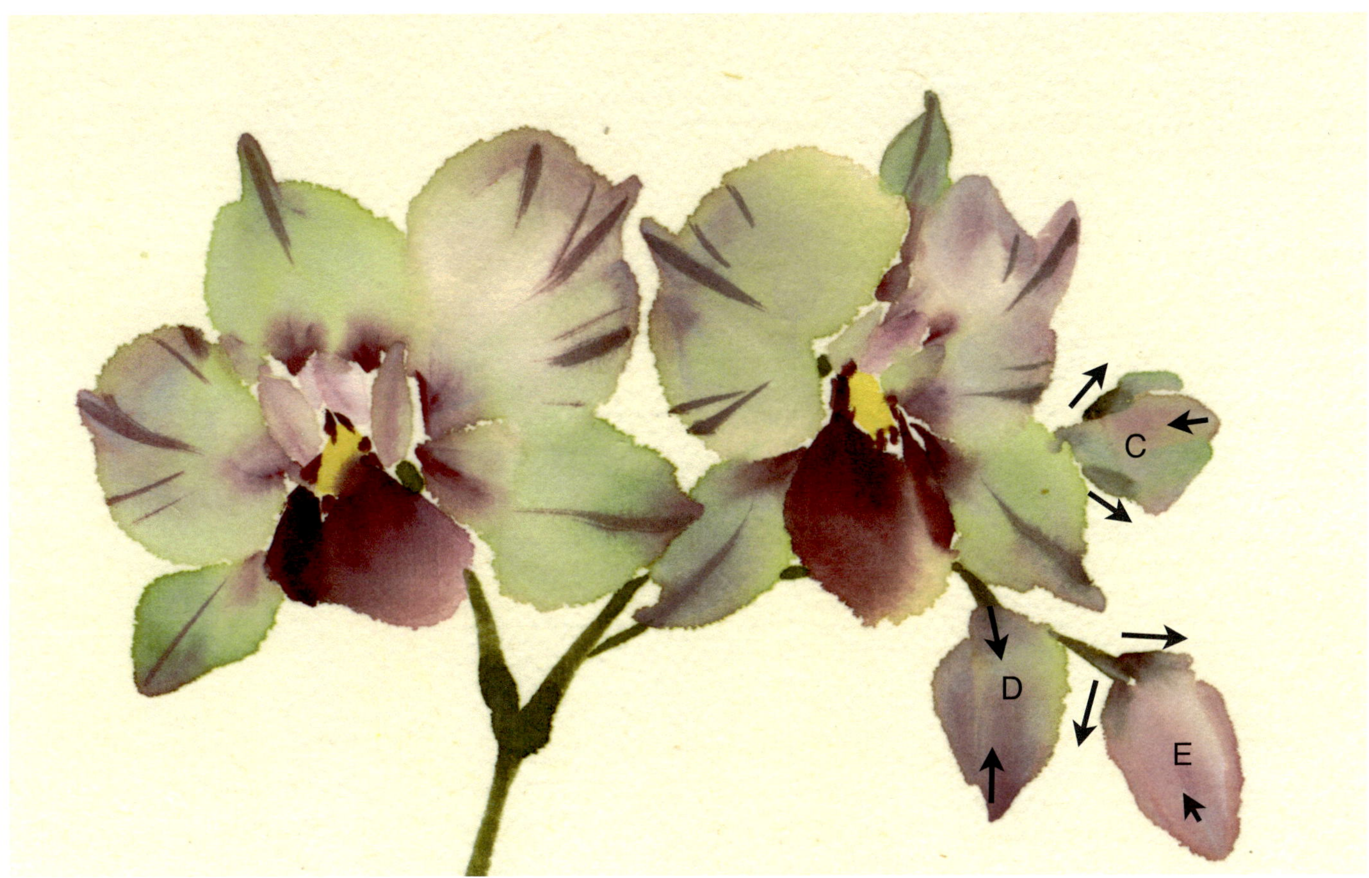


Buds

ℓ Flow

❖ White + Pink + White Green

Work the middle section of a bud (C).

❖ White Green + Light Green

Add strokes on both sides.

❖ Brown

Do shadows near the root of the bud.

❖ White Green + Pink + Magenta

Do another bud. Work strokes from the tip and the base and join them in the middle (D).

❖ Brown

Add a stem.

❖ White + Pink

Add a third bud to be the tip of the flower series. Work three strokes from the tip (E).

❖ Brown + Dark Red

Add base shadows and a stem.

I have used a variety of color combinations. They all seem to work. The colors really do not matter. The key is to show dark and light.

Leaves, Roots, and Stalk

♌ Large Flow

❖ Light Green + Dark Green

Work the topside of two leaves (F, G) with broad strokes.

❖ White Green + Light Green

Do a profile leaf showing its underside. Show a stem, do the body, extend the tip (H).

❖ Light Green + Brown

Work another profile leaf from the tip down. Add the root of the leaf upward (I).

❖ Light Green + Dark Green + Ink

Do a shadow leaf drooping to the right (J).

Add the shadow side of the profile leaf on the right. I love the composition so far.

♌ Flow

❖ Light Green + Brown

Join the flowers with stems. Work a stalk down into the middle of leaf group. Extend the stalk to connect the buds.

❖ Light Green + Brown

Add the root sections of the leaves like fish looking for the same food.

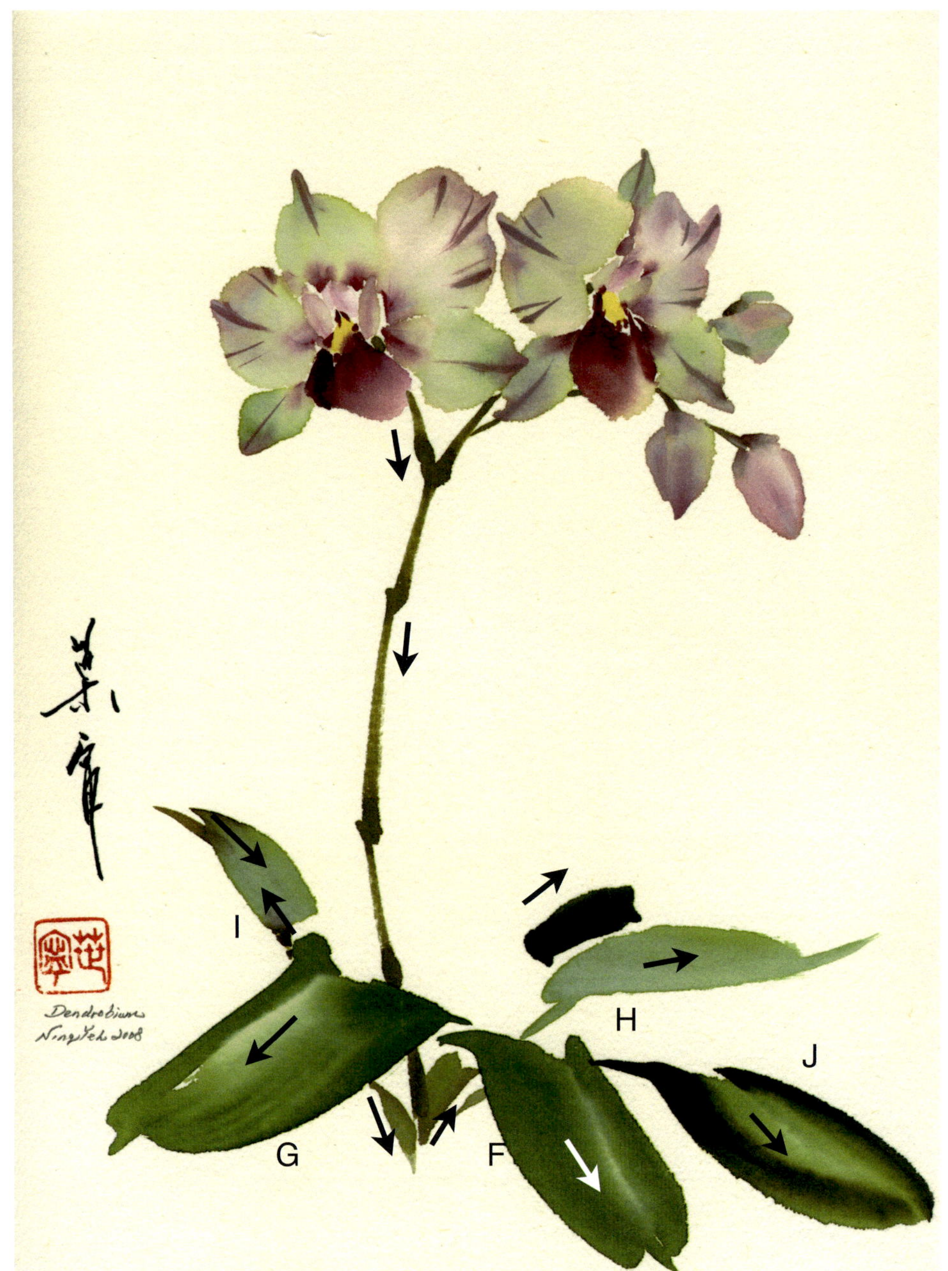


It took me seven years to complete my Ph.D. dissertation. My chairman had to tell me, “Ning, it is not that you will write only this one thing in your entire life. Get it done and move on…”

Nowadays, I do the best I can. Get it done and move on.

8036

# Dogwood

Ju lu
Zhū Yú: Dogwood

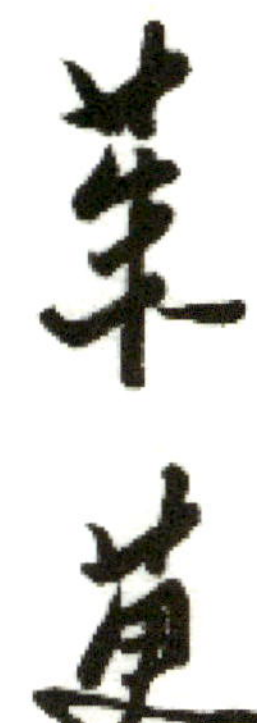


The two characters zhū and yú are used together as dogwood in ancient China. There are no other meanings. How cool! How authoritative!

Chinese translate the name Juliet with the character zhū. Yes, the love of Romeo's life.

**MATERIALS**

Paper: Double Shuen

Brushes
Flow, Large Orchid Bamboo, Happy Dot

❖ Colors
*Chinese*
Yellow
*Da Vinci*
White
*Schmincke*
Cadmium Red Deep
*Winsor & Newton*
Indigo, Permanent Magenta, Alizarin Crimson, Perylene Violet
*OAS*
Best Bottle Ink

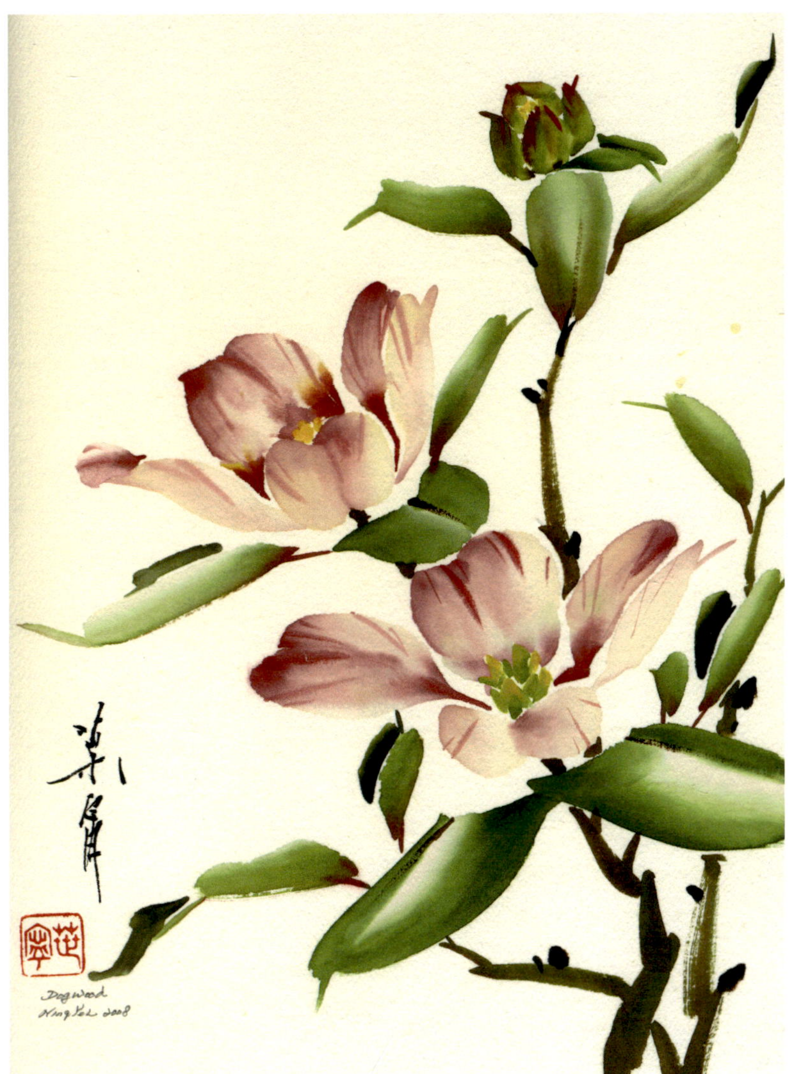

**PREPARATION OF COLORS**

Yellow: thick liquid
White: diluted + a touch of Yellow
Red: Cadmium Red Deep
Magenta: Permanent Magenta + Red
Pink: White + Magenta
Crimson: Alizarin Crimson + Red
Dark Red: Perylene Violet + Red
Light Green: Yellow + Indigo
Dark Green: Yellow + Indigo
Brown: Dark Red + Light Green
Ink

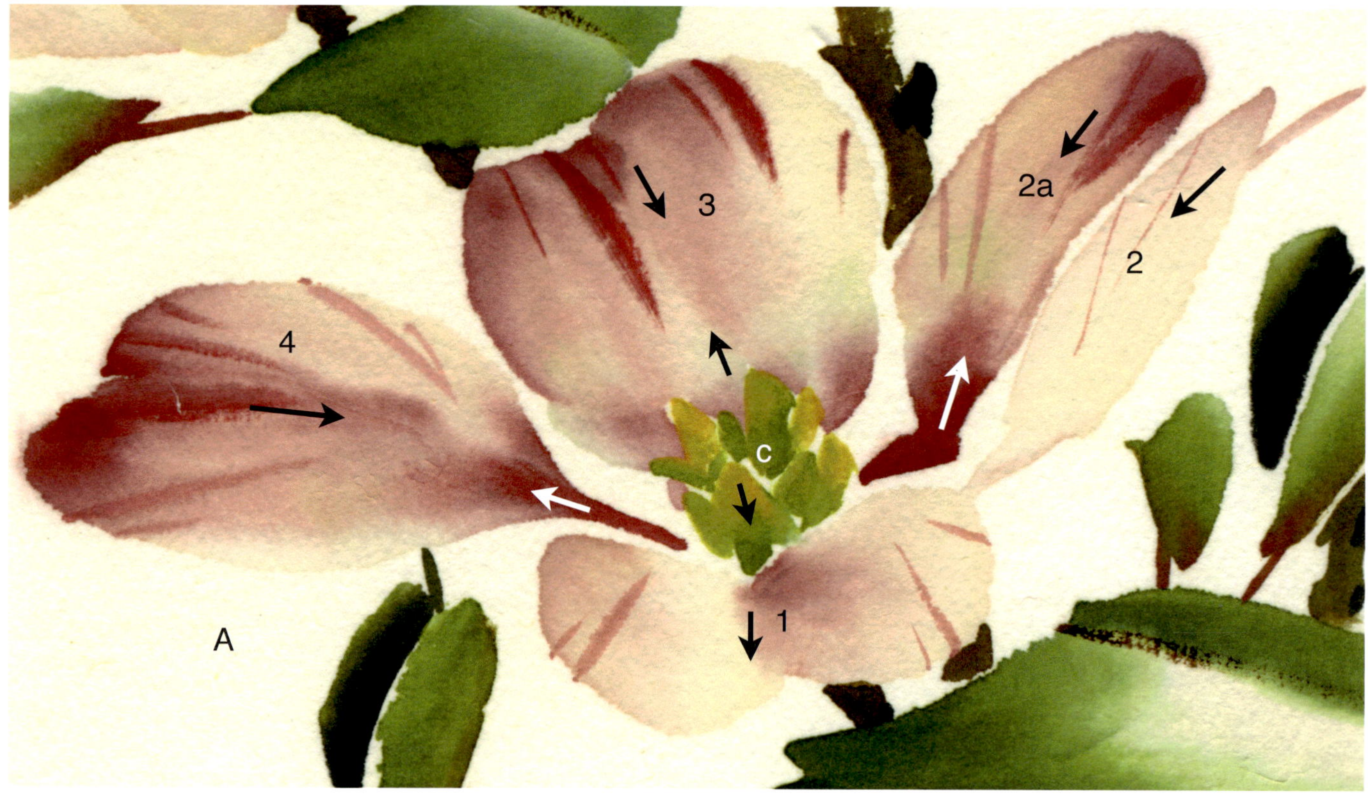


**STEPS**

Open Flower (A)
Petals
ℓ Large Orchid Bamboo
❖ White + Pink
Dogwood flowers have four petals. Work a "tongue" petal with two strokes using the side of the brush (1). Add a petal to the right showing its profile (2). Do the tip and body downward. Add the root of the petal attached to the corner of the tongue petal.

Center
ℓ Flow
❖ Light Green + Yellow
Do dots to show a pine cone shaped center (c).

❖ Light Green
Work the roots of the dots. Smooth the base and tie the center together.

ℓ Large Orchid Bamboo
❖ White + Pink + Magenta
Do the top petal. Show the tip. Arch the left shoulder. Add a small stroke to smooth the middle. Do the right side with a wrapping scoop. Leave the base area of the petal open (3).

Work the topside of the profile petal from outside in (2a).

Do a petal on the left with same strokes as the top petal (4). Make the petal longer, like arms reaching. The side petals balance each other.

ℓ Flow
❖ Pink + Magenta + Crimson + Dark Red
Work the roots of the petals from the center out.

We have a cheerful flower.

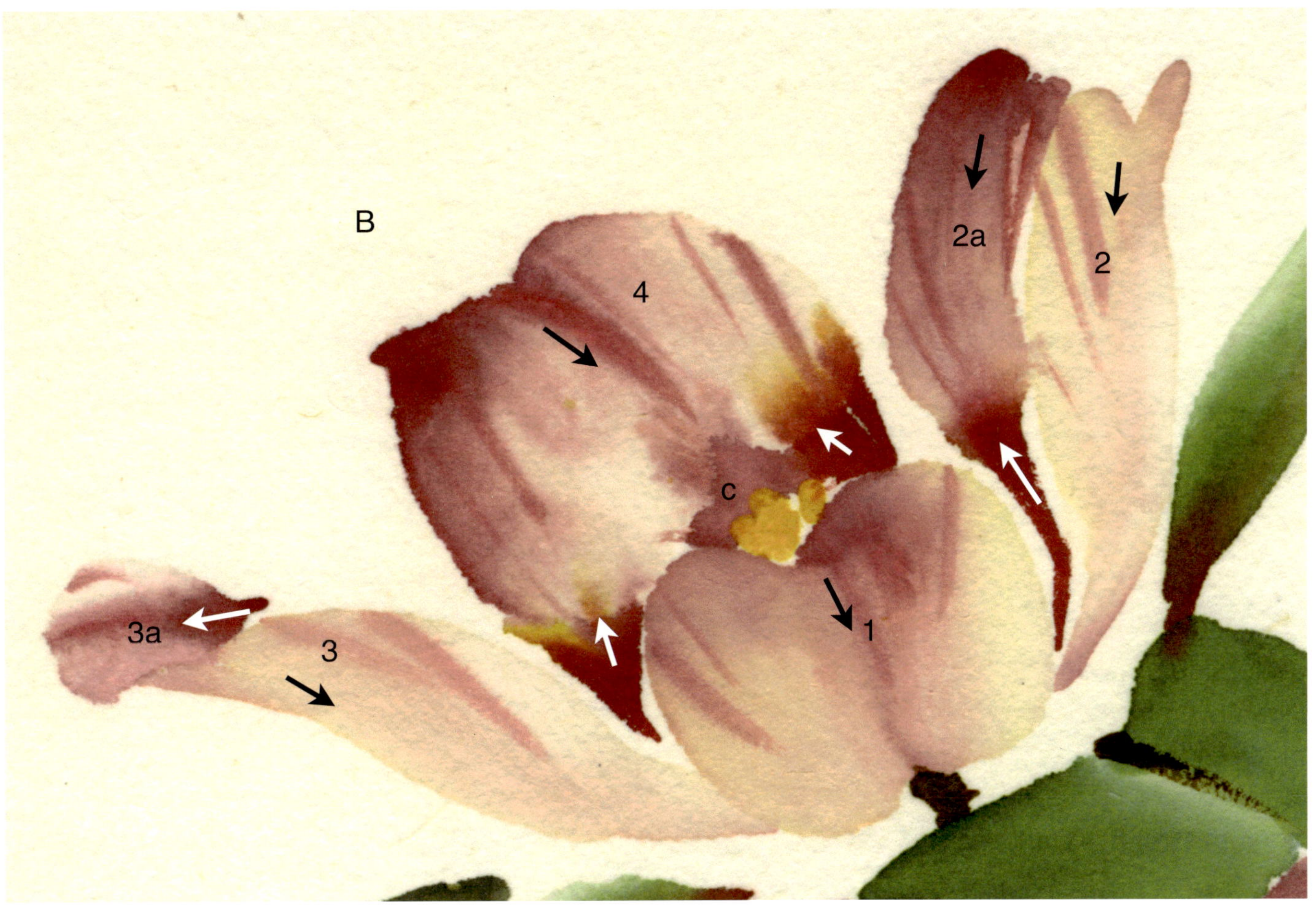


Profile Flower (B)
ᔓ Large Orchid Bamboo
❖ White + Pink
Show the backside of the center petal with three strokes (1). Arch the left shoulder. Add a stroke in the middle. Do the right side with a scoop.

Do profile petals on both sides from outside in. Add their roots from the center out (2, 3).

ᔓ Flow
❖ Yellow
Show the tip of the flower center with a few dots (c).

ᔓ Large Orchid Bamboo
❖ White + Pink + Magenta
Do the top petal with three strokes (4). Leave the base area open. Work the topside of the right profile petal from outside in (2a). Show the topside of the left profile petal (3a).

ᔓ Flow
❖ Crimson + Dark Red
Work the roots of the petals from the center out.

ᔓ Happy Dot
❖ Pink + Magenta + Crimson + Dark Red
Add veins on the petals. Do the topside petals first. The colors naturally become lighter on the underside of the petals. Cluster the lines into host and guest groups. Some are heavy, some are light. Do them long and short. Press and lift the strokes from the edge of the petals heading to the center.

Leaves

Leaves Showing Topside

♌ Large Orchid Bamboo

❖ Light Green + Dark Green

Do a pair of leaves below the full flower (1, 2).

Show a foreshortened leaf below the profile flower (3).

Bending Leaf

❖ Light Green + Dark Red

Do a leaf going up with its underside showing (4). Push two strokes up with an even top edge.

❖ Light Green + Dark Green

Work two strokes heading to the right to show the topside of the leaf (5).

Profile Leaves

❖ Light Green + Dark Red

Do a few pairs of profile leaves reaching to the left and the right Begin each leaf with a stem. Align the brush tip at the end of the stem, then press and lift a stroke to show the body of the leaf. I like to change the direction of the movement so the body does not line up straight with the stem. Vary the angle of the leaf tip, like a freeway exit, to create more variation (6-14).

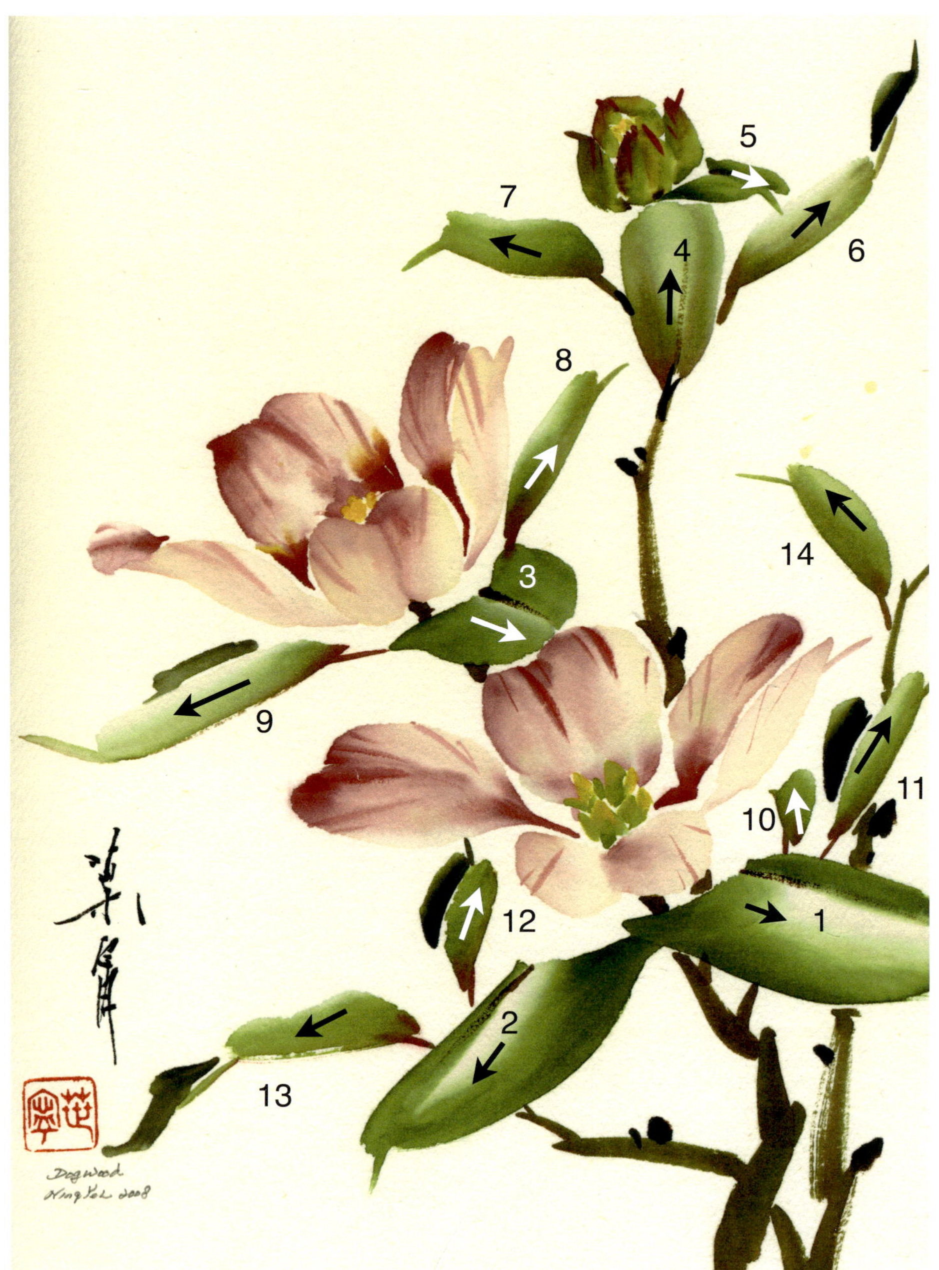

Branches

ᘏ Flow

❖ Light Green + Brown

Start below the lower flower. Do a branch leaping over the leaf group (1, 2). Add side twigs to connect the leaf group to the branch (3, 4).

Work twigs to tie the top flower and leaf groups down to the lower branches (5-6). Add a guest branch on the right. Cool (7).

❖ Light Green + Dark Green + Ink

Work dots on the branches.

❖ Light Green + Dark Green + Ink

Add the shadow side of some of the profile leaves.

Bud (B)

❖ Yellow + Light Green + Dark Red

Do a center petal first (1). Add side petals a little higher (2, 3).

❖ Dark Green

Connect the base of the petals into a “U” shape.

❖ Yellow

Add dots to show the bud center (c).

❖ Light Green + Dark Red

Do a petal in the back (4).

❖ Brown

Seal the base.

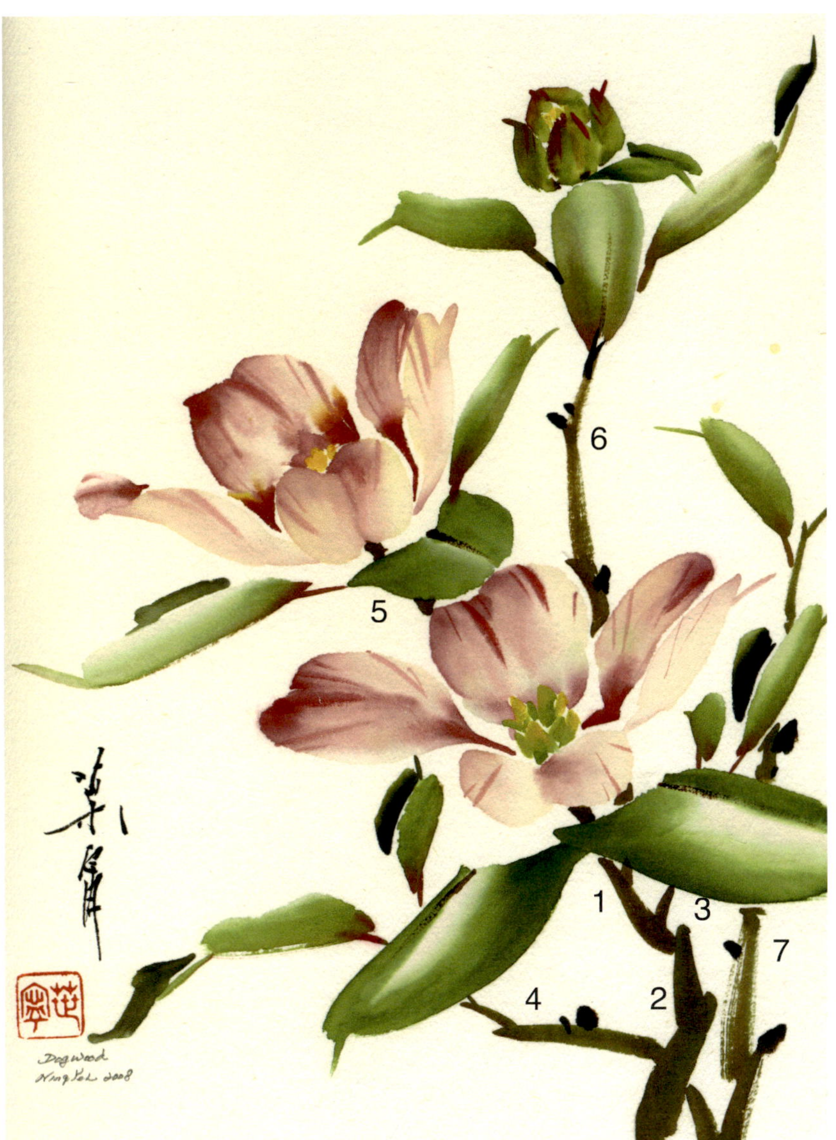


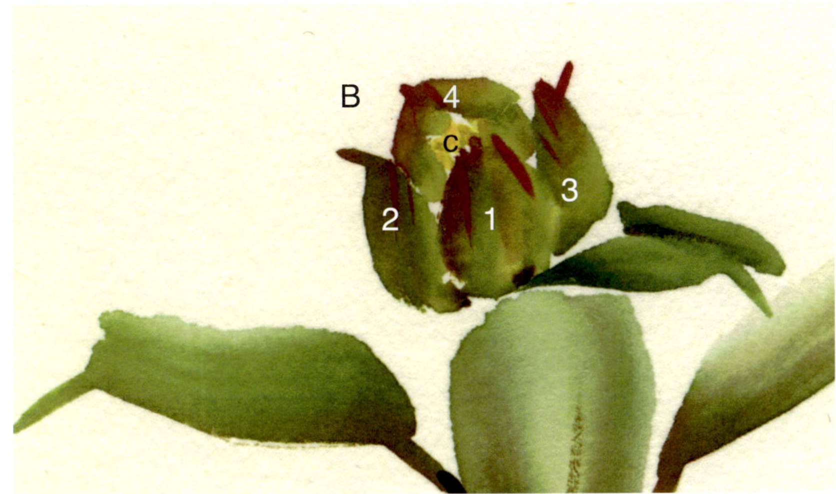


ᘏ Happy Dot

❖ Brown

Do a center vein for each of the open leaves.

❖ Dark Red

Add veins on the bud.

8037

# Dragon Head

Golden Spider Lily

Lung
Lóng: Dragon

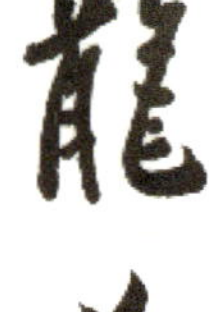

Shou
Shŏu: Head

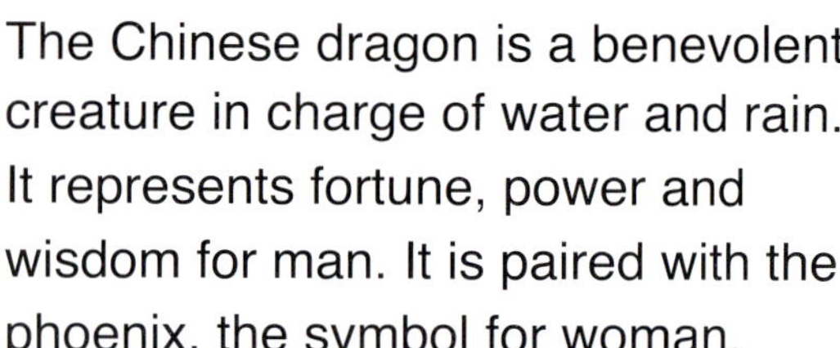

The Chinese dragon is a benevolent creature in charge of water and rain. It represents fortune, power and wisdom for man. It is paired with the phoenix, the symbol for woman.

This is why OAS has both Dragon and Phoenix brushes.

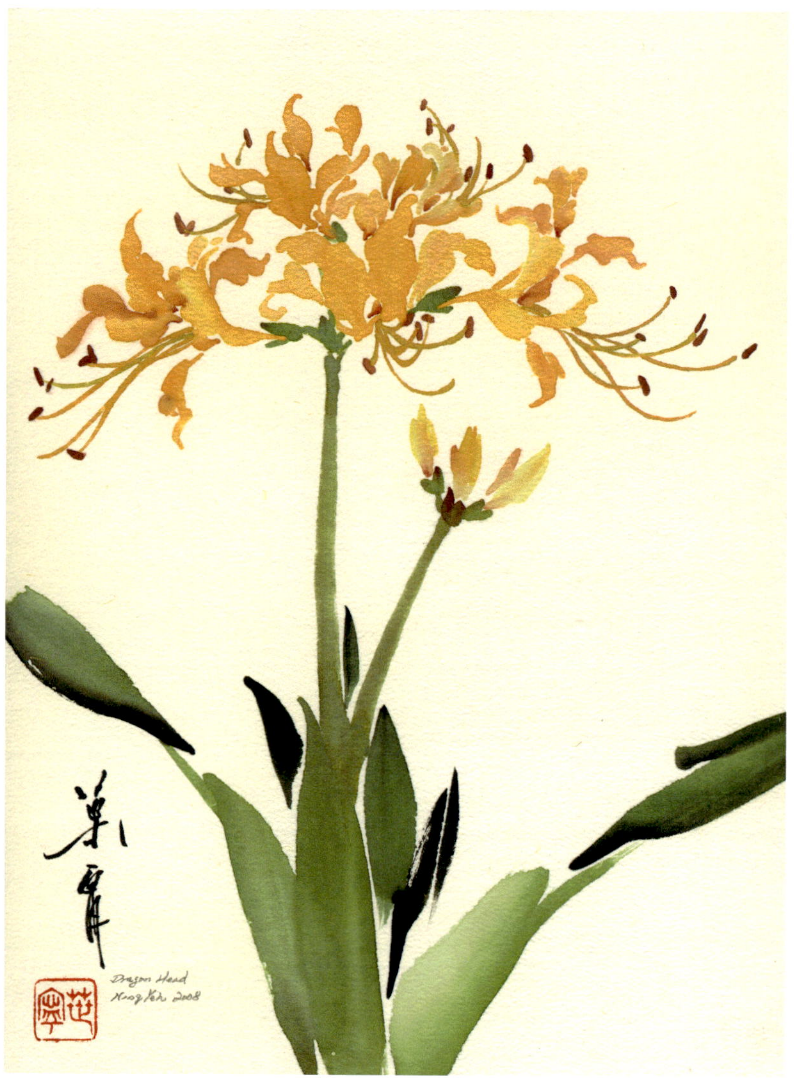

**MATERIALS**

Paper: Double Shuen

♌ Brushes
Flow, Happy Dot, Large Orchid
Bamboo

❖ Colors
*Chinese*
Yellow, Vermillion
*Da Vinci*
White
*Schmincke*
Cadmium Red Deep
*Winsor & Newton*
Indigo, Perylene Violet
*OAS*
Best Bottle Ink

**PREPARATION OF COLORS**

White: diluted
Yellow: Yellow + White
Vermillion: thick
Vermillion Yellow: Yellow + Vermillion
Red: Cadmium Red Deep + Vermillion
Dark Red: Perylene Violet + Red + Vermillion
Light Green: Yellow + Indigo
Dark Green: Yellow + Indigo
Brown: Dark Red + Light Green
Ink

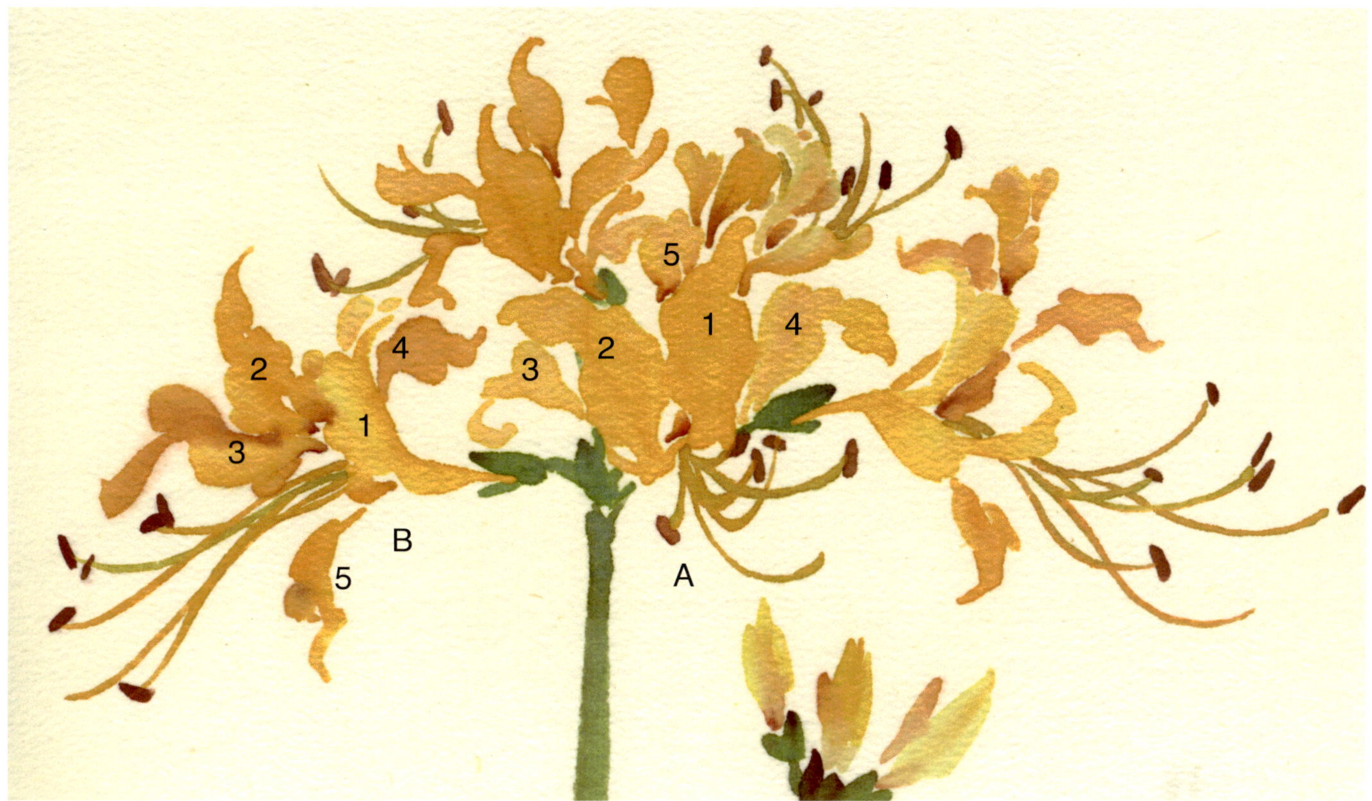


**STEPS**

Flowers

Center Flower (A)

ᔓ Flow

❖ Yellow + Vermillion Yellow

The dragon head has multiple flowers clustered on one stalk. Each flower has five curly petals flipping upward. Settle the base of the petal downward then reverse the stroke up. Work two strokes to show the main body of the petal. Add waves along both sides. Show a curly tip (1). Lead a petal out to the left like reversed check mark (2). Do one more petal on the left showing one side only (3). Add a petal on the right (4).

❖ Vermillion + Red

Show a petal above the center petal (5).

Flower on the Left (B)

❖ Yellow + Vermillion Yellow

Lead a profile petal out. Add ruffles on the left side (1).

❖ Vermillion

Show the other side of the folding petal peeking in and out.

❖ Vermillion Yellow

Work a petal above the folding petal (2).

❖ Vermillion + Red

Add the root of the petal. Work a companion petal (3). Elongate the tip.  Work one petal on the right side (4) to say "Hi!" to the center flower. Do a drooping petal (5).

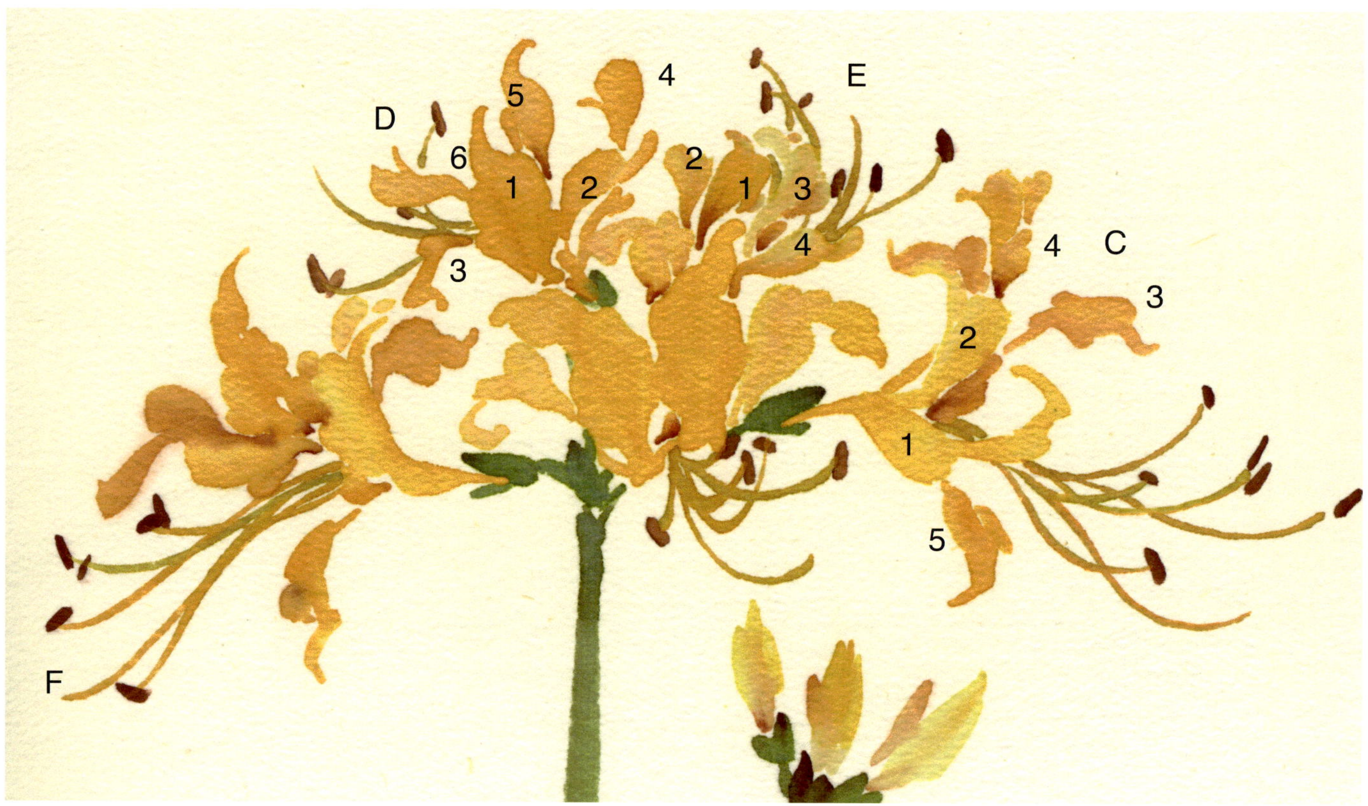


Flower on the Right (C)
❖ Yellow + Vermillion Yellow
Lead a profile petal out to the left (1). I like this. It's too bad that the petals come in clusters. It is like putting Brad Pitt in the formation of drummers at the 2008 Olympics Opening Ceremony. But, the formation is spectacular. Add one more profile petal on top (2).

❖ Vermillion + Red
Work the inside of the folding petal. Do a companion petal (3).

❖ Vermillion Yellow
Show a cross over petal (4).

❖ Vermillion + Red
Work the inside of the petal. Do a drooping petal (5).

Flower on the Top Left (D)
❖ Vermillion
Do a full petal showing its backside (1). Add a profile petal to its right (2).

❖ Vermillion + Red
Lead a skinnier petal out to the left side (3). Do a crossover petal on the right (4).

❖ Vermillion Yellow + Vermillion
Show a full petal in the back (5). Add a profile petal to keep it company (6). I know, I've lost count.

Flower on the Top Right (E)
❖ Vermillion Yellow + Vermillion + Red
Show a center petal (1). Add profile petals on both sides (2, 3, 4).

❖ Vermillion + Red
Work the inside of the folding petal.

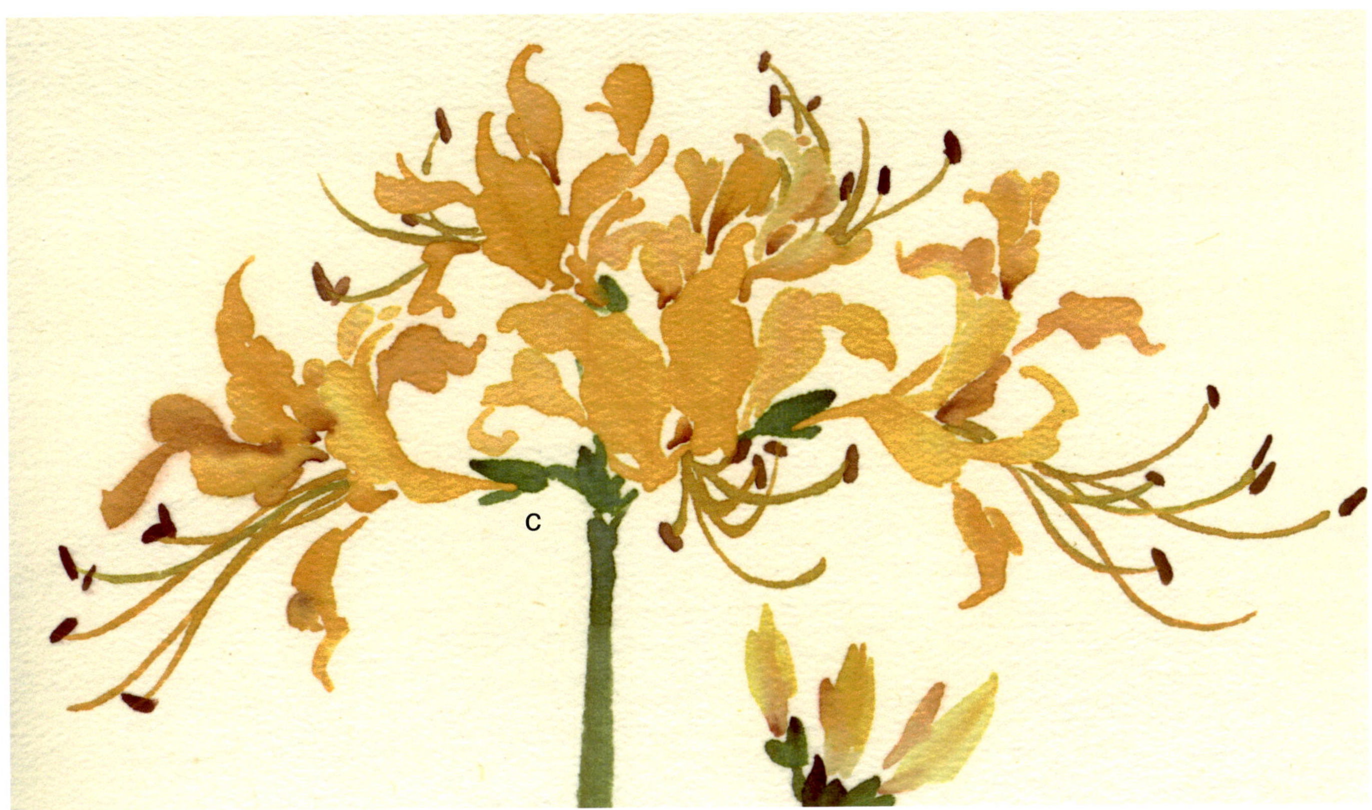


Calyx (c)
❖ Light Green + Dark Red
Add calyx dots below the flowers. Work stems to bring the flowers to the middle.

Stamens and Pollen
ᔓ Happy Dot
❖ Light Green + Vermillion Yellow
Do long curly lines leading toward the root of each flower. We can lead them in, or move them out. These lines add so much vitality to the composition. The dragons are coming to life.

ᔓ Flow
❖ Vermillion + Red + Dark Red
Work pollen dots on the tip of the lines. Sometimes we do a couple on one line to show overlapping. Too many lines can be trouble. Save one line for the lady.

Unlike most flowers, the lady is not prominent on this flower. Maybe it is because the dragon is the symbol of male.

There are plenty of fireworks now.

We like our happy dragons laughing out loud with their mouths wide open.

Buds

❖ Light Green + Dark Red
Work three sets of calyx dots two by two (c).

❖ Yellow + Vermillion Yellow
Do buds from the top with two strokes each (1, 2, 3).

❖ Red
Add small buds overlapping (4, 5).

❖ Vermillion + Red
Work the roots of the buds upward.

Leaves and Stalks

♌ Large Orchid Bamboo

❖ Light Green + Brown
Do an anchor leaf with its backside showing to house the flower stalks (A). Add a companion leaf in profile moving to the right (B).

♌ Flow

❖ Light Green + Brown
Add the stalks (C, D) to bring the flowers and buds into the leaf.

♌ Large Orchid Bamboo

❖ Light Green
Show one leaf on the left with a lighter underside (E).

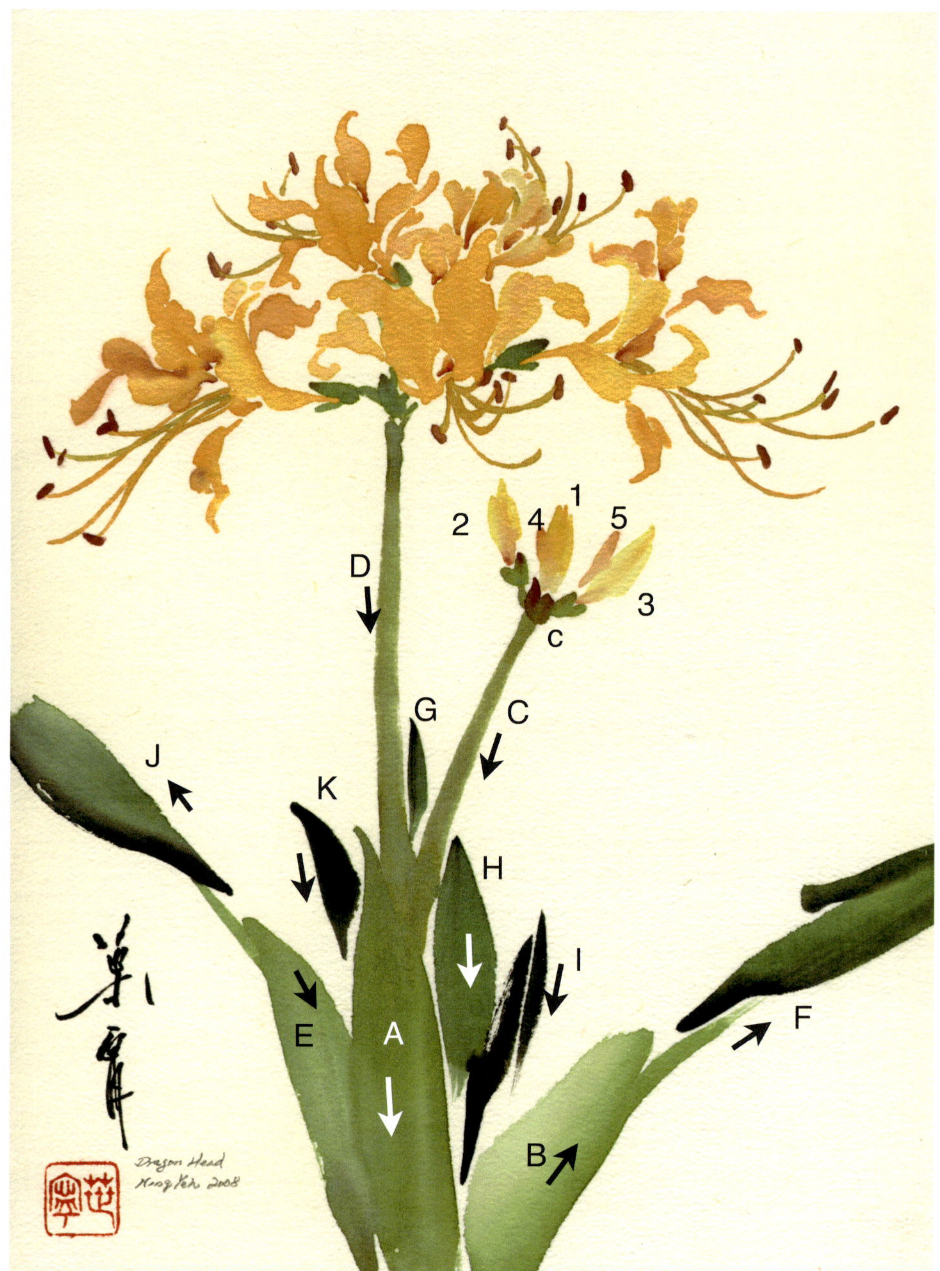


❖ Brown
Add the root of the leaf.

❖ Dark Green + Ink
Do leaves showing their topsides (F-K).

8038

# Dragon Pearl

Clerodendron, Bleeding Heart

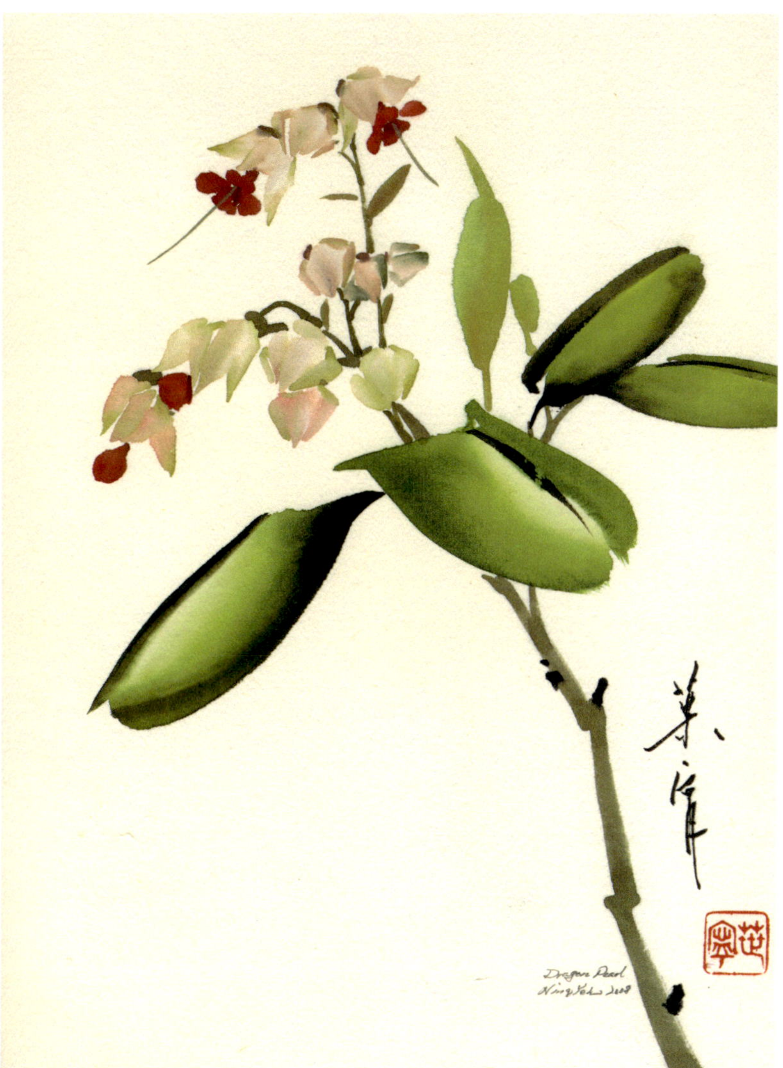

Lung
Lóng: Dragon

Tu
Tǔ: Spit

Ju
Zhū: Pearl

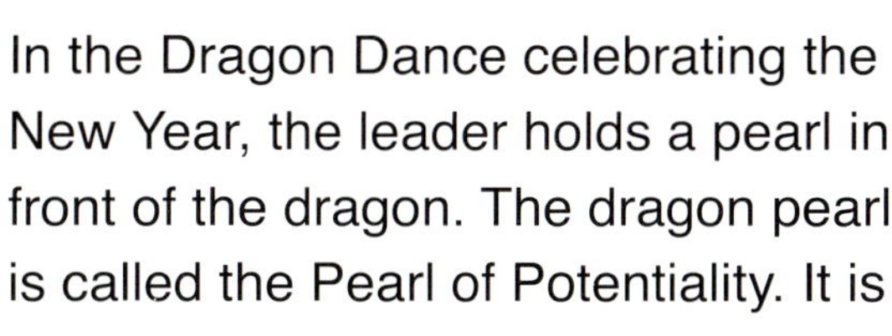

In the Dragon Dance celebrating the New Year, the leader holds a pearl in front of the dragon. The dragon pearl is called the Pearl of Potentiality. It is the dragon's source of power.

This is another plant that bears the name "bleeding heart." What is the matter with you guys?

**MATERIALS**

Paper: Double Shuen

Brushes
Flow, Large Flow, Small Mountain Horse, Large Orchid Bamboo

❖ Colors
*Chinese*
Yellow, Vermillion
*Da Vinci*
White
*Schmincke*
Cadmium Red Deep
*Winsor & Newton*
Indigo, Alizarin Crimson, Perylene Violet
*OAS*
Best Bottle Ink

**PREPARATION OF COLORS**

White: diluted
Yellow: thick liquid
Vermillion: thick
Red: Cadmium Red Deep
Crimson: Alizarin Crimson + Red
Dark Red: Perylene Violet + Red
Light Green: Yellow + Indigo
Dark Green: Yellow + Indigo
Pearl: White + Yellow + Light Green + Crimson
Beige: Pearl + Light Green
Ink

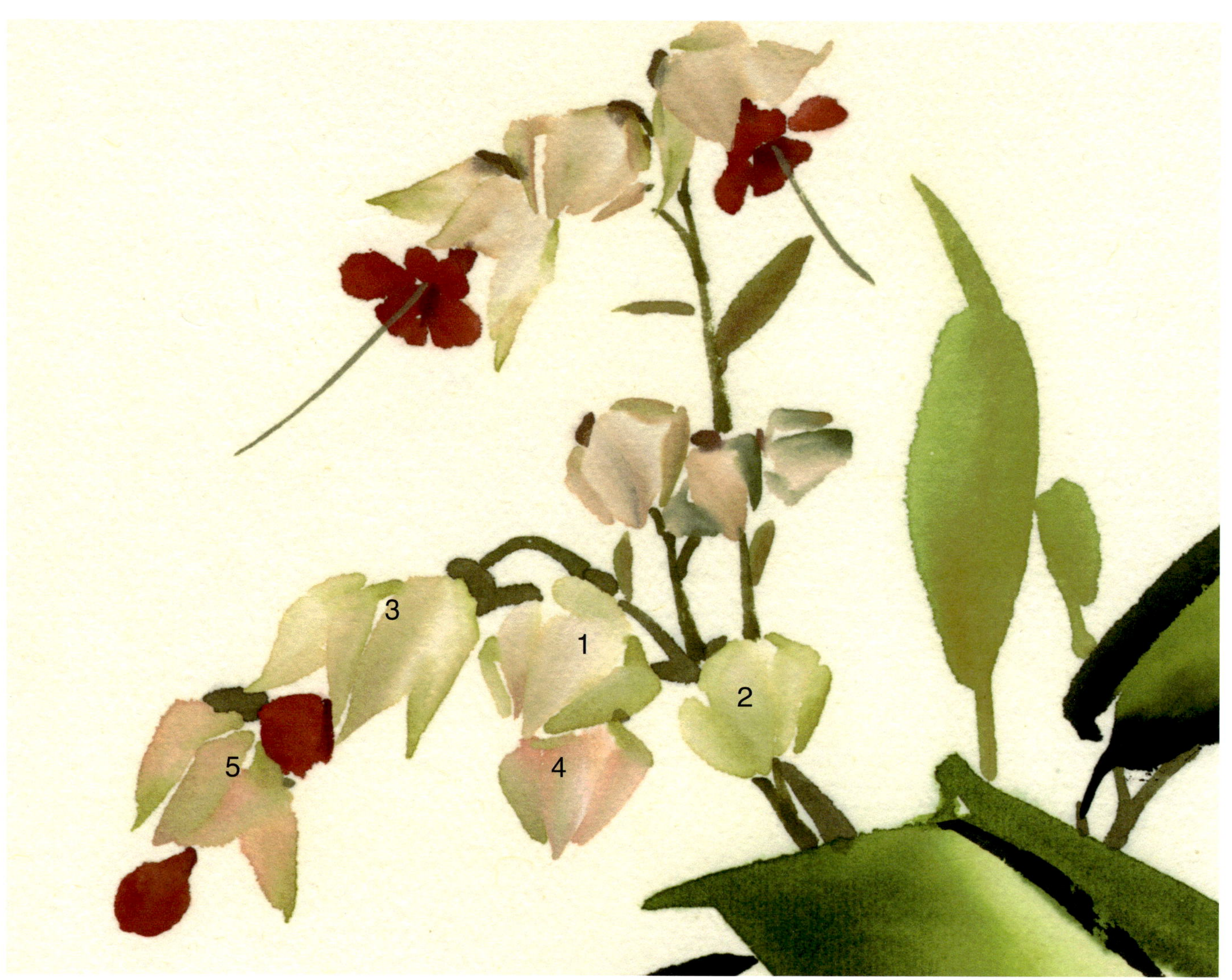


**STEPS**

Buds
♌ Flow
❖ White + Pearl + Beige
Show a drooping bud. Do a center petal with two strokes moving upward (1).

❖ Beige
Work petals on both sides and smooth the base.

Do another shy bud the same way (2).

Open Flower (3)
Show three pointed petals, each with two strokes. Do the center one first. Add skinnier petals on both sides. Work strokes to complete the base if needed.

❖ Vermillion + Crimson
Do a round pearl in red. Cool.

❖ Dark Red
Add a shadow.

❖ White + Pearl + Beige
Add another bud (4). There is some residue of red left on the brush. How nice.

❖ Pearl
Work one more flower with petals open (5).

❖ Vermillion + Crimson
Do a red pearl in the middle.

❖ Dark Red
Add a stem for the pearl.

Leaves and Branches

♌ Large Flow

❖ Light Green + Dark Green

The flower has dark leaves. They make the white petals show up more. Do a leaf moving to the right (1).

❖ Ink

Flip the brush. Work another leaf heading to the left (2). Cool. We add a couple more leaves on the right side (3, 4).

♌ Large Orchid Bamboo

❖ Light Green + Vermillion

Do a couple of leaves in profile (5, 6). Cozy.

♌ Flow

❖ Light Green + Dark Green + Dark Red

Work calyx dots at the base of the flowers (c). Add stems. Do a branch leaping over leaves. Add stems to connect the leaves and flowers onto the branch.

❖ Ink

Do some happy dots on the branch.

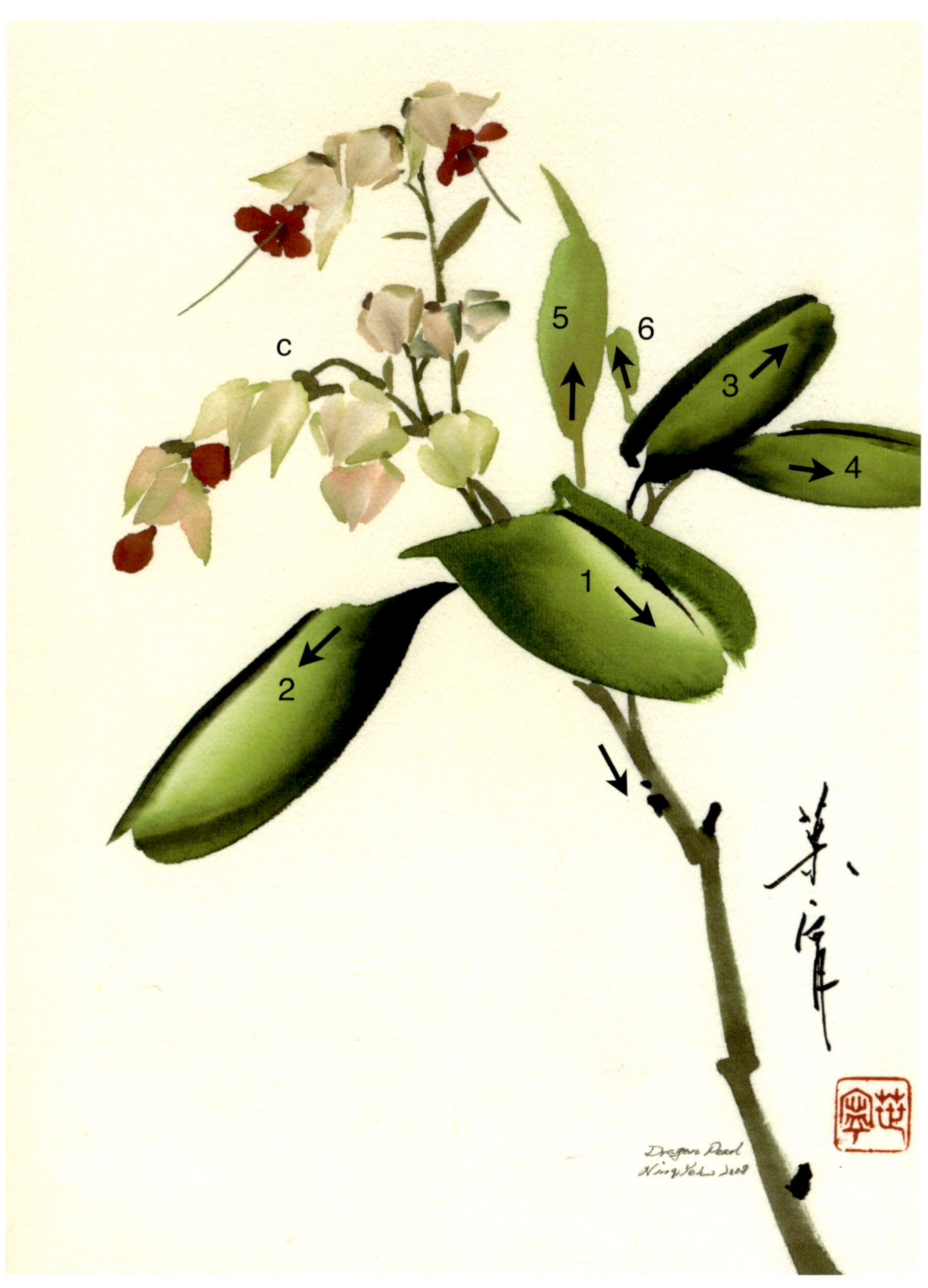

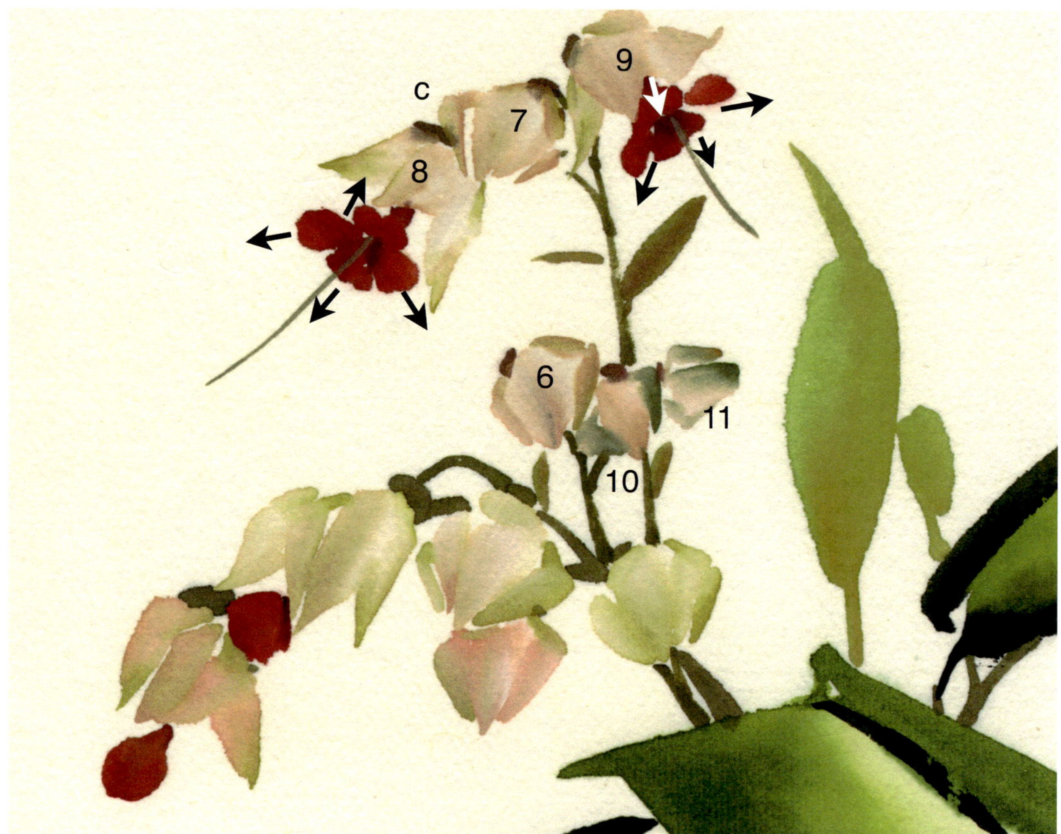


More Flowers

❖ White + Pearl

Work a bud as a liaison to a guest group of flowers above (6). Moving up, do a bud to anchor the top group (7).

Work an open flower on the left (8). Add another flower on the right as the high point of our composition (9).

❖ Light Green + Dark Red

Do some calyx dots at the base of the flowers (c).

❖ Vermillion + Crimson

When the pearl opens up, each one becomes a little flower. This is actually the real flower. This is the princess. The others are only the court ladies around her. We do two princesses.

❖ Dark Red

Seal the flower center. Add a stem to hold each flower.

♌ Small Mountain Horse

❖ Pearl + Beige

Add a dashing lady into or out from the center of the real flower. In reality, there may be more lines. For this composition, we keep it simple.

♌ Flow

❖ Pearl + Beige

Work a couple of buds to keep our liaison bud company (10, 11). One is a lonely number. Three is company.

❖ Mixture of Dark Red and Light Green

Add calyxes to the buds. Do stems to connect the flowers and buds to the branch.

♌ Small Mountain Horse

❖ Beige + Ink

Do a center vein on each of the full leaves.

♌ Flow

❖ Light Green + Dark Red

Add a few sheaths along the stems.

# 8039
# Dutch Iris

Iuan
Yuān: Ancient name
for sparrow hawk

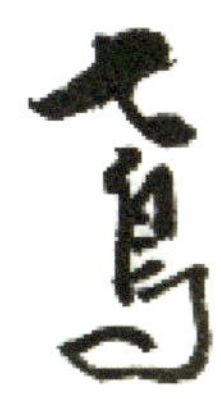

Uei
Wĕi: Tail

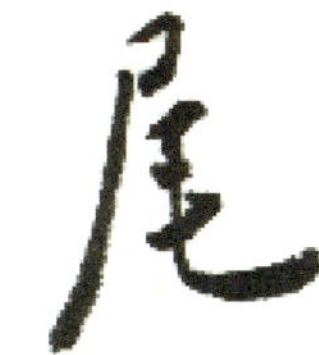

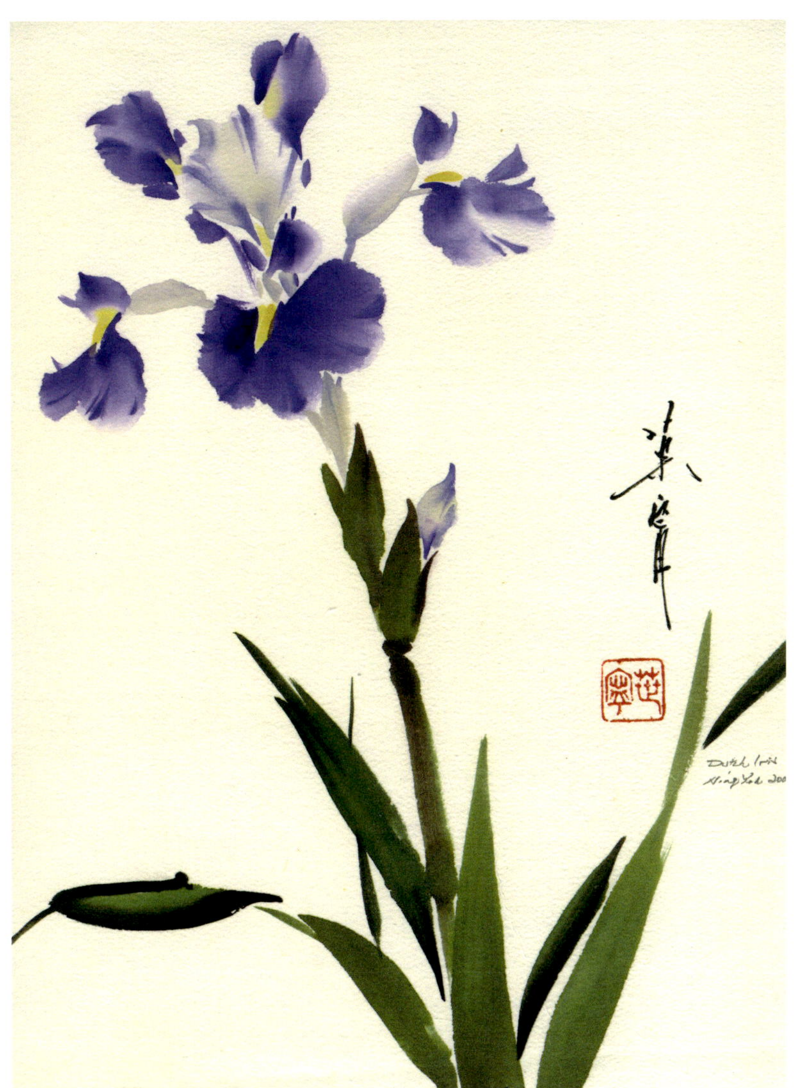

A distant uncle married a Dutch lady in Holland. I never met her. My mother showed me a photo of her when she mailed a toy for me. She was the only Dutch person I knew. I like Dutch people.

One of the terms I learned early was "go Dutch." Chinese never go Dutch. I doubt Dutch people do.

**MATERIALS**

Paper: Double Shuen

ᘯ Brushes
Large Orchid Bamboo, Flow, Small Mountain Horse

❖ Colors
*Chinese*
Yellow, Vermillion
*Da Vinci*
White
*Winsor & Newton*
Indigo, Ultramarine Violet, Winsor Violet, Perylene Violet
*OAS*
Best Bottle Ink

**PREPARATION**

White: diluted + a touch of Yellow
Yellow: thick liquid
Light Purple: Ultramarine Violet
Dark Purple: Winsor Violet
Light Green: Yellow + Indigo
Dark Green: Yellow + Indigo
Warm Green: Vermillion + Light Green
Brown: Perylene Violet + Dark Green
Ink

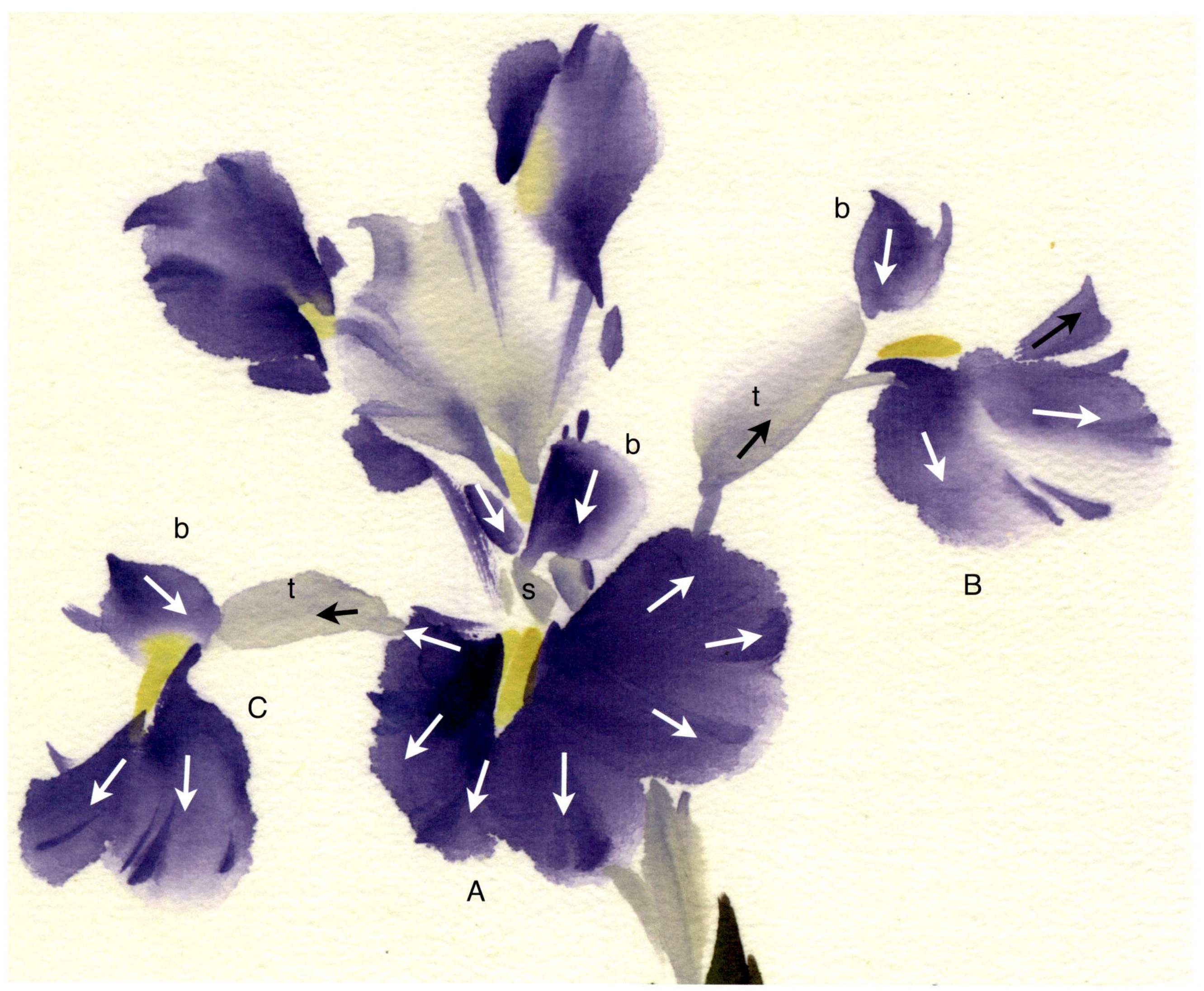


**STEPS**

Flower
Skirt Petals
There are three petals drooping down to form a skirt.
Middle Petal (A)
♌ Flow
❖ Light Purple + Purple
Show the orientation of the petal. Push strokes to the right—up, out, and down. Finish one side. Leave a gap open. Push strokes to the left. Make the left side smaller. Work two dots on top like butterfly wings (b).

❖ White + Light Purple
Add a short stem (s) below the butterfly with two strokes.

Side Petals (B, C)
Extend tubes from the corners of the middle petal out on both sides (t).

❖ Light Purple + Purple
Work strokes downward and outward. Add tips. Add pair of wing dots (b) above each tube tip.

Veins
♌ Small Mountain Horse
❖ Light Purple + Purple, keep the brush dry
Add veins. Work them from the outside edges of the petals inward. Press and lift. Show host and guest, long and short curves.

♌ Flow
❖ White + Yellow
Do markings below the butterfly dots.

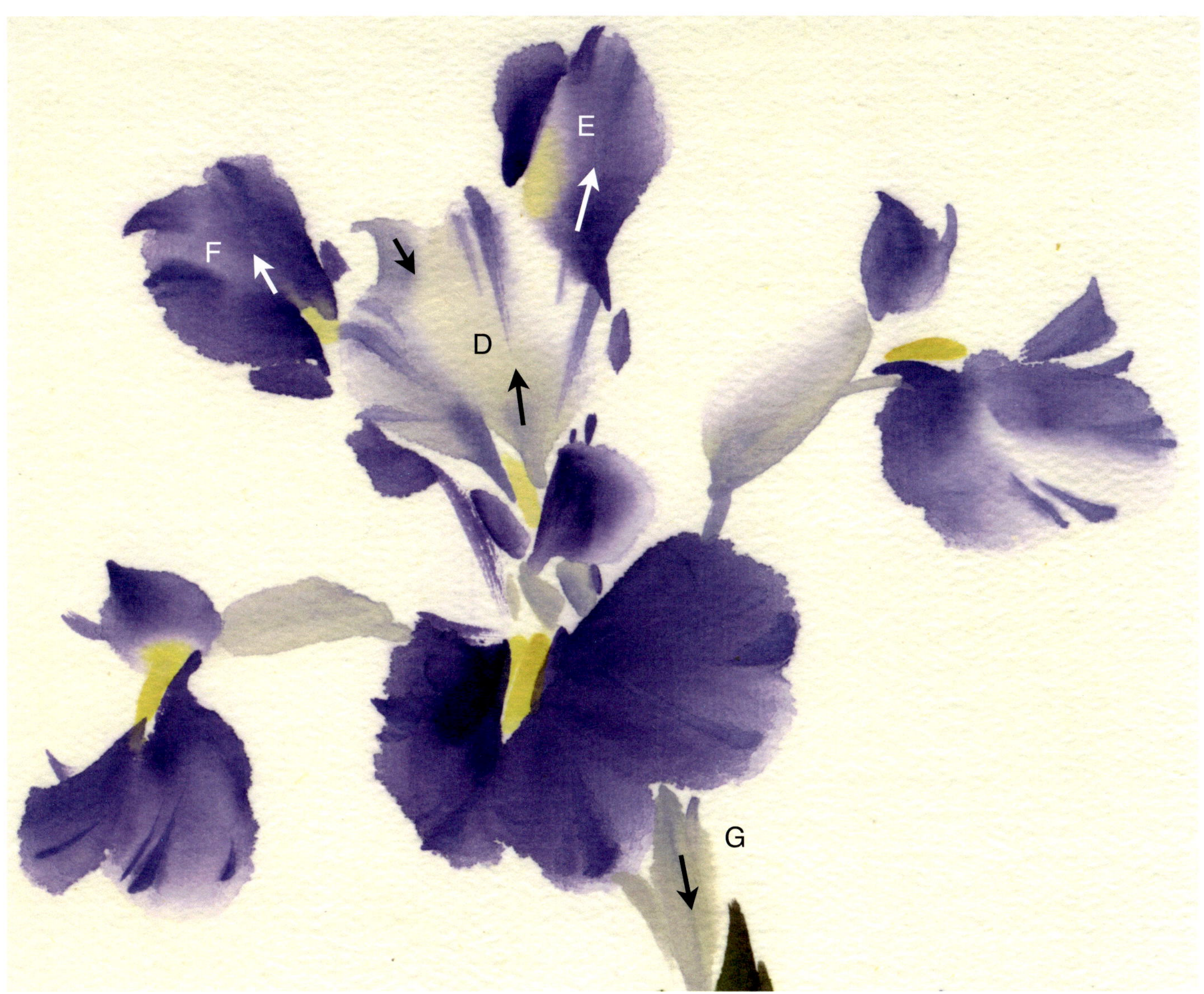


Crown Petals

There are three upright petals forming a crown.

Center Crown Petal

❖ White + Light Purple

Start with the petal roots then work two strokes upward wrapping each other. Add a tip downward. This petal is showing its backside (D).

Side Crown Petals (E, F)

❖ Light Purple + Purple

The side petals are showing their front sides and they are darker. Show the petal roots then work the petal with two strokes up. Add tips. We may show some ruffles in and out.

❖ White + Yellow

Add a touch of lighter yellow at the center near the root of each petal.

Veins

♌ Small Mountain Horse

❖ Light Purple + Purple

Add veins on the crown petals.

Trumpet

♌ Happy Dot

❖ White + Light Purple

Work a skinny tube below the middle of the flower (G).

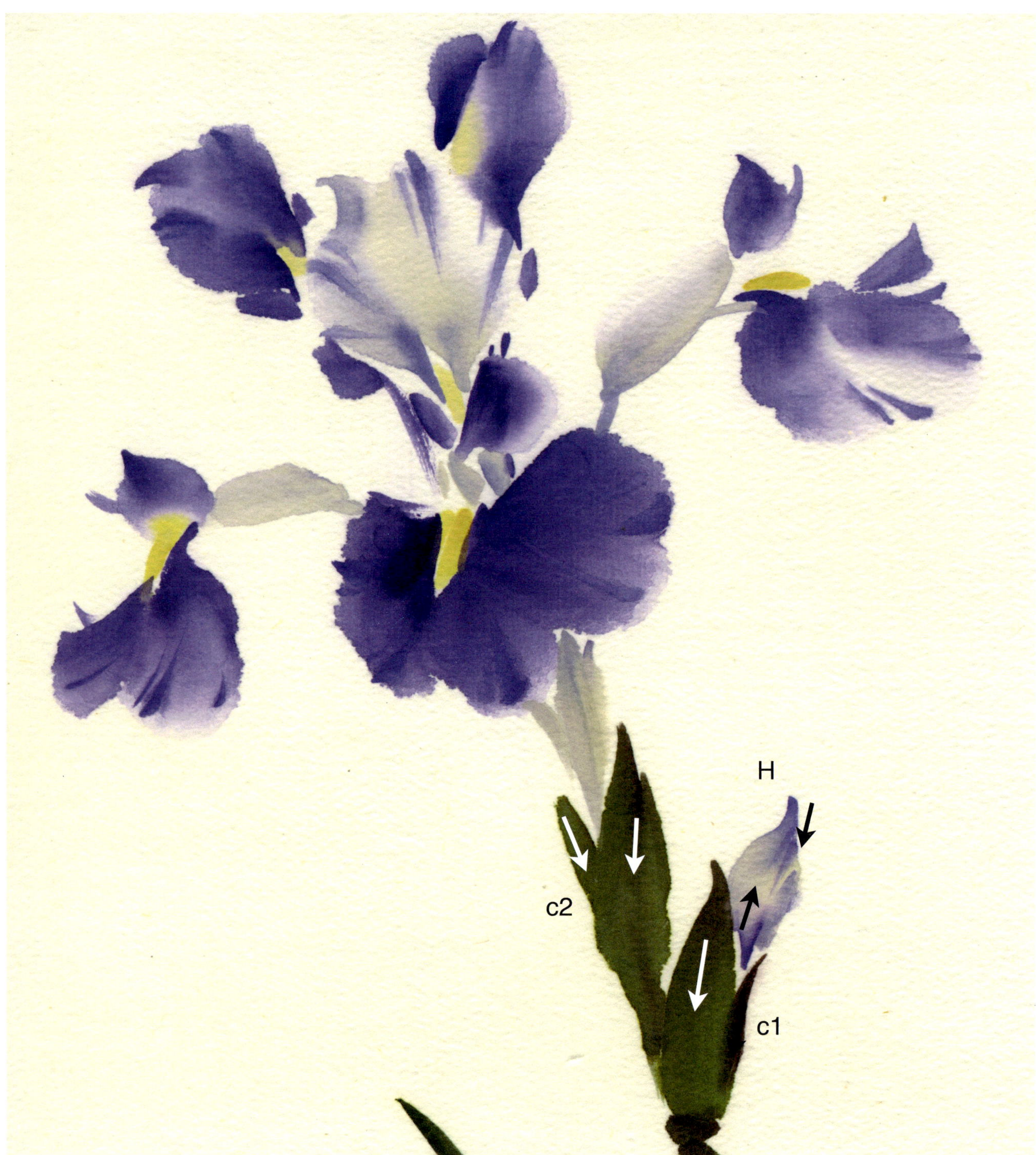


Calyx
ᔐ Large Orchid Bamboo
❖ Warm Green + Brown
Estimate where the stalk of the flower will travel. Work a calyx for a bud along the path of the stalk. Show a larger stroke on top and smaller one below. Tie them at the base (c1).

Work a calyx below the flower tube (c2). Connect the calyx roots with a stalk.

Bud (H)
ᔐ Flow
❖ White + Light Purple
Work the tip part of a bud with two strokes.

❖ Light Purple
Add the root of the bud.

ᔐ Small Mountain Horse
❖ Light Purple + Purple
Add veins on the bud.

Leaves

♌ Large Orchid Bamboo

❖ Light Green + Warm Green

Work a cluster of leaves showing their backsides. Do an anchor leaf (1) to house the stalk. Build a cluster with leaves on both sides (2, 3). They can move up or down, one or two strokes with added turns.

It is important to lead the leaves off the base of the paper to suggest more height.

❖ Brown

Run a stalk to bring the flower and bud into the leaves.

❖ Light Green + Dark Green + Ink

Do leaves showing their topsides. Work a crossing leaf on the right (4).

Add a leaf near the stalk (5). Work the tip. Show the body with two strokes. Add its root from the base up.

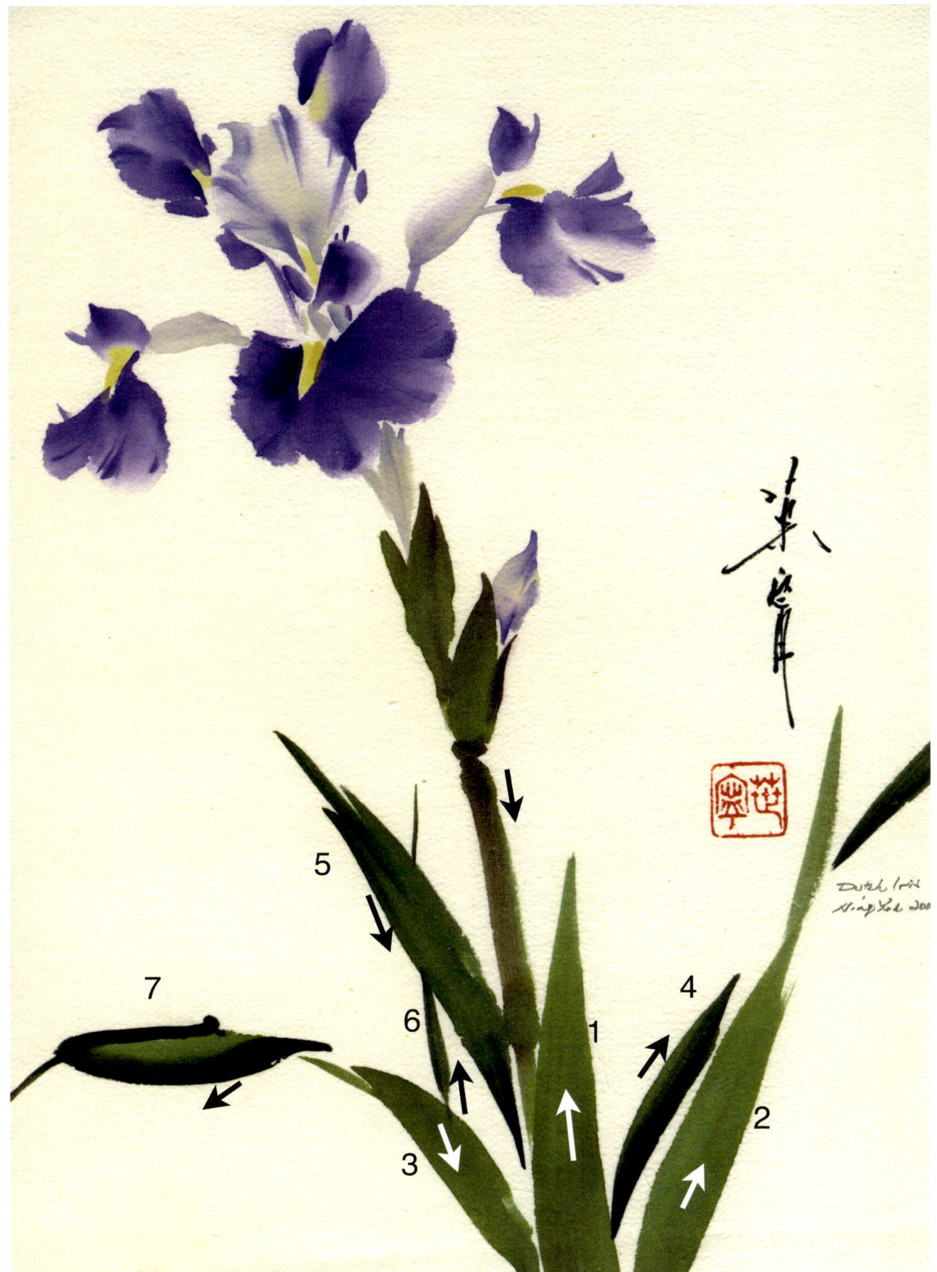


Cross with a small leaf (6). Say, "Excuse me, may I cross?"

Add the topside of the profile leaf heading to the left—the finale (7).

8040

# Eggplant

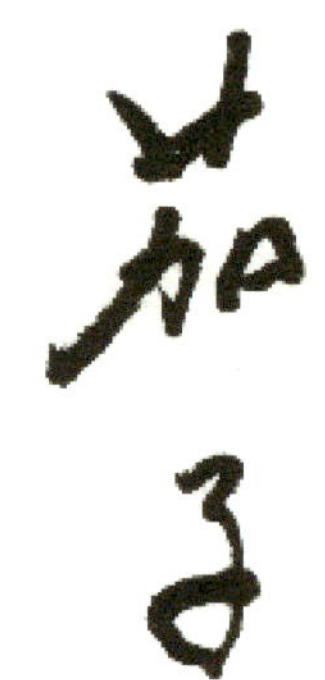

Chie
Qié: Eggplant

Tz
Zi: Fruit

Chinese flower painting is not about flowers. The fact that training begins with bamboo tells the story. Brush painting is about the expression of strokes, the rhythm of movement, contrast and harmony, the figure and space, the idea beyond what one sees, the joyful celebration of life.

Under the general title of flower painting, Chinese include fruits, vegetables, crops, trees and many more. Eggplant has one of the most beautiful purple colors. It also is shaped beautifully. The skin of the eggplant is shiny. It is a great subject to paint.

**MATERIALS**

Paper: Double Shuen

ᔓ Brushes
Flow, Large Flow, Happy Dot

❖ Colors
*Chinese*
Yellow
*Da Vinci*
White
*Schminke*
Cadmium Red Deep

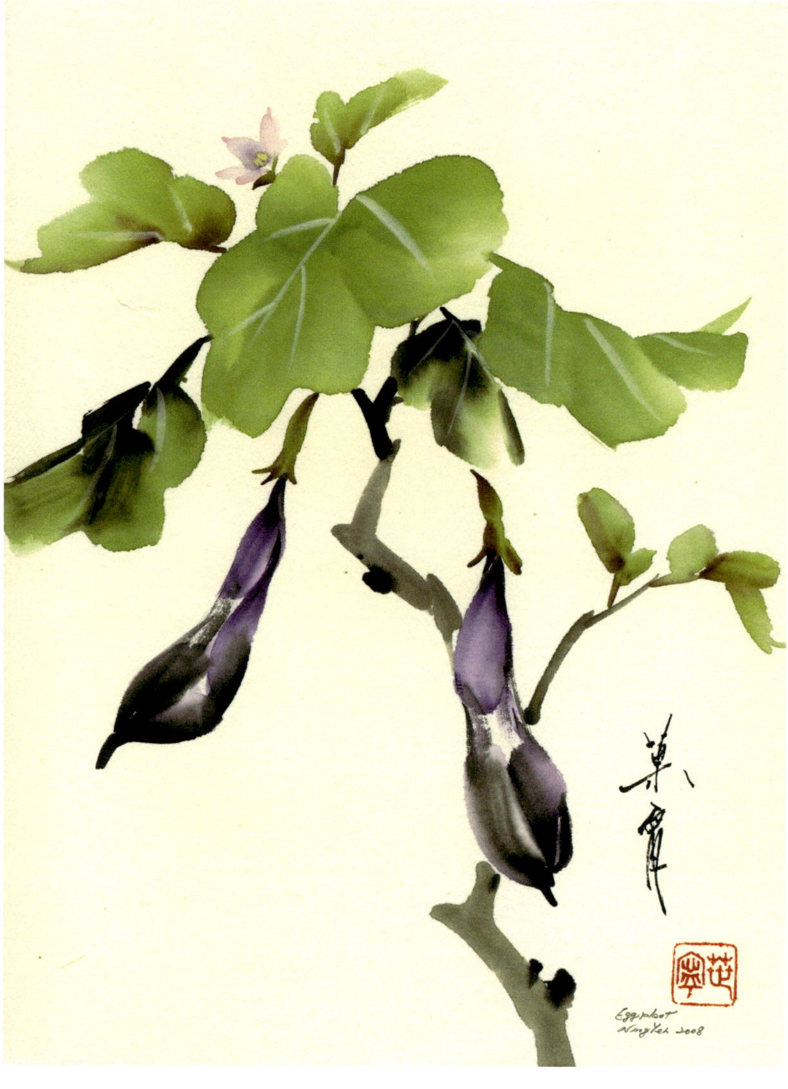

*Winsor & Newton*
Indigo, Ultramarine Violet, Winsor Violet, Perylene Violet, Permanent Magenta
*OAS*
Best Bottle Ink

**PREPARATION OF COLORS**

White: diluted
Yellow: Yellow + White
Light Purple: Ultramarine Violet
Purple: Winsor Violet + Perylene Violet
Red: Cadmium Red Deep
Dark Red: Perylene Violet
Light Green: Yellow + Indigo
Dark Green: Yellow + Indigo
Pink: Permanent Magenta + Red
Brown: Dark Red + Dark Green
White: pasty
Ink

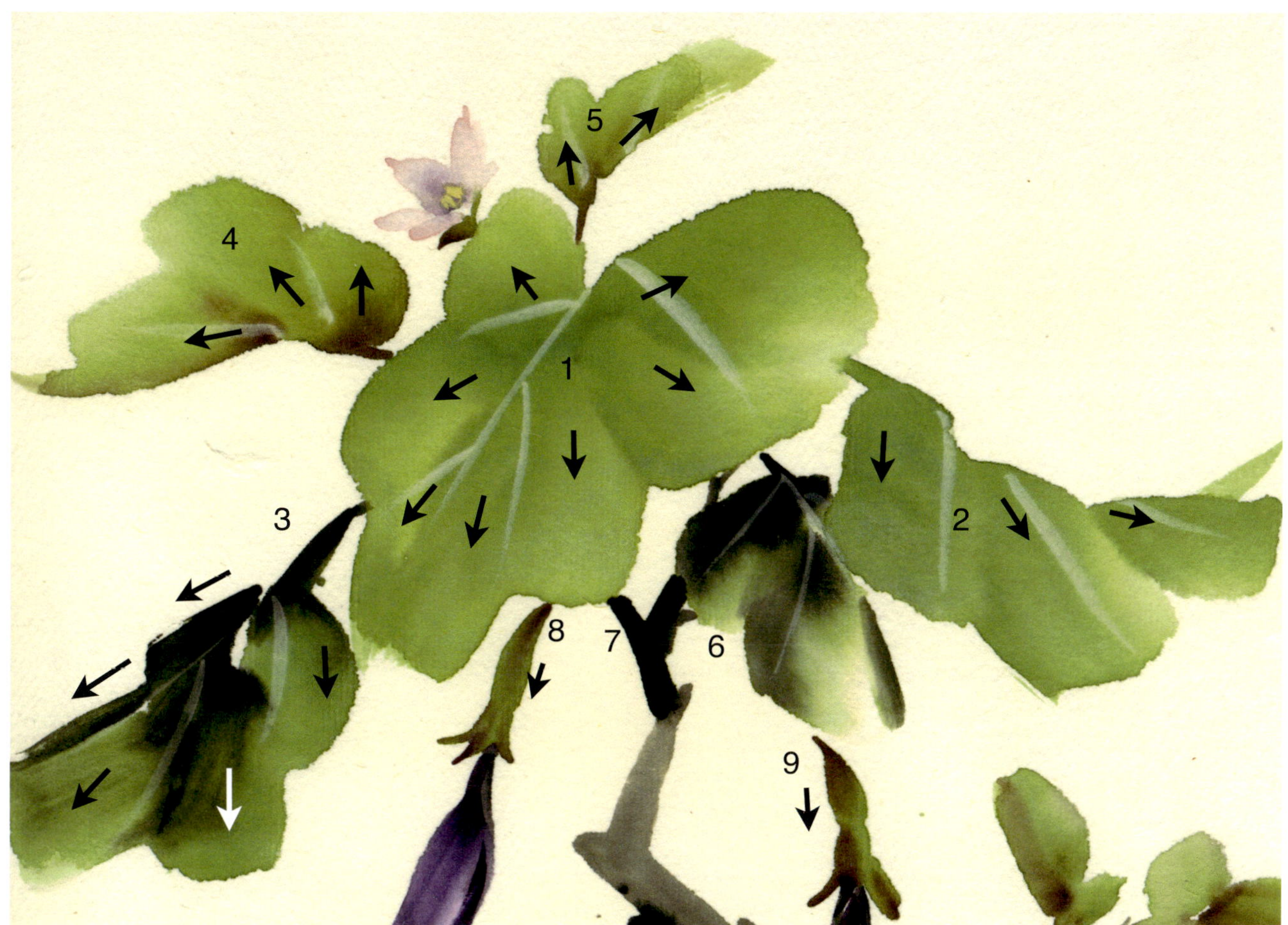


## STEPS

ℒ Large Flow
❖ Light Green + Dark Green
Set the orientation of the leaf with a centerline. Push strokes out to form the right side of the leaf. Do the left side smaller (1).

Add a leaf drooping to the right (2).

❖ Dark Green + Ink
Balance the composition with a shadow leaf on the left (3).

❖ Light Green + Dark Red
Work a pair of profile leaves on top with their undersides showing (4, 5).

ℒ Happy Dot
❖ Pasty White + Light Green
Do veins with pasty white and a dry brush while the leaves are still wet. Work center veins on fully opened leaves. Alternate the side veins. Profile leaves do not need to show center veins.

ℒ Flow
❖ Light Green + Dark Green + Ink
Add a shadow leaf (6).

ℒ Happy Dot
❖ Pasty White + Light Green
Work the veins on the shadow leaf.

ℒ Flow
❖ Light Green + Dark Red
Do stems to hold the eggplants (7). Add a set of calyx dots to each stem (8, 9).

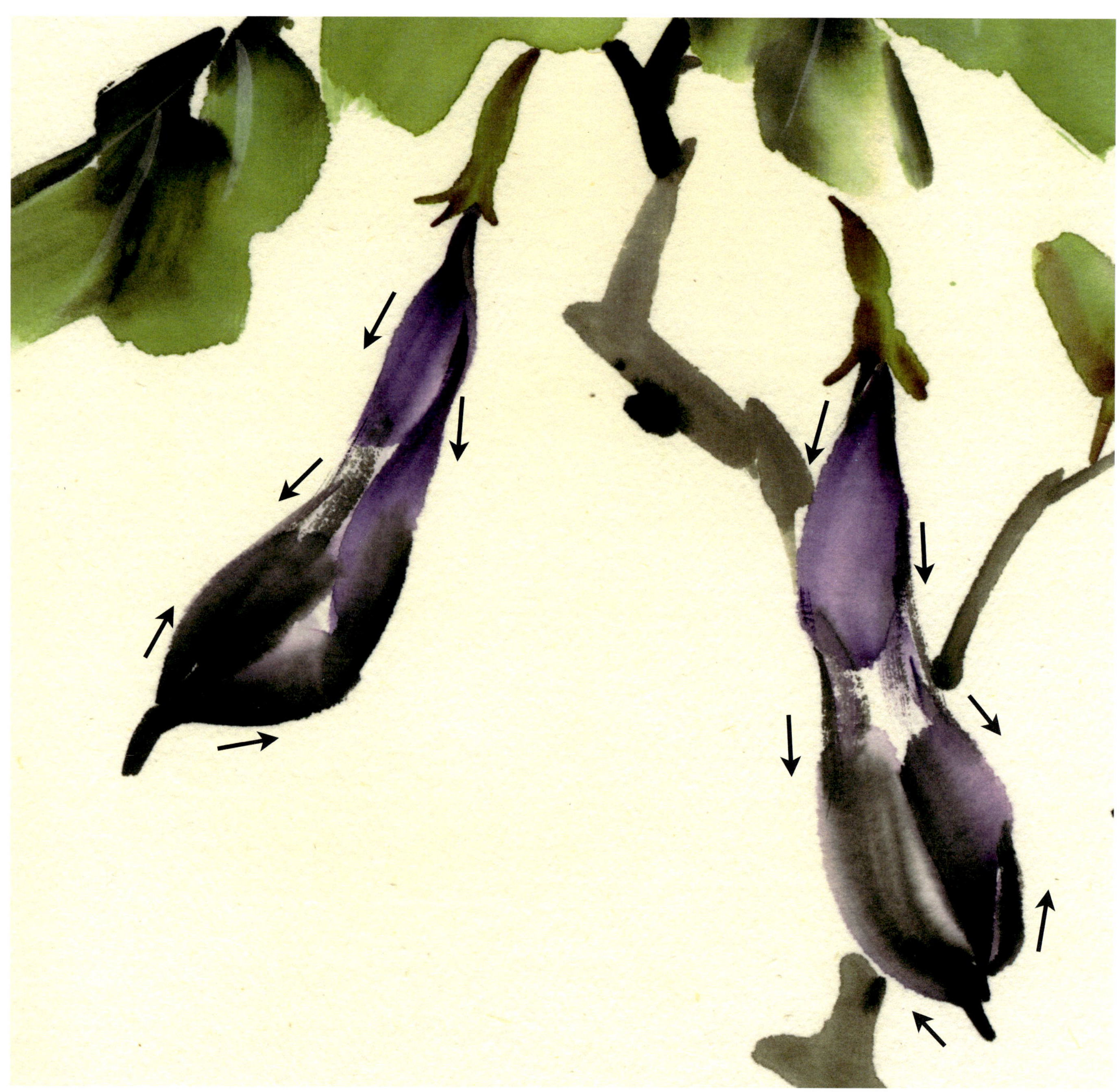

❖ Light Purple + Dark Purple
Do the top of the eggplants with two strokes from the calyx down.

❖ Light Purple + Dark Purple + Ink
Make the lower part of the eggplants fuller. Work strokes from the base up.

❖ Split the brush tip open and soften the colors a little with water.
Do strokes to connect the middle portions of the eggplant. Tighten the waistline.

No matter what we do. It is a self-portrait of sorts, or an ideal version of a self-portrait.

❖ White + Light Purple
Show lighter colors in the middle. Leave some space open.

❖ Brown
Do the branches. Make the lower sections wider.

❖ Ink
Add stems to bring the leaves into the branches. Do more twigs. Land a few happy dots on the branches.

❖ Light Green + Dark Red
Work a pair of profile leaves as a guest group.

❖ White + Pink
Do a flower with five pointed petals. Work the petals from outside in.

❖ Light Purple + Dark Purple
Seal the center of the flower.

❖ Light Green + Dark Red
Add a calyx below the flower.

❖ Yellow + White
Do the center of the flower with up to five dots.

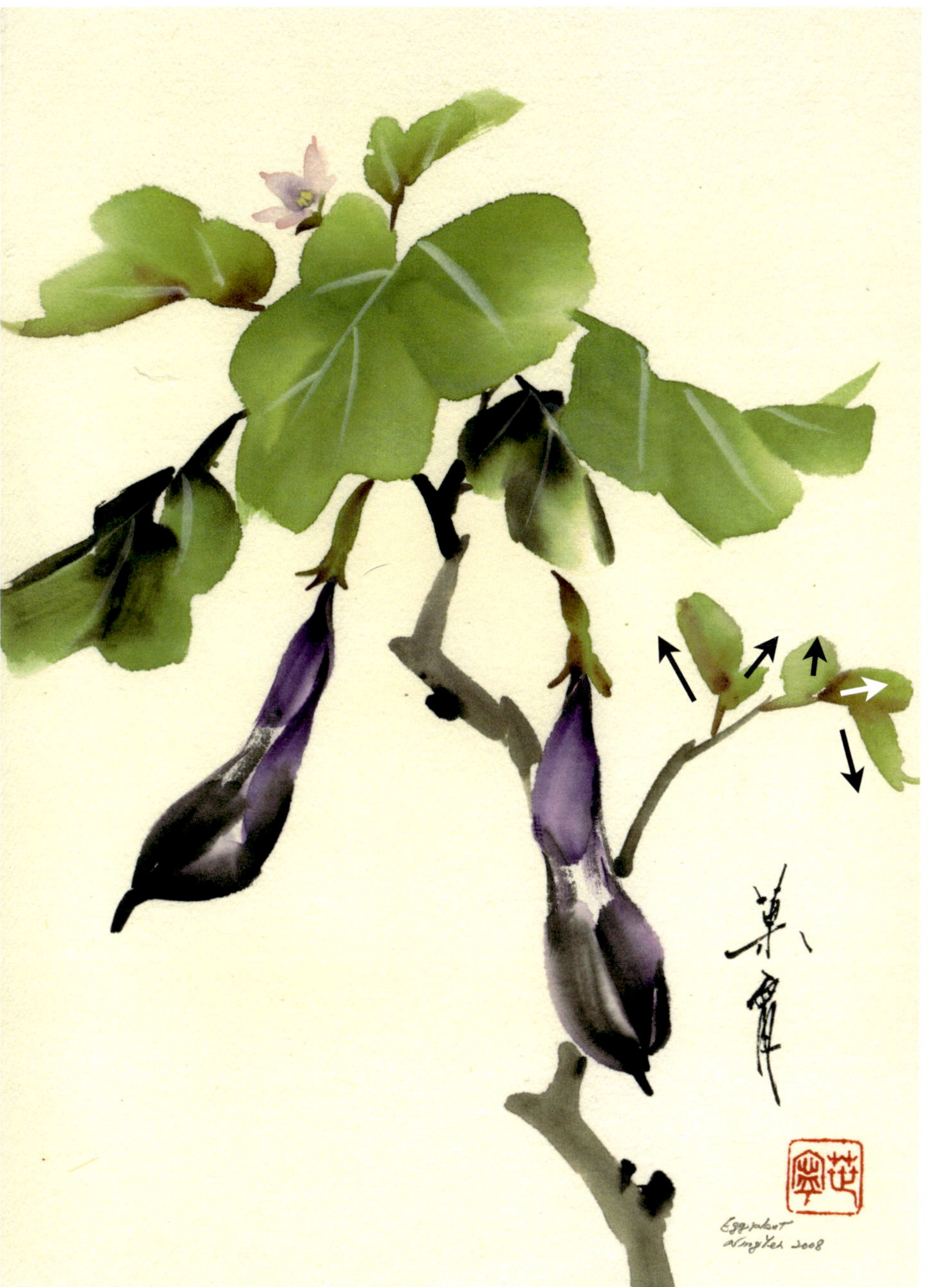

We have a simple composition that includes everything about the eggplant.

One Eggplant

Before the lesson, I did a little warm up. One eggplant turned out. I like to share it with you.

♌ Flow

❖ Light Green + Dark Red

Do a stem (1). Add a calyx below the stem (2).

♌ Large Flow

❖ Purple

Do the top part of eggplant.

❖ Ink

Work the lower part of the eggplant from the base up.

❖ Split the brush tip open. Connect the top and lower parts, showing the waist of the eggplant.

❖ Light Purple

Show a suggestion of light in the middle. Leave some space open to heighten the contrast.

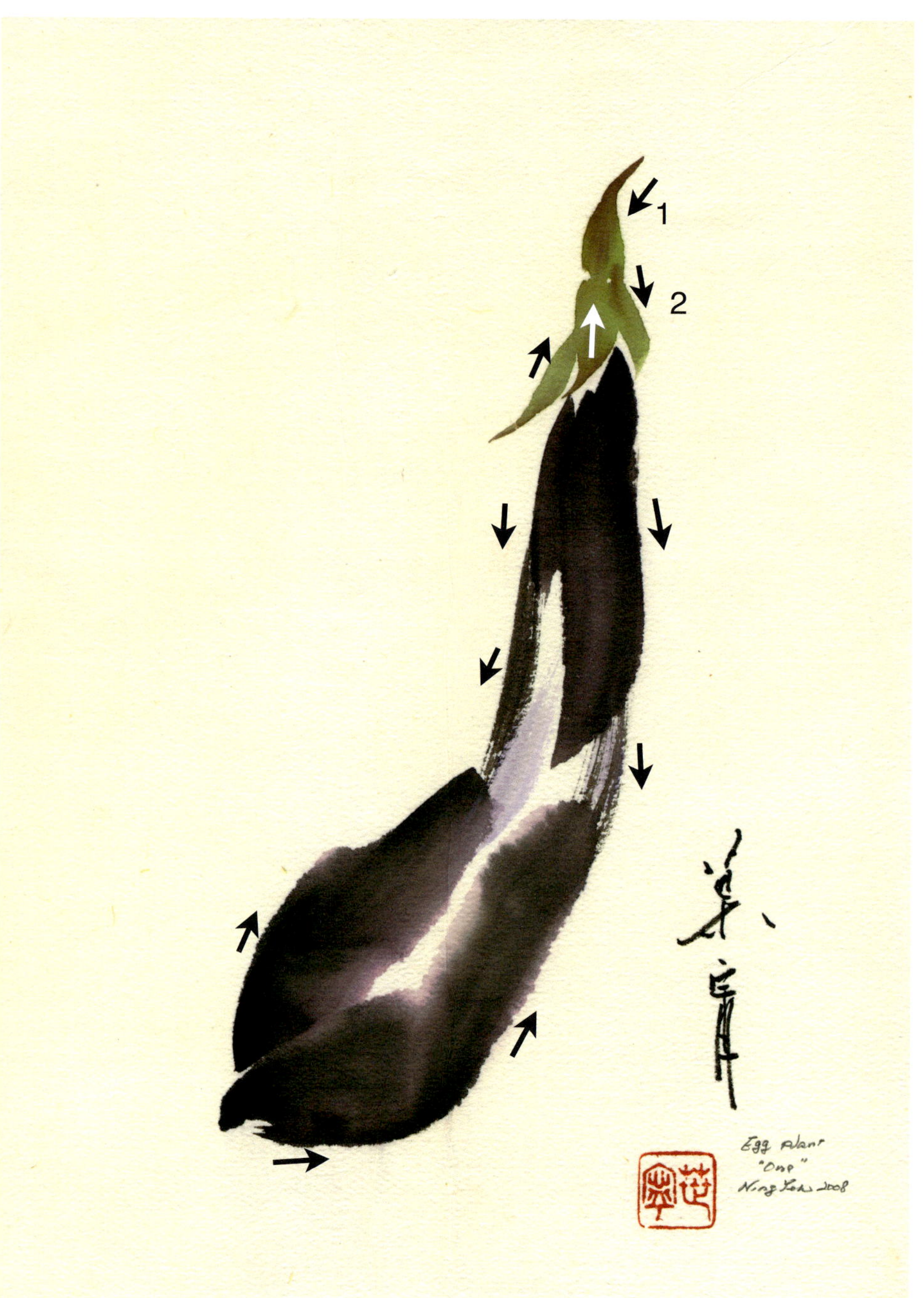

8041

# Forget-Me-Not

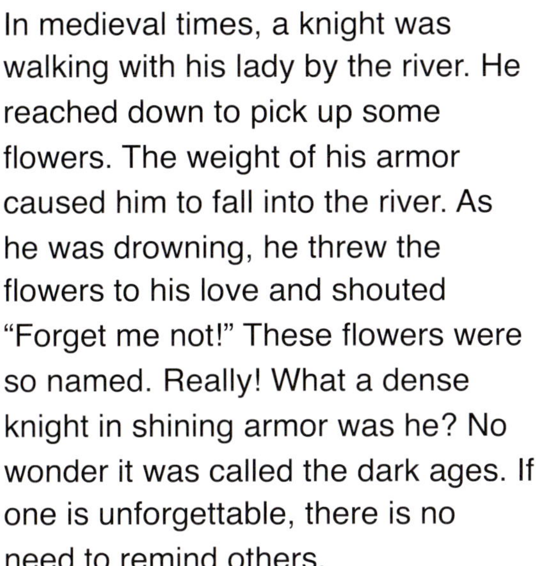


U
Wù: Not

Uang
Wàng: Forget

Uo
Wǒ: Me or I

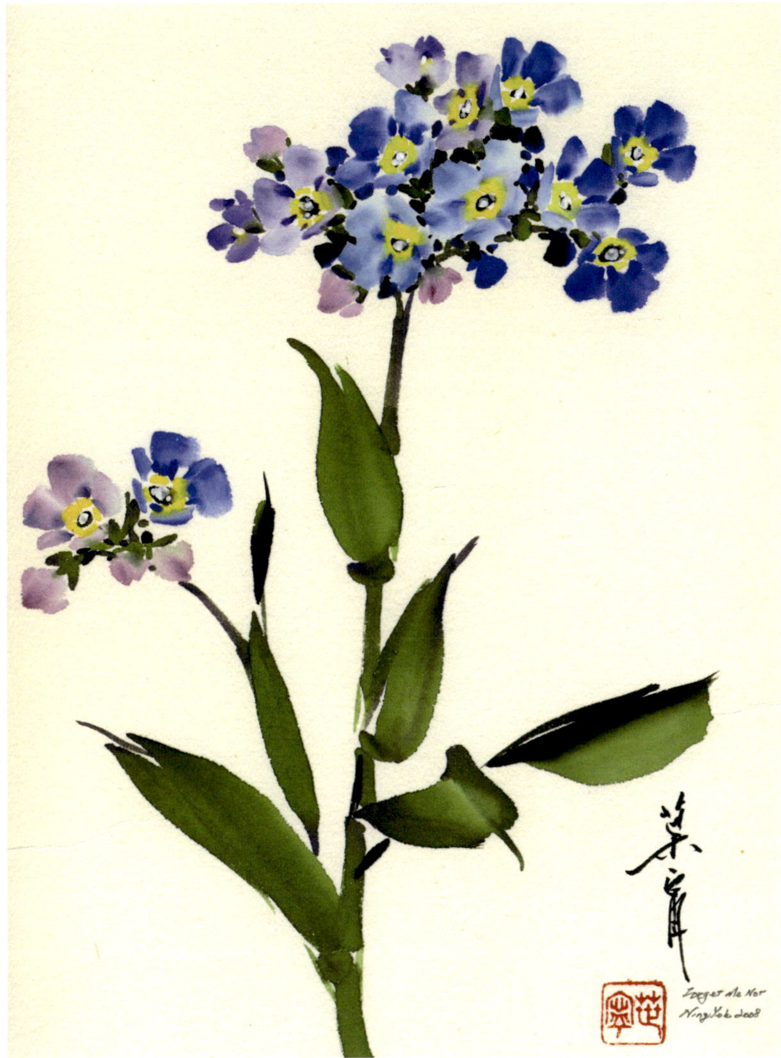

In medieval times, a knight was walking with his lady by the river. He reached down to pick up some flowers. The weight of his armor caused him to fall into the river. As he was drowning, he threw the flowers to his love and shouted "Forget me not!" These flowers were so named. Really! What a dense knight in shining armor was he? No wonder it was called the dark ages. If one is unforgettable, there is no need to remind others.

Forget-me-not comes in multiple colors from blue to red. Yes, I am blue when you are not with me. I turn pink when you are around.

## MATERIALS

Paper: Double Shuen

Brushes
Large Orchid Bamboo, Flow

❖ Colors
*Chinese*
Yellow, Vermillion
*Da Vinci*
White
*Winsor & Newton*
Indigo, Cerulean Blue, Winsor Blue (Green Shade), Ultramarine Violet, Winsor Violet, Permanent Magenta, French Ultramarine
*OAS*
Best Bottle Ink

## PREPARATION

White: diluted
Yellow: thick liquid
Light Blue: Cerulean Blue
Blue: French Ultramarine
Dark Blue: Winsor Blue
Magenta: Permanent Magenta
Light Purple: Ultramarine Violet
Purple: Winsor Violet
Light Green: Yellow + Indigo
White: pasty
Ink

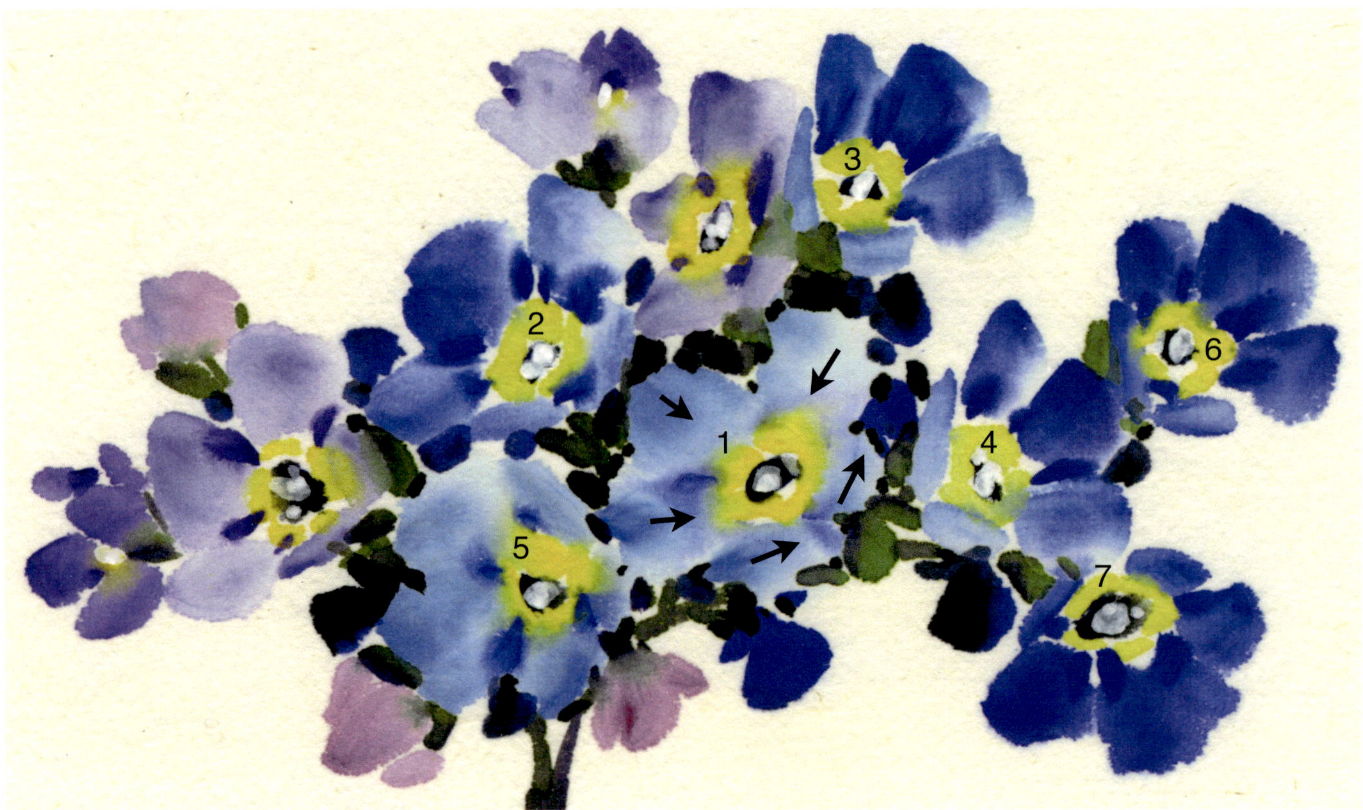


**STEPS**

Flowers
Host Group (1-7)
Each flower has five petals. The flower center has a yellow ring. Work flowers in a cluster. Begin with center ones. Do the rest of the flowers facing outward so their roots can join the center.

ℓ Flow
❖ Dark Blue + Ink
Work an oval dot for the center of the flower.

❖ Yellow
Do five small strokes around the center.

Petals
❖ White + Light Blue (1, 5)
❖ Light Blue + Blue (2, 3, 4)
❖ Blue + Dark Blue (6, 7)
The center flowers are light. We make flowers on the right side darker to add dimension to our cluster.

Work five petals. Do the top center petal with two strokes. Add side ones from outside in. Work the front lip petals moving sideways.

Shadows on Petals
❖ Blue (1, 5)
❖ Blue + Dark Blue (2, 3, 4)
❖ Dark Blue (6, 7)
Add shadows on the petals. There are five white strips between the petals. I do not paint them but use shadows to make their presence felt.

We have a cluster of blue flowers. Let us work on some purple ones.

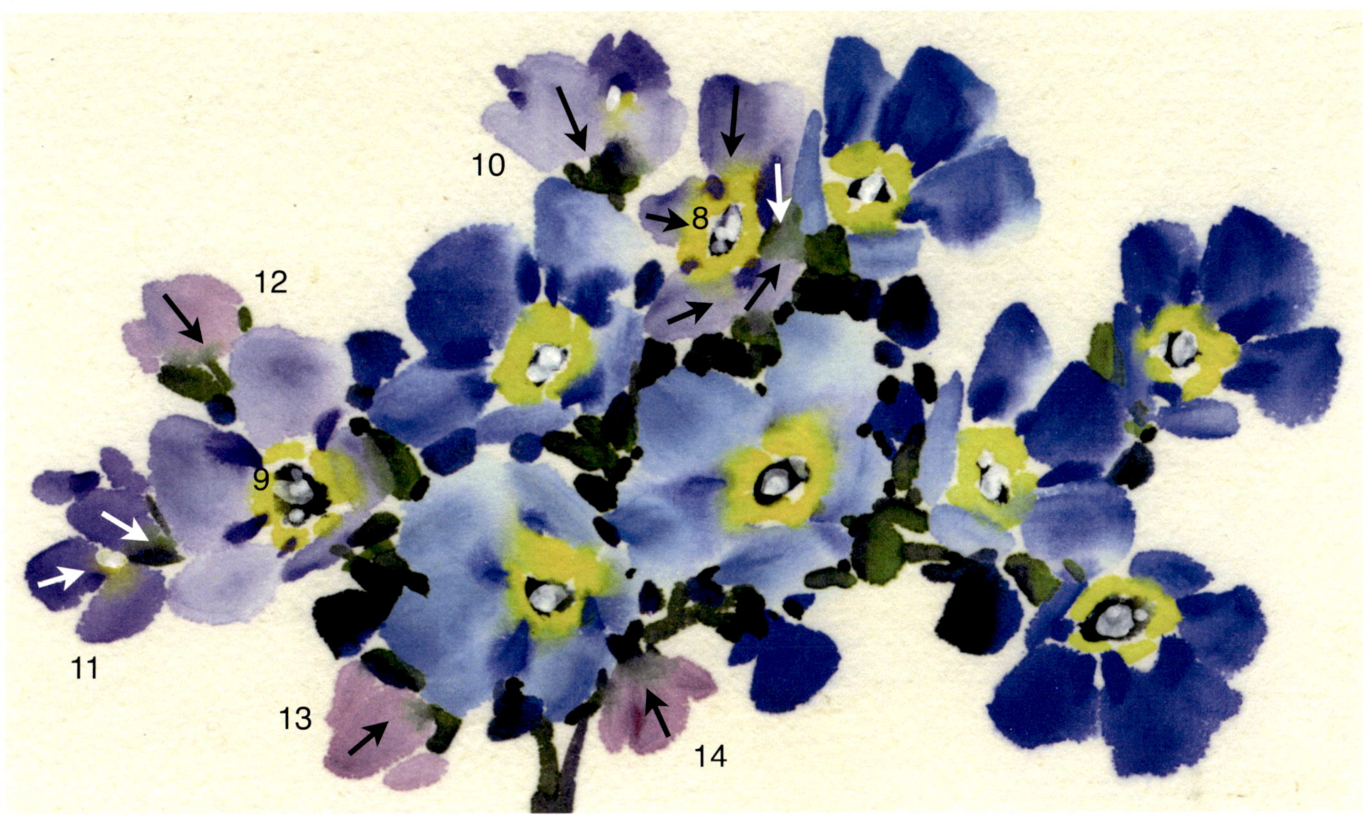


❖ Purple + Ink
Do the center dots of the flowers.

❖ Yellow
Work the rings.

❖ White + Light Purple
Show two fully opened flowers with light purple (8, 9). Work petals to show a profile flower on top (10).

❖ Light Purple + Purple
Add shadows to the open flowers.
Show the front facing petals of the profile flower. Work another profile flower. Do the petals that are showing their backsides (11).

❖ Purple
Do the front facing petals of the profile flower.

❖ Yellow
Suggest a hint of yellow in the center of the profile flowers.

❖ Purple
Add shadows to the profile flowers.

❖ White + Pink + Light Purple
Do some buds in pink (12, 13, 14).

❖ Green + Purple
Work up to three calyx dots below each of the flowers and buds.

We have a beautiful host cluster.

Guest Group

❖ Ink

Do center dots. They tell the flowers where to go.

❖ Yellow

Work the rings.

❖ White + Light Blue + Blue

Do a full flower in blue (1).

❖ Dark Blue

Add shadows.

❖ White + Pink + Light Purple

Work the second flower in purple pink (2).

❖ Light Purple + Purple

Add shadows.

❖ White + Pink

Do a bud (3).

❖ Green + Purple

Add calyx dots below the flowers. Work stems to bring the side flowers to the center.

❖ White + Pink

Do a couple more buds (4, 5).

❖ Green + Purple

Do calyx dots.

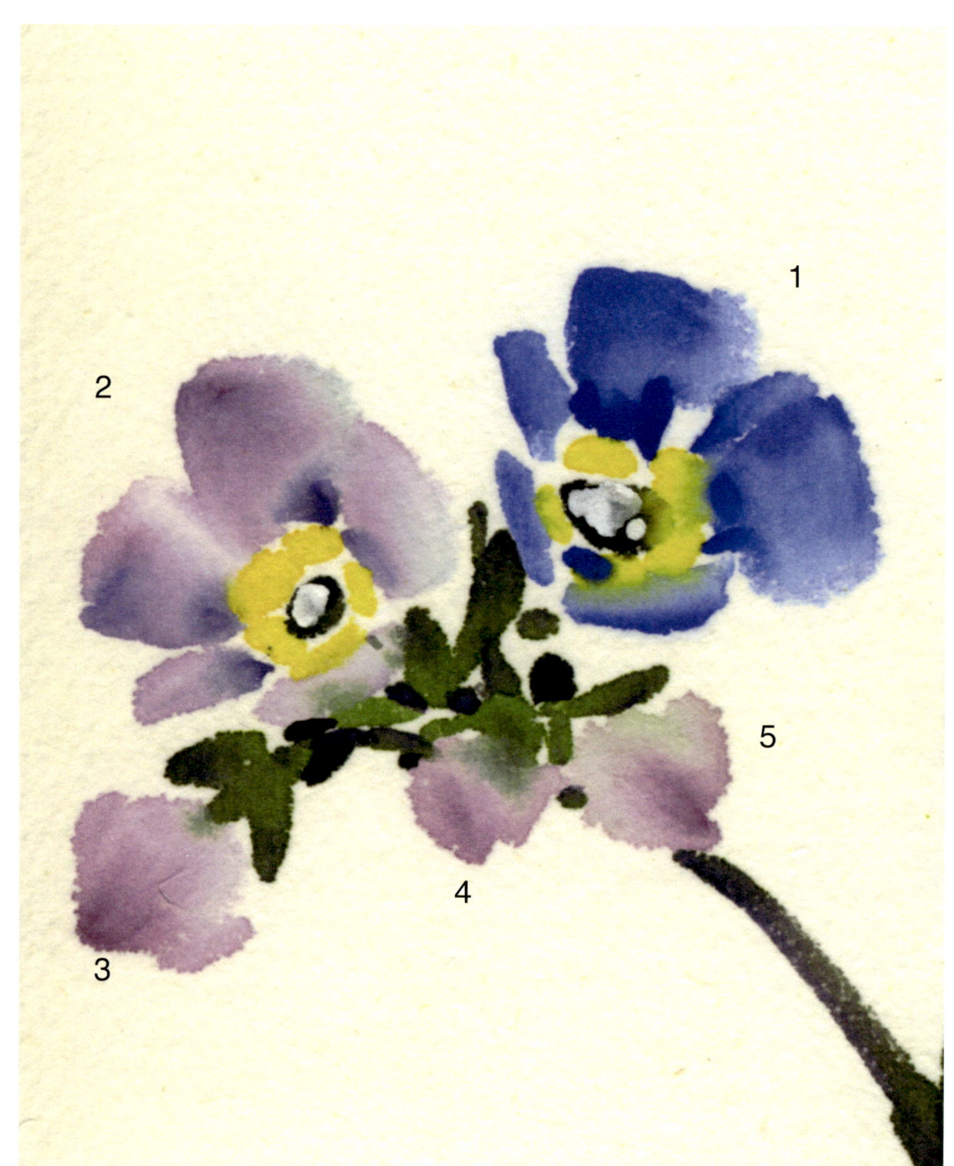

Leaves

ꝭ Large Orchid Bamboo

❖ Green + Purple

Do a couple of leaves along the projected stalk. The leaves are showing their backsides (1, 2). Show the tip of the leaf. Work the body with two strokes. Add a base to each leaf.

❖ Green + Ink

Do a foreshortened leaf reaching downward to the right (3).

❖ Green + Purple

Work a leaf showing its backside moving strokes from the left into the projected stalk (4).

❖ Green + Purple

Run a stalk down from the host flower group. Thread through the roots of the leaves along the way (5).

❖ Green + Purple

Work a profile leaf heading toward the guest flower group (6).

❖ Green + Ink

Work a shadow leaf moving to the right. Add the tip of the profile leaf on the left (7, 8).

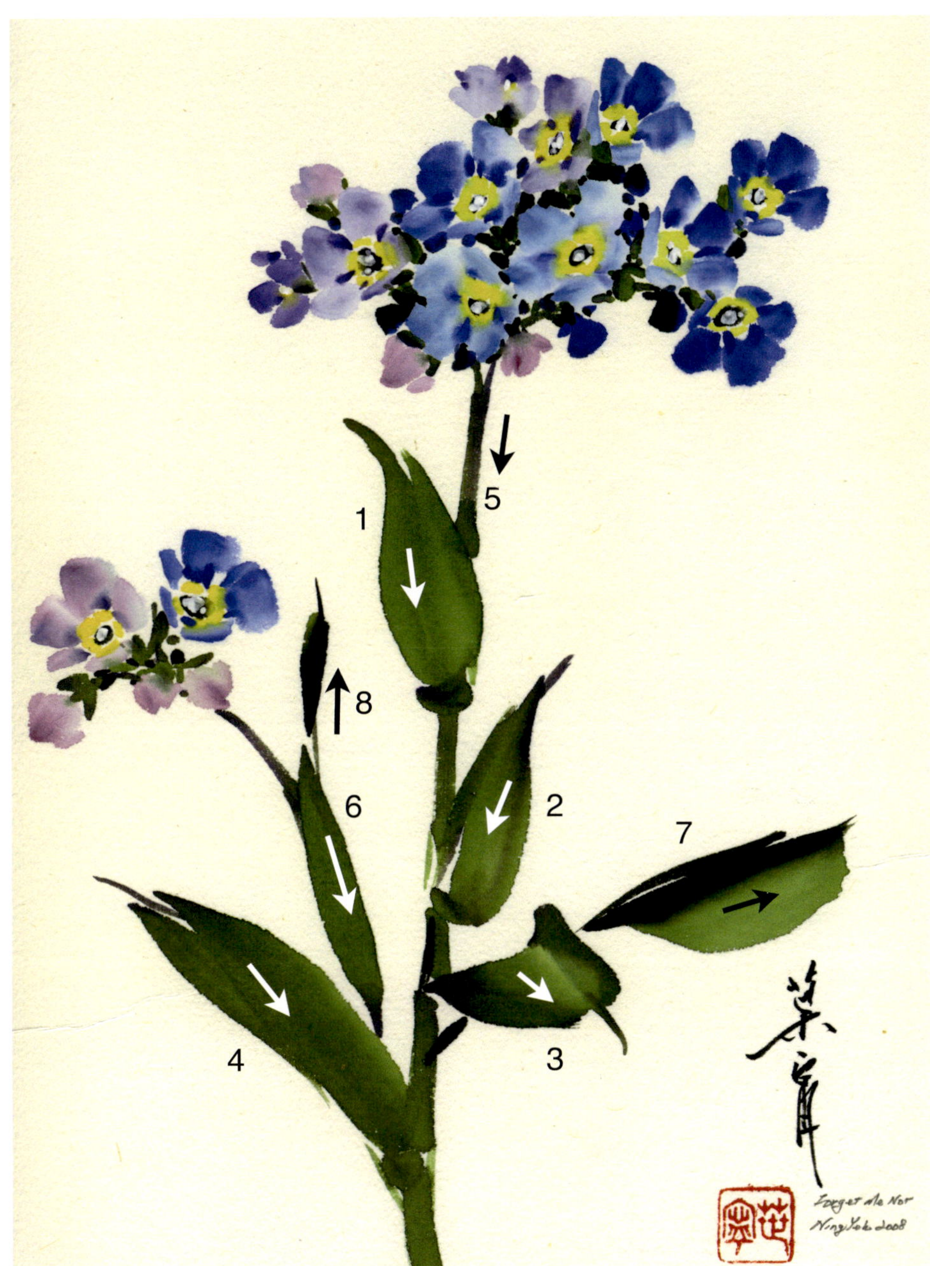


ꝭ Flow

❖ Blue + Dark Blue + Purple

Add shadow flowers to tighten the flower cluster and to add depth.

❖ Green + Purple

Work stems to connect the flowers. Add a stalk to bring the guest flower group down into the main stalk.

❖ Pasty White

Add up to three bright dots to the center of the flowers.

8042

# Foxglove

Jr
Zhǐ: Pointing

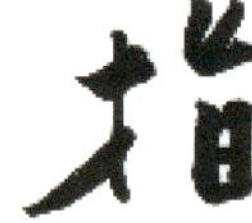

Ding
Dǐng: Top

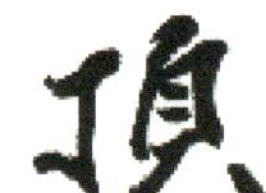

When Weyerhaeuser asked me to do a painting to celebrate the new forest after the devastation caused by Mt. St. Helen, the company took me on a helicopter to study the landscape. When we landed, tall foxgloves were my first sight. I used the flowers as the foreground for the forest painting. To me, the flower represents the spirit of rebirth.

**MATERIALS**

Paper: Double Shuen

Brushes
Large Flow, Flow, Small Mountain Horse

❖ Colors
*Chinese*
Yellow
*Da Vinci*
White
*Schmincke*
Cadmium Red Deep
*Winsor & Newton*
Indigo, Perylene Violet
*OAS*
Best Bottle Ink

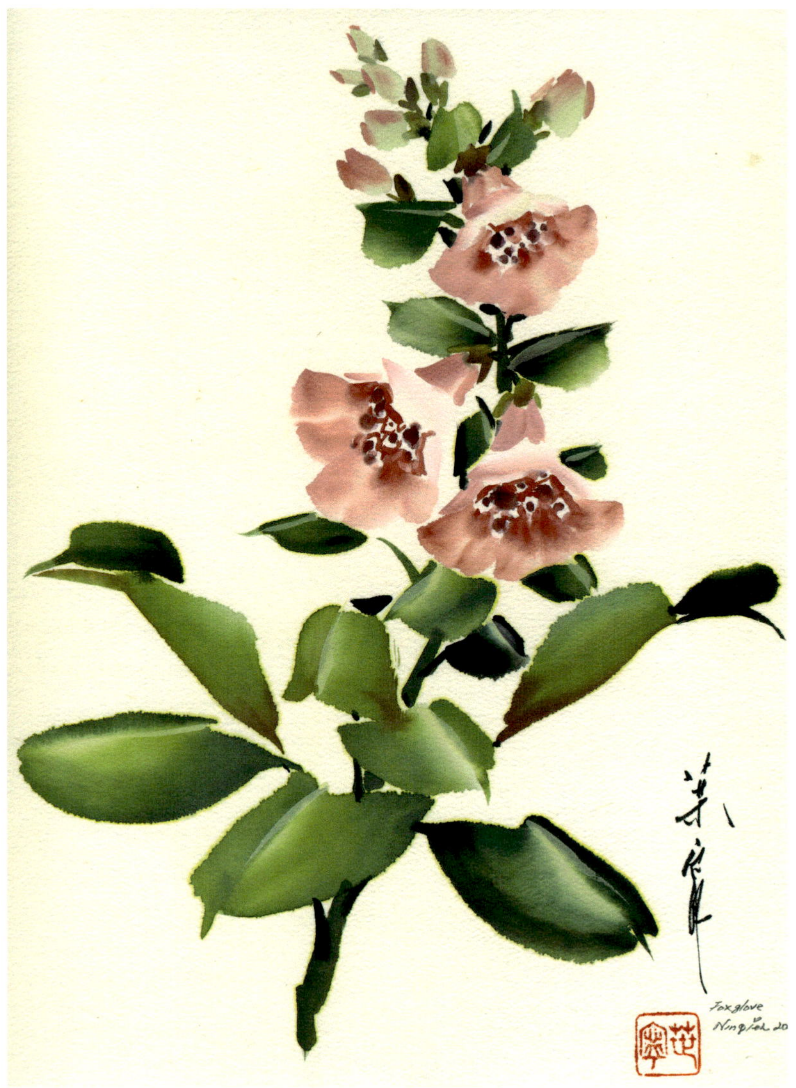


**PREPARATION OF COLORS**

Yellow: thick liquid + White
White: diluted
Red: Cadmium Red Deep
Pink: White + Red
Dark Red: Perylene Violet + Red
Light Green: Yellow + Indigo
Dark Green: Yellow + Indigo
Ink

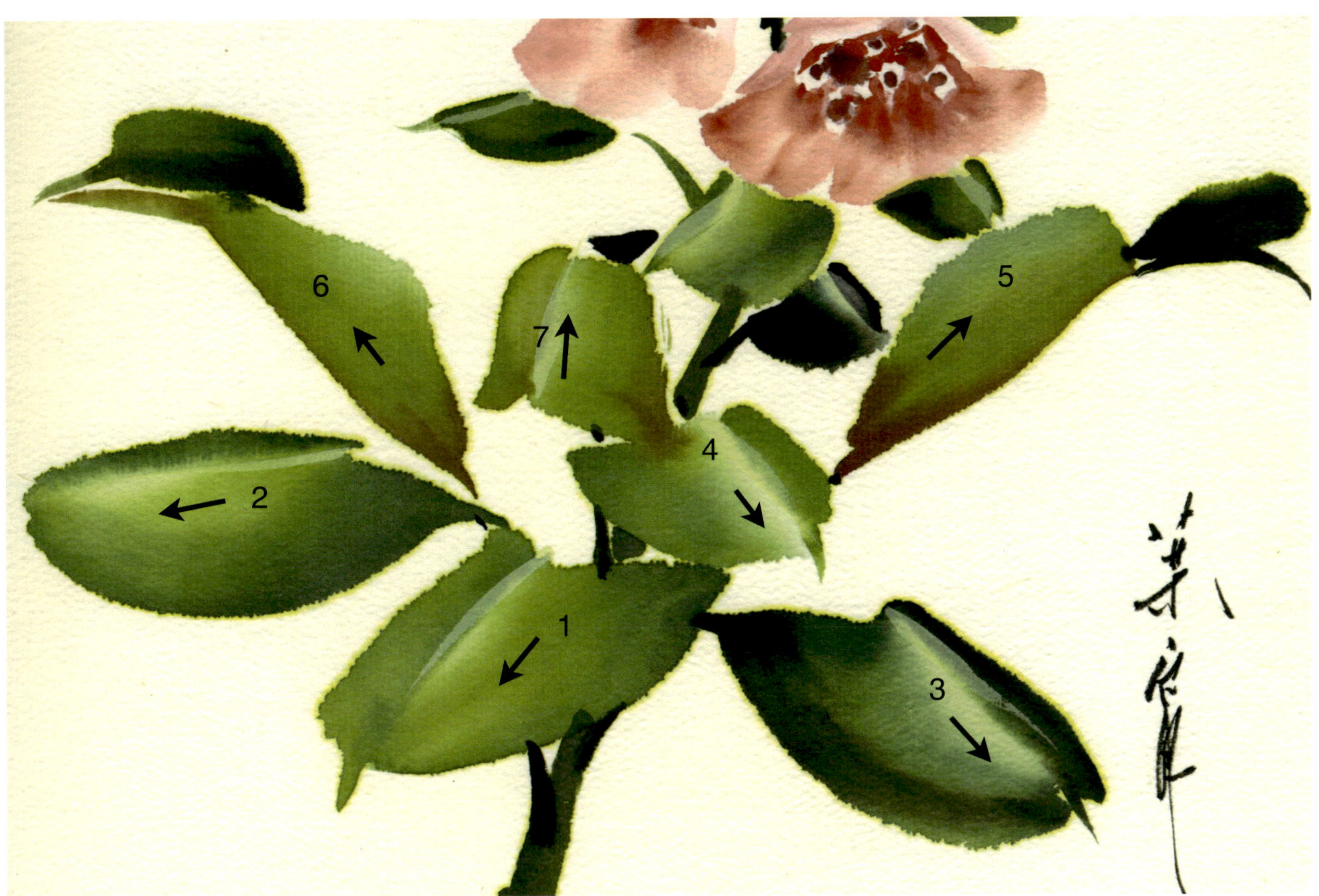


**STEPS**

Leaves

♌ Large Flow

❖ Light Green + Dark Green

Do a group of large leaves forming a skirt near the base. These leaves are drooping and showing their topsides. Work one in the center (1). One moves to the left (2).

❖ Dark Green + Ink

Do a shadow leaf heading to the right (3).

❖ Light Green + Dark Green

Work a foreshortened leaf above the skirt (4).

❖ Separate some Dark Red for leaves. Load Light Green + Dark Red

Do profile leaves showing their undersides (5, 6). They reach diagonally upward like cheerful arms creating a valley. Work another short leaf in the middle with its backside showing (7).

❖ Dark Green + Ink

Add the topsides of the profile leaves.

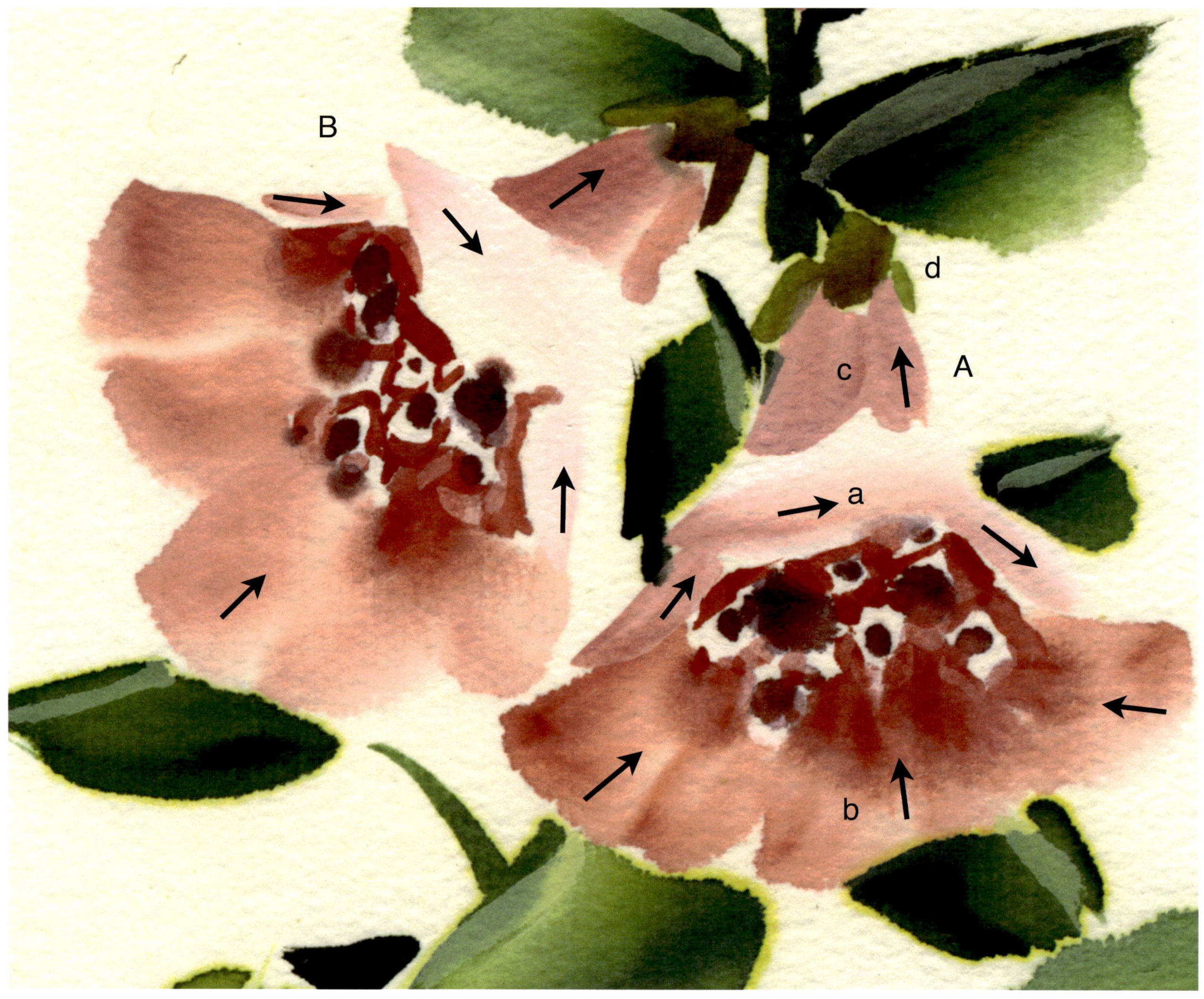


Flowers

♌ Flow

❖ White + Pink

The trumpet-shaped flowers droop down from a stalk. Make an invisible mark where the projected stalk will be before working the flowers. Do two flowers in the middle (A, B). Show the top edge of the trumpet opening with three strokes for each flower (a).

❖ White + Pink + Red

Work petal strokes from outside into the center of the trumpet opening (b). Leave space open in the center.

❖ Dark Red

Work dots in the center of the Trumpet.

❖ White

Circle each center dot with a white ring. The rings may be invisible. Do them anyway.

❖ Pink + Red

Seal the remaining pockets in the center.

❖ White + Pink

Work strokes to show a tube behind each trumpet opening (c).

❖ Light Green + Dark Red

Add calyx dots at the end of the tubes (d).

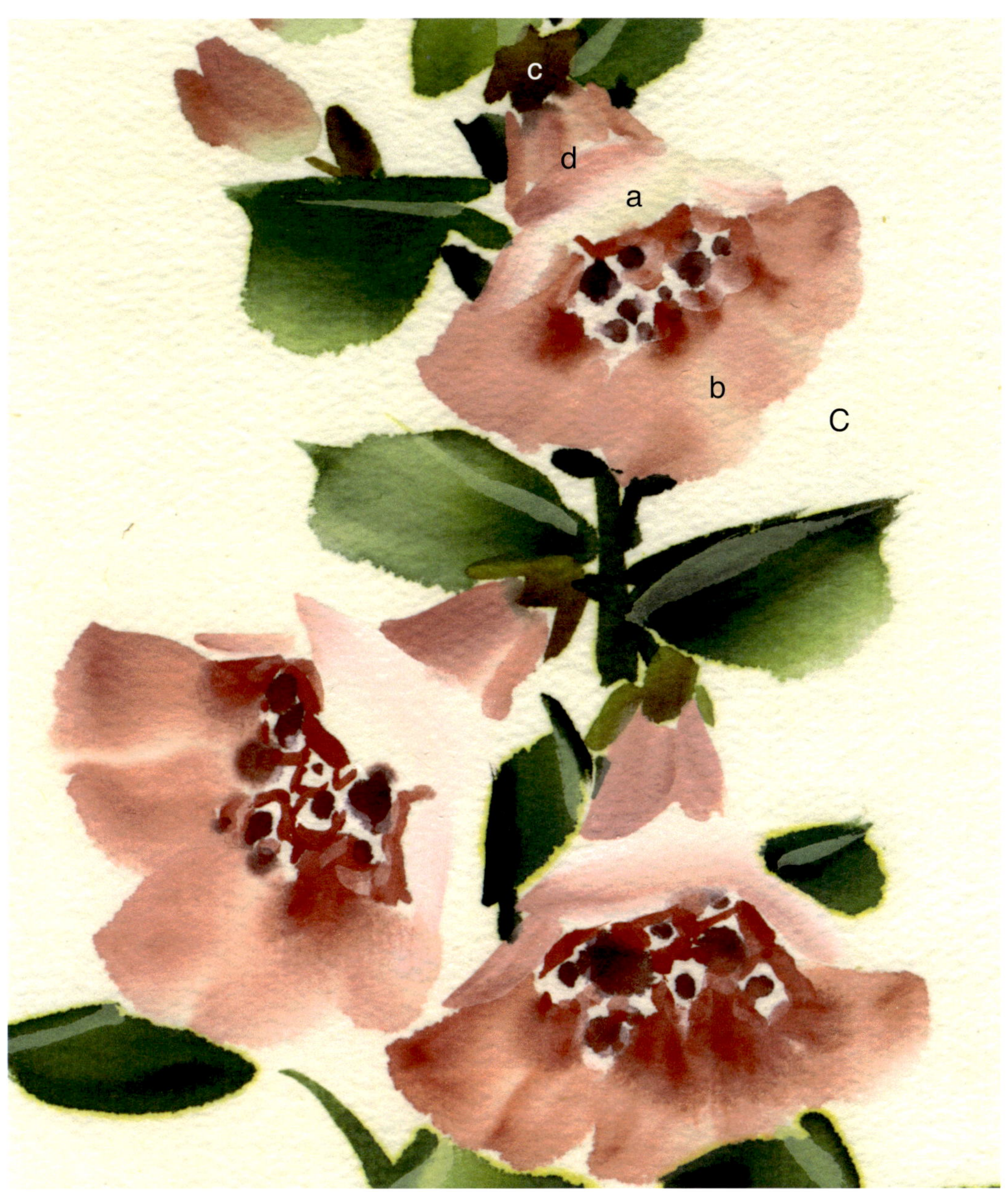


❖ White + Pink
Put one smaller flower on top (C). Show the top edge of the trumpet opening (a).

❖ Dark Red
Work dots in the center.

❖ White
Do a ring around each dot.

❖ White + Pink
Work petal strokes from outside into the center of the trumpet opening. Leave space open in the center (b).

❖ Pink + Red
Seal the remaining pockets in the center.

❖ Light Green + Dark Red
Add calyx dots at the end of the tubes. Leave a little distance from the trumpet opening (c).

❖ White + Pink
Work a tube from the calyx to the trumpet opening (d).

I have changed the sequence of strokes. I am not showing off here. Sometimes it just takes a little doing to figure out a better way. Other times, it may take years.

More Leaves

❖ Light Green + Dark Green

Do a drooping leaf below the lower flower (8).

❖ Dark Green + Ink

Do a leaf by the root of each flower (9, 10, 11).

❖ Mix a Brown by using Light Green + Dark Green + Dark Red

Add a stalk. Thread it through the middle of our composition. Add stems to connect each flower and leaf onto the stalk (12).

❖ Dark Green + Ink

Do a few more leaves. Add stems to bring them home.

Buds

❖ Light Green + Dark Red

Do sets of calyxes with two or three dots each.

❖ White + Pink

Set the buds. Work each bud with one or two strokes above the calyx. Add smaller buds on the very top.

❖ Light Green + Dark Red

Wrap calyx dots below the new buds.

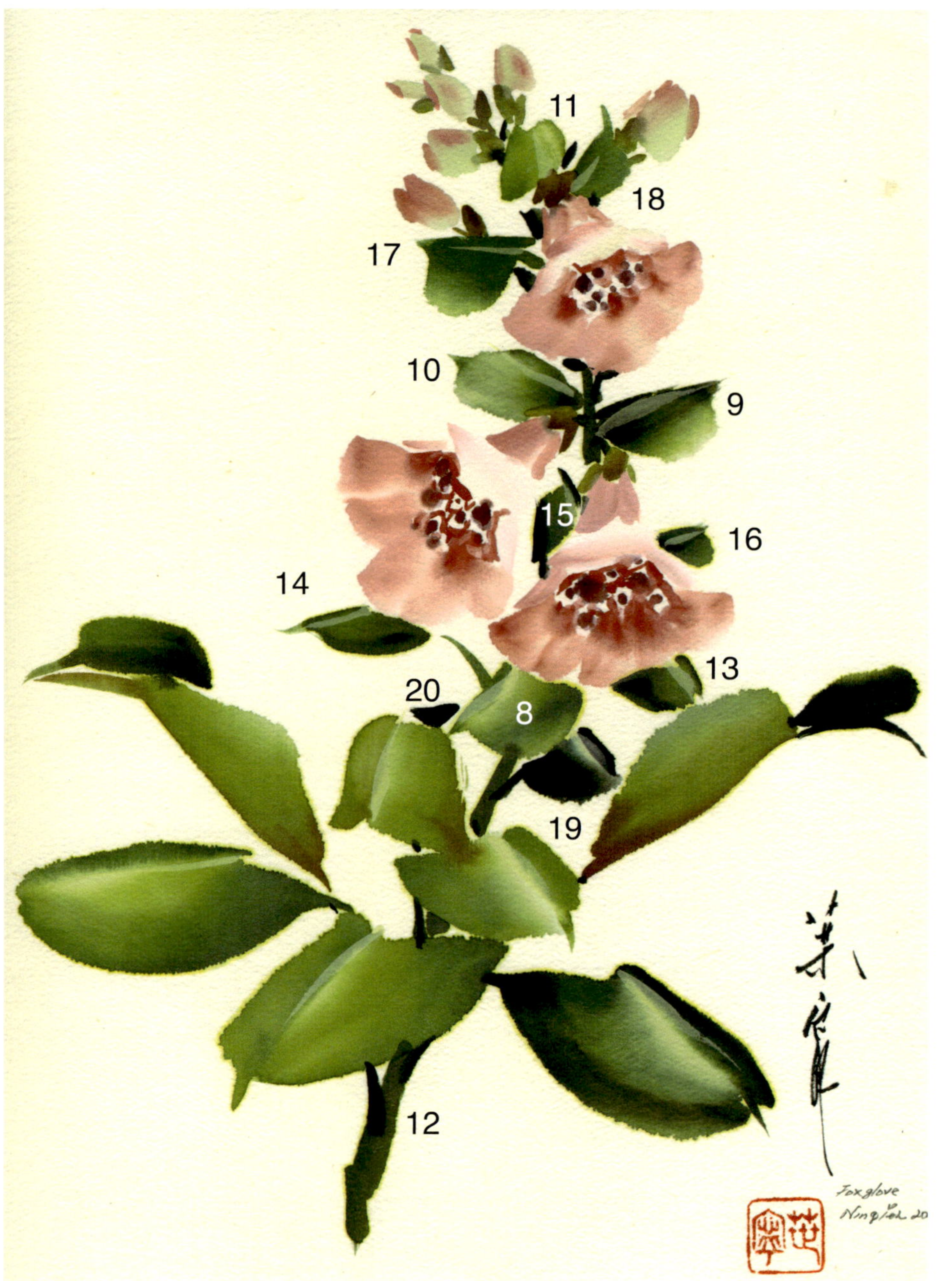


❖ Pink + Red

Turn the lower buds into teenagers by adding some side petals.

❖ Dark Green + Ink

Add more shadow leaves (13-20).

❖ Pink

Add a touch of shadow to the top buds.

♌ Small Mountain Horse

❖ Yellow + White

Do center veins on the fuller leaves.

8043

# Freesia

香蒼蘭

Shiang
Xiāng: Fragrant

Tsang
Cāng: Green

Lan
Lán: Orchid

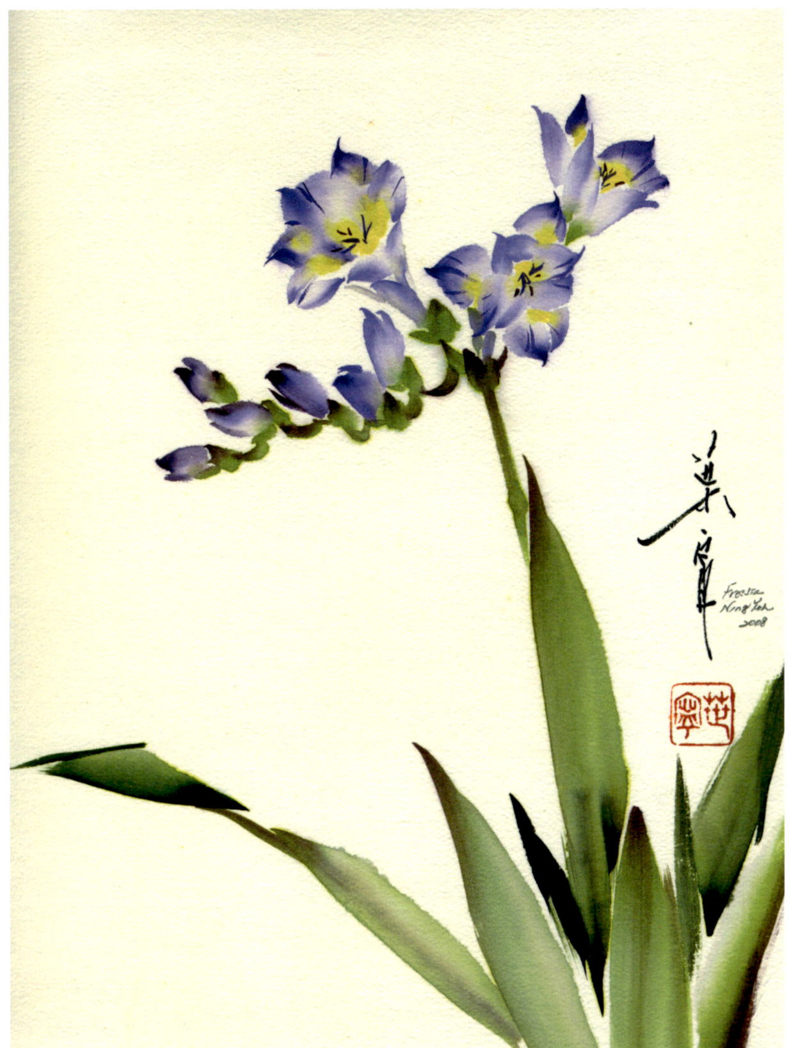

Freesia comes in an orderly row, like well-behaved kindergarteners on their first day of school. When I first worked on the flowers, I behaved like the parents outside the window—tight.

Small flowers are meant to be joyful. With just a few petals, we can do whatever we want with them. Indeed, it is free-sia.

School is out and the fish are jumping.

## MATERIALS

Paper: Double Shuen

♌ Brushes
Large Orchid Bamboo, Flow, Happy Dot

❖ Colors
*Chinese*
Yellow
*Da Vinci*
White
*Winsor & Newton*
Indigo, Winsor Violet, Perylene Violet
*OAS*
Best Bottle Ink

## PREPARATION OF COLORS

White: diluted
Yellow: thick liquid + White
Light Purple: White + Winsor Violet
Dark Red: Perylene Violet
Purple: Winsor Violet
Light Green: Yellow + Indigo
Dark Green: Yellow + Indigo
Ink

**STEPS**

Leaves

♌ Large Orchid Bamboo

❖ White + Light Green + Dark Red

Freesia leaves are in vertical clusters around the flower stalk. Do three leaves showing their backsides from the top down. Work each leaf with two strokes (1, 2, 3). The tall one will be hosting the flower stalk.

Add a profile leaf reaching to the right from the base up (4).

❖ Dark Green + Ink

Add the root of the overlapping leaf (3a).

❖ White + Light Green + Dark Red

Work a profile leaf moving the stroke in from the left side (5)

❖ Light Green + Dark Green + Ink

Do the topside of the profile leaf (5a). Add a few shadow leaves to thicken the cluster (6, 7, 8).

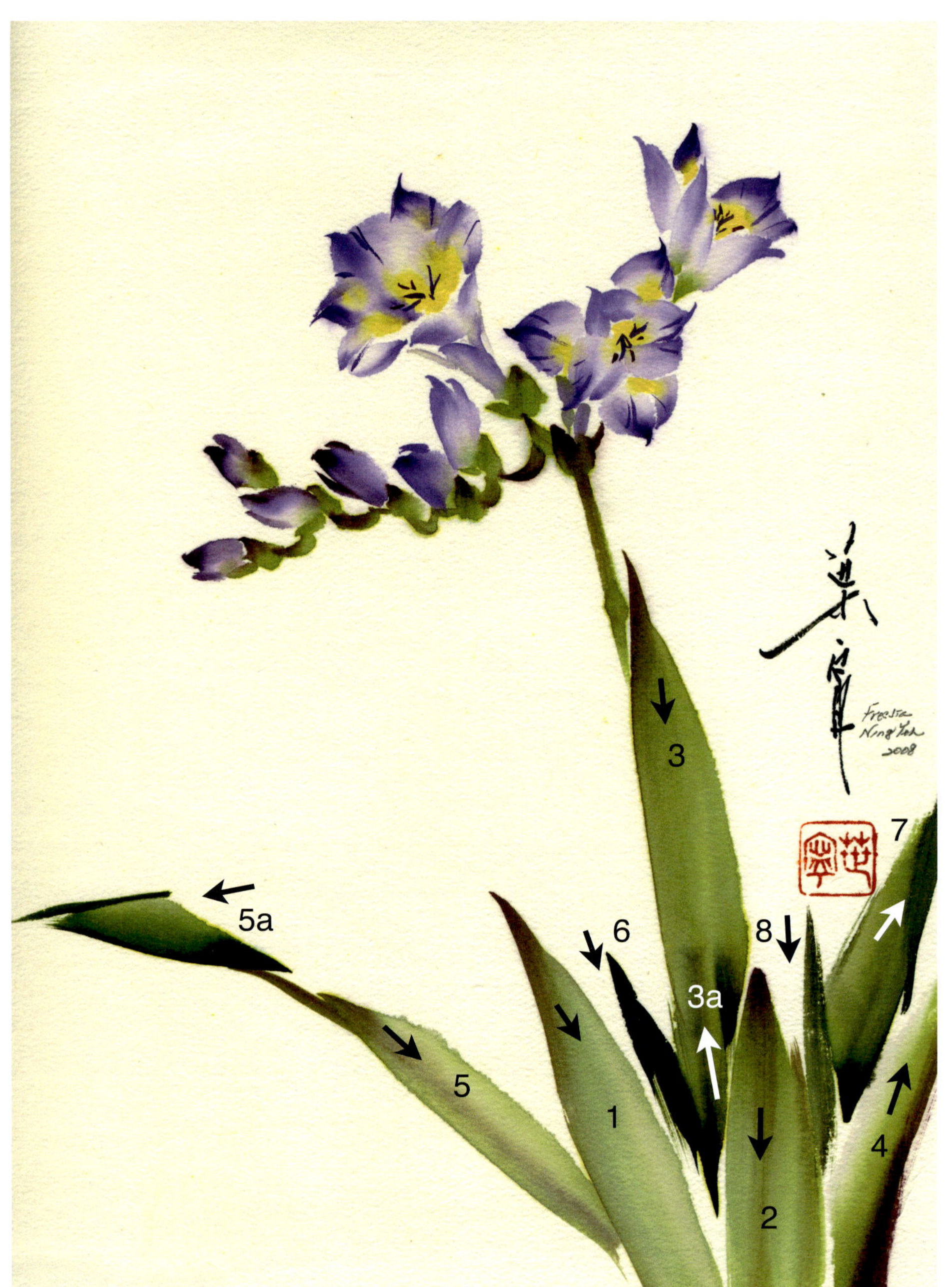

Flowers

Flower Facing Front (A)

ℒ Flow

❖ White + Light Purple

Work three petals from outside in to form a triangle (a). Leave the center open.

❖ Light Purple + Purple

Do three petals from outside in to form another triangle (b).

❖ Yellow

Add yellow to the center of the inside triangle and to the middle of each petal on the outside triangle.

❖ Light Green + Dark Red

Do a base (calyx) below the flower (c). This base will be the grand central station for all the flowers.

Add a stalk to bring the calyx into the tall leaf (d).

❖ White + Light Purple + Light Green

Work a tube to bring the flower into the base (e).

Flower Going Left (B)

❖ White + Light Purple

Do a foreshortened petal (f). Work a petal on each side to form a "U" shape. Add a fuller top petal.

❖ Light Purple + Purple

Do petals on both side of the top petal and add their roots.

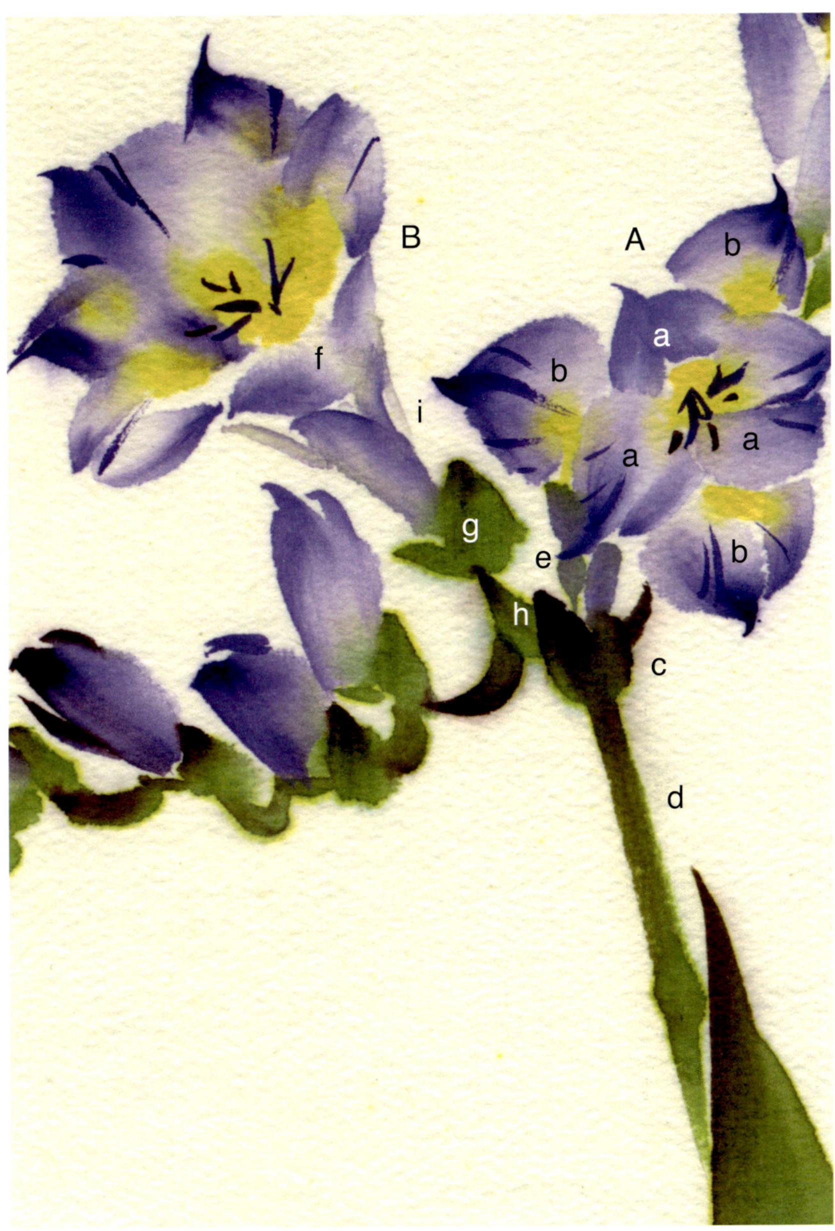


❖ Yellow

Add yellow to seal the flower center and the middle area of each top petal.

❖ Light Green + Dark Red

Do a set of calyx dots below the flower (g). Lead the calyx into the base of the first flower with a stem (h).

❖ White + Light Purple

Work a tube below the middle of the flower to connect it into the calyx (i).

❖ Light Green

Add a touch of light green to the root of the tube.

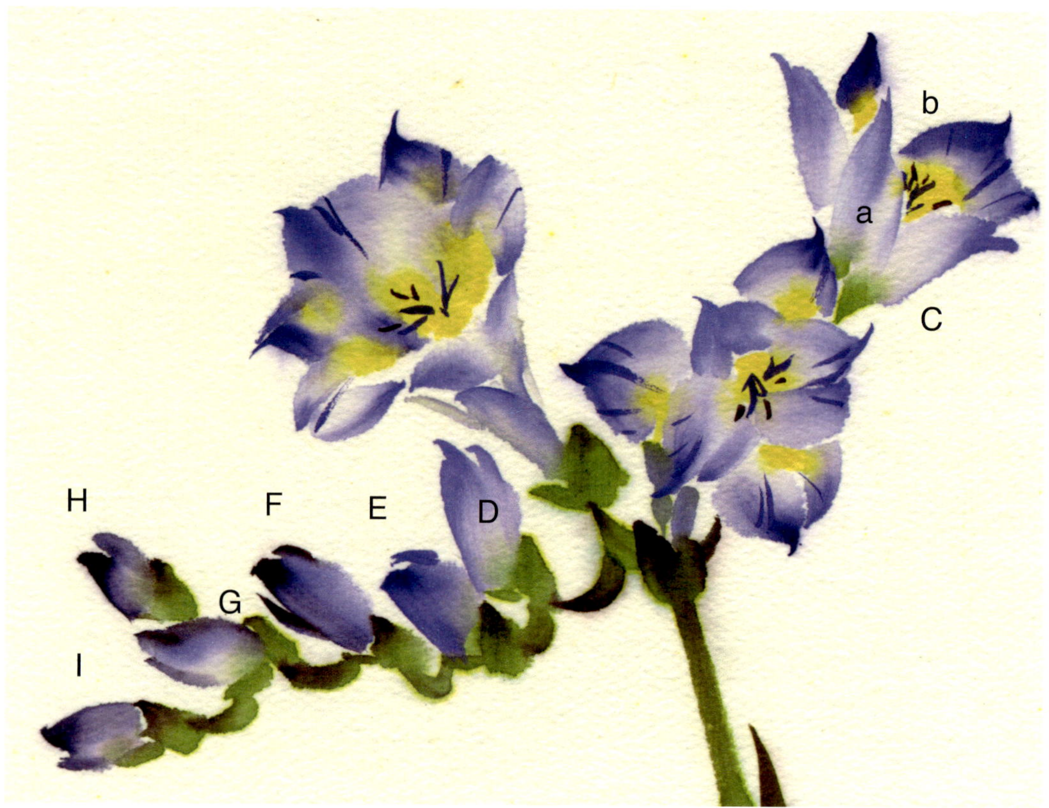


Profile Flower (C)

❖ White + Light Purple
Work three petals showing their backsides (a). Start with the center one and add the side ones.

❖ Light Green
Add roots of the petals from the base up.

❖ Light Purple + Purple
Do three petals showing their topside (b).

❖ Yellow
Add yellow to the center area of the flower.

❖ Light Green + Dark Red
Lead a stem into the base.

❖ White + Light Purple
Work a bud with two strokes (D).

❖ Light Purple + Purple
Add more buds to the left with darker colors (E, F).

❖ Purple + Dark Red
Continue moving left with smaller buds. Freesia loves to line up her buds. We want to inject some variations (G, H, I).

❖ Light Green + Dark Red
Add calyx dots below each bud. Connect the root of each calyx—one onto the next with a curved stem. Now they are all together.

❖ Light Green
Add a touch of green to the root of the bud, if so desired.

♌ Happy Dot

❖ White + Light Purple + Purple
Work some veins on the petals.

❖ Purple
Do the lady in the center of the flower with five arms. Add a stem below if needed.

❖ Dark Red
Show three gentlemen dots next to the lady.

8044

# Fuchsia

Dau
Dǎo: Upside down

Jin
Jīn: Gold

Jung
Zhōng: Clock

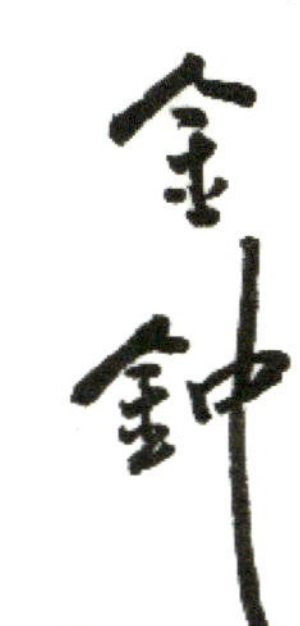

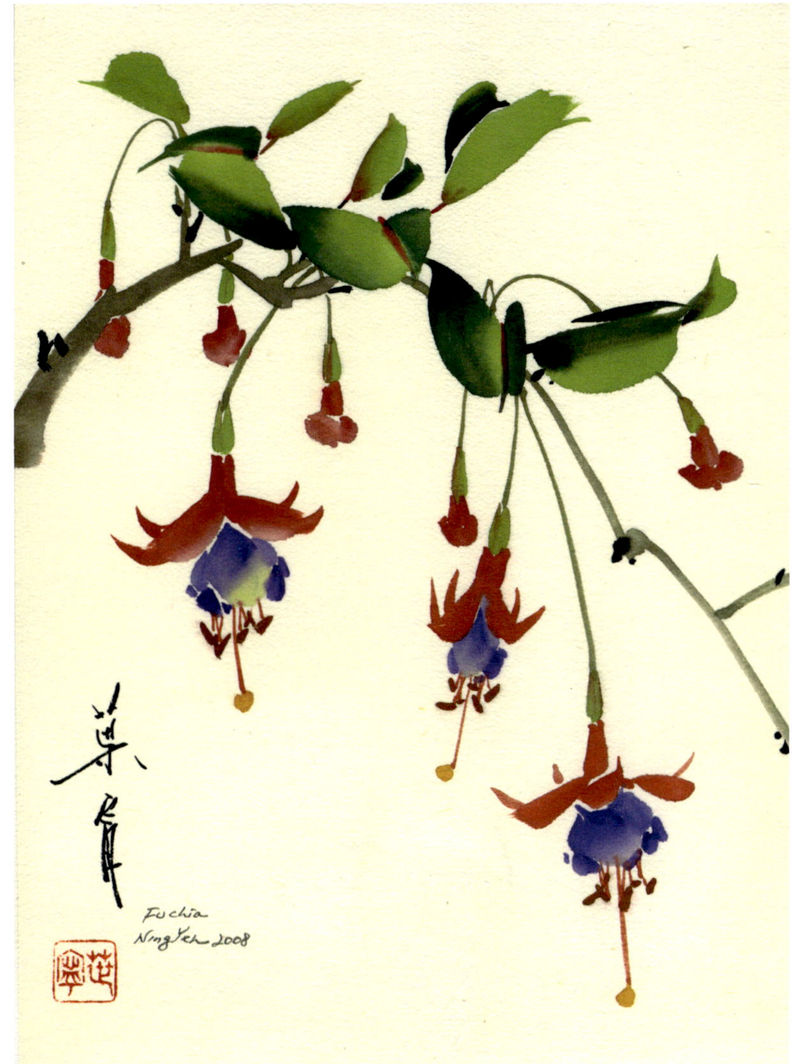

To me, fuchsia is a ballerina with long legs and a ruffled tutu.

My buddies and I used to row boats during our summer vacations on Taichung Lake. There was this wooden bridge. Whenever a girl was about to walk across the bridge, we would race our boat under it.

Now, I hang a basket of fuchsia. No sweat.

**MATERIALS**

Paper: Double Shuen

ᔕ Brushes
Large Orchid Bamboo, Flow, Fine Mountain Horse

❖ Colors
*Chinese*
Yellow
*Da Vinci*
White
*Schmincke*
Cadmium Red Deep
*Winsor & Newton*
Indigo, Alizarin Crimson, Winsor Violet, Ultramarine Violet
*OAS*
Best Bottle Ink

**PREPARATION OF COLORS**

Yellow: thick liquid + White
White: diluted
Red: Cadmium Red Deep
Crimson (Dark Red): Alizarin Crimson + Red
Light Purple: Ultramarine Violet
Purple: Winsor Violet + Ultramarine Violet
Light Green: Yellow + Indigo
Dark Green: Yellow + Indigo
Brown: Light Green + Red
Ink

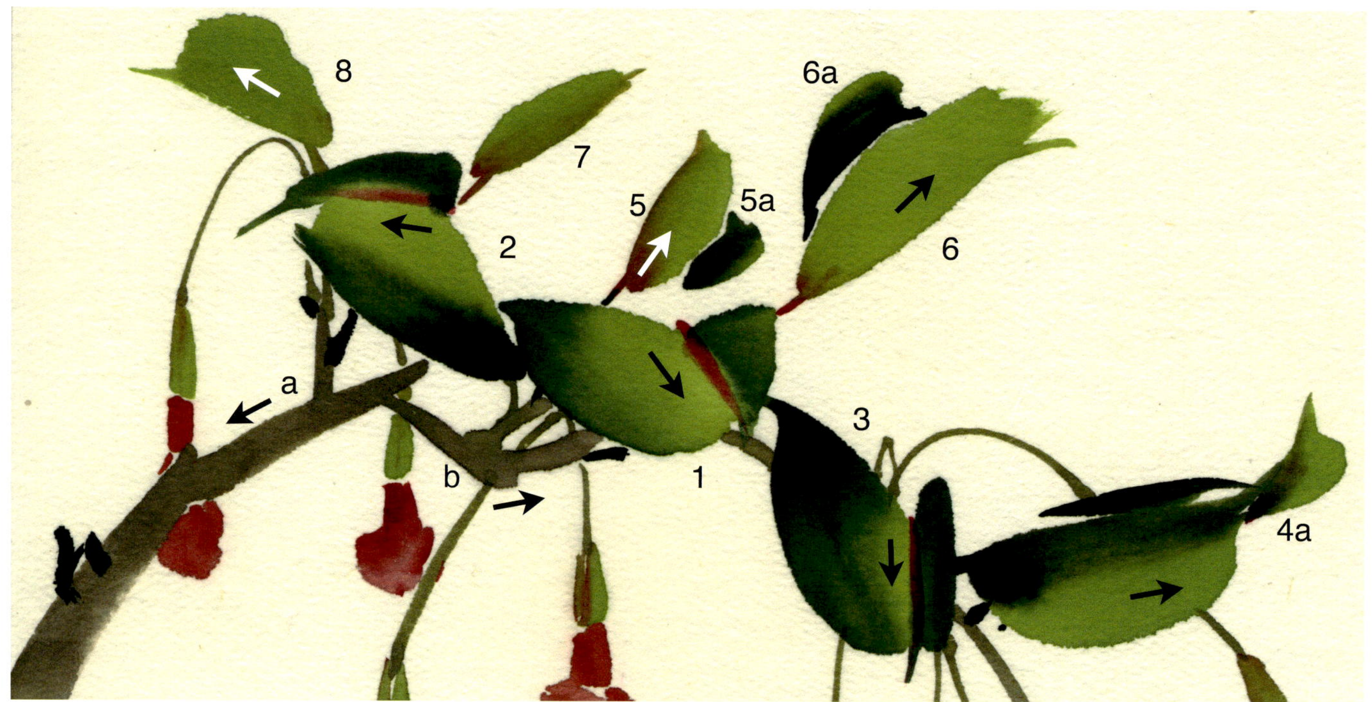


**STEPS**

Leaves
ᔓ Large Orchid Bamboo
❖ Light Green + Dark Green
Do some heart-shaped drooping leaves.
Show a leaf going to the right (1).
Work one side fuller. Move half way over to the right to do the second stroke.

❖ Dark Green + Ink
Reverse the brush. Work a leaf going left (2).
Show one more leaf on the right (3).
Work a profile leaf showing one side. Lead the tip to the right (4).

❖ Light Green + Crimson
Work pairs of profile leaves above showing their undersides (5, 6, 7, 8). Add the underside of the profile leaf going to the right (4a).

❖ Dark Green + Ink
Work the topside of the profile leaves (5a, 6a).

Branches
❖ Brown
Do a "Y" and extend the main branch down (a). Widen the strokes as they moves down. Lead branches to the right (b). Thread through the leaves and move down to the right.

ᔓ Flow
❖ Brown + Ink
Add twigs and dots.

Veins
ᔓ Fine Mountain Horse
❖ Crimson
Do center veins on the full leaves.

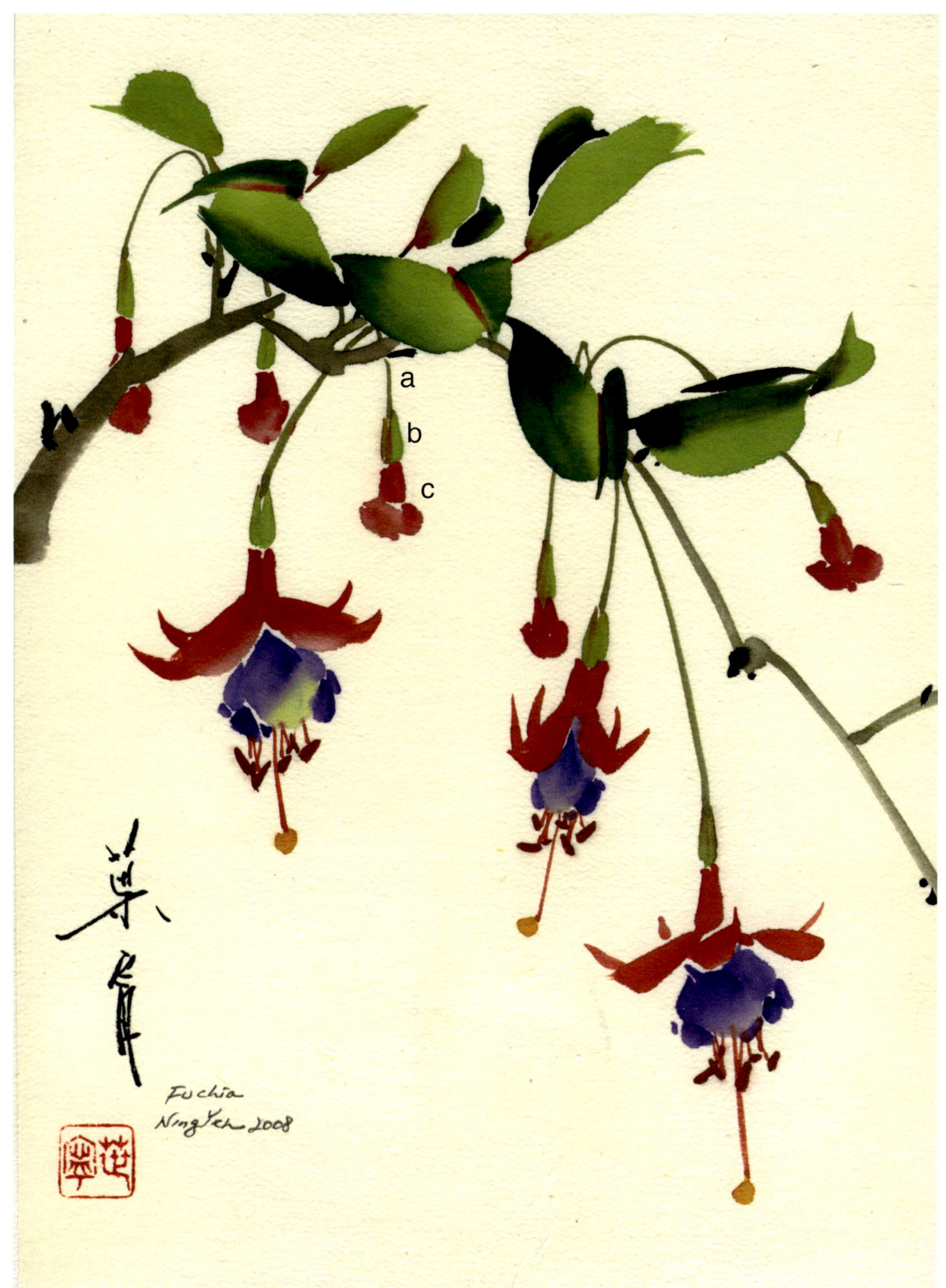


Stems

❖ Brown

Run loops of stems to hold the flowers. Do the main cluster on the right. Work a guest group on the left (a).

Calyxes

♌ Flow

❖ Light Green + Crimson

Add calyxes at the end of the stems, each with two wrapping strokes (b).

Buds

❖ White + Yellow + Red + Crimson

Work each bud with two strokes from the calyx to show a tube. Do a round ball below the tube. Add a tip (c).

These buds are so cute. We tend to forget the flowers. Do try to save some calyxes. Do not add buds to all of them.

Flowers

Wings

Each flower has four wings below the tube. We like to show them with different attitudes. Show a tube with strokes moving downward from the calyx. Swing strokes outward and add wing tips flipping upward (a).

Skirts

❖ White + Yellow + Light Purple

Do the front of the skirt below the wings. Slide a stroke diagonally downward from the middle of the flower. Add more strokes if needed (b).

❖ Light Purple + Purple

Create ruffles with dots (c). Each skirt has multiple layers.

ᔓ Fine Mountain Horse

❖ Crimson

Show stamens (d). They come out from the tube above. Keep them bundled in the middle of the skirt. Show an extra long center pistil in line with the tube.

ᔓ Flow

❖ Crimson + Brown

Add happy pollen dots at the tips of the stamens (e).

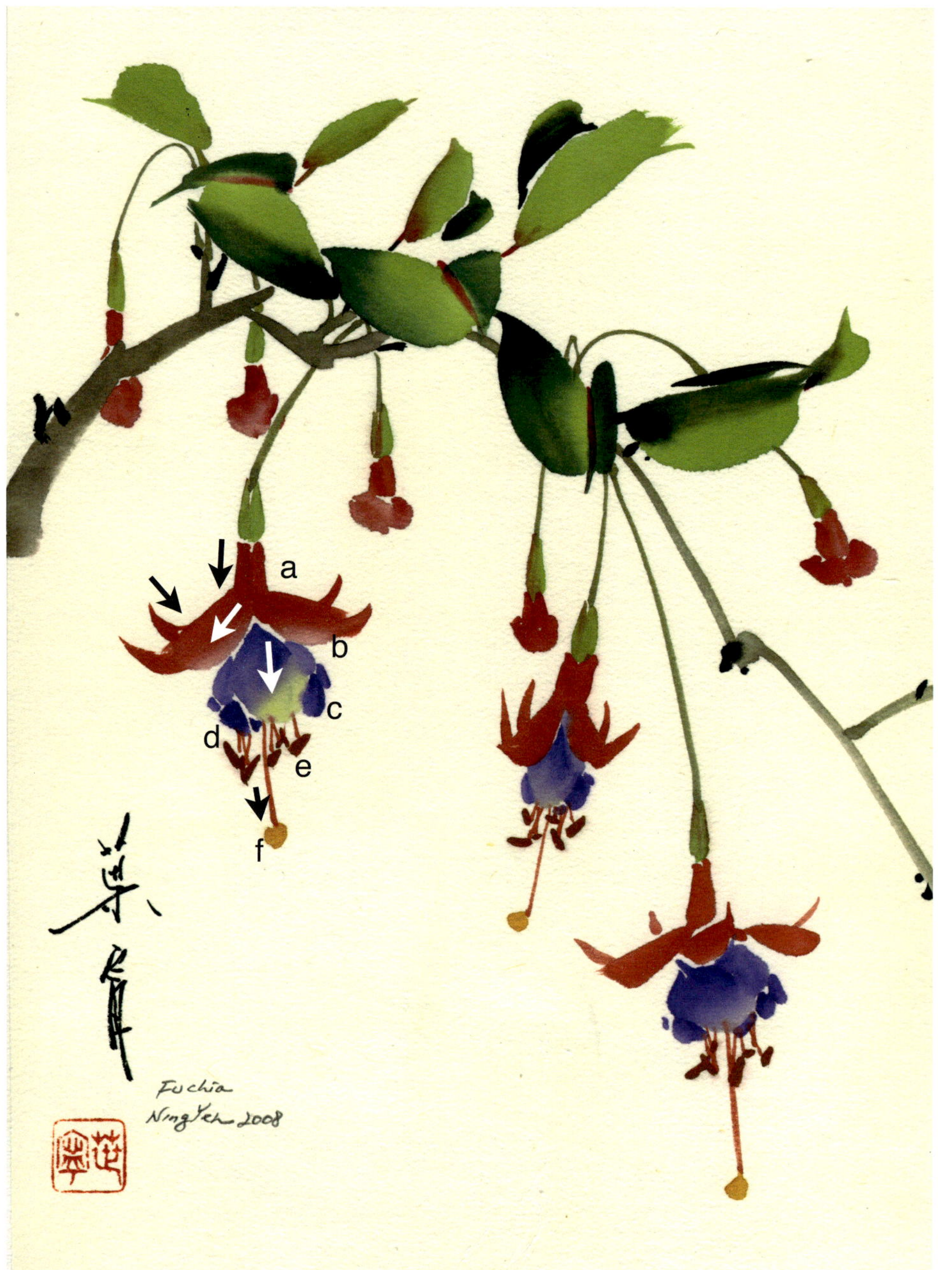


❖ Yellow + Red

Do a round dot in gold on the long pistil to show the lady for each flower (f).

ᔓ Large Orchid Bamboo

❖ Light Green + Crimson

Add a set of profile leaves.

We have a family of cheerful dancers.

8045

# Geranium

Tian Ju
Tiān Zhú: India
(ancient name)

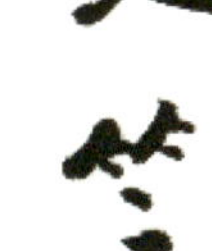

Kuei
Kuí: Type of flower

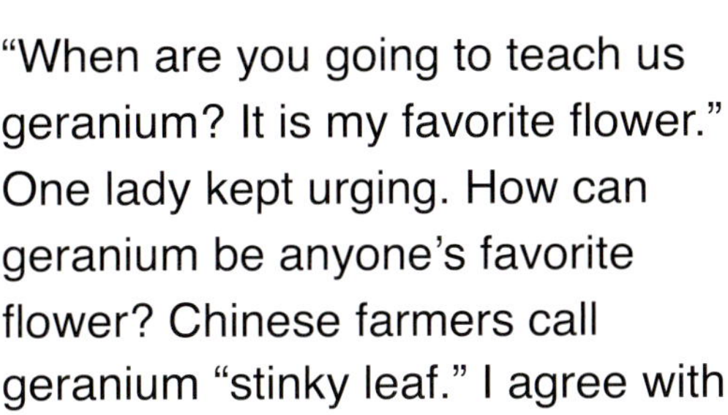

"When are you going to teach us geranium? It is my favorite flower." One lady kept urging. How can geranium be anyone's favorite flower? Chinese farmers call geranium "stinky leaf." I agree with the farmers.

I studied the flower closely for a month and taught the lady's class. I am now addicted to the smell of geranium leaf. I did win the National Teaching Excellence Award three times. I feel I deserve another one.

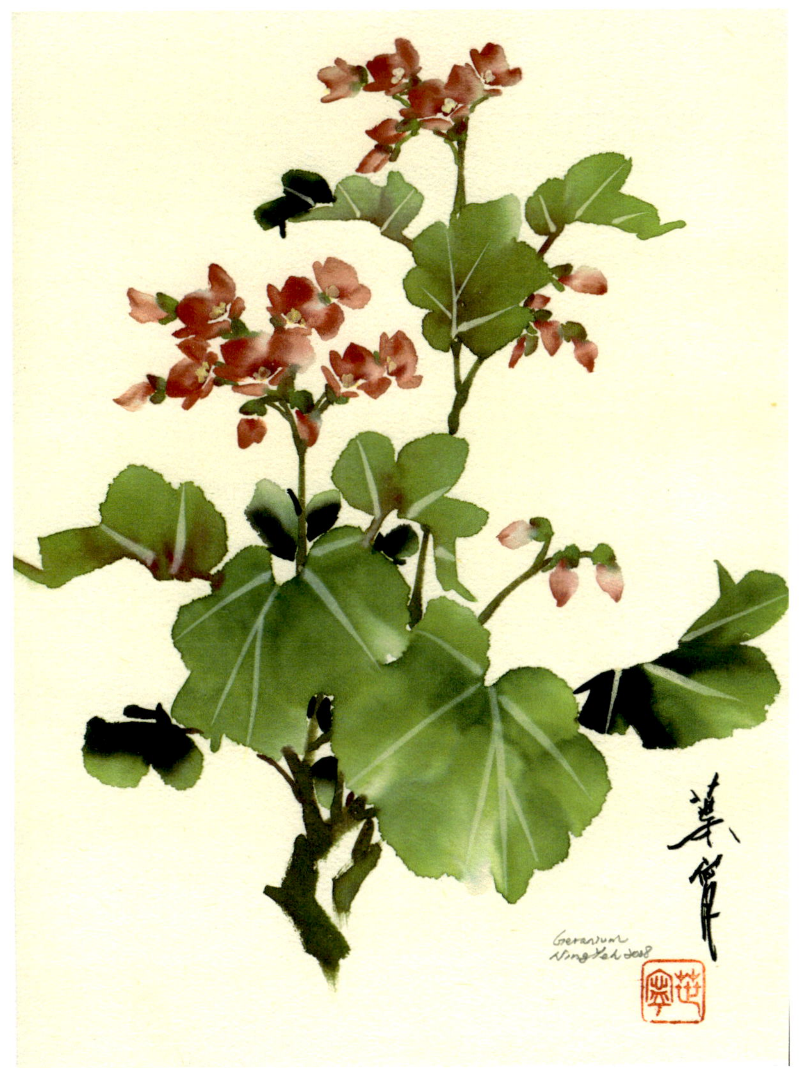

**MATERIALS**

Paper: Double Shuen

♌ Brushes
Flow, Large Flow, Small Mountain Horse

❖ Colors
*Chinese*
Yellow
*Da Vinci*
White
*Schmincke*
Cadmium Red Deep
*Winsor & Newton*
Indigo, Alizarin Crimson, Perylene Violet
*OAS*
Best Bottle Ink

**PREPARATION OF COLORS**

Yellow: thick liquid
White: diluted
Light Green: Yellow + Indigo
Dark Green: Yellow + Indigo
Red: Cadmium Red Deep
Pink: White + Cadmium Red Deep
Crimson: Alizarin Crimson + Red
Dark Red: Perylene Violet + Red
White Yellow: pasty White + thick Yellow
Brown: Light Green + Dark Red
Ink

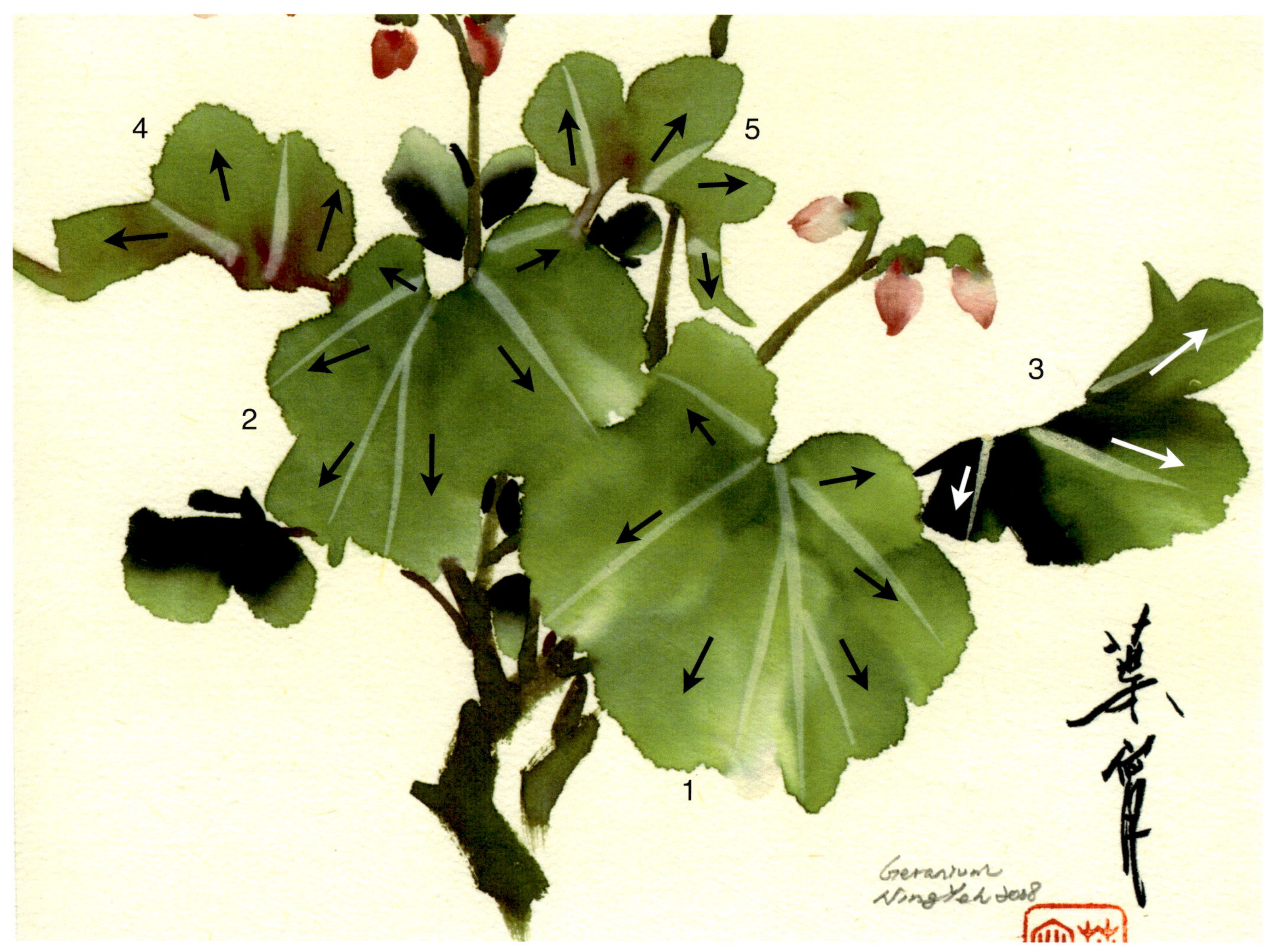


**STEPS**

Leaves

♌ Large Flow

❖ Light Green + Dark Green

Geranium has heart-shaped leaves with ruffled edges. Do a leaf going to the right (1). Work strokes from the center of the heart outward. Do the left side first then do the right side smaller. Balance the first leaf with another leaf a little higher and going to the left (2).

❖ Dark Green + Ink

Do a profile leaf going to the right showing its topside (3).

❖ Light Green + Dark Red

Work a pair of profile leaves showing their undersides (4, 5).

Branches

♌ Flow

❖ Brown

Do main branches. Show a "V" below the leaves. Move down with a trunk. Connect the leaves into the branches with twigs and stems.

Veins

♌ Small Mountain Horse

❖ White Yellow

Add veins to the leaves. Do each full leaf with a center vein, alternating the side ones. Radiate the veins from the center out.

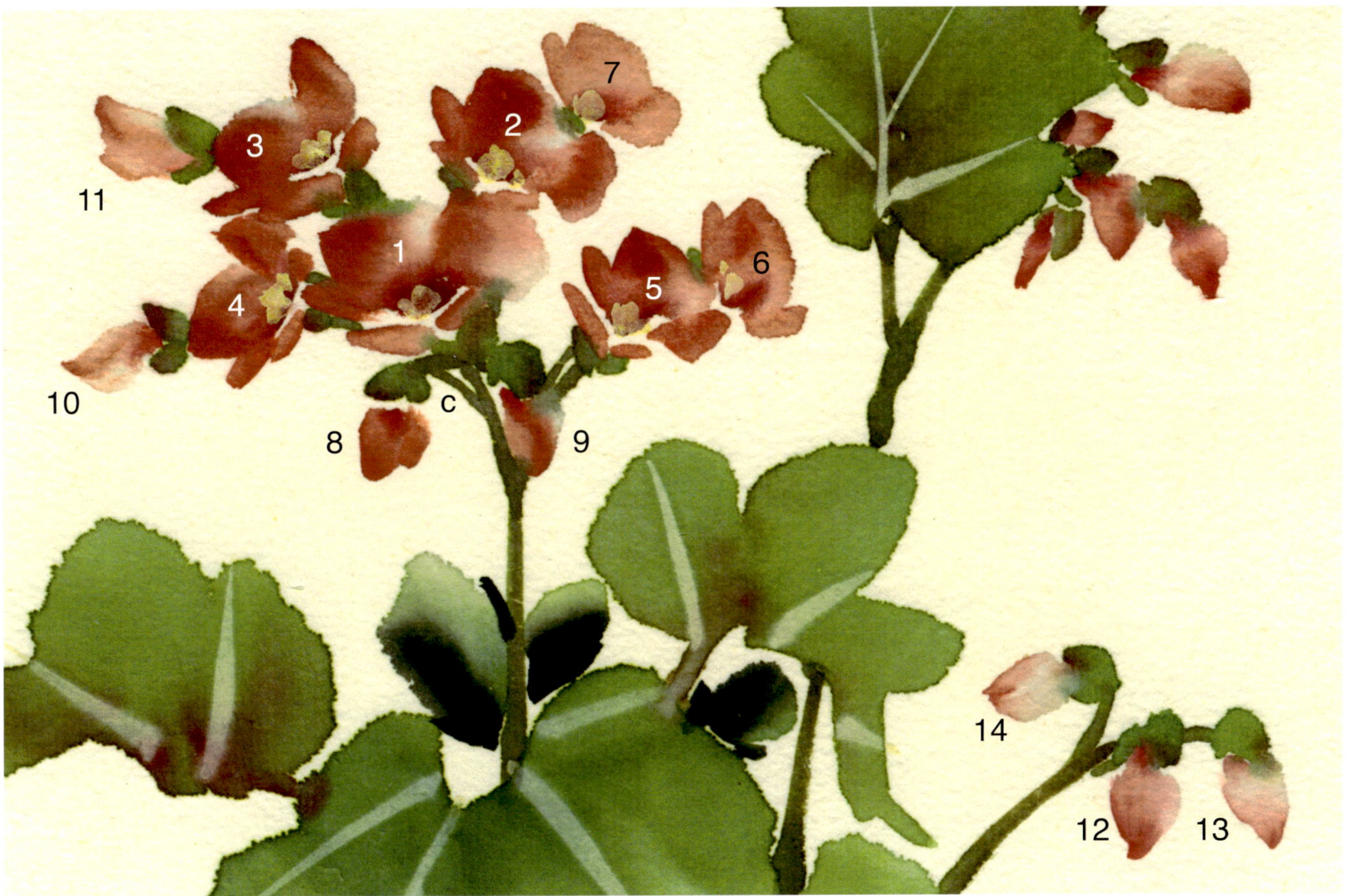


Flowers

♌ Flow

❖ Pink + Red + Crimson

Do full flowers with five petals each. Make the top center one fuller. Add the side ones from outside in. Front petals are shaped like lower lips. Work them from side to side. Leave the center area open. Cluster the flowers so their roots can join together. Keep the flower formation tight with petals touching one another (1-7).

❖ Crimson + Dark Red

Seal the center of each flower.

❖ Light Green + Dark Red

Do calyx dots below the flowers. Add sets of calyx dots for buds (c).

❖ White + Pink + Red

Work buds by moving strokes from the tip toward the calyx (8-11).

❖ Crimson

Add the roots of the buds moving strokes from the calyx outward.

❖ Brown (Light Green + Dark Red)

Work a main stalk in the middle of the flower cluster below the buds. Add stems to lead flowers and buds onto the stalk.

❖ Light Green + Dark Red

Do calyx dots for a guest group of buds (12-14).

❖ White + Pink + Red

Work buds from their tips.

❖ Red

Add the roots of the buds.

❖ Brown

Do a stalk to bring the guest buds into the branches. Add stems to connect to the buds.

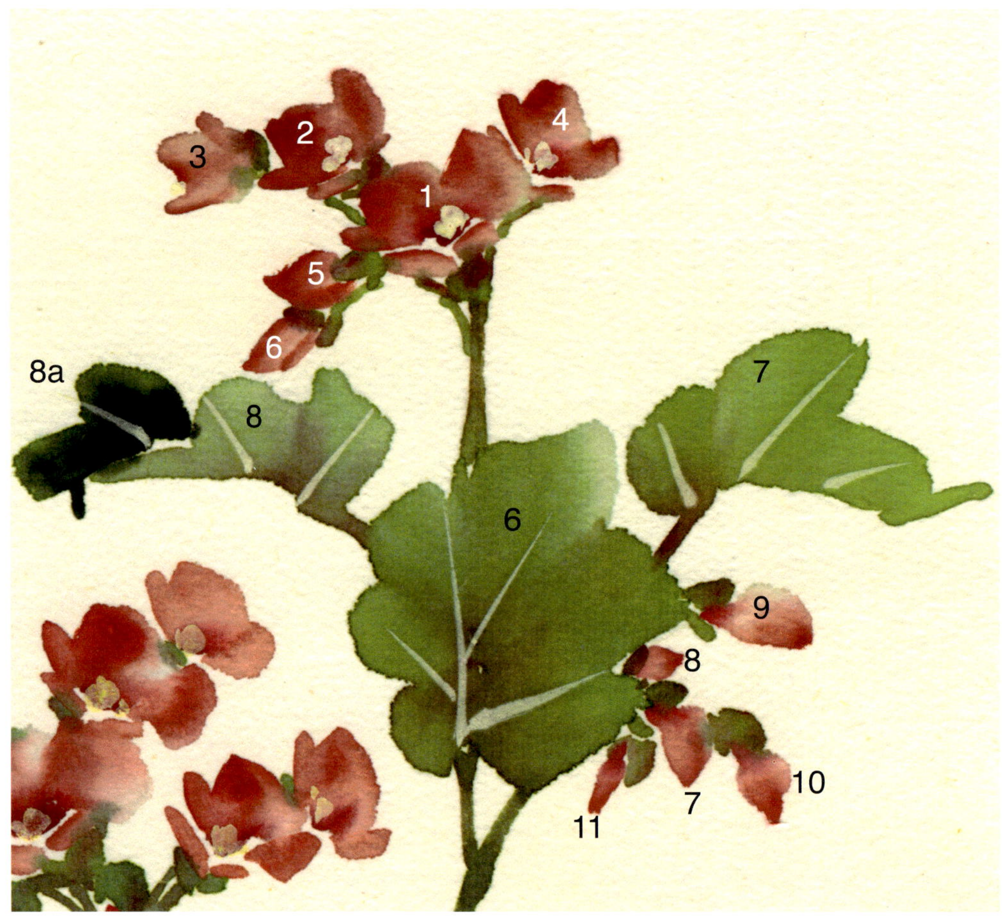


More Leaves

♌ Large Flow

❖ Light Green + Dark Red

Work a guest group of leaves on top. Do a center leaf (6) showing its underside (backside). Add a pair of folding leaves also showing their undersides (7, 8).

❖ Dark Green + Ink

Show the topside of a profile leaf (8a).

♌ Flow

❖ Dark Green + Dark Red

Connect the leaves with stems. Work a stalk downward onto branches below.

♌ Small Mountain Horse

❖ White Yellow

Add veins to the leaves.

More Flowers

❖ Pink + Red + Crimson

Do a cluster of flowers on top (1-4).

❖ Crimson + Dark Red

Seal the center of the flowers.

❖ Light Green + Dark Red

Work calyx dots below the flowers.

❖ White + Pink + Red

Add buds (5, 6).

❖ Light Green + Dark Red

Do a stalk below the center of the flower group. Lead the flowers into the stalk with stems. Add more calyx dots.

❖ White + Pink + Red

Work more buds (7-11).

❖ Crimson + Dark Red

Finish the roots of the buds.

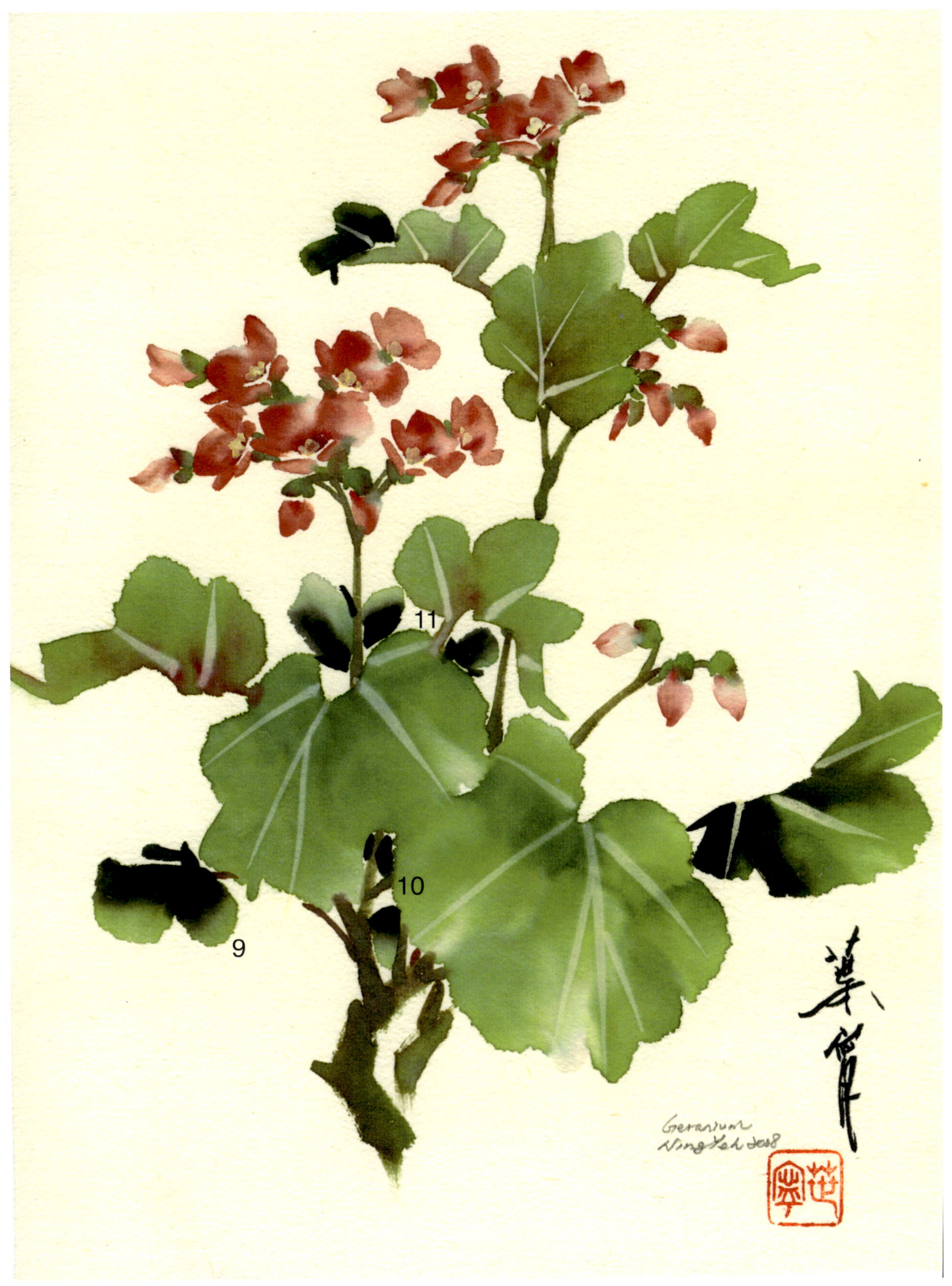


❖ Light green + Dark Green + Ink
Work a few shadow leaves (9-11).

❖ Light Green + Dark Red
Add stems to connect the leaves.

❖ White Yellow
Do up to three bright dots at the center of each flower.

# 8046
# Ginger Lily

Jiang
Jiāng: Ginger

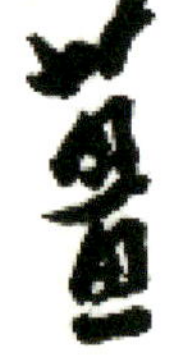

Lan
Lán: Orchid

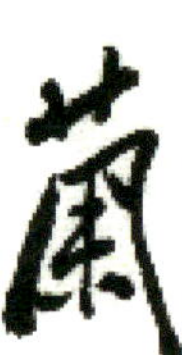

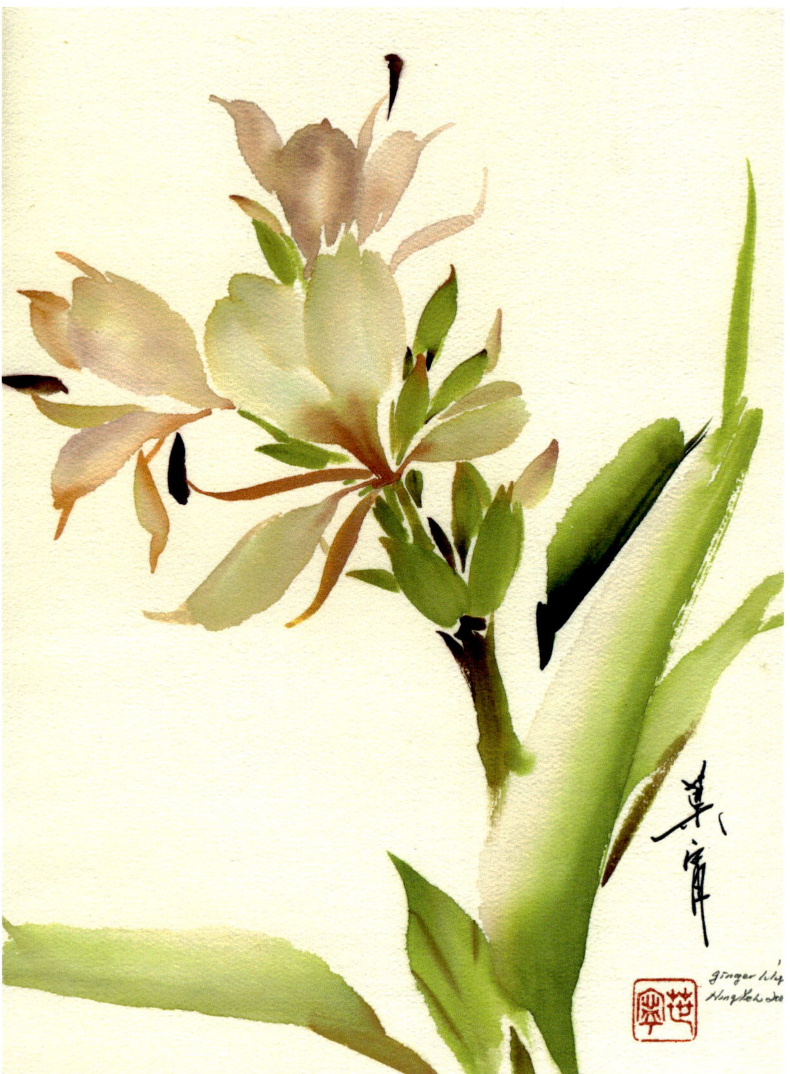

Behind the little shack en route to Kailua in Oahu, I dropped some melon juice from my shaved ice on the white ginger lily.

To paint white flowers on white paper really is not a problem. White flowers pick up colors around them. A little injection of other colors into the white is all we need.

I love the flower. Simple, yet it has all the fun things.

**MATERIALS**

Paper: Double Shuen

ℓ Brushes
Flow, Large Flow

❖ Colors
*Chinese*
Yellow, Vermillion
*Da Vinci*
White
*Schmincke*
Cadmium Red Deep
*Winsor & Newton*
Indigo, Perylene Violet
*OAS*
Best Bottle Ink

**PREPARATION OF COLOR**

Yellow: thick liquid
Vermillion: thick
White: diluted
Light Green: Yellow + Indigo
Dark Green: Yellow + Indigo
Red: Cadmium Red Deep
Pink: Red + pasty White
Dark Red: Perylene Violet + Red
Cream: White + Light Green + Yellow + Vermillion + Pink
Ink

**STEPS**

Flowers
Host Flower (A)
ℓ Large Flow
❖ White + Cream
Work two petals from top down like butterfly wings. Show the tip and work two strokes (1, 2).

ℓ Flow
❖ Cream + Vermillion + Pink
Do the base of the petals from bottom up (b).

❖ White + Cream + Vermillion + Pink
Work petals reaching to the sides. Do the right side smaller (3). Extend the left side petal longer. Add the tip (4).

❖ Cream + Vermillion + Pink
Do a stamen (s).

❖ Yellow
Add an extra tongue petal (t). I do really know what to call this one.

❖ Vermillion + Dark Red
Land an impressive pollen dot (p). Cool.

Profile Flower (B)
❖ White + Cream + Vermillion + Pink
Work a petal from the top down (1).

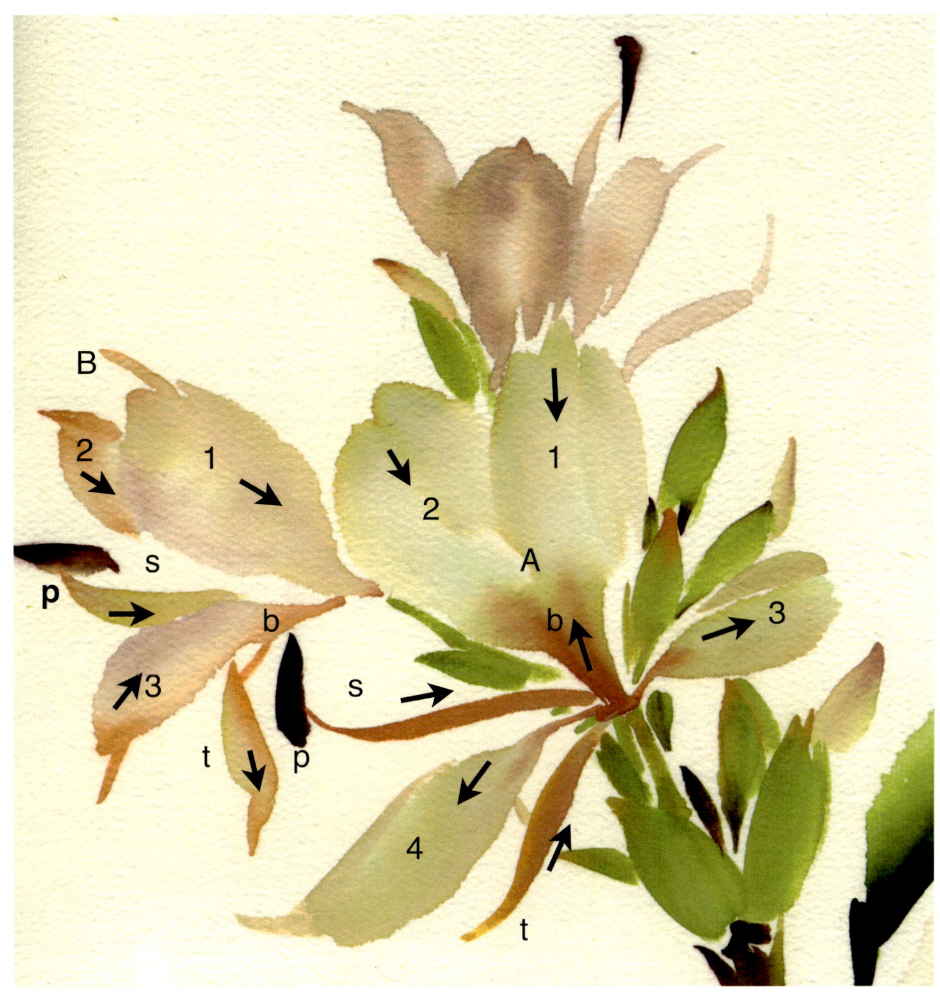


❖ Pink
Add the base of the petal.

❖ Vermillion + Pink
Show the other side of the pair of wings (2). Work a petal below the wings from tip inward (3).

❖ Pink
Add the root of the petal.

❖ Vermillion + Pink
Do a stroke to show the stamen (s). Add a tongue below (t).

❖ Dark Red
Lay a bossy pollen dot (p).

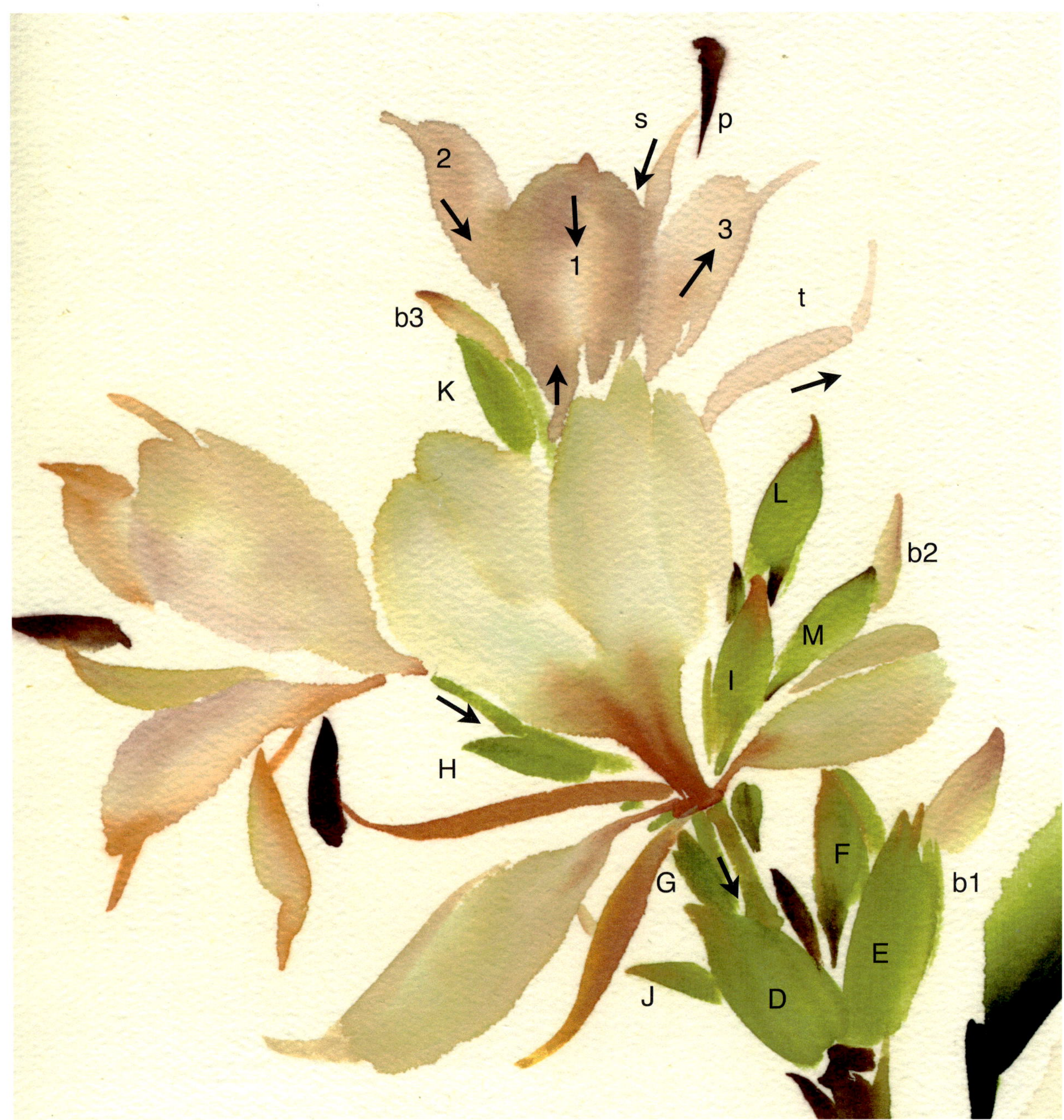


Top Flower (C)

❖ White + Cream + Vermillion + Pink

Do a center petal (1). Work petals on both sides (2, 3). Show skinnier stamen (s) and tongue (t) strokes.

❖ Vermillion + Dark Red

Add a pollen dot (p).

Calyx Dots and Buds

❖ Cream + Light Green + Vermillion + Pink

Show a cluster of larger calyx dots below the flowers (D, E, F). Add smaller ones a little higher (G-M).

❖ Light Green + Vermillion

Work stems to bring the flowers into the calyx.

❖ Dark Green + Dark Red

Add roots for the calyx dots.

❖ Cream + Vermillion + Pink

Do a few buds peeking out of the calyx dots (b1-b3)

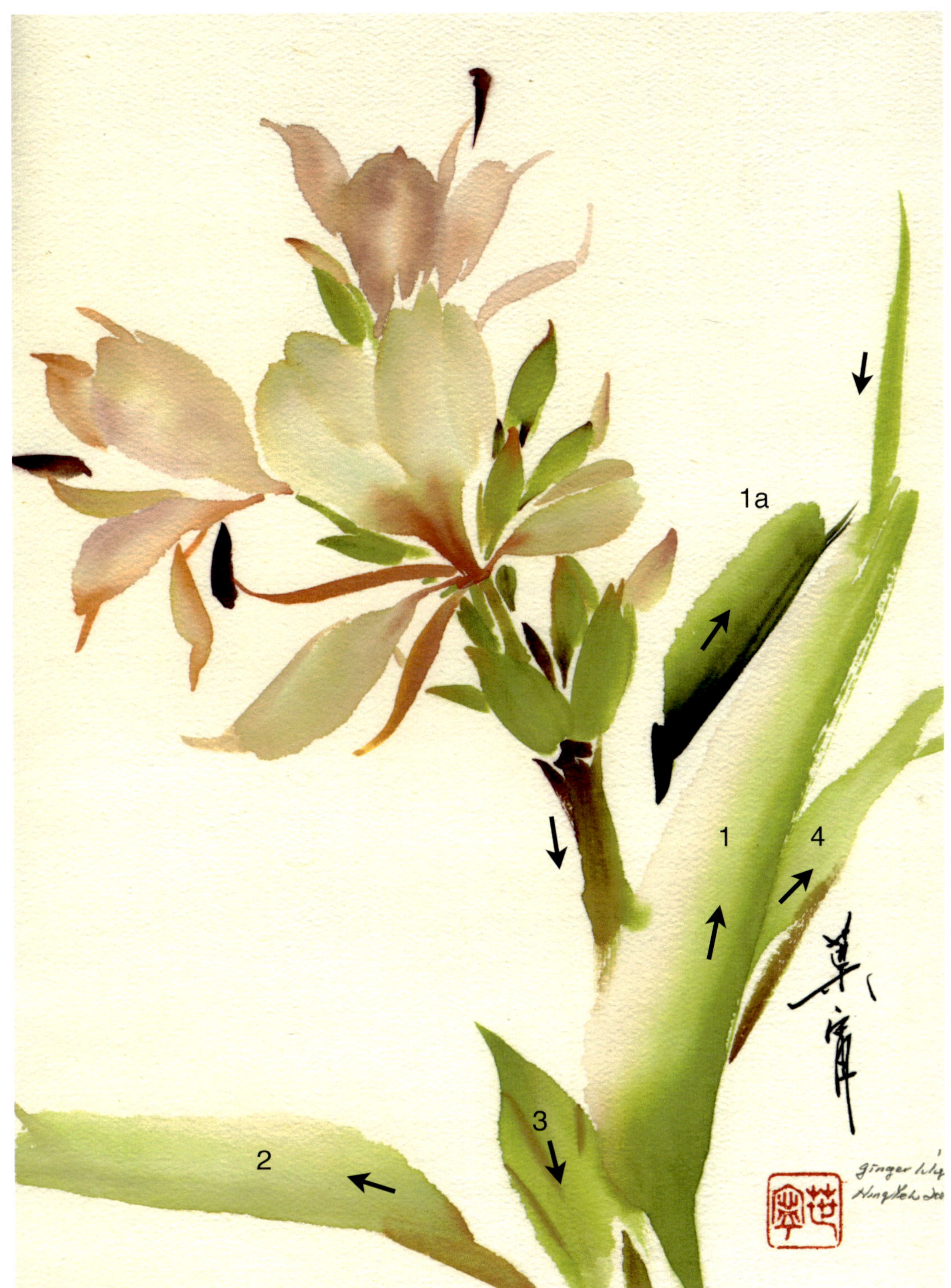


Leaves and Stalk
♌ Large Flow
❖ Cream + Light Green
Do one leaf (1) showing its backside. Move the stroke upward. Add the tip. Wow.

❖ Dark Green + Ink
Show the topside of the leaf (1a).

❖ Cream + Light Green + Vermillion
Work one leaf sideways to the left (2).

❖ Light Green
Add a couple of smaller leaves (3, 4).

♌ Flow
❖ Light Green + Dark Red
Work a stalk to bring the flower clusters into the leaves. Add a few vein lines on the leaves.

8047

# Gladiolus

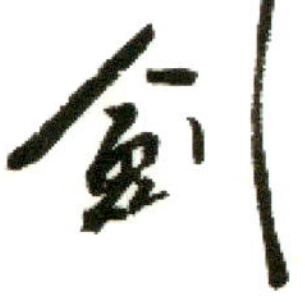

Jian
Jiàn: Sword

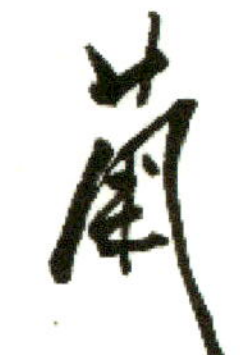

Lan
Lán: Orchid

Gladiolus is jiànlán, or sword orchid, in Chinese.

Flower painting is a combination of velvety petals and bold leaves or branches. In between grace and strength, there is that delightful sense of celebration—happy dots like children. People enjoy our painting because it is a joyful family portrait of harmony.

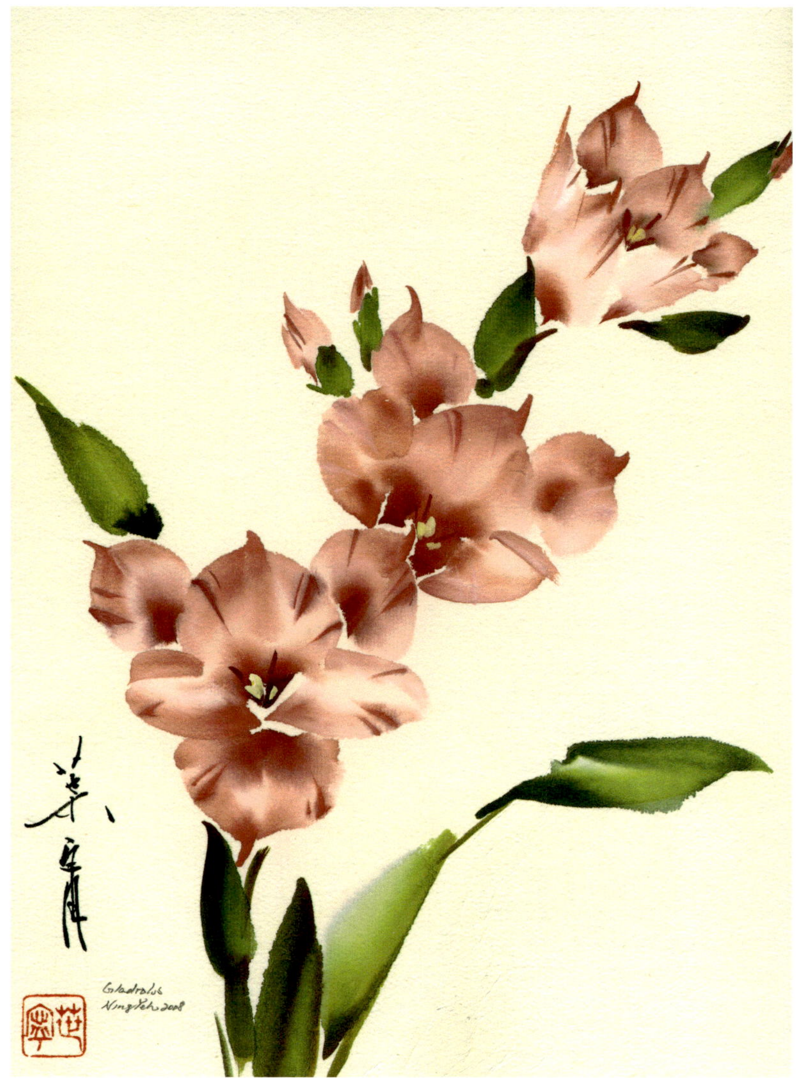

**MATERIALS**

Paper: Double Shuen

ℰ Brushes
Flow, Large Orchid Bamboo, Small Mountain Horse

❖ Colors
*Chinese*
Yellow
*Da Vinci*
White
*Schmincke*
Cadmium Red Deep
*Winsor & Newton*
Indigo, Permanent Magenta, Alizarin Crimson, Perylene Violet
*OAS*
Best Bottle Ink

**PREPARATION OF COLORS**

Yellow: thick liquid
White: diluted + a touch of Yellow
Red: Cadmium Red Deep
Magenta: Permanent Magenta + Red
Crimson: Alizarin Crimson + Red
Dark Red: Perylene Violet + Red
Light Green: Yellow + Indigo
Dark Green: Yellow + Indigo
Ink

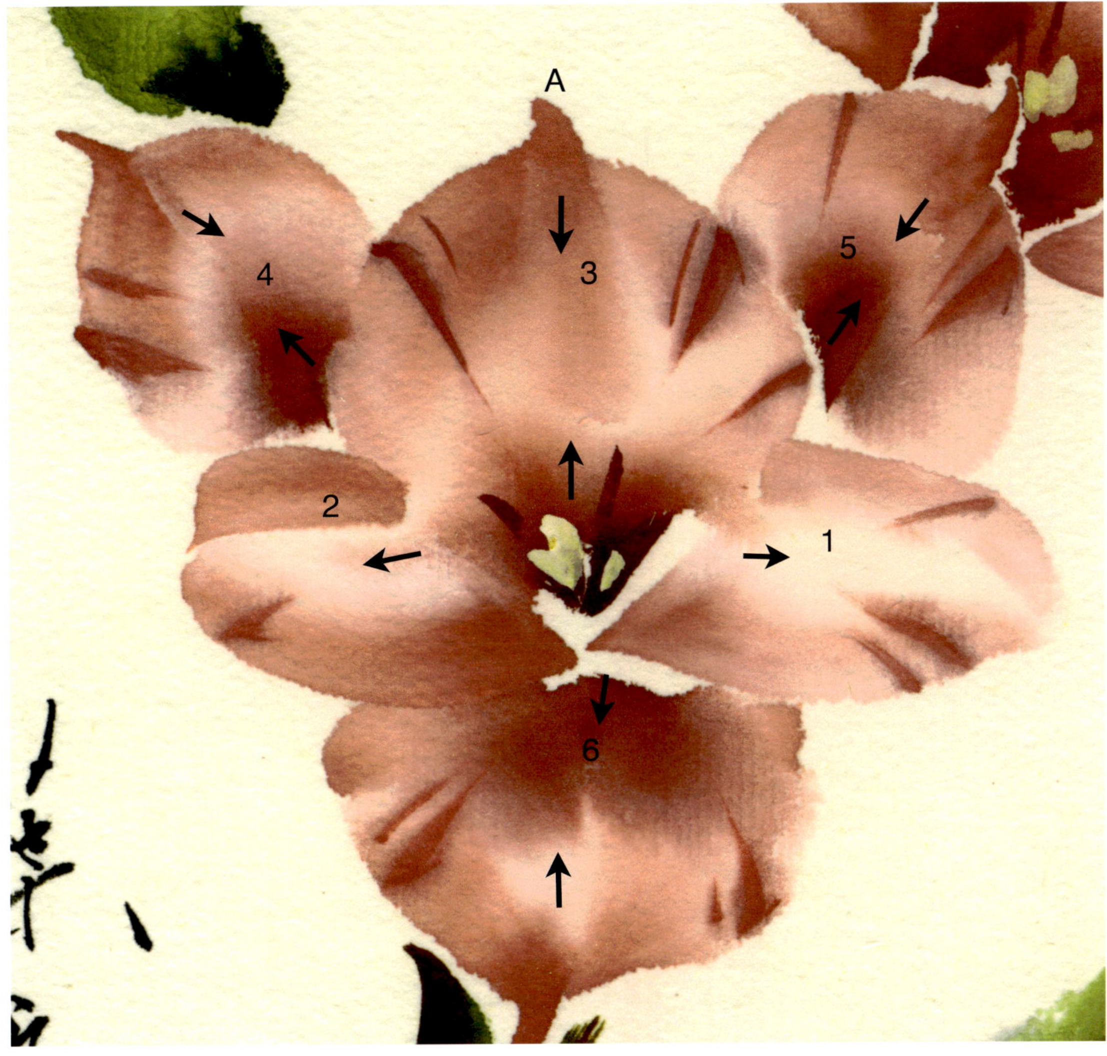


**STEPS**

Flowers

Base Flower (A)

ᔕ Flow

❖ White + Magenta

Each flower has two sets of triangles each formed by three petals. Work a set of petals reaching out on both sides (1, 2). Add a top petal with three strokes (left, middle, and right) moving from the top down (3). Add dots on both sides of the petal to show ruffles. Leave the center area of the flower open. This is the inside triangle.

Do three petals from outside in (4, 5, 6). Work each petal with two strokes. Add ruffle dots if needed. Leave the middle areas of the petals open. This is the outside triangle.

❖ Magenta + Crimson + Dark Red

Seal the center area of the flower and the middle areas of the outer petals with a lower the boom motion.

ᔕ Small Mountain Horse

❖ Magenta + Crimson + Dark Red

Work veins to show wrinkles on the petals. Do them from the outside edges moving inward. Press and lift. Show host and guest. Do two strokes together, one apart. Make them long and short, thick and thin, like fountains splashing out from the center.

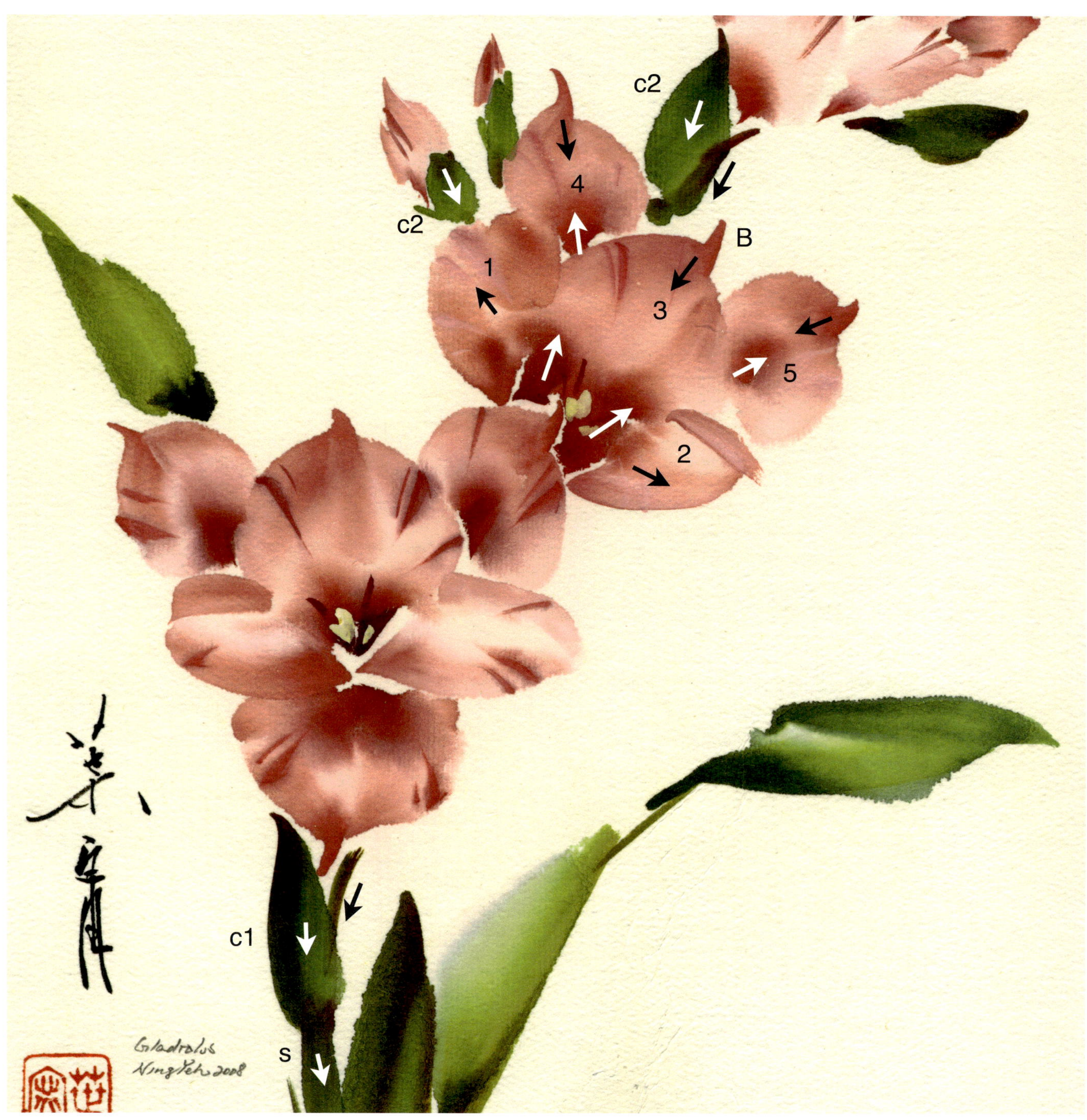


Middle Flower (B)

♌ Flow

❖ White + Magenta

Do three petals to form an inside triangle (1, 2, 3). Add a couple of petals to show the top of the outside triangle (4, 5).

❖ Magenta + Crimson + Dark Red

Seal the center area of the flower. Lower the boom from the base upward.

♌ Small Mountain Horse

❖ White + Magenta + Crimson + Dark Red

Add veins.

♌ Large Orchid Bamboo

❖ Light Green + Dark Red

Work a set of calyx dots (c1) below the base flower and extend a stem (s).

Do a couple more sets of calyx dots on top (c2).

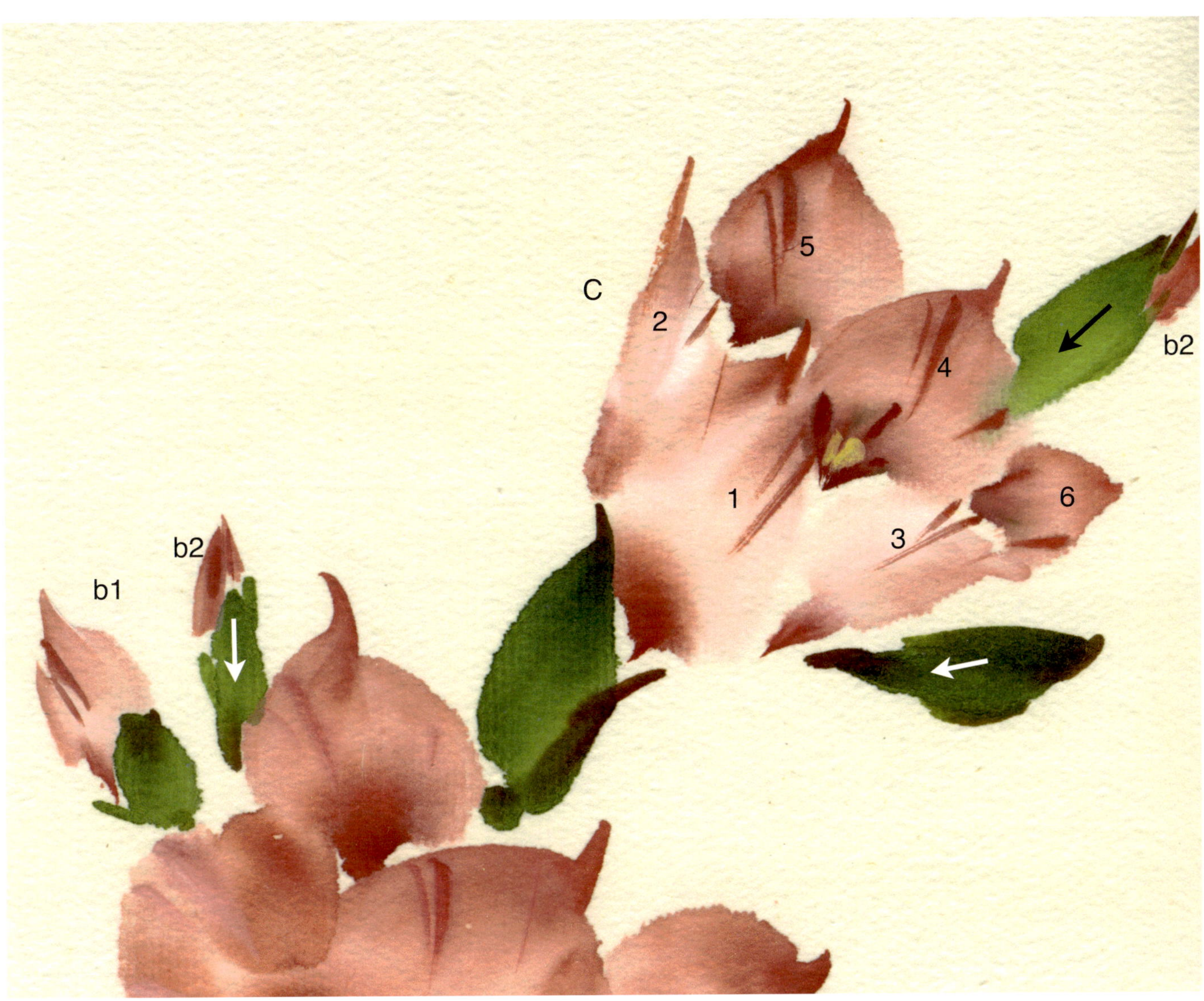


Profile Flower (C)
ᘐ Flow
❖ White + Magenta
Work a front layer of petals showing their backsides. Do a petal in the middle from the top downward (1).

❖ Magenta + Crimson
Add the root of the petal from the calyx upward.

❖ White + Magenta
Work petals on both sides (2, 3).

Show a bud (b1).

Add a layer of back petals from the top downward (4, 5, 6).

❖ Magenta + Crimson + Dark Red
Seal the center between the two petal layers. Lower the boom from the base upward.

ᘐ Large Orchid Bamboo
❖ Light Green + Dark Red
Work a few more calyx dots around the profile flower. Add stems.

ᘐ Flow
❖ White + Magenta
Show a couple of buds (b2).

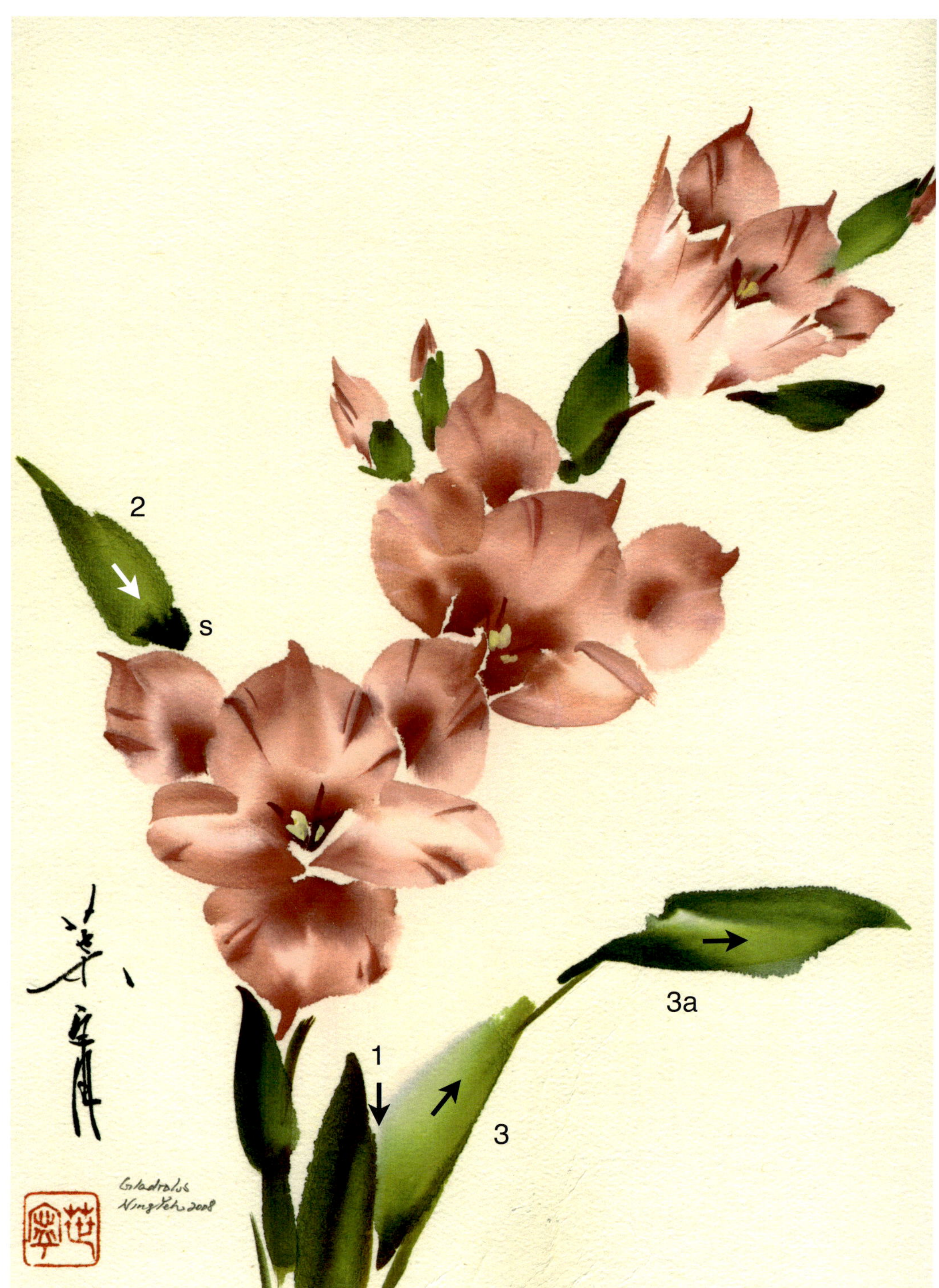


♌ Small Mountain Horse
❖ White + Magenta + Crimson + Dark Red
Add veins to the flower and buds.

♌ Flow
❖ Pasty White + Yellow
Work three impressive dots in the center of each flower to show the tip of the lady.

❖ Crimson + Dark Red
Do three skinny gentlemen in each flower center to keep the lady company.

♌ Large Orchid Bamboo
❖ Light Green + Dark Red
Add a few leaves (1, 2, 3).

❖ Light Green + Dark Green + Ink
Show the topside (3a) and add shadows to the leaves (s).

8048

# Gloxinia

Ian
Yán: Rock

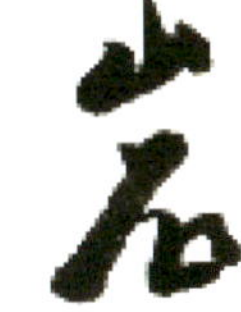


Tung
Tóng: Tree name

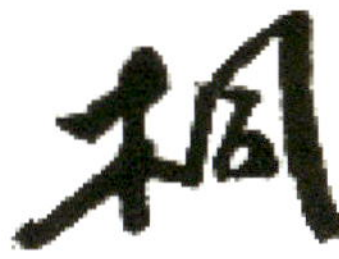


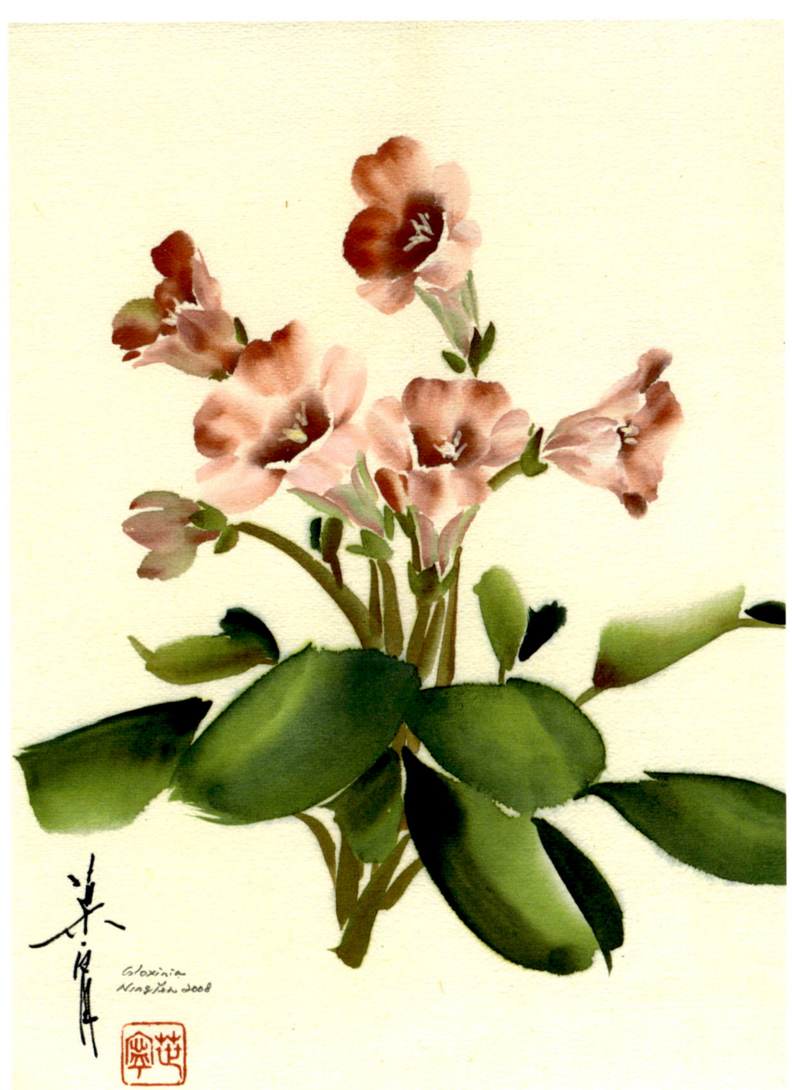

I know very little about the plant. I just love the showy velvety flowers and the spirited long ovate leaves. It is a wonderful subject.

As with everything else in America, there is a Gloxinia Society. In case further information is needed.

**MATERIALS**

Paper: Double Shuen

ꝭ Brushes
Large Orchid Bamboo, Flow, Large Flow, Happy Dot

❖ Colors
*Chinese*
Yellow
*Da Vinci*
White
*Schmincke*
Cadmium Red Deep
*Winsor & Newton*
Indigo, Perylene Violet
*OAS*
Best Bottle Ink

**PREPARATION OF COLORS**

Yellow: thick liquid
White: diluted + a touch of Yellow
Red: Cadmium Red Deep
Pink: White + Red
Dark Red: Perylene Violet + Red
Light Green: Yellow + Indigo
Dark Green: Yellow + Indigo
Brown: Dark Red + Light Green
Ink

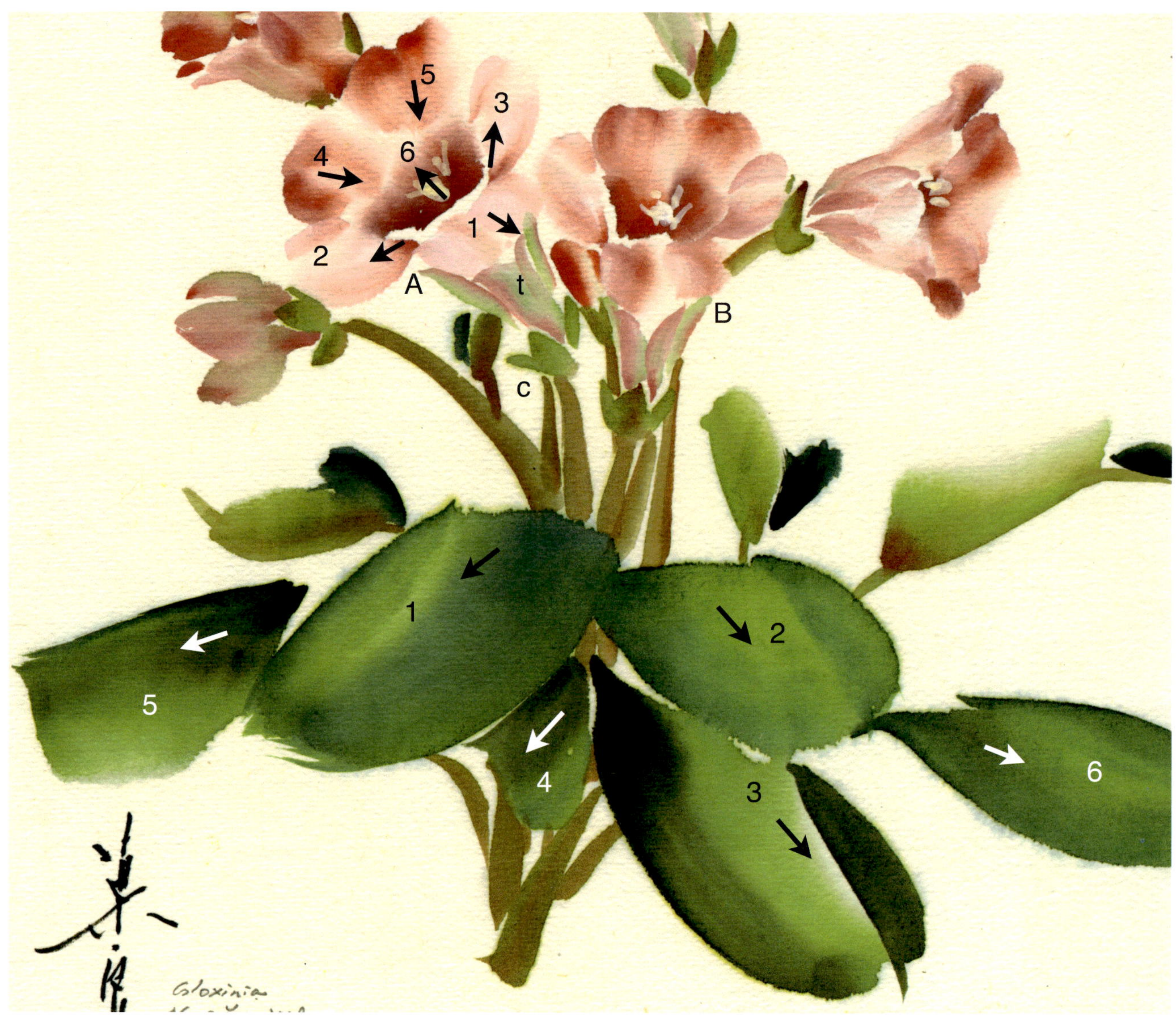


**STEPS**

Leaves

ℒ Large Flow

❖ Light Green + Dark Green

Do a couple of center leaves to anchor the composition (1, 2).

❖ Light Green + Dark Green + Ink

Expand the leaf cluster into a skirt. Show a couple of shadow ones below (3, 4), and reach out on both sides (5, 6).

Flowers

ℒ Flow

❖ White + Pink

Each flower has five petals opening from a full-bodied tube. Work two host flowers (A, B). Do each flower with three petals in the front forming a "U" shape (1-3).

❖ Pink + Red

Do two petals from the top down to complete a circle. Leave the center area open (4,5).

❖ Red + Dark Red

Seal the center with upward strokes.

❖ Light Green + Dark Red

Leave room for the flower tube. Do a set of calyx dots for each flower. Up to three dots for each set (c).

❖ White + Pink

Work a full-bodied tube (t) to bring the flower into the calyx.

Stalks

❖ Brown

Do stalks for each leaf and flower. Working from the lower center leaves, bring two stalks together to form the root of our plant (a). End the rest of the stalks higher to show they are behind. Together, the root of the stalks form an arrow shape.

Right Profile Flower (C)

❖ White + Pink

Work foreground petals showing their backsides. Do the center petal (1). Make the side petals a little higher (2, 3).

❖ Red

Work the background petals with more red (4, 5).

❖ Red + Dark Red

Seal the center of the flower.

Extend strokes showing the top of the side petals (2a, 3a).

❖ Light Green + Dark Red

Work calyx dots for the flower (c).

❖ White + Pink

Add the tube of the flower (t).

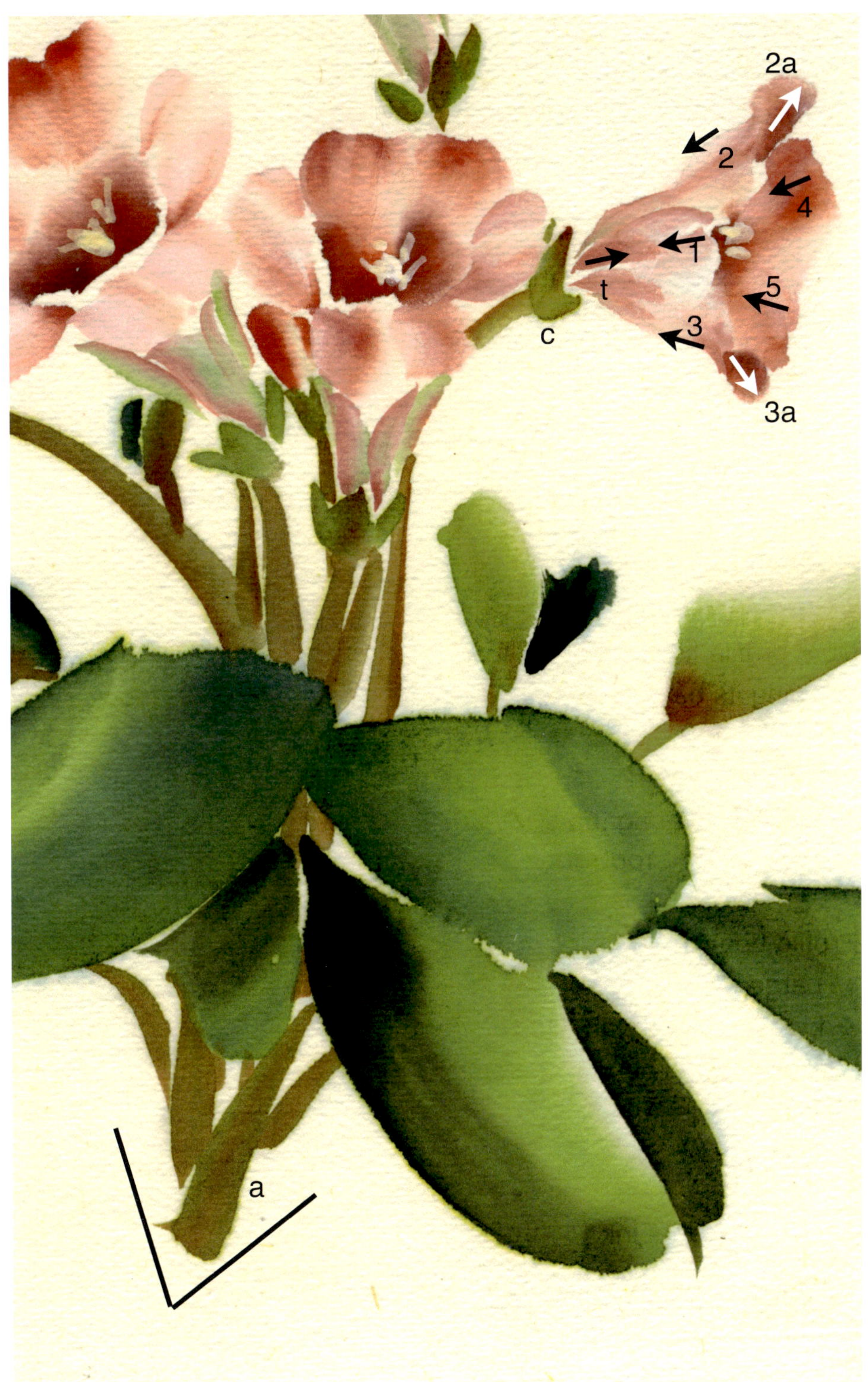

Top Flower (D)
Do the petals and the center of this flower the same way as Flower A.

❖ Light Green + Dark Red
Work calyx dots (c) for the top flower and for a flower on the left (yet to come).

❖ White + Pink
Add a tube (t) to bring the flower into the calyx.

❖ White + Pink
Do a profile flower showing its backside (E).

❖ Brown
Add stalks to bring the flowers into the root.

Profile Leaves
♌ Large Orchid Bamboo
❖ Light Green + Dark Red
Work two pairs of profile leaves showing their undersides (7-10).

❖ Dark Green + Ink
Add the topsides of the profile leaves (a).

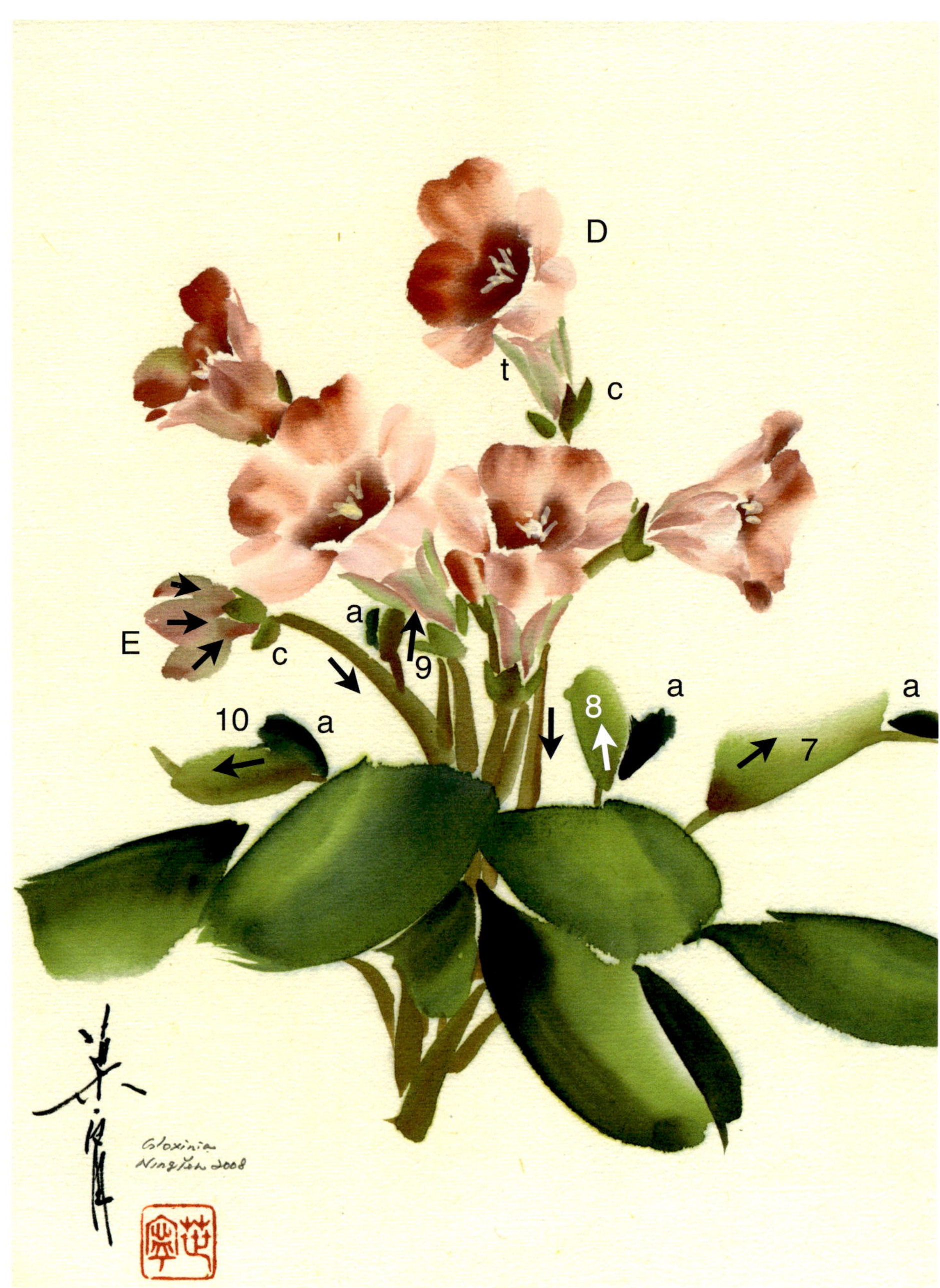

Left Profile Flower (F)
𝔑 Flow
❖ White + Pink
Work a layer of three petals showing their undersides (1, 2, 3).

❖ Pink + Red
Add the front-facing petals of the flower (2a, 3a, 4, 5).

❖ Red + Dark Red
Seal the center of the flower. Add a bud in the center area of the composition. Add shadows at the root.

❖ Brown
Work calyx dots below the flower and the bud. Add stalks.

𝔑 Happy Dot
❖ Pasty White + Yellow
Add a few dots in the center of the flowers.

The flower has a lady with octopus arms going crazy in the center. We do not want to encourage such excessive behavior.

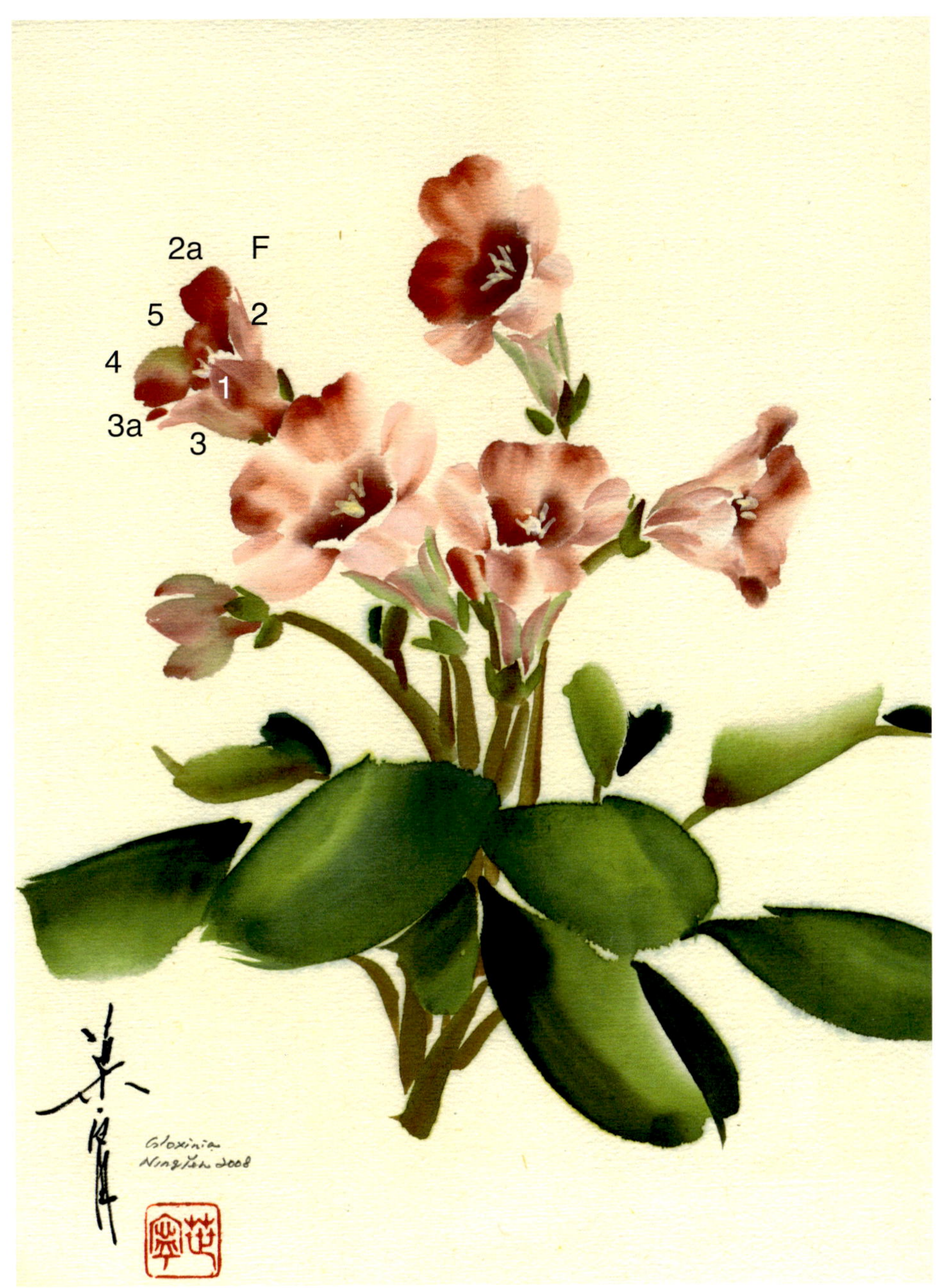

8049

# Gourd

Hu Lu
Hú Lú: Gourd

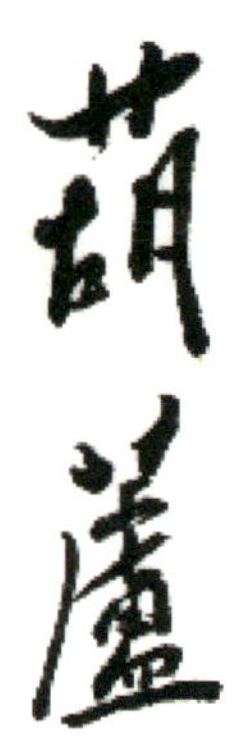


Chinese deities used giant gourds to carry wine. Chinese see gourd as a token of mystery. It is hard to find out what is inside. It may not always be complimentary. Many times, a gourd has nothing inside.

Gourd is a fantastic subject. It can be any shape. Its crinkled leaves can be many shapes. Its vine can go anywhere. One can do anything.

There should never be a lesson on how to paint gourd. This is how wonderful the subject is.

**MATERIALS**

Paper: Double Shuen

♌ Brushes
Large Flow, Flow, Small Mountain Horse

❖ Colors
*Chinese*
Yellow, Vermillion
*Winsor & Newton*
Indigo, Perylene Violet
*OAS*
Best Bottle Ink

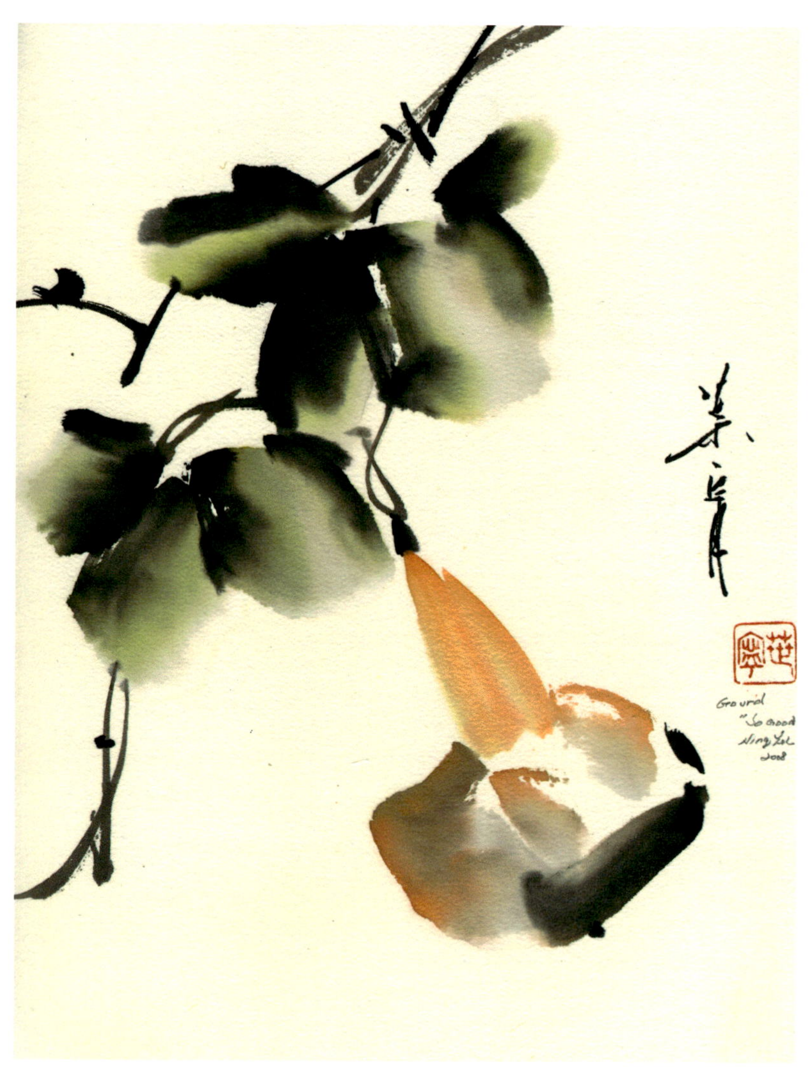

**PREPARATION OF COLORS**

Yellow: thick liquid
Vermillion: thick
Dark Red: Perylene Violet + Vermillion
Light Green: Yellow + Indigo
Dark Green: Yellow + Indigo
Brown: Vermillion + Ink
Ink
Medium Ink: Ink + Water

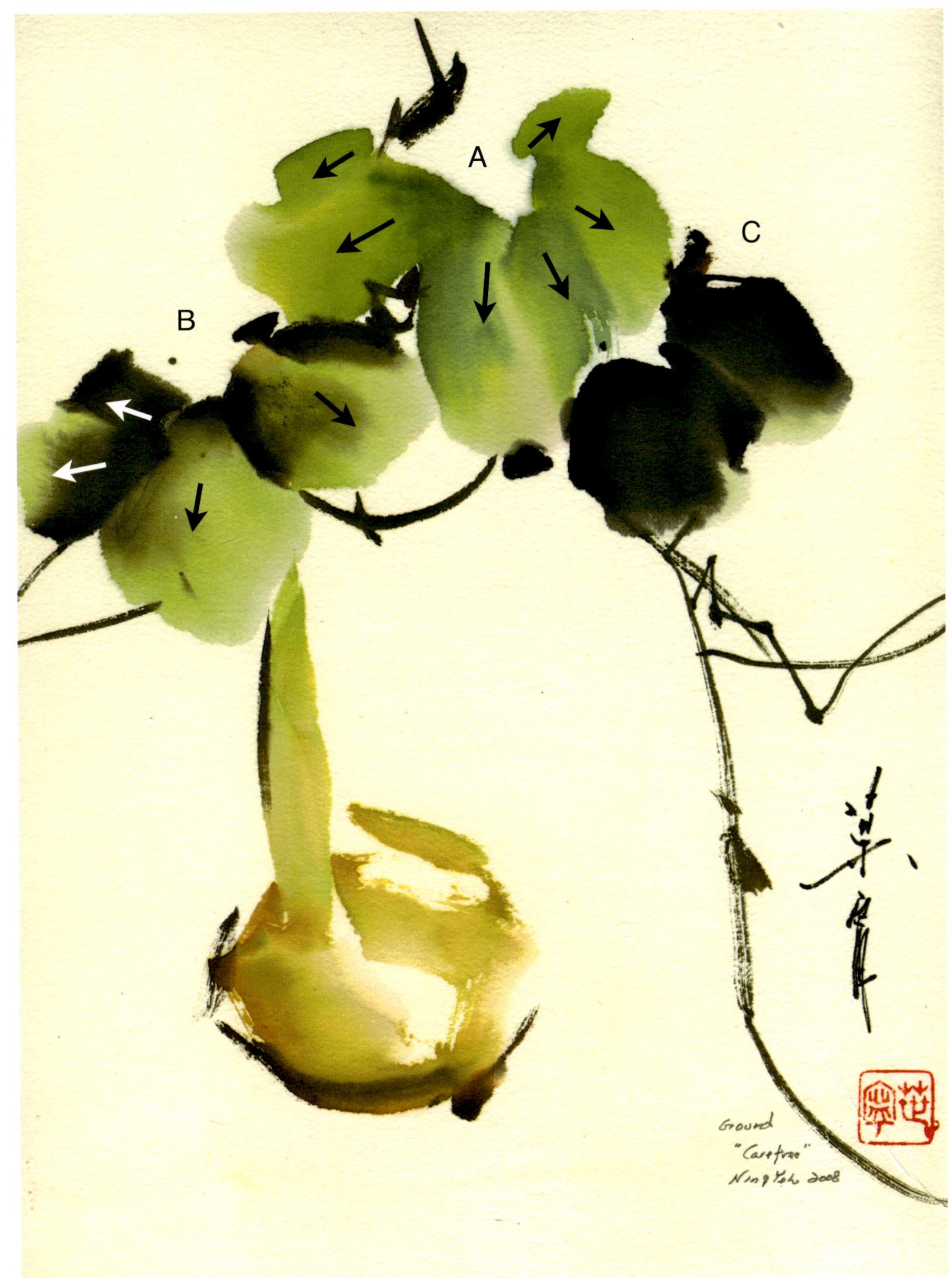


**STEPS**

Composition 1
Leaves
♌ Large Flow
❖ Yellow + Light Green + Dark Green
Do a leaf in the upper middle area of the paper (A). Show five sections of the leaf. Work the left side with a large stroke. Add a small stroke to show the top section. Do the center section with two strokes. Make the right side smaller with two sections.

❖ Ink
Work a leaf heading to the left (B).
Use bold strokes. Show the spontaneous blending of colors.

Do a shadow leaf on the right with more Ink (C). Express character with each stroke. Bring contrasting elements into harmony: wet and dry, dark and light, big and small, shape and space.

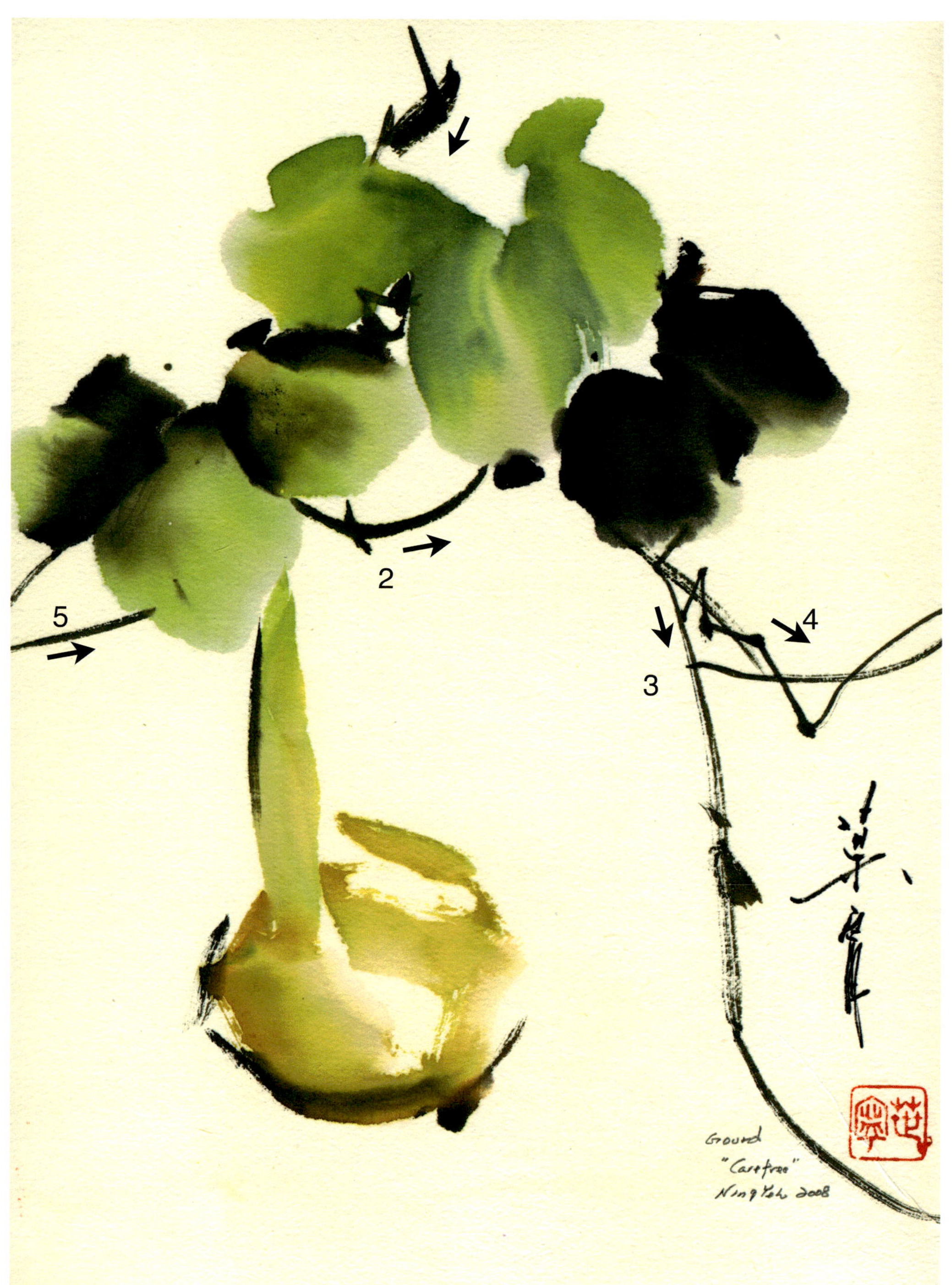


Vines

♌ Small Mountain Horse

❖ Light Green + Brown

Do vines from the top with heavier strokes (1). Run through the middle and lower area of the leaves (2). Extend finer vines downward (3) and to the right with energetic curves (4). Work vines on the left side (5). Show their nature by adding playful partners that twist and turn.

Gourd

♌ Flow

❖ Yellow + Light Green

Extend a long tube from the leaves down.

❖ Brown

Work the body of the gourd. Show contrast. Capture dynamic spontaneity.

❖ Dark Red + Brown + Ink

Do shadow strokes and dot the base. Add just a few more dots. This is so cool.

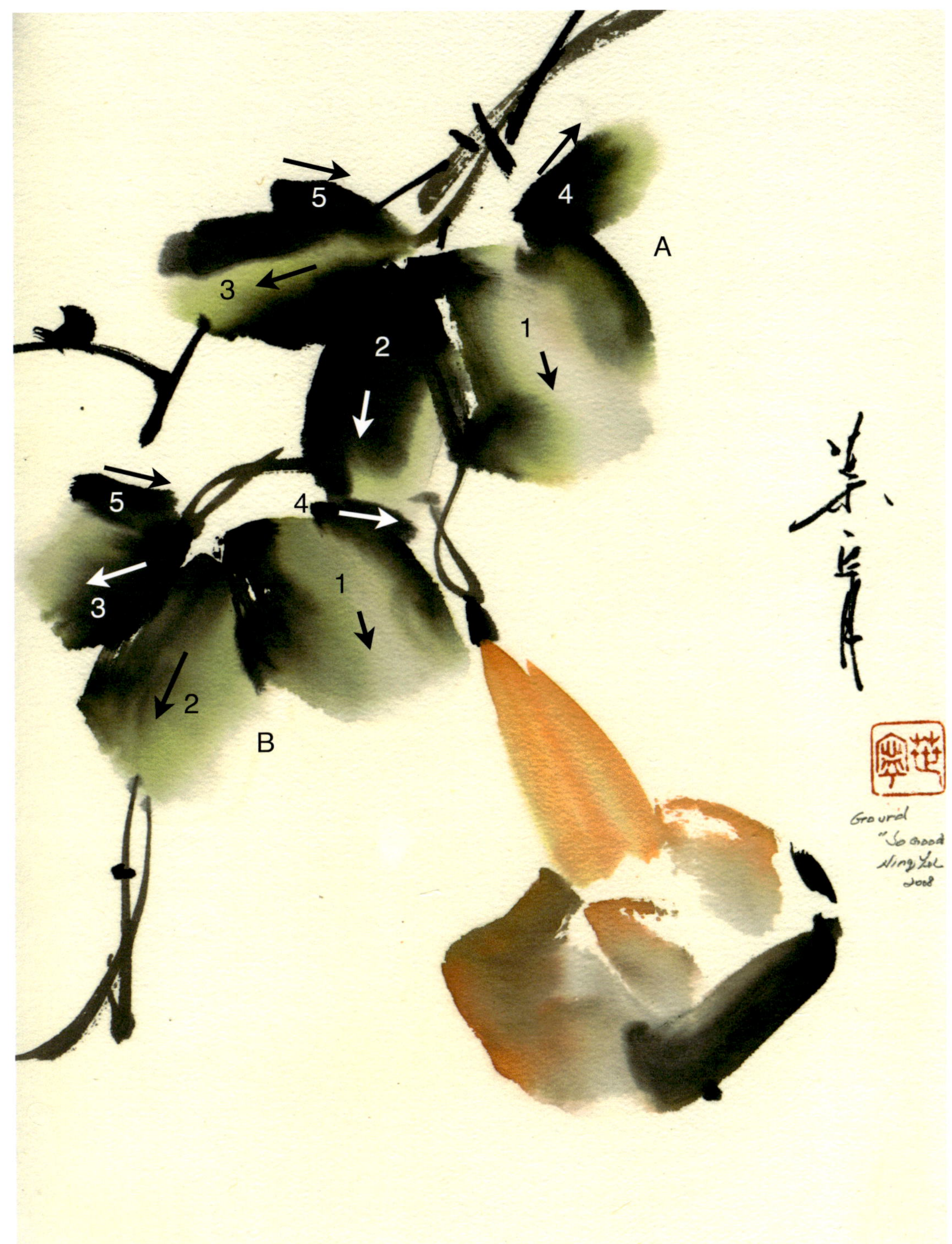


Composition 2

Leaves (A, B)

♌ Large Flow

❖ Yellow + Light Green + Dark Green + Dark Red + Brown + Ink

These leaf strokes are the essence of brush painting. This is why brush painting is so much fun. Never mind the shapes. Just enjoy how the incredibly sensitive paper responds to the strokes. Watch the velvety blending of various colors (1-5).

Vines

♌ Small Mountain Horse

❖ Light Green + Dark Red + Brown + Medium Ink

Now, the delightful, rhythmic, playful vines dance through the splashing ink. Students here do well with these clever turns because English writing has many moves.

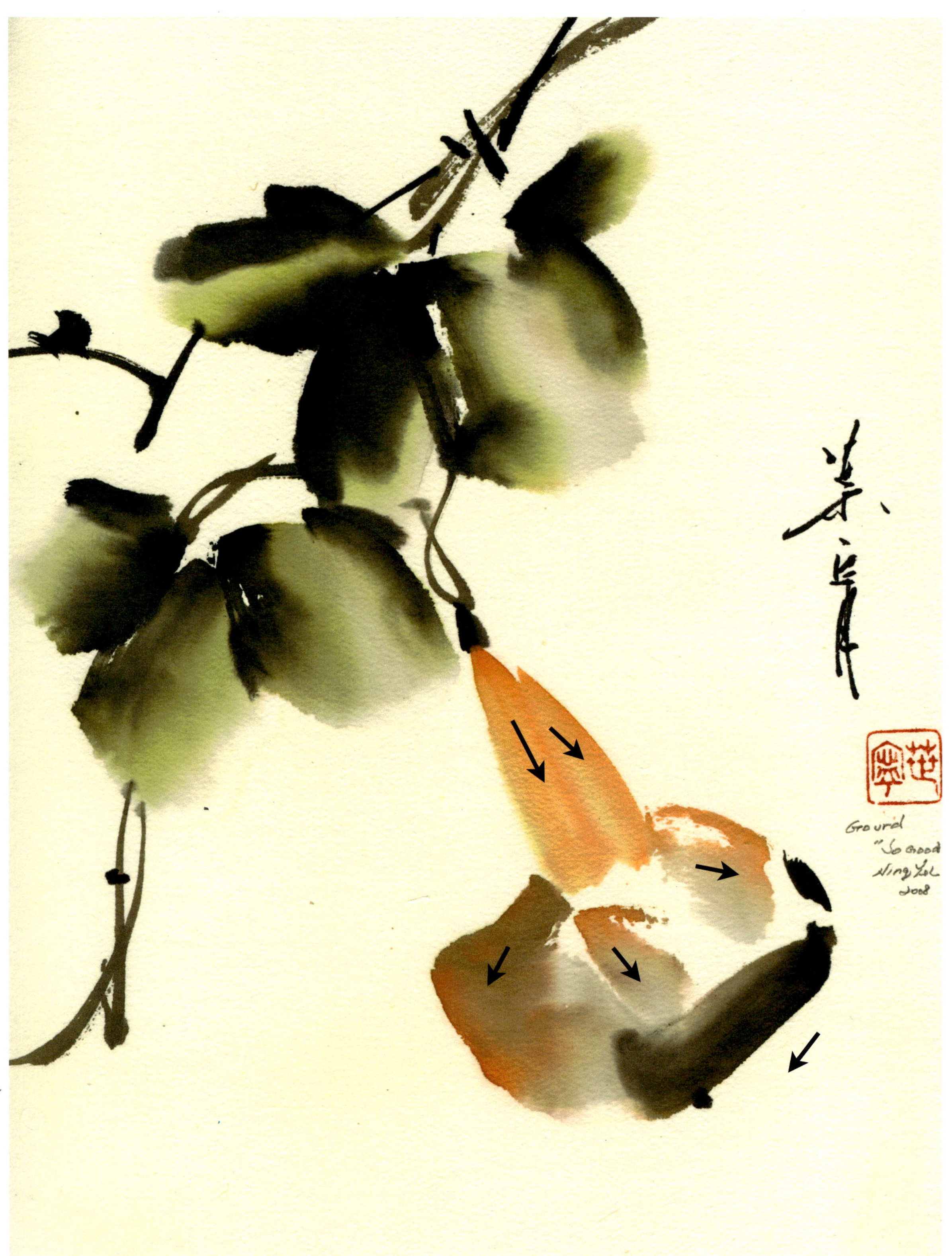

Gourd

♌ Large Flow

❖ Yellow + Vermillion

Work the neck of the gourd.

❖ Vermillion + Brown

Do the voluptuous body.

❖ Brown + Ink

Show the base of the gourd.

♌ Flow

❖ Ink

Add dots on top and below the gourd. Fire a few happy dots at will. A masterpiece in no time.

8050

# Grape

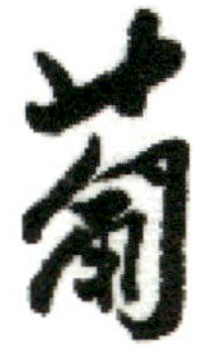

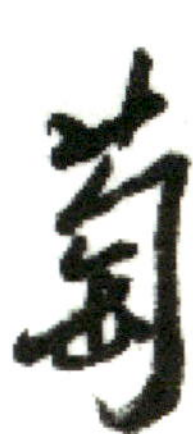

Pu Tau
Pú Tao: Grape

Grape is pútao in Chinese. Pú means "crawling." Tao has the connotation of being intoxicated with joy. It is a good name for a fruit that provides so many moments of inspiration for all.

Turpan, along the Silk Road, is China's grape capital. Turpan is 154 meters below sea level but surrounded by snow-capped mountains. It is the hottest spot in China. The streets of Turpan are completely covered by grape canopies. I really enjoyed the warmth of the people there.

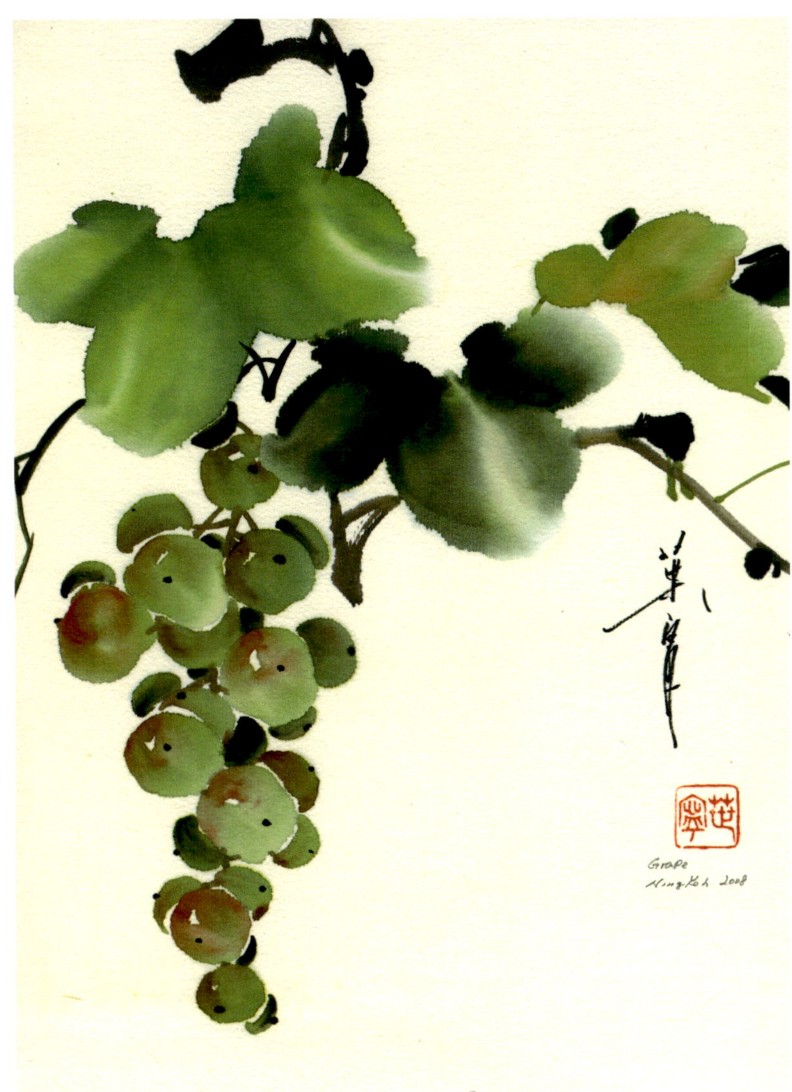

**MATERIALS**

Paper: Double Shuen

Brushes
Large Flow, Flow, Small Mountain Horse

❖ Colors
*Chinese*
Yellow, Vermillion
*Da Vinci*
White
*Schmincke*
Cadmium Red Deep
*Winsor & Newton*
Indigo, Perylene Violet
*OAS*
Best Bottle Ink

**PREPARATION OF COLORS**

Vermillion: thick
White: diluted
Red: Cadmium Red Deep
Dark Red: Perylene Violet + Red
Light Green: Yellow + Indigo
Dark Green: Yellow + Indigo
White Green: White + Light Green
Brown: Vermillion + Ink
Ink

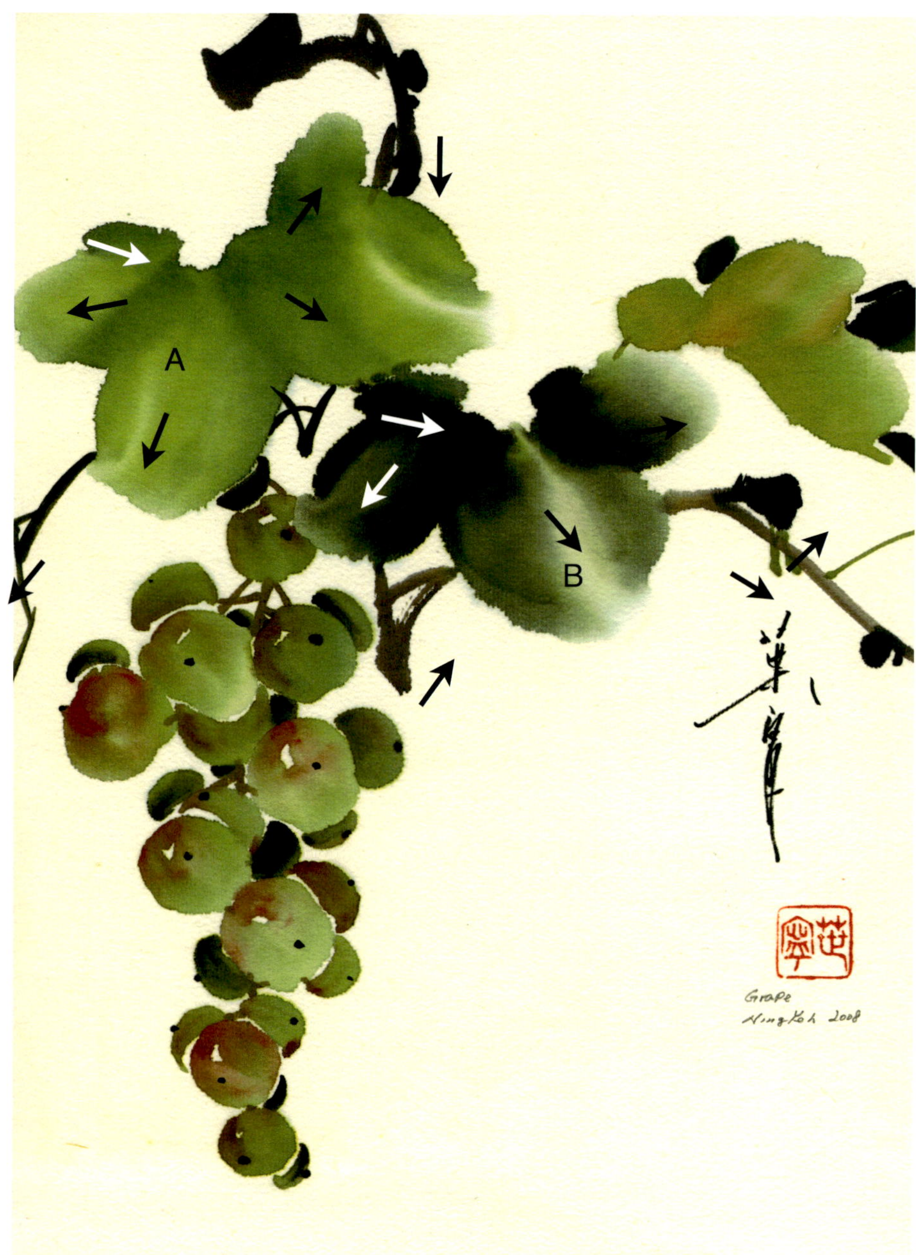


**STEPS**

Leaves
♌ Large Flow
❖ Light Green + Dark Green
Each leaf has five sections. Do a leaf heading left on the upper left side of the painting (A). Work two strokes to show the right side. Do the center section with two strokes. Make the sections overlap each other. Show the right side and top sections each with one stroke.

❖ Dark Green + Ink
Work a shadow leaf heading to the right (B). I do grape leaves with a wet brush. The edges naturally show some ruffles. I love the color variations on the leaf.

Vines
♌ Small Mountain Horse
❖ Brown
Work vines with bold turns. Curve the strokes. Begin from the top with heavier strokes. Leap through the leaves. Move the main branch to the right and off the paper.

♌ Flow
❖ Dark Green + Ink
Add happy dots along the vines.

Grapes

♌ Flow

❖ White Green + Light Green + Red

Estimate where the main stem of the grape cluster will be. Put grapes along the imaginary stem. Use mostly the brush tip to do the left side of each grape. Begin with less pressure. Work the lower part with more pressure. Use more of the brush body to do the right side with a scoop motion. Leave a small space to show the light on the fruit.

Think of the cluster like our body. Show upper shoulders and lower leg parts. Vary the spacing of the fruits, and show some overlapping (1-6).

❖ Light Green + Dark Green + Red + Dark Red

Work darker ones overlapping the existing fruit. Keep a hairline space between the grapes. Connect the fruits into a continuous shape (7-16).

❖ Light Green + Dark Green + Red + Dark Red + Ink

Place one grape closer to the leaves. We will add more grapes in the shadow to add depth to our cluster (17-21).

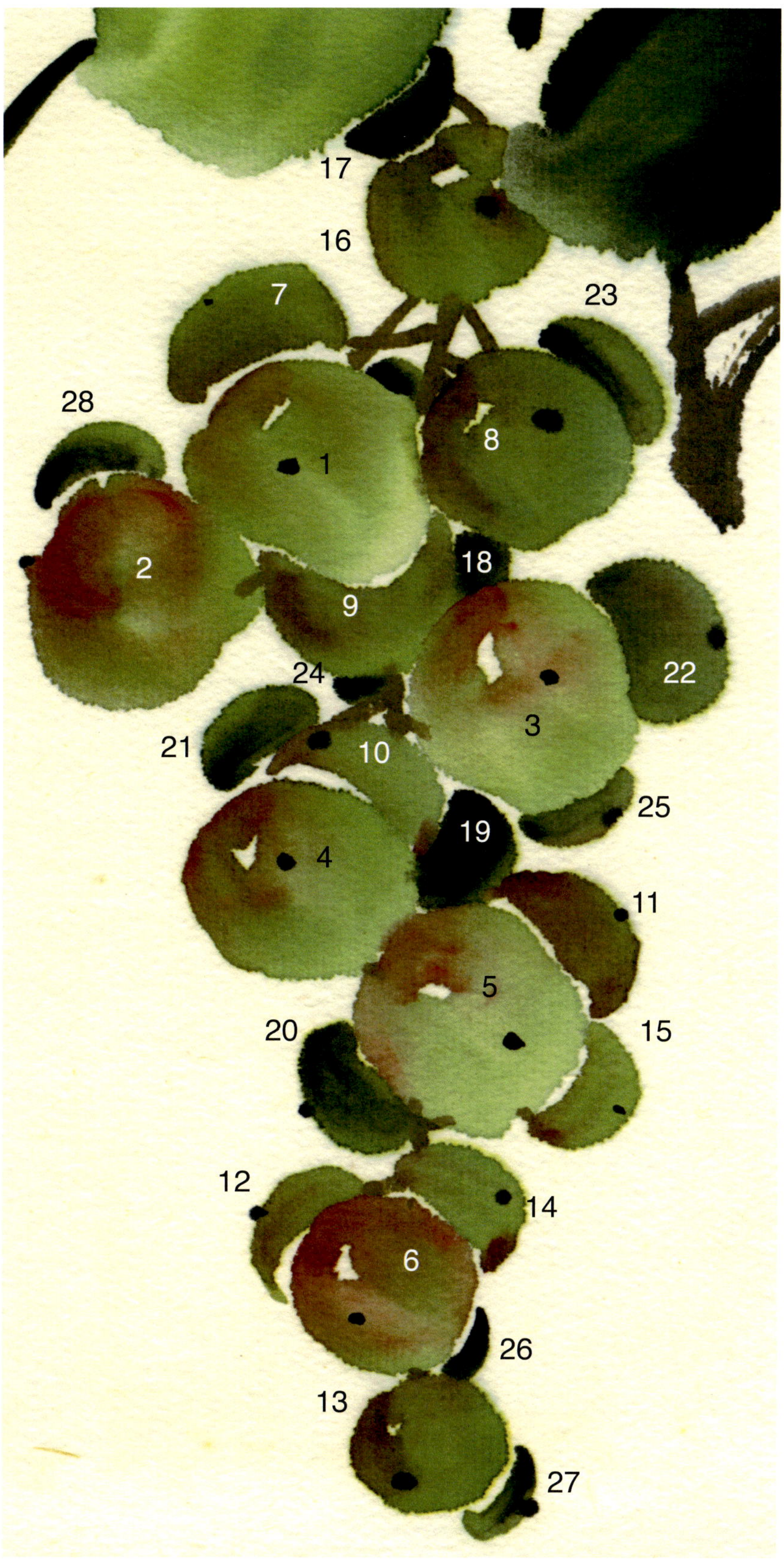


❖ Brown + Ink

Add the center stem. Alternate side stems along the center stem reaching to the grapes.

❖ White Green + Light Green + Red + Dark Red + Ink

Show more grapes (22-28).

❖ Ink
Place a dot on each grape according to its location. Dot the center one in the middle. Side ones have dots on the side. Top ones dot higher and lower ones lower. Is this dot called the "navel?" This is where the stem ends.

This is where you, grape master, will tell the world that you know what you are doing. Do not underestimate the dot.

♌ Large Flow
❖ Light Green + Vermillion
Do a profile leaf (C). Show the underside. Work the middle section with two strokes upward. Add a small section on the left. Elongate the right side. Show the tip like a "freeway exit."

❖ Dark Green + Ink
Show the topside of the profile leaves.

♌ Small Mountain Horse
❖ Brown
Add the leaf stem.

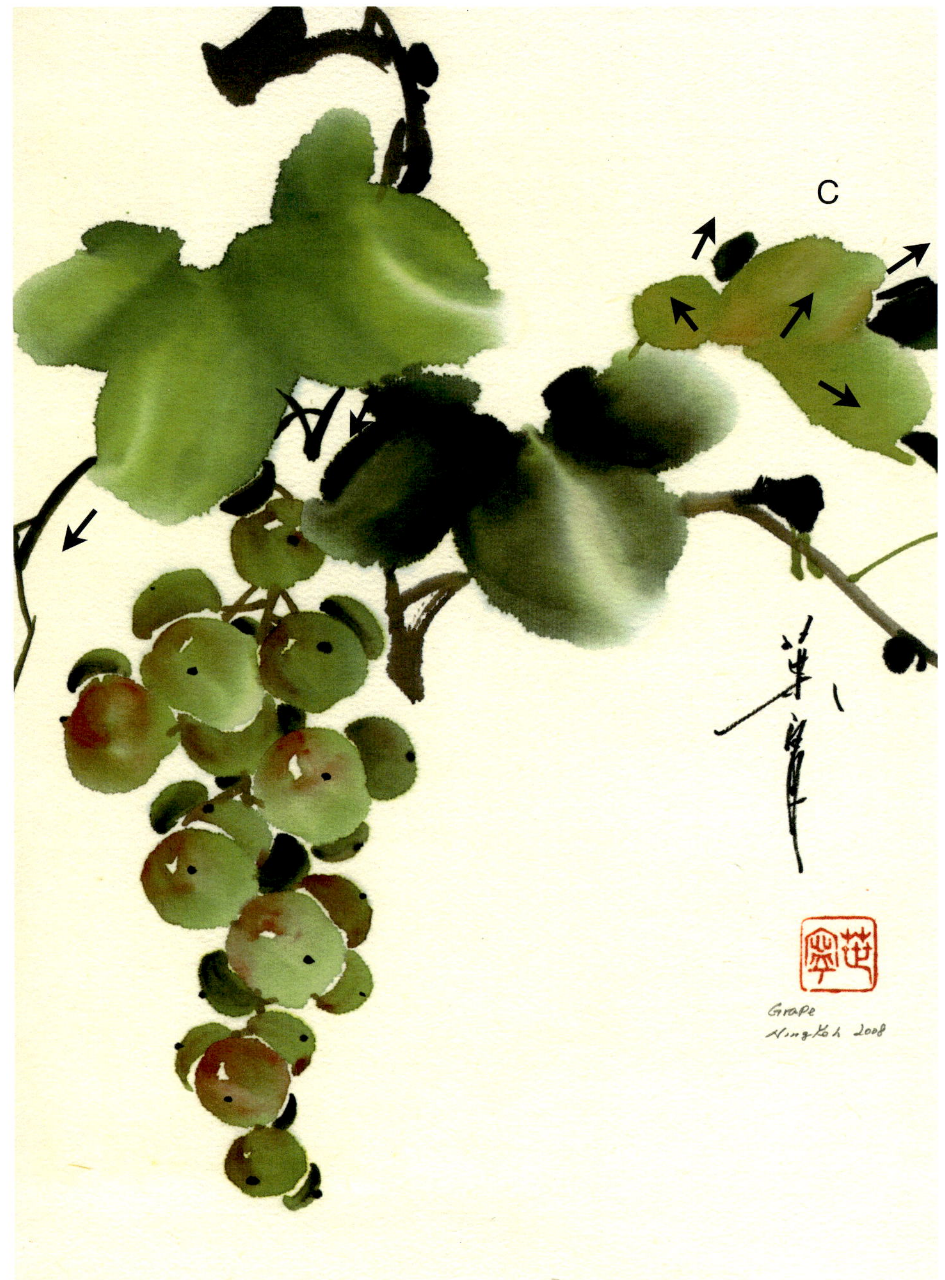


❖ Ink
Run a shadow vine cluster to the left and a playful companion to the main branch.

8051

# Heavenly Bamboo

Tian Ju

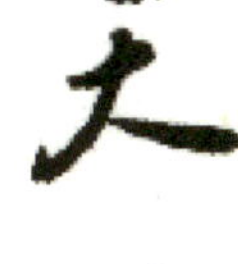

Tiān Zhú: India

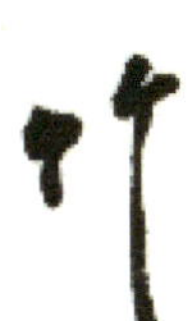

Jwu

Zhú: Bamboo

I pick a subject like this to teach during the holiday season. I start the class with berries and go holiday shopping. When I return, students would still be adding berries. They never notice the teacher leave.

**MATERIALS**

Paper: Double Shuen

Brushes
Large Orchid Bamboo, Flow, Small Mountain Horse

❖ Colors
*Chinese*
Yellow, Vermillion
*Schmincke*
Cadmium Red Deep
*Winsor & Newton*
Indigo, Alizarin Crimson, Perylene Violet
*OAS*
Best Bottle Ink
Gold

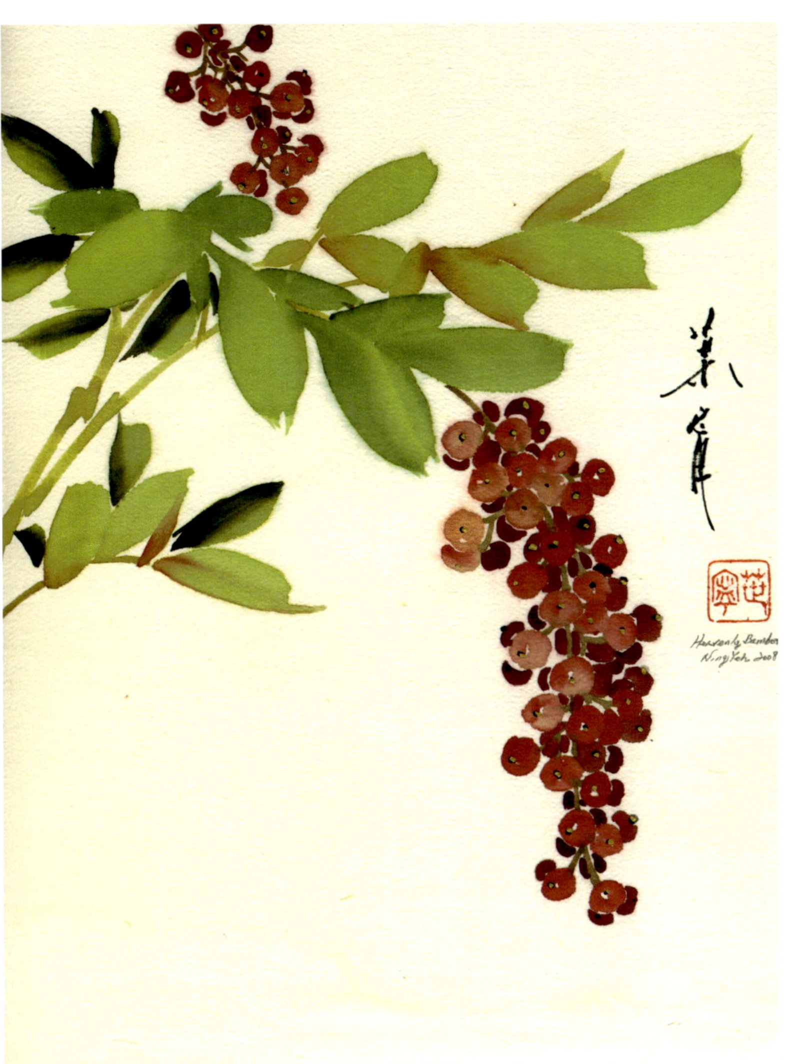

**PREPARATION OF COLORS**

Yellow: thick liquid
Vermillion: thick
White: diluted
Light Green: Yellow + Indigo
Dark Green: Yellow + Indigo
Red: Cadmium Red Deep
Crimson: Alizarin Crimson + Red
Dark Red: Perylene Violet + Red + Crimson
Brown: Dark Red + Dark Green
Ink
Gold

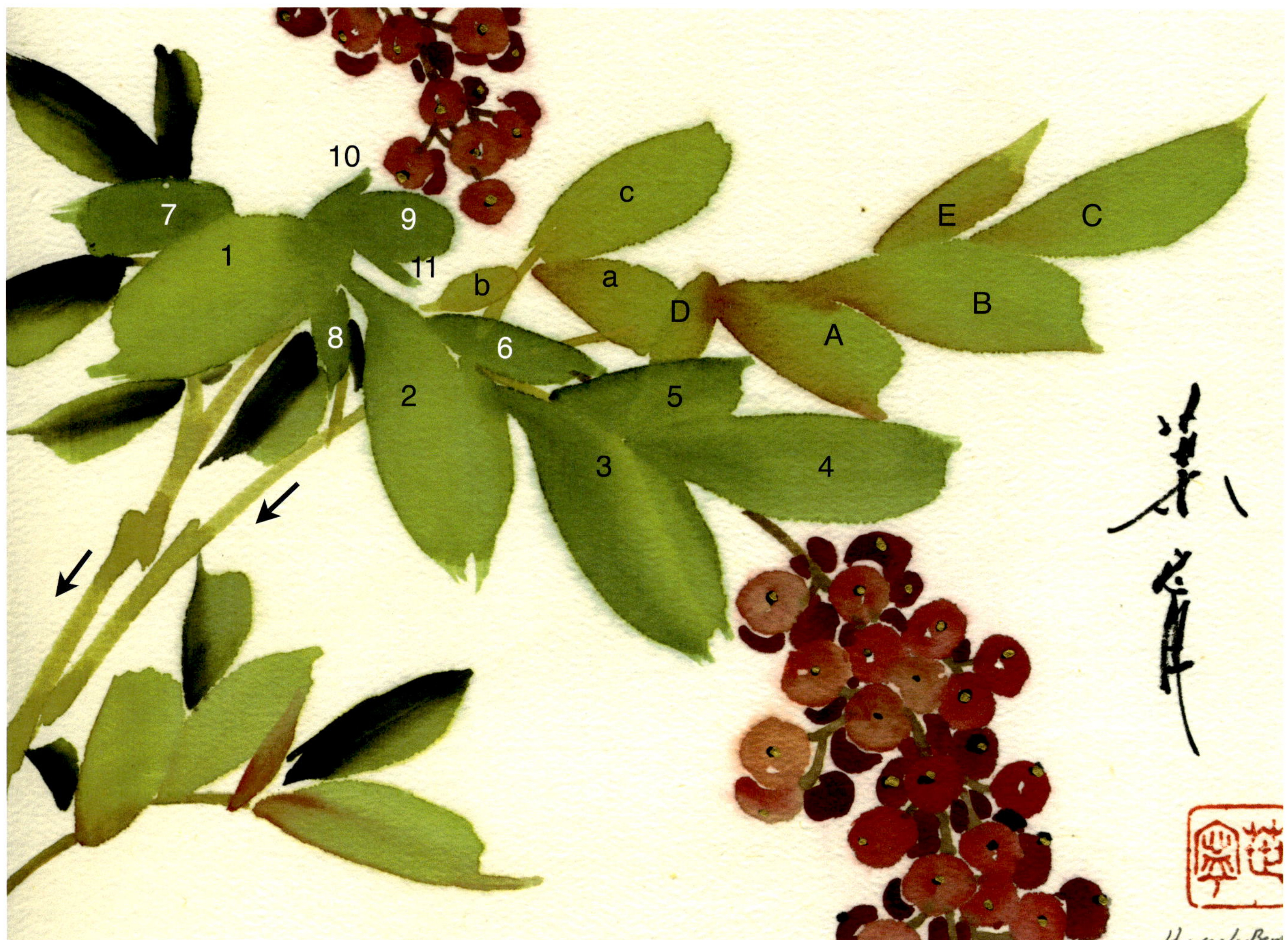


**STEPS**

Leaves

♌ Large Orchid Bamboo

❖ Light Green + Dark Green

Each leaf cluster hosts multiple leaves sharing the same stem. Work three drooping leaves. Do a base leaf heading to the left with two strokes (1). Work a middle leaf (2). Add a leaf on the right (3). Link the leaves.

Extend two leaves to form a tip group (4, 5). Add a small partner to the middle leaf (6). Work small leaves on both sides of the base leaf (7, 8).

Show three leaves in the opposite direction to the base leaf (9, 10, 11).

❖ Light Green + Red

Heavenly bamboo leaves have multiple colors. Do two clusters of leaves showing some red colors (A-E and a-c).

Branches

♌ Small Mountain Horse

❖ Light Green + Vermillion + Brown

Add leaf stems and branches.

♌ Large Orchid Bamboo

❖ Light Green + Dark Green + Ink

Do a few shadow leaves.

♌ Small Mountain Horse

❖ Brown

Add leaf stems.

Berries

♌ Flow

❖ Vermillion + Red + Crimson

Mark an invisible stem for the berry cluster with your finger. Work a long series of berries along the projected stem. Do the berries in the middle of the series first with lighter colors.

Do each berry with curved strokes moving left and right. Round off the base. Occasionally leave a spot open on the body to suggest light. Once started, it is hard to stop (1-31).

❖ Brown

Thread a main stem through the middle of the berry cluster. Do more stems to link the berries.

❖ Red + Crimson + Dark Red

Work more berries. Carve along the existing berries. Go behind the stems with darker berries in the shadow. Leave hairline spaces between them. Connect the berries into a continuous series. We like the cluster to show interesting borders. Berries are not soldiers marching in formation.

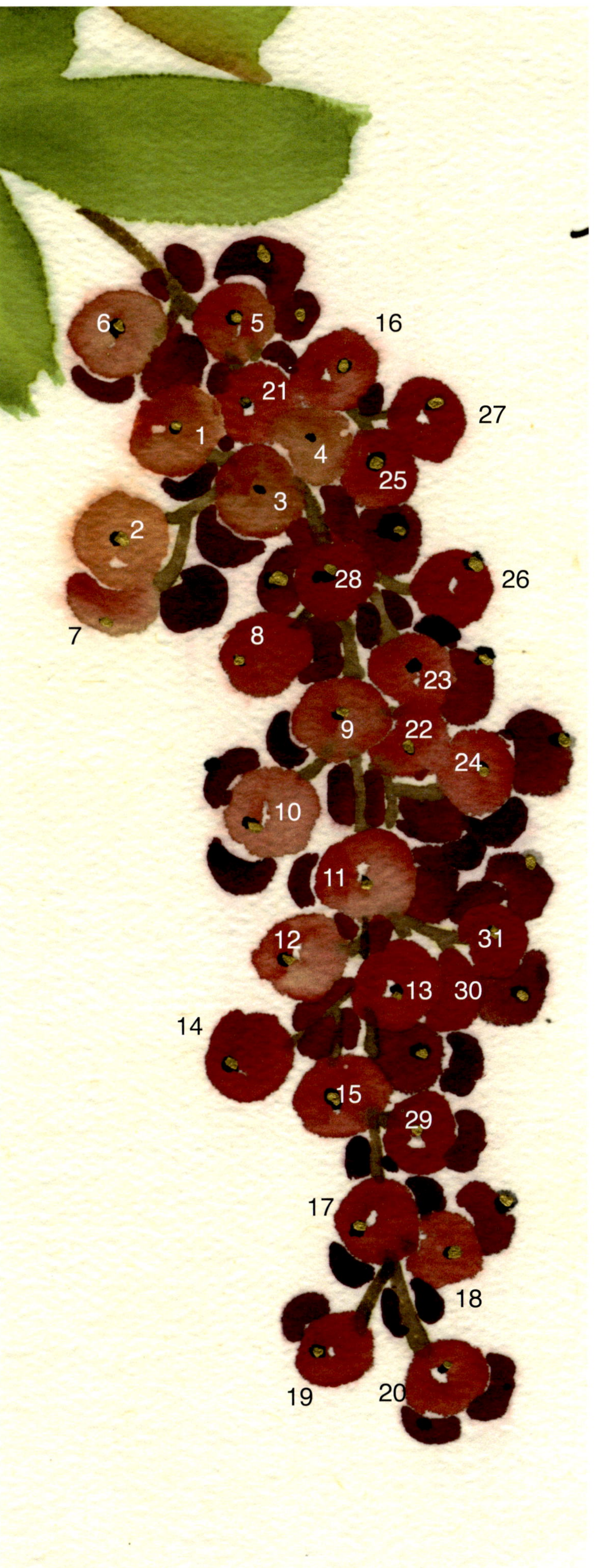

❖ Ink
Place a dot on each berry according to its location. Dot the center berry in the middle. Side ones have dots on the side. The back ones may not show dots because they are facing away from us.

❖ Gold
Land a touch of gold on top of the ink dots. I love the combination of gold and ink. Gold makes things cheerful and adds a touch of the holiday spirit.

Now, we want a guest group of berries.

❖ Vermillion + Red + Crimson
Work the lighter ones first. It is an interesting idea to hang a series from the top. This is all we need to suggest that the plant is much larger (1-9).

❖ Brown
Work a center stem through the berries. Add side ones to link the berries. Add some stems for berries yet to come.

❖ Dark Red
Do more berries. Carve along the existing berries. Go behind the stems with darker berries in the shadow. Leave hairline spaces between them.

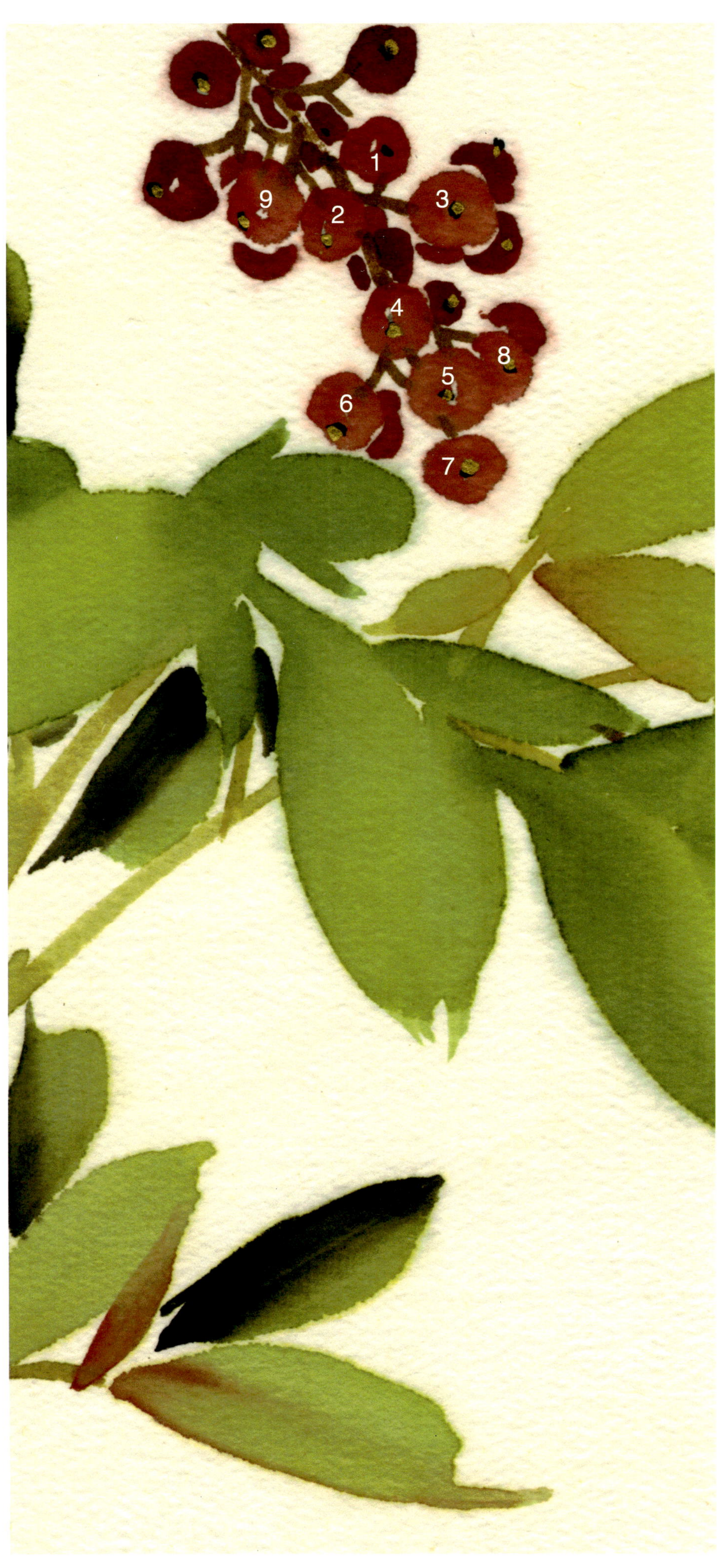

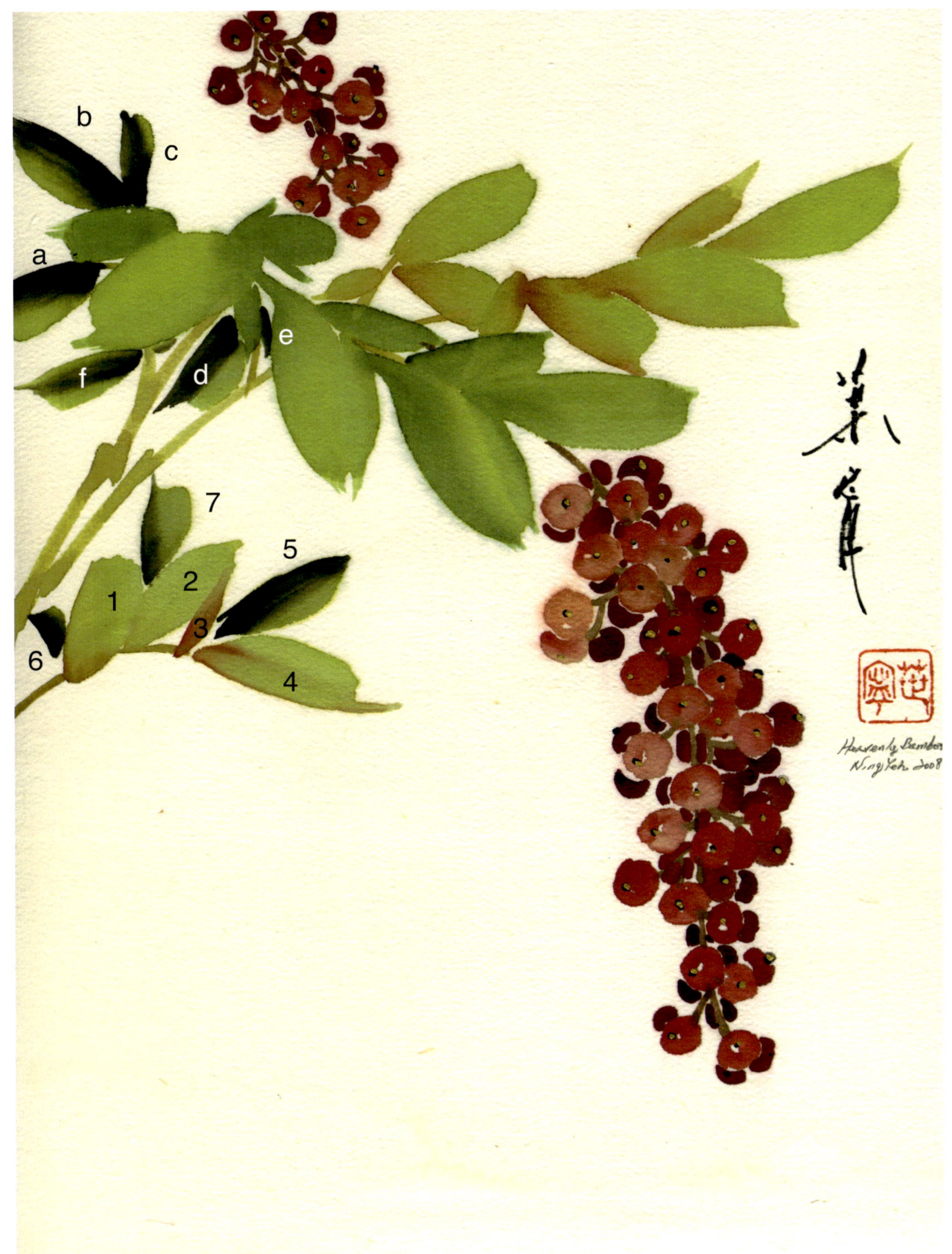


❖ Ink
Place a dot on each berry according to its location.

❖ Gold
Accent the ink dots with Gold.

More Leaves
♌ Large Orchid Bamboo
❖ Light Green + Red
Work a guest group of leaves (1-4).

♌ Small Mountain Horse
❖ Light Green + Vermillion + Brown
Work a stem to link the leaves.

♌ Large Orchid Bamboo
❖ Light Green + Dark Green + Ink
Add more shadow leaves (5-7, a-f).

♌ Small Mountain Horse
❖ Brown
Connect the leaves with stems.

8052

# Hibiscus

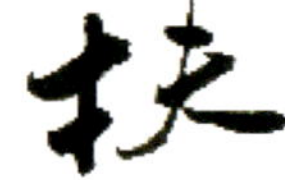


Fu
Fú: Support

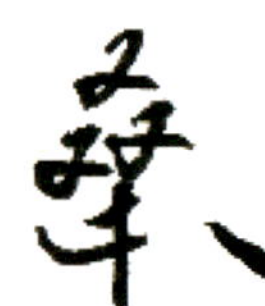


Sang
Sāng: Mulberry

I raised silk worms when I was in grade school. These worms are incredible eating machines. They are very picky eaters. One day, I ran out of mulberry leaves. In a panic, I fed the worms with hibiscus leaves. The leaves are shaped the same. The worms had no eyes anyway. They would not know the difference, I thought.

These worms were fussy little guys. They refused to eat. After some intense persuasion (I used a feather to brush the head of the worm, as any good silk worm tender was told to do), they reluctantly began to eat. They soon had the runs and were pretty sick for a while. It was not a pretty sight. These worms would have nothing to do with hibiscus.

**MATERIALS**

Paper: Double Shuen

♌ Brushes
Large Flow, Flow, Small Mountain Horse, Happy Dot

❖ Colors
*Chinese*
Yellow

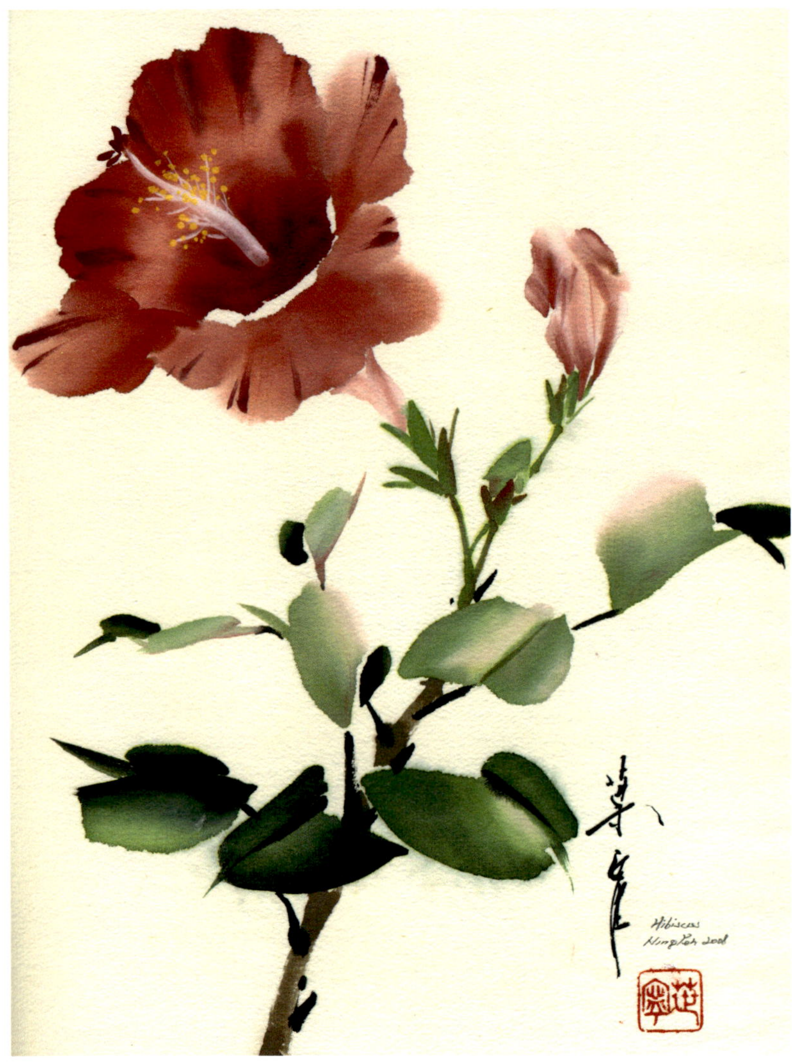

*Schmincke*
Cadmium Red Deep
*Winsor & Newton*
Indigo, Alizarin Crimson, Perylene Violet
*OAS*
Best Bottle Ink

**PREPARATION OF COLORS**

Yellow: thick liquid
White: diluted
Light Green: Yellow + Indigo
Dark Green: Yellow + Indigo
Red: Cadmium Red Deep
Crimson: Alizarin Crimson + Red
Dark Red: Perylene Violet + Red + Crimson
Brown: Dark Red + Dark Green
Ink

**STEPS**

Flower

Petals

ᔓ Large Flow

❖ White + Red

Each flower has five serrated petals. Work a center petal with two downward strokes. Add small strokes on both sides (A). Add a petal on each side to form a "U" shape (B, C).

❖ Red + Crimson

Work two top petals with strokes moving from the outside into the center (D, E). Leave the center area of the flower open.

❖ Rinse and dry the brush

Extend the roots of the top petals with a few dry strokes. Soften the hard edges of the roots.

❖ Red + Crimson + Dark Red

Build wide walls above the lower petals. Leave a hairline space. Lower the boom to seal the center of the flower.

Veins

ᔓ Small Mountain Horse

❖ White + Red + Crimson + Dark Red

Add veins beginning from the outside edges of the petals moving inward. Press and lift with curving lines. Do darker petals first. Spread the veins like splashing fountains.

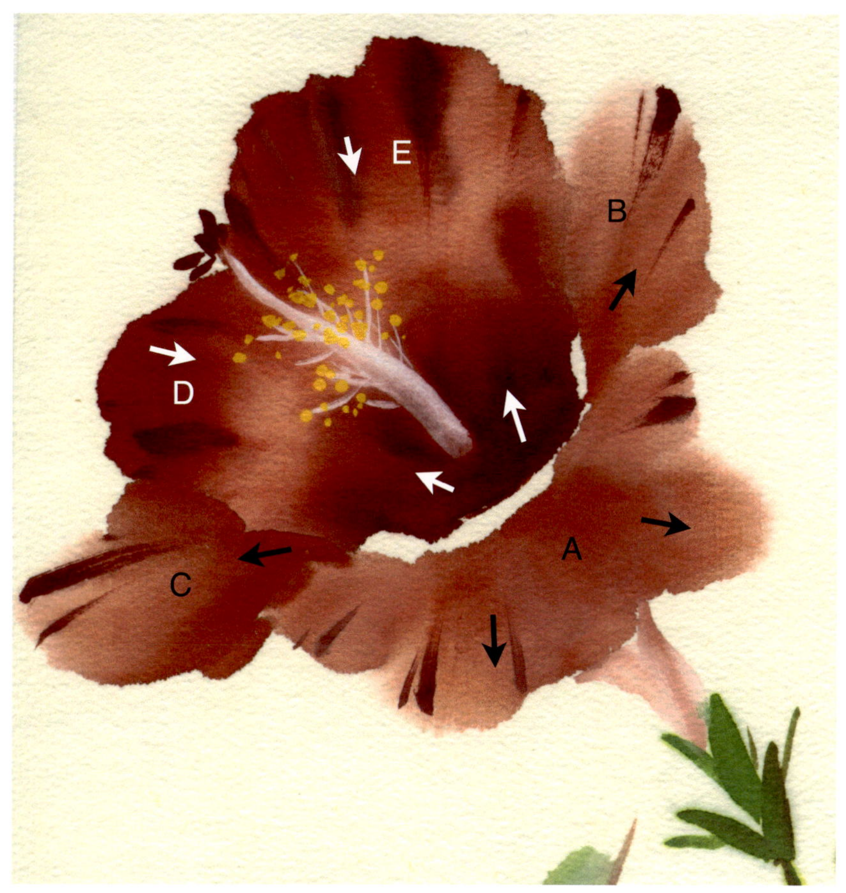


Pistil

ᔓ Flow

❖ White + Red + pasty White

Do a bossy pistil into the center of the flower.

Stamens

ᔓ Happy Dot

❖Pasty White

Add fine stamens with varying lengths at the midsection of the pistil.

Pollen

ᔓ Flow

❖ Pasty White + Yellow

Do pollen dots near the tips of the stamens.

Lady

❖ Dark Red

Do the lady with five impressive dots on top of the pistil.

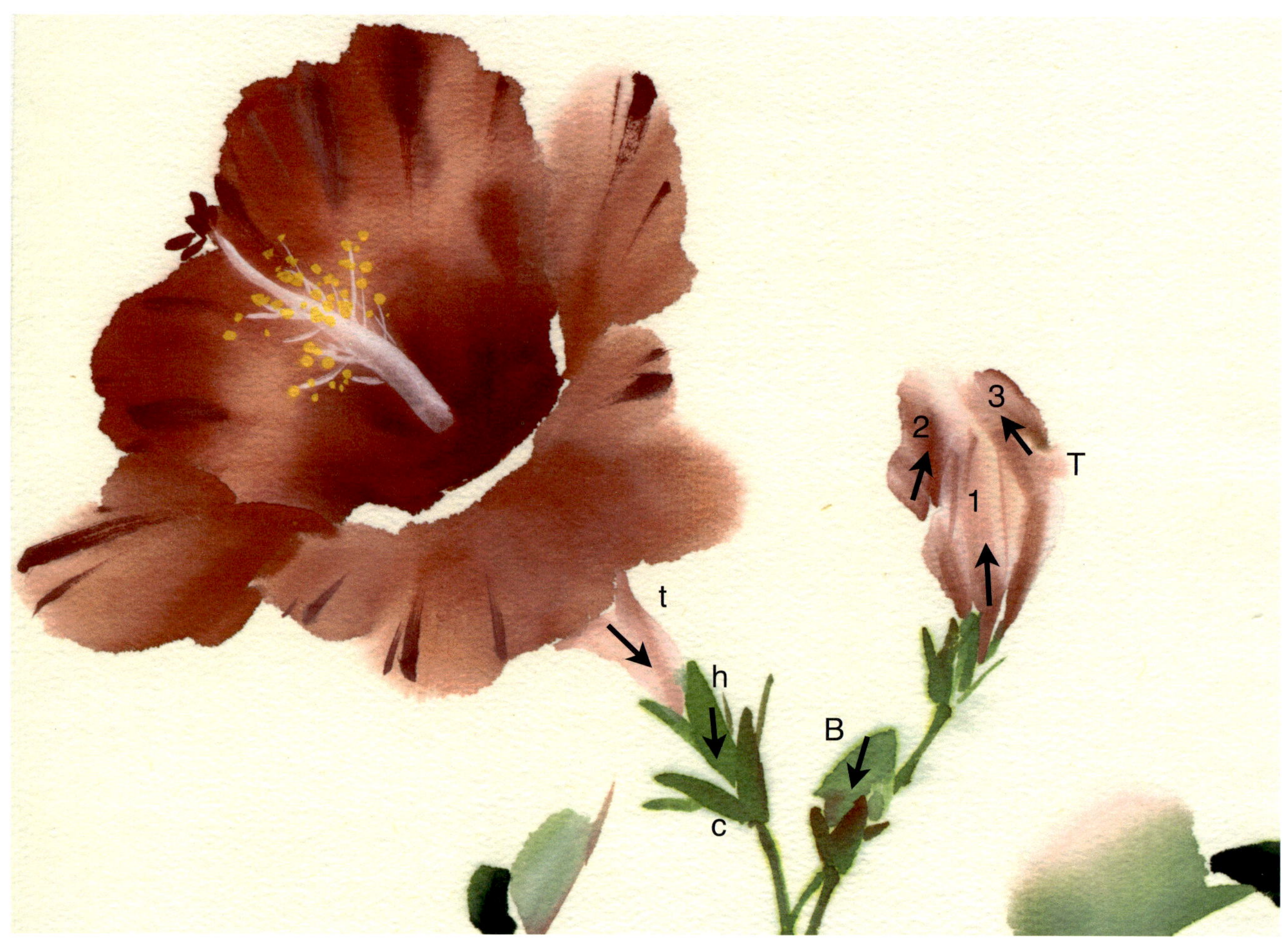


Trumpet
❖ White + Red
Work a trumpet below the flower (t).

Calyx
ᔓ Happy Dot
❖ Light Green + Red
Do calyx dots a little distance away from the trumpet (c).

ᔓ Flow
❖ Light Green
Work a cup to house the trumpet on top of the calyx dots (h).

Buds
ᔓ Happy Dot
❖ Light Green + Red
Do two more sets of calyx dots for a teenage flower and a small bud.

Teenager (T)
ᔓ Flow
❖ White + Red
Work one petal showing its backside above the calyx dots (1).

❖ Crimson
Add petals on top bowing to the middle (2, 3).

❖ Light Green
Work a cup between the petals and calyx dots.

Small Bud (B)
Show the top part of a small bud.

❖ Red
Add the roots of the small bud.

ᔓ Small Mountain Horse
❖ White + Red + Crimson + Dark Red
Add veins on the petals of the teenager.

Leaves

ᘓ Large Flow

❖ White + Red + Light Green

Mark the course of the stalk with your finger. Work an anchor leaf flipping upward with its backside showing (1). Add profile leaves on both sides of the anchor leaf (2, 3).

❖ Light Green + Dark Green

Do a drooping leaf showing its topside (4).

❖ Dark Green + Ink

Work two shadow leaves moving to the left (5, 6). Add the topsides of the profile leaves (2a, 3a).

Stems and Branches

ᘓ Flow

❖ Light Green + Red

Add stems below the flowers and the bud. Bring them into the anchor leaf.

❖ White + Brown, mix into Beige

Do a branch downward from the base of the anchor leaf. Leap over the leaves below.

❖ Dark Green + Ink

Add more branches to link to the side leaves.

❖ Ink

Do a few dots on the branches.

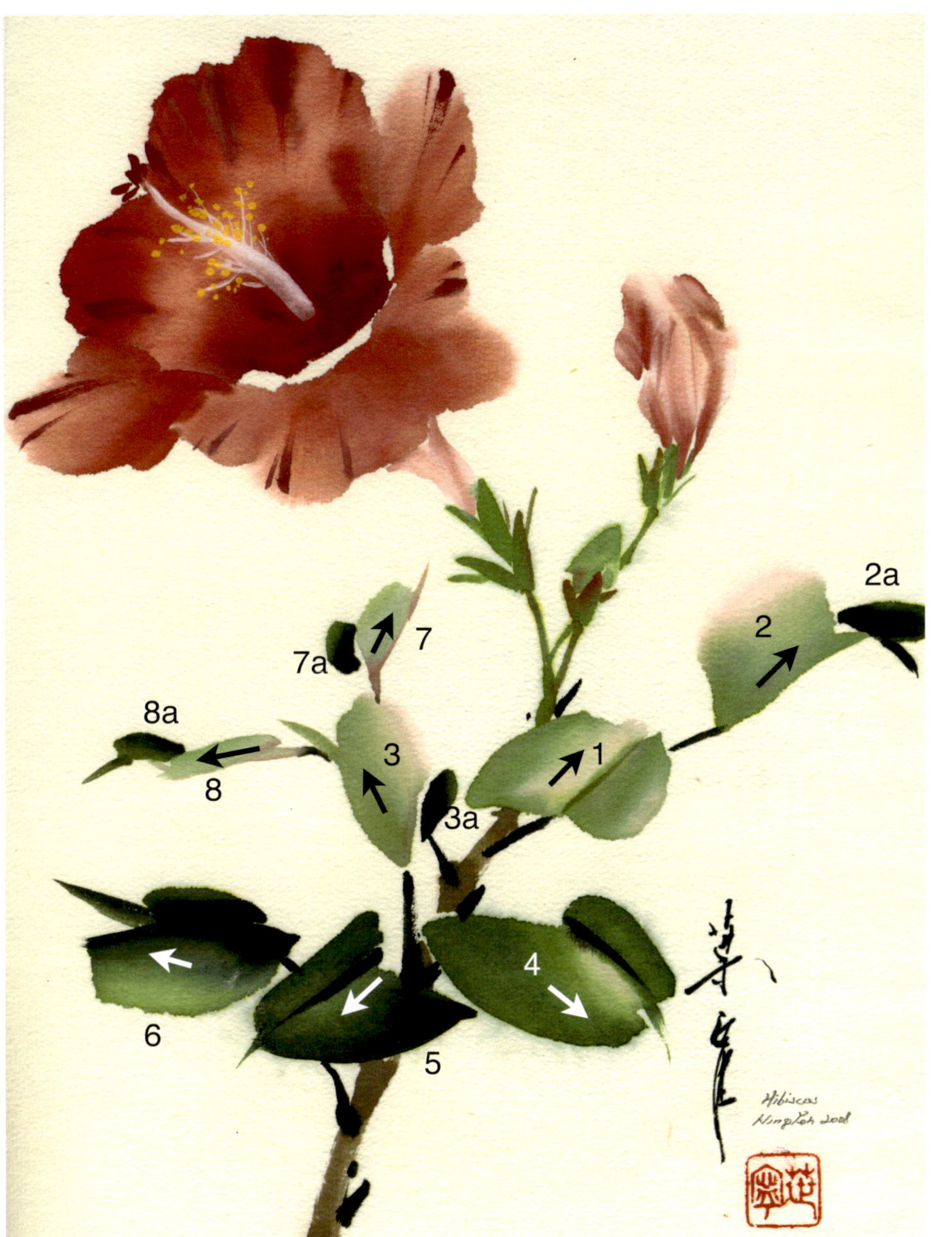


ᘓ Small Mountain Horse

❖ Dark Green + Ink

Add a center vein on each leaf. (Profile leaves do not show center veins).

ᘓ Flow

❖ White + Light Green + Red

Work a pair of profile leaves on the left side (7, 8).

❖ Light Green + Dark Green + Ink

Show the topside of the new profile leaves (7a, 8a).

❖ Brown + Ink

Add stems and branches to bring the leaves home.

8053

# Hibiscus

Multi-layered

Fu
Fú: Support

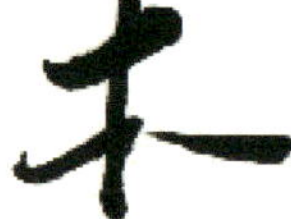

Sang
Sāng: Mulberry

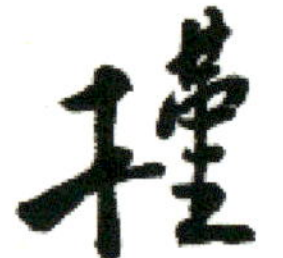

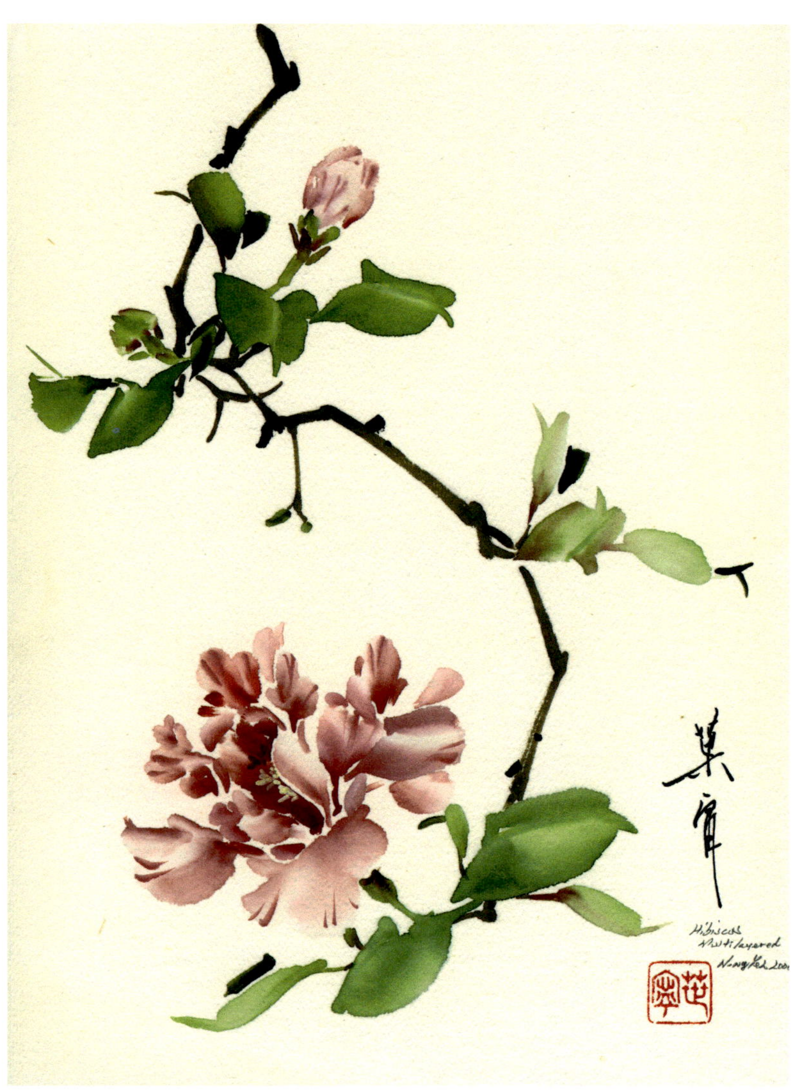

There are hundreds of species of hibiscus in south China with different names. It is a flower that is both showy and easy to care for.

Hibiscus is the national flower of South Korea where many of my students come from. They spoil me rotten. I do this flower in their honor.

**MATERIALS**

Paper: Double Shuen

♌ Brushes
Flow, Large Flow, Small Mountain Horse, Happy Dot

❖ Colors
*Chinese*
Yellow
*Da Vinci*
White
*Schmincke*
Cadmium Red Deep
*Winsor & Newton*
Indigo, Permanent Magenta, Alizarin Crimson, Perylene Violet
*OAS*
Best Bottle Ink

**PREPARATION OF COLORS**

Yellow: thick liquid
White: diluted
Light Green: Yellow + Indigo
Dark Green: Yellow + Indigo
Red: Cadmium Red Deep
Magenta: Permanent Magenta + Red
Crimson: Alizarin Crimson + Red
Dark Red: Perylene Violet + Crimson
Brown: Perylene Violet + Light Green
Ink

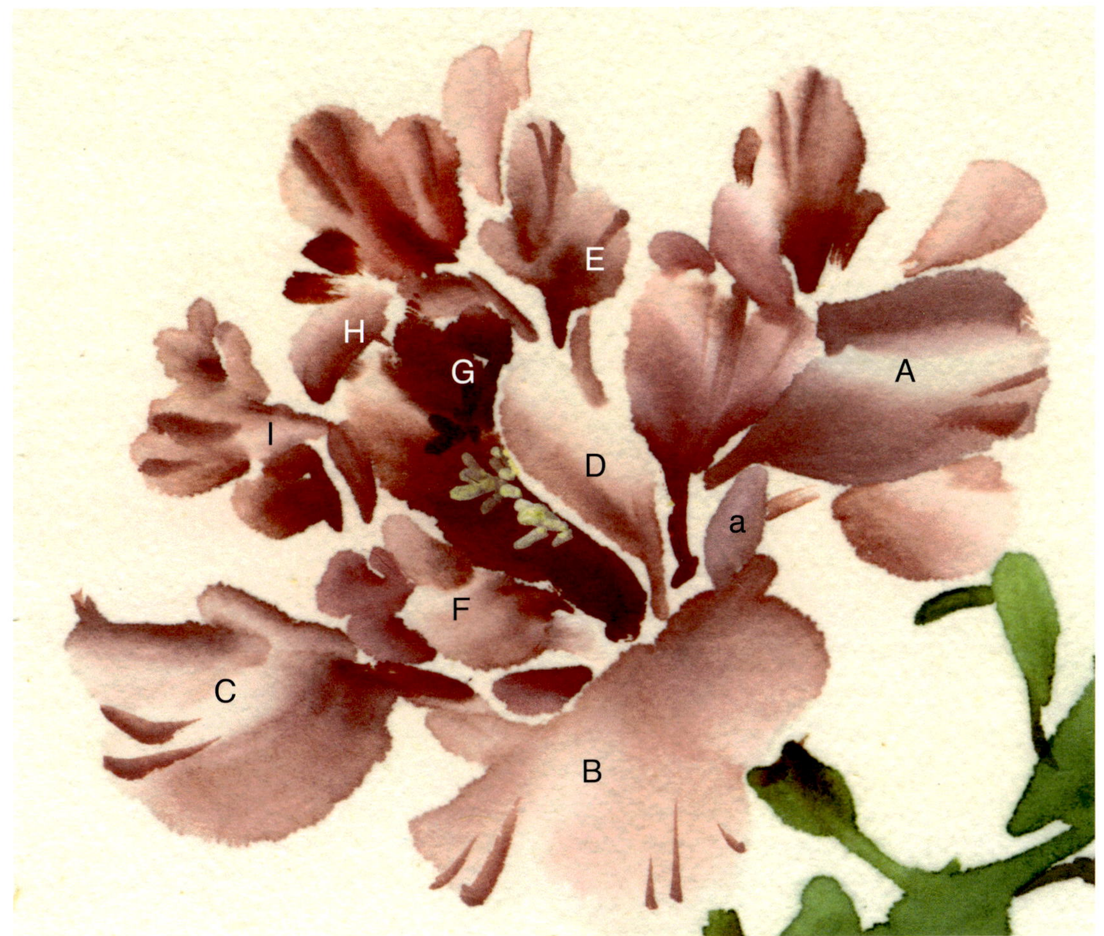


**STEPS**

Flower

Skirt Petals

♌ Flow

❖ White + Magenta

Do a skirt at the base of the flower with three petals. Show a handle and lead a petal to the right with two strokes (A).

❖ White

Extend a stroke below the petal to show its underside (a).

❖ White + Magenta

Turn the brush and work a series of strokes to do a center petal (B).

❖ Magenta + Red

Do a petal reaching to the left side (C). The three petals form a "U" shape.

Crown Petals

❖ White + Magenta

Now, think about doing a little vertical flower inside the "U" shape. Do a folding petal on the right side. Show the base. Press to the left to do the body. Extend a tip (D).

❖ Magenta + Red

Show folds along the top edge (E). Work the the topside of another folding petal (F).

❖ White

Add the underside of the left petal.

❖ Magenta + Red + Crimson + Dark Red

Do a dark petal between the two petals. Move strokes upward (G).

❖ White + Magenta + Red

Show some folds along the top edge of the dark petal (H). Extend a profile petal on top (I).

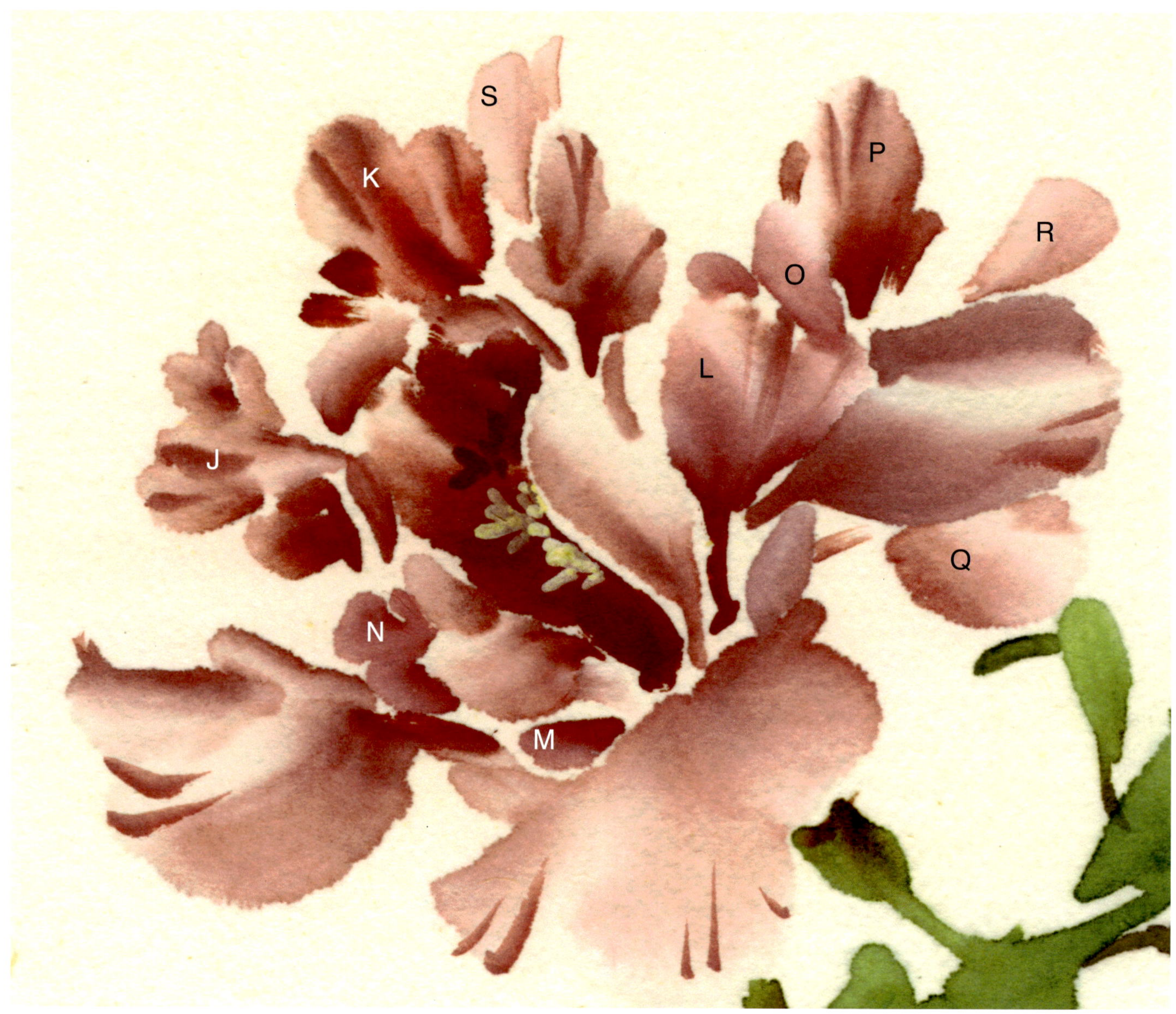


❖ Magenta + Red + Crimson
Work the inside of the profile petal (J). Add strokes to show one more petal on top (K).

❖ White + Magenta + Red + Crimson + Dark Red
Insert petals on both sides between the skirt and the crown petals (L, M, N). Add a couple of folds to the petal on the right side (O).

Right Side
❖ White + Magenta + Red + Crimson
Extend a few petals on the right side of the flower to accentuate the flower movement to the left (P-S). We have a multi-faceted flower.

ℌ Happy Dot
❖ White + Magenta + Red
Add veins to the petals selectively.

ℌ Flow
❖ Pasty White + Yellow
Do pollen dots along the centerline of the flower into a vertical series.

❖ Dark Red
Add up to five lady dots on top of the pollen series.

Leaves

ℓ Large Flow

❖ Light Green + Dark Green

Work leaves in clusters. Do a center leaf (1) and a leaf going to the right (2).

❖ Light Green + Dark Red

Show a profile leaf going to the left (3).

Teenager (T)

ℓ Flow

❖ Light Green + Dark Red

Do calyx dots (c) . Extend a tube below with two strokes (t). Add a stem. Hibiscus has two layers of calyxes. Do a top layer above the calyx dots.

❖ White + Magenta

Work a center petal.

❖ Magenta

Do side petals bowing to the middle.

Veins

ℓ Happy Dot

❖ White + Magenta

Add veins on the petals.

Baby Bud (B)

ℓ Flow

❖ Light Green + Dark Red

Do calyx dots. Work the top part of the bud with strokes moving down and out.

❖ Light Green + Dark Red

Add the base of the bud.

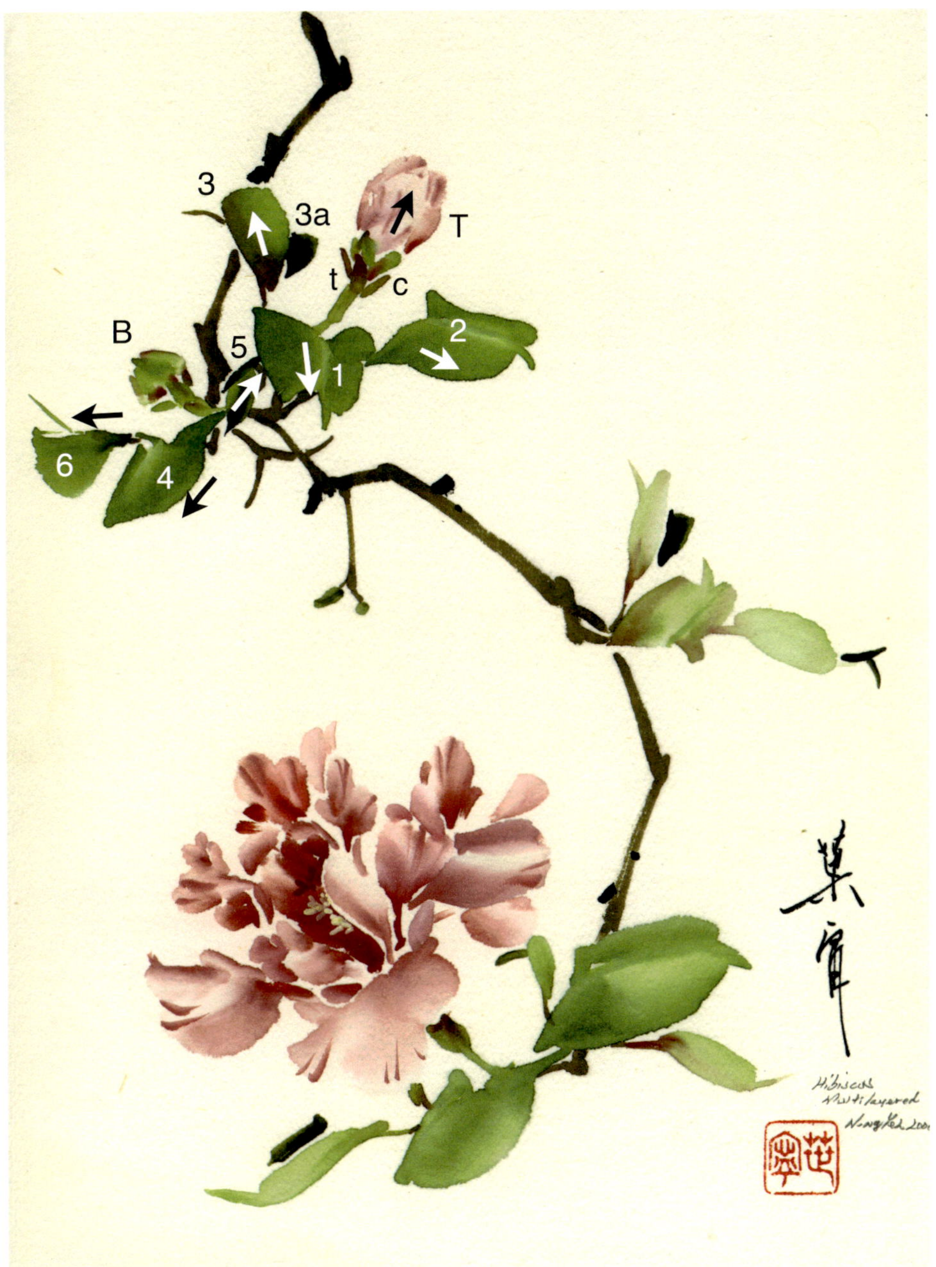


Leaves Below the Bud

ℓ Large Flow

❖ Light Green + Dark Green

Work a center leaf (4).

❖ Ink

Add leaves on both side of the center leaf (5. 6). Do the topside of a profile leaf (3a).

ℓ Flow

❖ Light Green + Dark Red

Work a tube below the bud. Extend a stem to connect the bud to the center leaf below.

Leaves Below the Flower

♌ Large Flow

❖ Light Green + Dark Green

Do two leaves below the flower (7, 8).

♌ Flow

❖ Light Green + Dark Red

Work a tube below the flower (t). Add a stem.

Liaison Leaf Cluster

♌ Large Flow

❖ Light Green + Dark Red

Work a center leaf flipping upward showing its underside (9). Add profile leaves on both sides (10, 11). Expand the leaf skirt below the flower by adding more profile leaves (12, 13, 14).

Branches

♌ Flow

❖ Brown

Bring the bud and the teenager together with branches. Work the main branch from the top down. Link it to the rendezvous point of the bud and teenager. Extend to the liaison leaf cluster. Connect leaves with stems. Add side twigs. Reach down to the leaf cluster below.

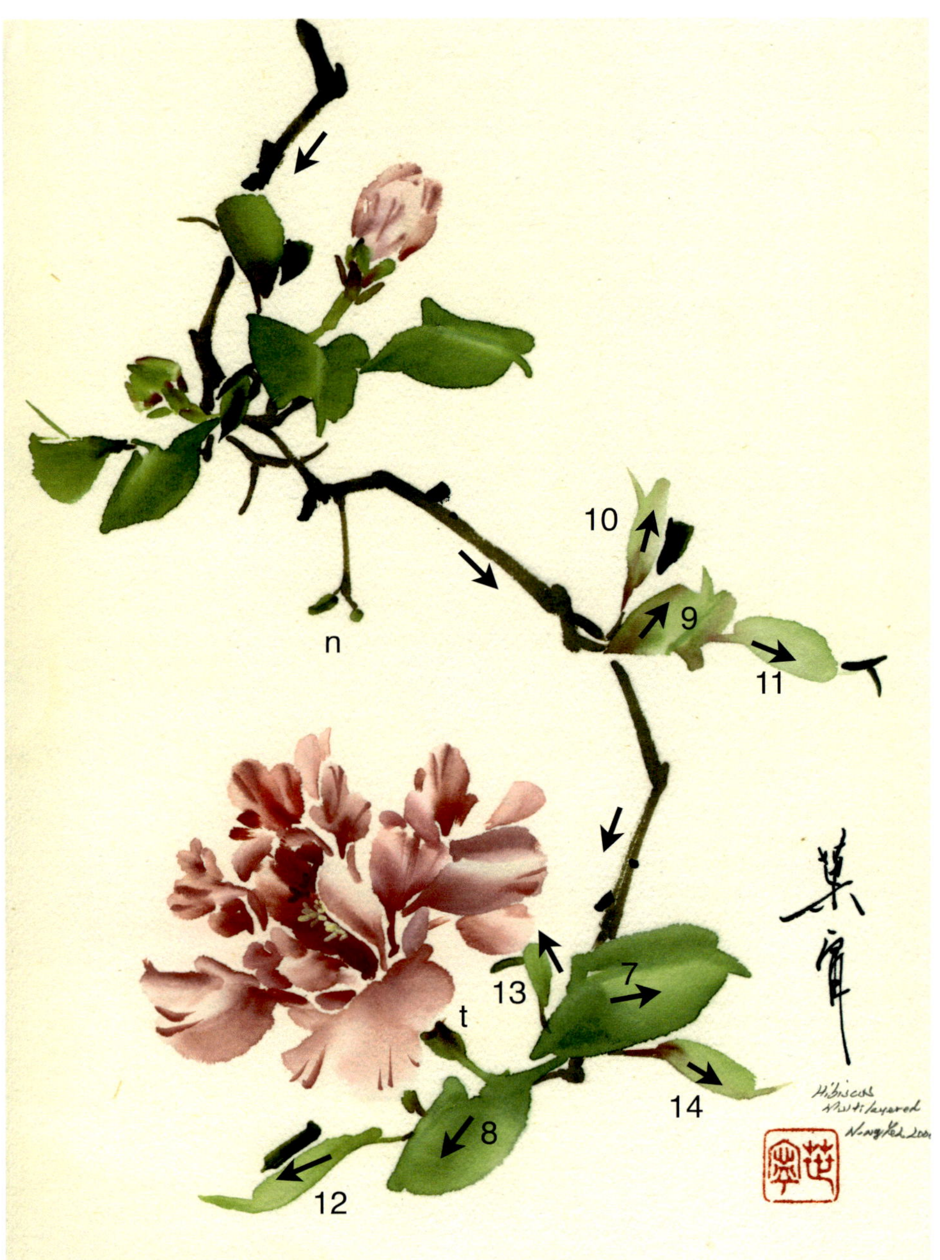


❖ Brown + Ink

Happy dot time always indicates a sign of relief.

❖ Light Green + Dark Green + Ink

Do the topsides of a few folding leaves. Add a few dots to show signs of new growth (n).

Veins

♌ Small Mountain Horse

❖ White + Yellow + Light Green

Add center veins to the leaves.

8054

# Holly

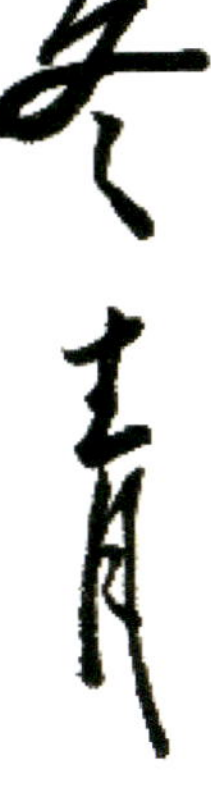


Dung
Dōng: Winter

Ching
Qīng: Green

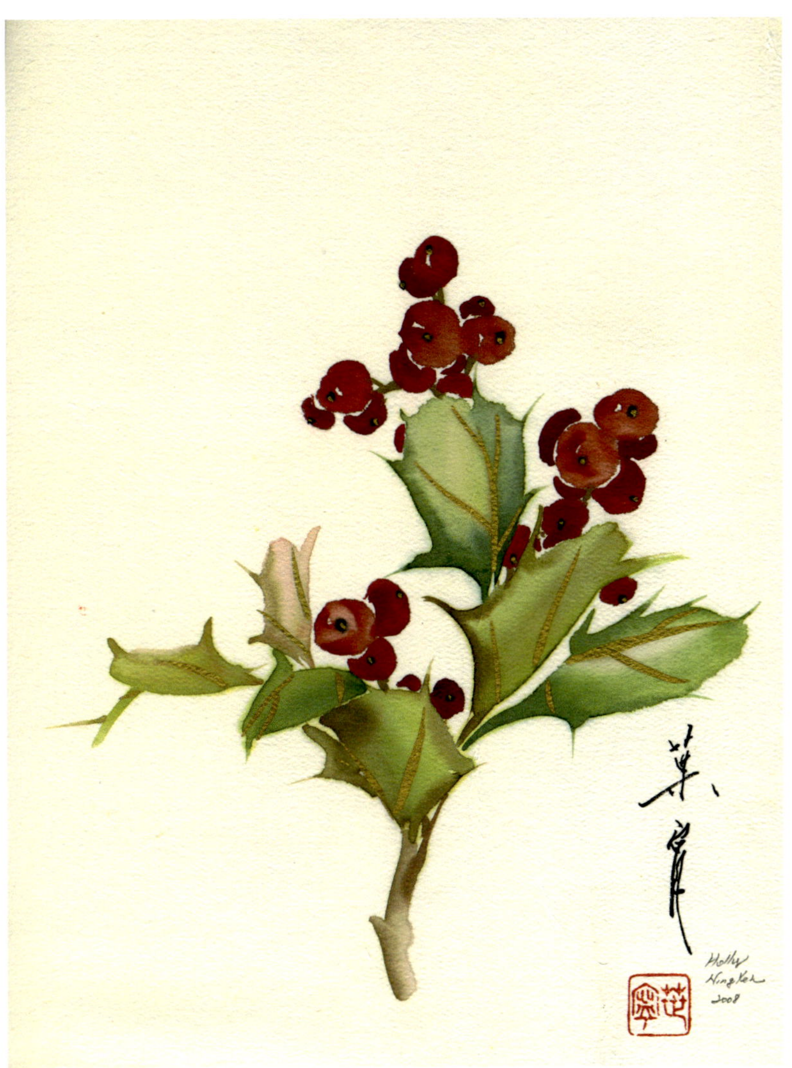

Holly has a wonderful Chinese name that means winter green. Besides surviving winter, the holly wood is hardy and is used for chess pieces and piano keys. These virtues really add meaning to holly as a symbol for endearing friendship.

Holly is also fun to do. The Mountain Horse brush makes the leaves of holly a piece of cake.

**MATERIALS**

Paper: Double Shuen

Brushes
Large Flow, Flow, Small Mountain Horse

❖ Colors
*Chinese*
Yellow
*Schmincke*
Cadmium Red Deep
*Winsor & Newton*
Indigo, Alizarin Crimson, Perylene Violet
*OAS*
Best Bottle Ink
Gold

**PREPARATION OF COLORS**

Yellow: thick liquid
Light Green: Yellow + Indigo
Dark Green: Yellow + Indigo
Red: Cadmium Red Deep
Crimson: Alizarin Crimson + Red
Dark Red: Perylene Violet + Red + Crimson
Brown: Dark Red + Dark Green + Light Green
Ink
Gold

## STEPS

Leaves
♌ Large Flow
❖ Light Green + Dark Green
Do the topside of a leaf (A).

❖ Light Green + Brown
Work the underside (A1). Make sure the center vein expresses the continuity between the top and the underside of this leaf.

♌ Small Mountain Horse
❖ Light Green + Brown
Work the edge of the leaf. Do curves showing sharp points on both ends. (Do the second curve by leaving the tip of the first curve alone).

♌ Large Flow
❖ Light Green + Brown
Do the underside of a profile leave (B). Show the stem. Press to do the body. Extend the tip like a freeway exit.

♌ Small Mountain Horse
❖ Light Green + Brown
One cannot wait to do the edge of the leaf. Run some curves along the top edge of the profile leaf.

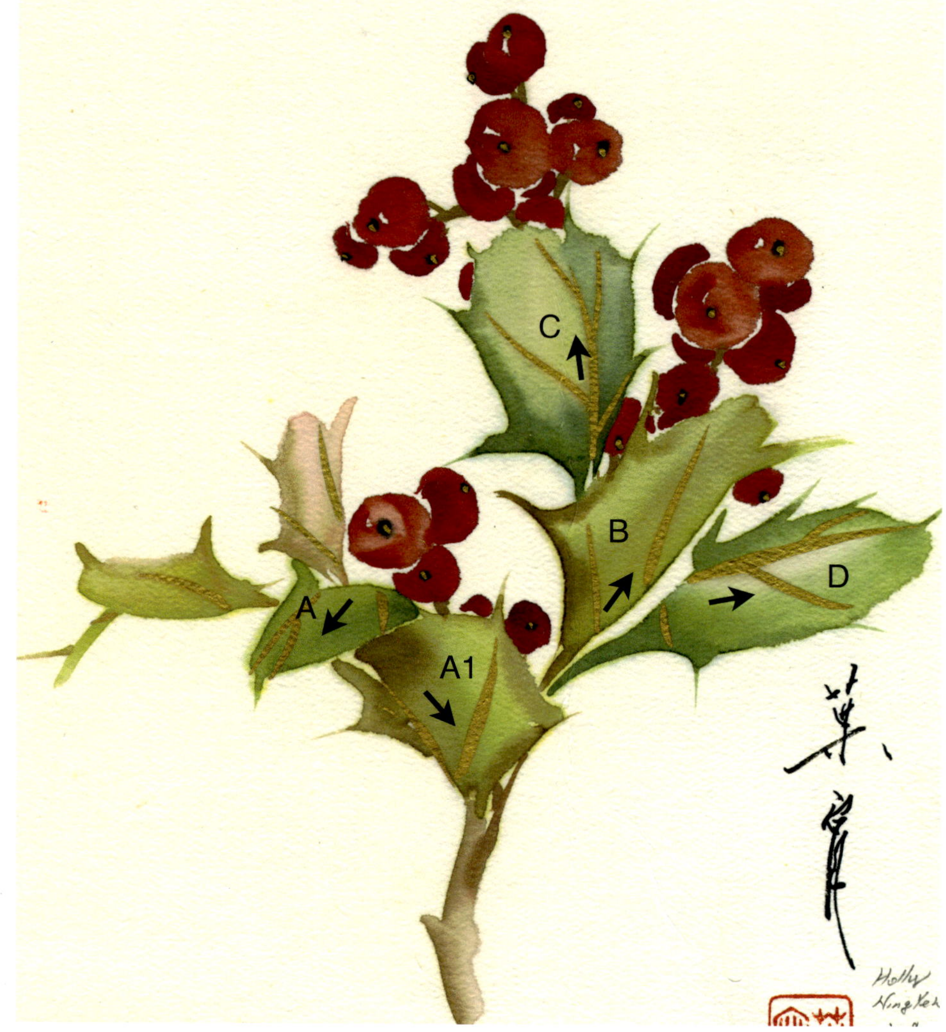


♌ Large Flow
❖ Light Green + Dark Green
Work two leaves showing their topsides (C, D).

♌ Small Mountain Horse
❖ Light Green + Dark Green
Run curves to form the points. The colors should be the same as the leaves. We really want the edges to integrate with the leaves.

There is no need to run the curves for the entire leaf.

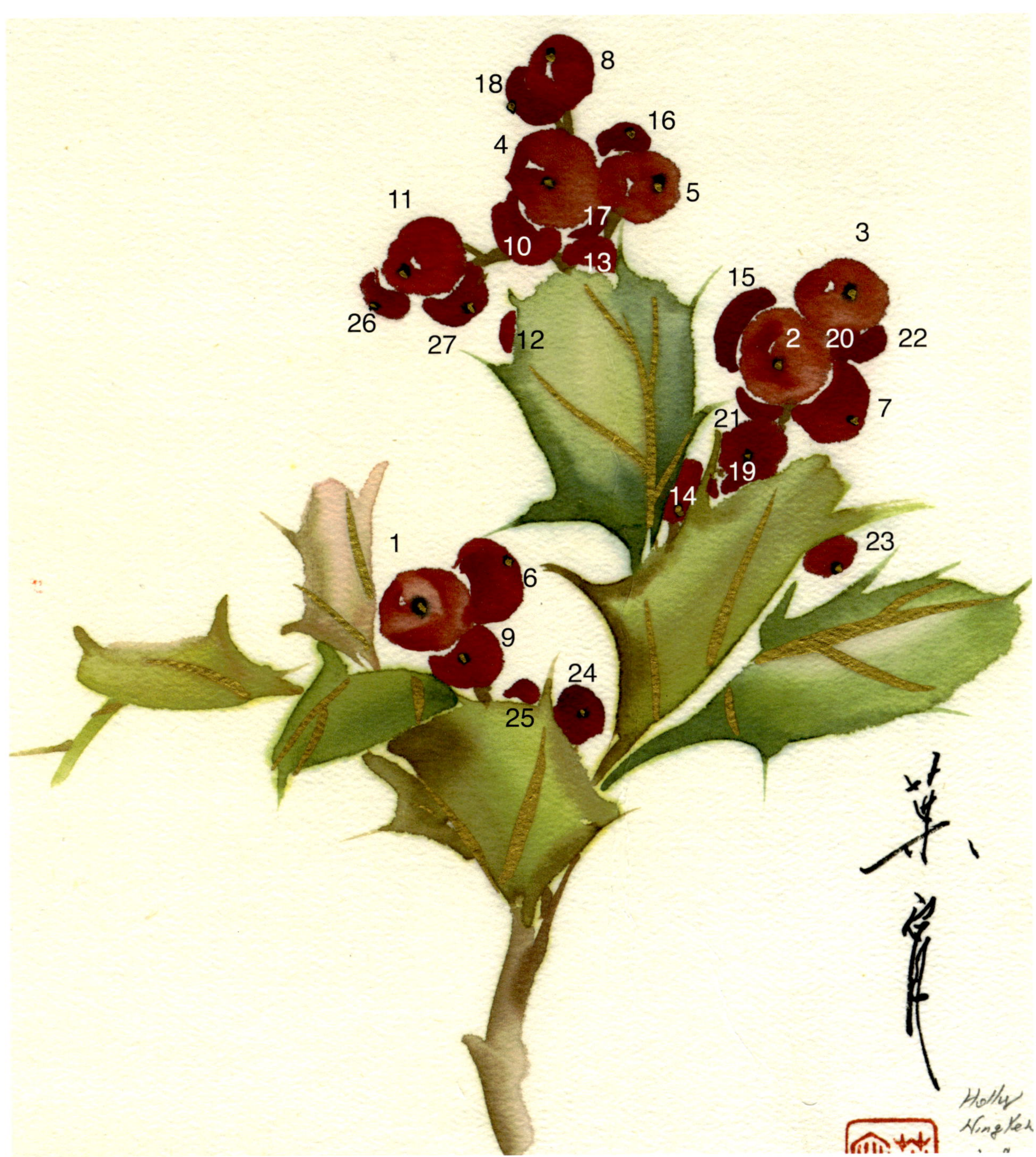


Branch

ᔓ Flow

❖ Brown

Do the branch and add stems to bring the leaves into the branch.

Berries

❖ Red

Work the berries into circles with rounded strokes. Leave a tiny space to express light on each full-bodied berry. Let the spot happen naturally. If it happens, great! If not, don't stress over it. Settle the berries into three groups. Do a host. Accompany the hosts with guests (1-5).

❖ Crimson + Dark Red

Work more berries. Show them overlapping each other. Leave a hairline space between the berries. Develop each group with a host cluster and a guest cluster. Show some berries playing hide and seek (6-27).

Guest Leaves
❖ Light Green + Red
Do a couple of smaller profile leaves.

♌ Small Mountain Horse
❖ Light Green + Red
Add the thorny edges.

♌ Flow
❖ Brown
Link the berries with stems. Bring them home to the leaves and branches below.

❖ Dark Red + Ink
Add dots on the berries. The dots should relate to the orientation and location of each berry in the group. Center berries have center dots. Side ones show dots on the side. The back ones do not get any.

♌ Small Mountain Horse
❖ Gold
Work shiny veins on the leaves.

♌ Flow
❖ Gold
Accent the dot with a touch of gold to bring the holiday spirit to all.

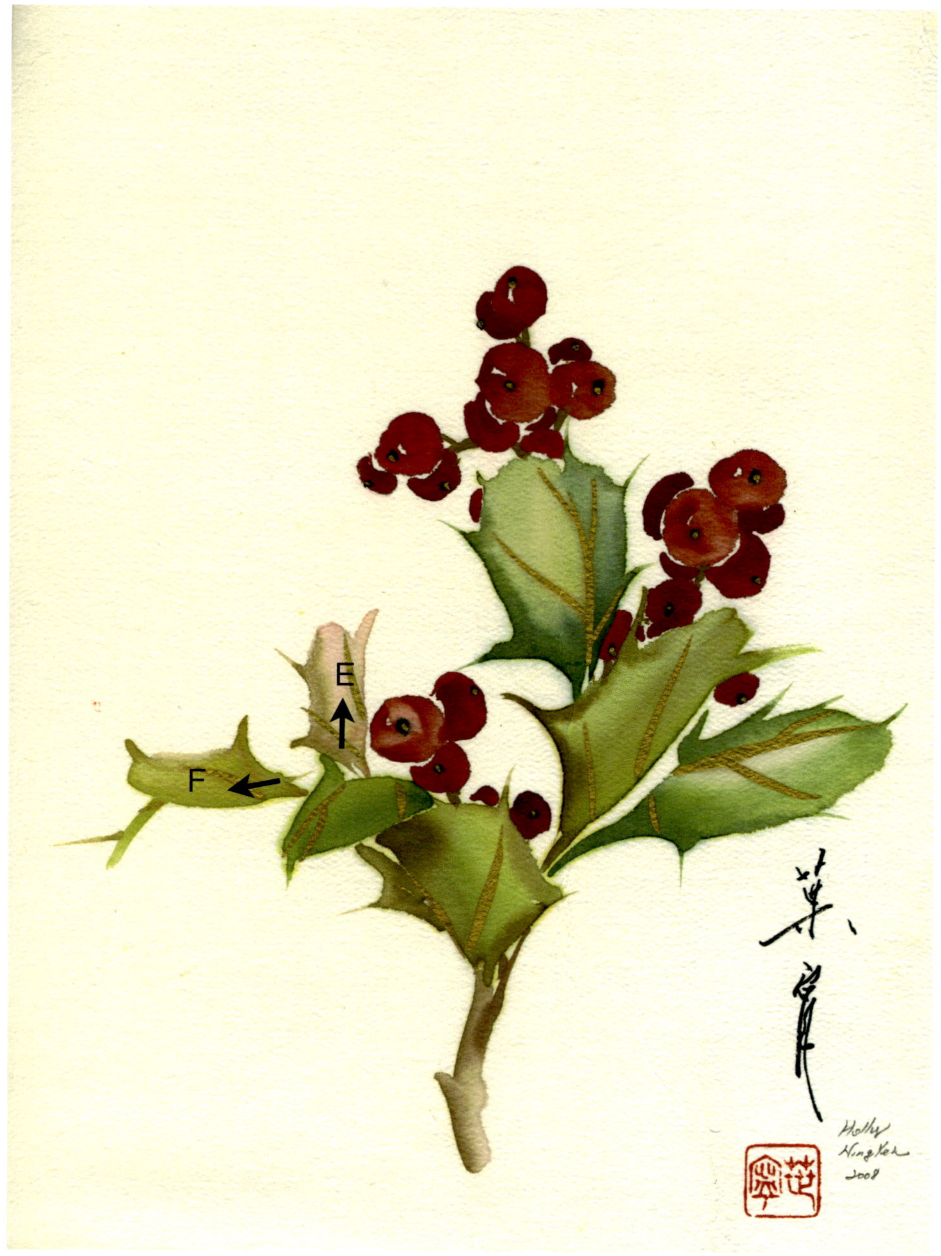

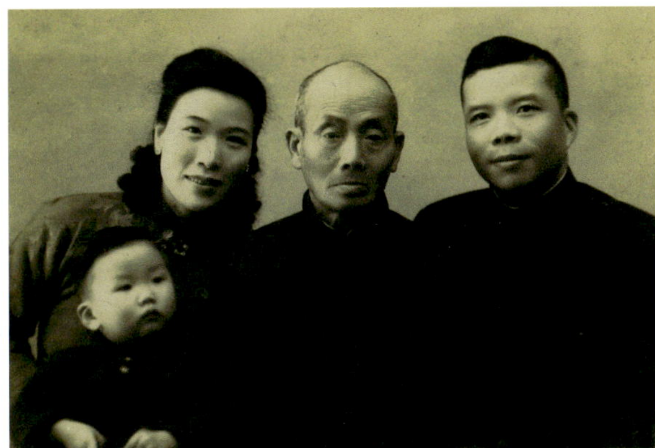

*Ning with parents and grandfather in China, 1948*

# About the Artist

Ning Yeh was born in China into a family with an artistic tradition of many generations.

Ning Yeh's art training began early after the family moved to Taiwan in 1949.

As a top high school student, he became a draft choice of Taiwan's best university in humanities studies. In 1969, Ning Yeh accepted scholarships in America. He received his Ph.D. degree from Claremont Graduate University at The Claremont Colleges.

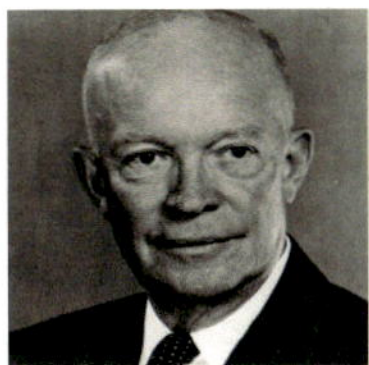

THE WHITE HOUSE
WASHINGTON

July 6, 1960

Dear General Yeh:

Mrs. Drumright has personally forwarded to me your scroll painting. She also sent me a translation of the more than generous dedication that you attached to the scroll. I am truly overwhelmed by your comments and by your kindness.

I understand that we share both our vocation (at least my vocation of some forty-odd years) and an avocation (although you are an outstanding artist and I am but a rank amateur). I am sorry that we did not have an opportunity when I was in Taipei to meet to discuss our many common interests.

With my warm thanks and best wishes,

Sincerely,

Dwight D. Eisenhower

*A gracious letter from President Eisenhower to Ning's father, a renowned horse painter and a general in Chiang Kai-shek's army.*

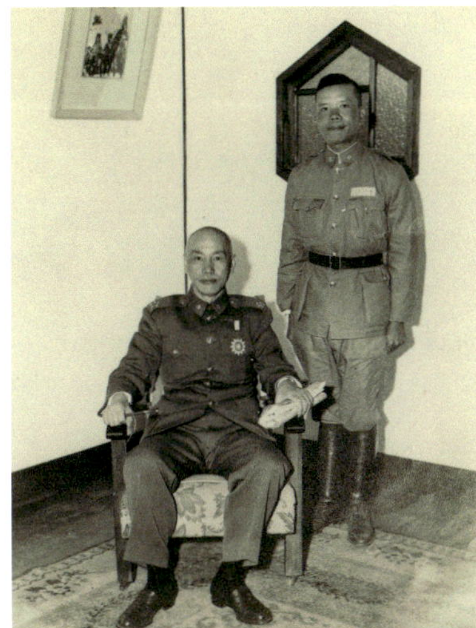

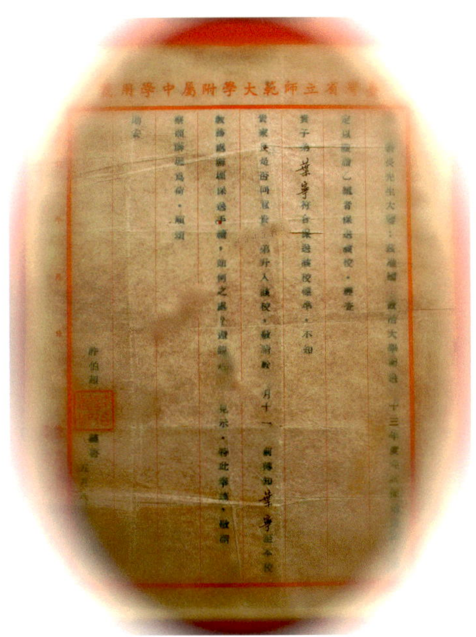

*Top draft choice of Taiwan's best university in humanity studies, 1964*

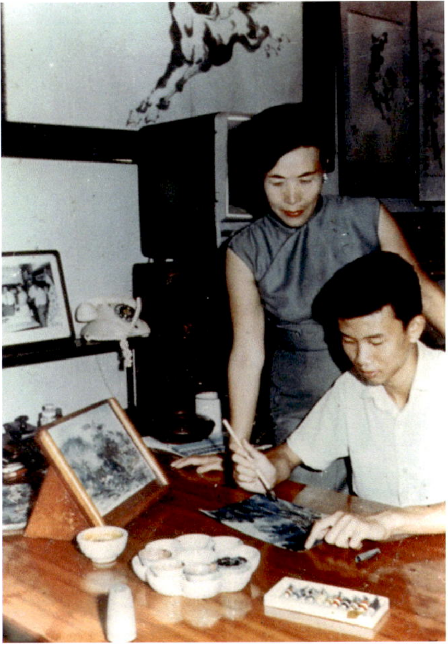

*Painting in Taiwan with mother's supervision, 1964*

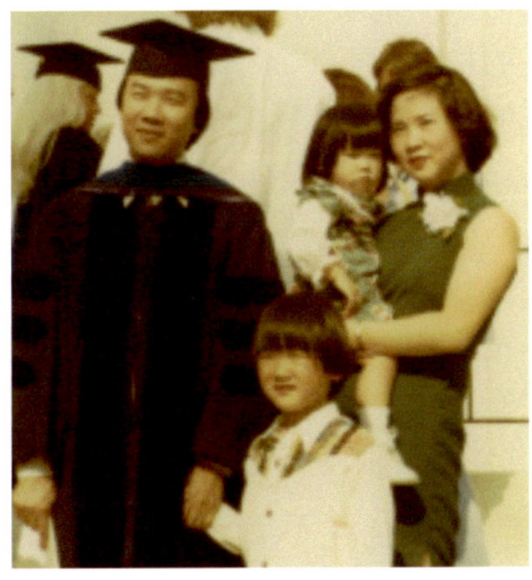

*Ph.D. from Claremont with wife Lingchi, son Evan, and daughter Jashin, 1978*

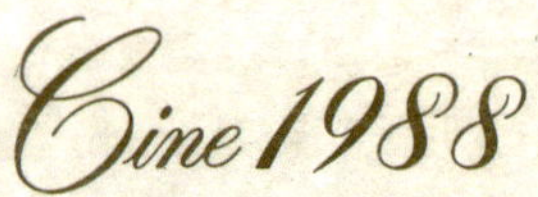

The Council on International Nontheatrical Events
congratulates
Ning Yeh
Artist
for the motion picture

Head Of The Horse

selected for its excellence to represent the
United States of America in international
motion picture events abroad and awards to it

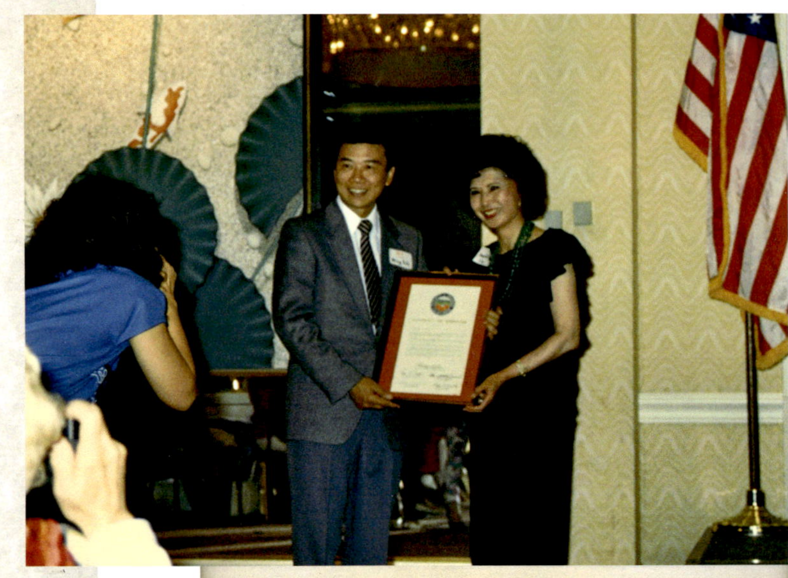

ACADEMY
OF
TELEVISION ARTS & SCIENCES

40th ANNUAL
LOS ANGELES AREA EMMY AWARDS

*Honors*
NING YEH
ARTIST/ACADEMIC ADVISOR

*for contributing to the winning of an*
*Area Award*

INSTRUCTIONAL SERIES
CHINESE BRUSH PAINTING
SERIES
KOCE

State of California

**March Fong Eu**
**Secretary of State**

"THE GREAT SEAL OF THE GREAT STATE OF CALIFORNIA"

The Great Seal of the State of California was adopted at the Constitutional Convention of 1849. Thirty-one stars are displayed, one for each state which comprised the Union at the time. Beneath them appears the motto, Eureka! The peaks of the Sierra Nevada stand for the grandeur of Nature. Shipping on San Francisco Bay typifies commerce. A miner laboring with pick, rocker and pan represents industry. Agricultural wealth is seen in a sheaf of wheat and clusters of grapes. Keeping watch over this tableau is the armored figure of Minerva who, in classical mythology, was goddess of the arts and sciences, wise in peace and war. Like the political birth of California, she was born full grown from the brain of Jupiter, father of the gods and guardian of law and order. At her feet is a grizzly bear, independent and formidable, symbolizing the State of California. The Secretary of State is the keeper of the Great Seal.

By token of the Great Seal, the California Secretary of State extends to

NING YEH

sincere appreciation for the beauty of his art and its philosophy, commends his dedication to preserving this exquisite art form through his teaching and offers best wishes for every success with his new telecourse and in all future endeavors. This seal is offered as a token of lasting friendship.

Subscribed this 9th day of August, 1987

March Fong Eu
MARCH FONG EU
Secretary of State

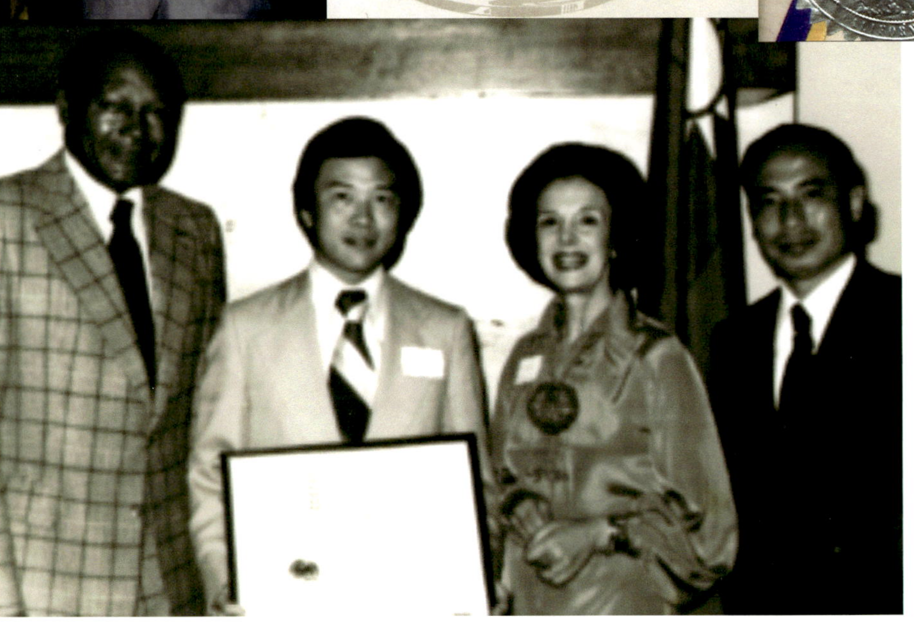

*Ning Yeh's art has received many special awards and recognition: the Golden Eagle, the Emmy, the Great Seal of California, and special a Merit Award presented by Mrs. Dorothy Chandler, and Mayor Tom Bradley, among others.*

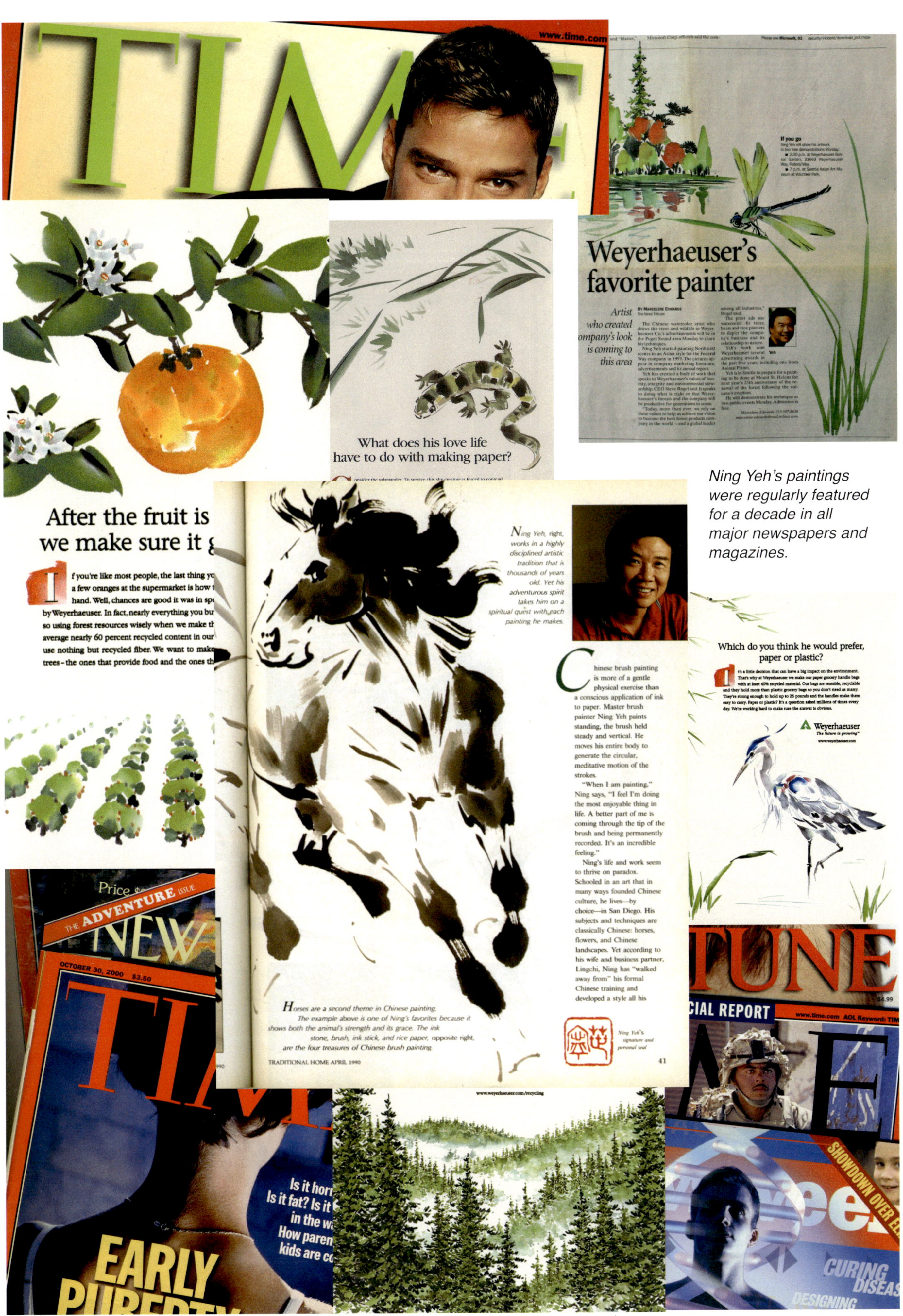

# Weyerhaeuser's favorite painter

*Artist who created company's look is coming to this area*

By Marcelene Edwards
The News Tribune

The Chinese watercolor artist who draws the trees and wildlife in Weyerhaeuser Co.'s advertisements will be in the Puget Sound area Monday to share his techniques.

Ning Yeh started painting Northwest scenes in an Asian style for the Federal Way company in 1999. The pictures appear in company marketing literature, advertisements and its annual report.

Yeh has created a body of work that speaks to Weyerhaeuser's values of honesty, integrity and environmental stewardship, CEO Steve Rogel said. It speaks to doing what is right so that Weyerhaeuser's forests and the company will be productive for generations to come.

"Today, more than ever, we rely on these values to help us achieve our vision to become the best forest products company in the world – and a global leader among all industries," Rogel said.

The print ads use watercolor fir trees, bears and tree planters to depict the company's business and its relationship to nature.

Yeh's work won Weyerhaeuser several advertising awards in the past five years, including one from Animal Planet.

Yeh is in Seattle to prepare for a painting to be done at Mount St. Helens for next year's 25th anniversary of the renewal of the forest following the volcano's eruption.

He will demonstrate his technique at two public events Monday. Admission is free.

Yeh

**If you go**

Ning Yeh will show his artwork in two free demonstrations Monday:

- 2:30 p.m. at Weyerhaeuser Bonsai Garden, 33663 Weyerhaeuser Way, Federal Way.
- 7 p.m. at Seattle Asian Art Museum at Volunteer Park.

---

*Ning Yeh, right, works in a highly disciplined artistic tradition that is thousands of years old. Yet his adventurous spirit takes him on a spiritual quest with each painting he makes.*

Chinese brush painting is more of a gentle physical exercise than a conscious application of ink to paper. Master brush painter Ning Yeh paints standing, the brush held steady and vertical. He moves his entire body to generate the circular, meditative motion of the strokes.

"When I am painting," Ning says, "I feel I'm doing the most enjoyable thing in life. A better part of me is coming through the tip of the brush and being permanently recorded. It's an incredible feeling."

Ning's life and work seem to thrive on paradox. Schooled in an art that in many ways founded Chinese culture, he lives—by choice—in San Diego. His subjects and techniques are classically Chinese: horses, flowers, and Chinese landscapes. Yet according to his wife and business partner, Lingchi, Ning has "walked away from" his formal Chinese training and developed a style all his

*Horses are a second theme in Chinese painting. The example above is one of Ning's favorites because it shows both the animal's strength and its grace. The ink stone, brush, ink stick, and rice paper, opposite right, are the four treasures of Chinese brush painting.*

*Ning Yeh's signature and personal seal*

TRADITIONAL HOME APRIL 1990 41

---

## Which do you think he would prefer, paper or plastic?

It's a little decision that can have a big impact on the environment. That's why at Weyerhaeuser we make our paper grocery handle bags with at least 40% recycled material. Our bags are reusable, recyclable and they hold more than plastic grocery bags so you don't need as many. They're strong enough to hold up to 25 pounds and the handles make them easy to carry. Paper or plastic? It's a question asked millions of times every day. We're working hard to make sure the answer is obvious.

Weyerhaeuser
*The future is growing*™
www.weyerhaeuser.com

---

What does his love life have to do with making paper?

---

After the fruit is
we make sure it

If you're like most people, the last thing yo
a few oranges at the supermarket is how t
hand. Well, chances are good it was in sp
by Weyerhaeuser. In fact, nearly everything you bu
so using forest resources wisely when we make t
average nearly 60 percent recycled content in our
use nothing but recycled fiber. We want to mak
trees – the ones that provide food and the ones th

---

www.weyerhaeuser.com/recycling



*Ning Yeh's paintings were regularly featured for a decade in all major newspapers and magazines.*

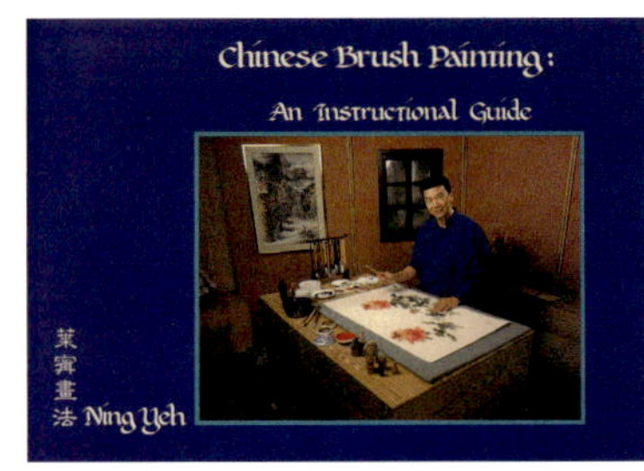


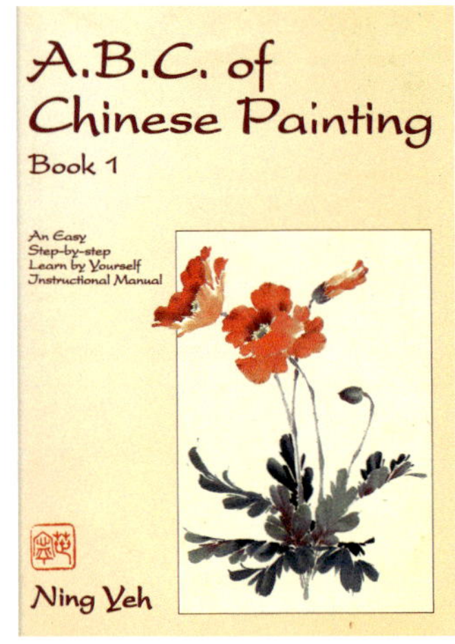


Landscape Lessons Book 1

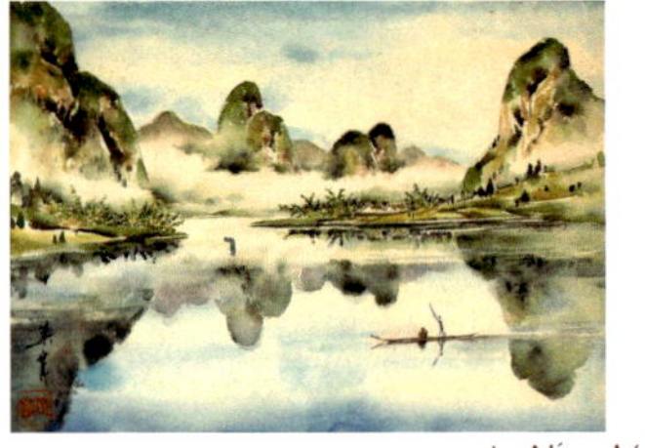

by Ning Yeh

Landscape Lessons

Book 2

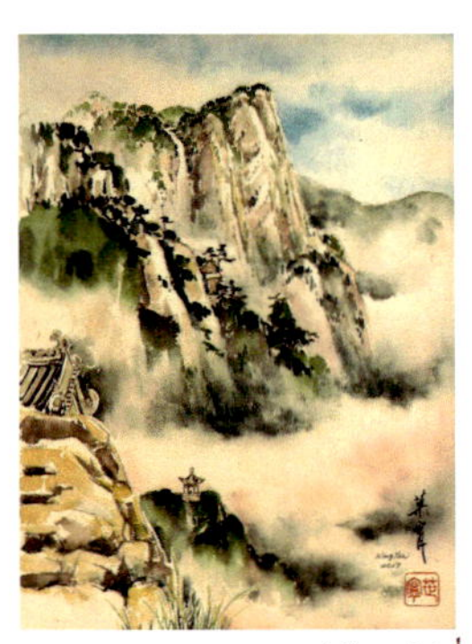

by Ning Yeh

Dr. Yeh became a full-time art professor in 1972. He is a three-time recipient of the National Teaching Excellence Award.

In 1987, his first instructional television series, *Chinese Brush Painting with Ning Yeh*, won the Emmy Award for Best Instructional Series.

In 1997, *Chinese Flower Painting with Ning Yeh (1 and 2)* began airing on PBS stations. In the 2000s, Dr. Yeh released his fourth television series *Chinese Animal Painting*. These TV series have had 25 years of continuous airing in the United States.

Dr. Yeh has published many books and art albums. His instructional books, *Chinese Brush Painting: An Instructional Guide* and *A.B.C. of Chinese Painting,* are best sellers with repeated editions.

Dr. Yeh lives in Huntington Beach, California. His family owns Oriental Art Supply Company which has provided the best painting materials for over 40 years.

*108 Flowers* represents his most endearing teaching effort in sharing the magic of brush painting. It is simple, fun, and dynamic with profound spiritual fulfillment. It is comprised of state-of-the-art videos and detailed step-by-step books. It will bring years of joy to art lovers everywhere.

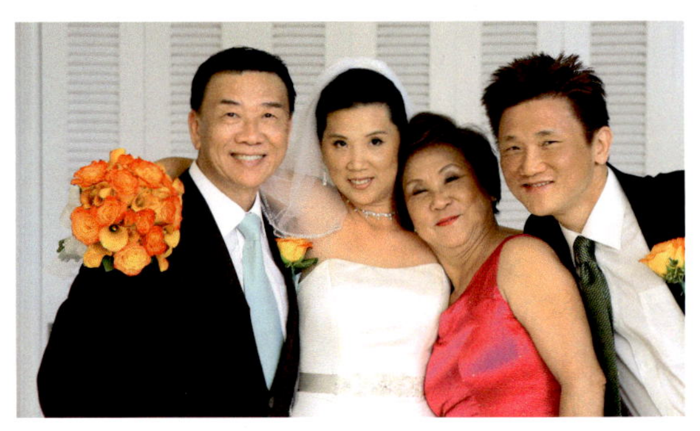

*Ning, Lingchi, Evan, and Jashin Yeh, 2012*
www.orientalartsupply.com

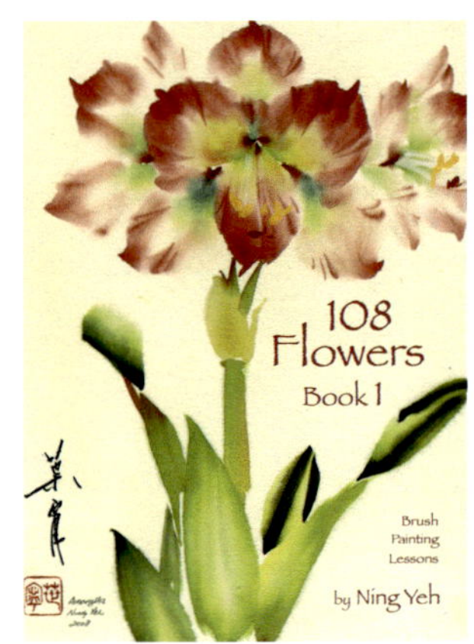


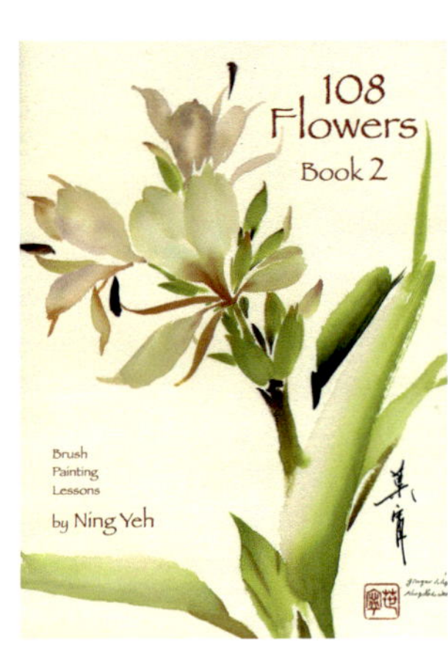


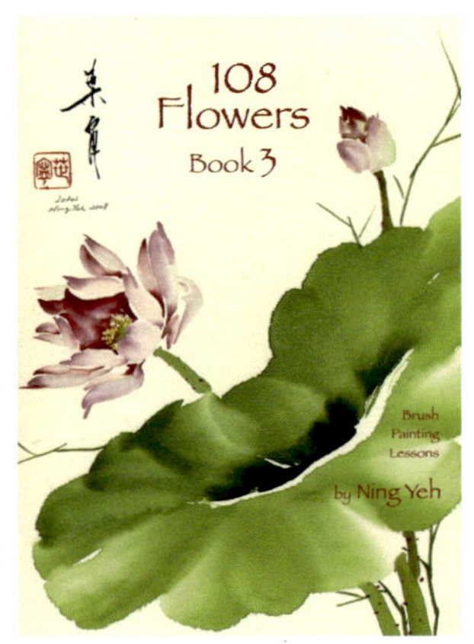


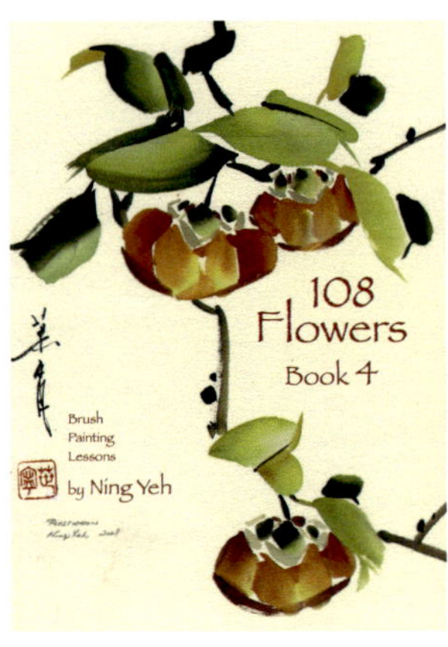